HOW TO

PROPERLY PLAN YOUR 'TOTAL ESTATE WITH A LIVING TRUST,

WITHOUT THE LAWYER'S FEES

The National Living Trust Kit

By Benji O. Anosike, B.B.A., M.A., Ph.D.

First Revised Edition, 2001

Copyright © 1995 and 2001 by Benji O. Anosike

Library of Congress Cataloging-in-Publication Data

Anosike, Benji O.
 How to properly plan your 'total' estate with a living trust, without the lawyer's fees : the national living trust kit / by Benji O. Anosike.-- 1st rev. ed.
  p. cm.
 Includes bibliographical references and index.
 ISBN 0-932704-54-9 (alk.paper)
  1. Living trusts--United States--Popular works. 2. Living trusts--United States--Forms. 3. Estate planning--United States--Popular works. I. Title.

KF734.Z9 A56 2001
346.73052--dc21

2001017174

Printed in the United States of America

ISBN: 0-932704-54-9

Library of Congress Catalog Number:

Published by:
 Do-It-Yourself Legal Publishers
 60 Park Place #1013,
 1930 Glenview Road Newark, NJ 07102
  Glenview, Illinois

SelfHelper Law Update Service

The laws governing the creation of Trusts, Wills, Living Wills, Powers of Attorney, and other related estate planning instruments addressed in this manual, as well as the forms and formal procedures for using them, can and do change every now and then. Nevertheless, this necessitates at least two things: first, that a book such as this be revised and updated as frequently as possible, and, secondly, that readers as well as publishers be vigilant, always on the look out for possible significant changes that might occur.

We'll appreciate your assistance in helping us keep track of, and with, this task. *If you should come across any "local" rules or form(s) or procedure(s) that are particular to your state or county or locality, or any that are new or significantly different from the ones provided in this manual, we'll like to know about it. Simply send us a written note specifying the law or procedure and/or enclosing a blank copy of the form(s).* Such material will be of valuable help to us in any subsequent next editions and future updates and revisions. However, in addition to that, the Do-It-Yourself Legal Publishers researchers will further research into the matter and send you instructions on the new law or the use of the material, where necessary or specifically requested by the reader.

The Selfhelper Law Update Service Response Form

The Do-It-Yourself Legal Publishers • **60 Park Place #1013** • Newark, NJ 07102

Dear Publisher,

Here's the information you invited in your HOW TO PROPERLY PLAN YOUR 'TOTAL' ESTATE WITH A LIVING TRUST, as follows (*Check applicable paragraphs & add details*):

☐ I find that the laws/procedures/forms* for my county/state* seem to have changed (to be significantly different) from the one(s) in the book in the following ways:

_____

_____

☐ Copy of the new or different form(s) is/are hereby enclosed.

My Name is: _____

Address: _____

Zip: _____

Phone No. ( ) _____

IMPORTANT: Please do NOT rip out the page. Consider others! Just make a photocopy and send that!

*Cross out the inapplicable terms or words

Dedication

This Book is Lovingly Dedicated to...

Ezinne Ndiem Anosike

...thank you, Ezie, for being so loving and caring to your daddy...for literally saving and sustaining your daddy's life. Oh yes. You've made it all more than worthwhile for me!

The Publisher's Disclaimer

It remains for us, the Publishers, to assure our readers that we have diligently researched, checked and counterchecked every bit of information contained in this manual to ensure its accuracy and up-to-dateness. Nevertheless, we humans have never been noted for out infallibility, no matter how hard the effort! Furthermore, details of laws, rules, or procedures do change from time to time. And, with specific respect to estate planning, or trust-making, and the like, the specific details of rules or procedures (though generally not the law or the broad basic principles themselves) often differ from one state to another. Nor is this relatively short manual conceivable intended to be an encyclopedia on the subject, containing the answer or solution to every issue on the subject. *THE READER IS THEREFORE FOREWARNED THAT THIS MANUAL IS SOLD AND DISTRIBUTED WITH THIS DISCLAIMER:* The publisher (and/or the author) does not make any guarantees of any kind whatsoever, or purport to engage in rendering professional or legal service, or to substitute for a lawyer, an accountant, financial or estate planner, a tax expert, or the like. Where such professional help is legitimately called for in your specific or other cases, it should be sought accordingly.

—Do-It-Yourself Legal Publishers

CREDITS:

Cover design, art direction, typesetting and illustration, by Amy R. Feigenbaum and Suzanne Feigenbaum of Rivanne Advertising Creative Desktop Publishing Services, Brooklyn, NY.

Other Books By The Author

On Estate Planning:

• How To Probate, Administer & Settle An Estate Yourself, Without The Lawyer's Fees
• How To Plan Your 'Total' Estate With A Will & Living Will, Without The Lawyer's Fees

On Other Subjects:

• How To Form Your Own Profit Or Non-Profit Corporation Without A Lawyer
• How To Buy Or Sell Your Own Home Without A Lawyer or Broker
• How To File Chapter 11 Business Bankruptcy Without A Lawyer
• How To Settle Your Own Auto Accident Claims Without A Lawyer

Table of Contents

FOREWORD:
THE PUBLISHER'S MESSAGE

To All Our Readers:

The fundamental ingredient of any sound estate plan is simply this: that it be a reflection of the individual's own true desires and wishes. And, equally, a fundamental goal and objective of a sound estate plan is to allay a profound human concern—the desire for order and orderliness in passing on property to loved ones, the deep yearning to be able to do so in an environment as free of family feuds and ill-feelings as possible.

The message of *How To Properly Plan Your Total Estate With A Living Trust Without The Lawyers' Fees*, is very simple: that, for the most part, the answer to sound estate planning and peace of mind for you, as well for your heirs and loved ones, is the LIVING TRUST (preferably in combination with the Will and other related instruments) and an organized estate; and that, with that tool in place as the centerpiece of your estate plan, you and your estate stand to reap a myriad of benefits—principally protection of your surviving spouse, or your heirs and other loved ones from being condemned to the much-dreaded "agony" and horrendous delays and expenses of having to probate your estate, and the elimination or substantial reduction of estate taxes.

Driven by the author's concern that, in his words, "with the increasing proliferation of the Living Trust among more and more Americans in recent times, the danger, indeed the actual evidence, abounds that there's a pronounced reduction in the quality of the Living Trust documents being offered by even the lawyers and professionals of the trade," the book consciously sets about redressing the potential tilt today to mediocrity in the making of Living Trusts. And the book hugely succeeds. It provides you, in a simple, non-technical, easy-to-understand language, knowledge of the following, among others:

- What is the (Revocable) Living Trust and what it is all about.
- Other devices of estate planning (Joint Ownership, the Will, the Living Will, the Durable Financial and Medical Power of Attorney, the Insurance Trust, etc.) and how they compare with the Living Trust, and the advantages of the Living Trust.
- How, why and under what circumstances the Living Trust works (should be employed) in combination with, and as a complement to other estate planning methods.
- What a good, well-written Living Trust should contain (the language, the provisions, the consideration, etc.)
- Why, over and beyond having a Living Trust, it is imperative to organize an estate, and how exactly to do just that, so as to truly avoid having to have the estate subjected to probate in spite of having the Living Trust
- How and why the basis of an orderly and simplified settling of your estate and disposition of an estate's property, is to have a good Living Trust and an organized estate
- Which of the three basic forms of the Revocable Living Trust—the A, the A-B, or the A-B-C forms—is most suited for you

As the use and popularity of the Living Trust continues to grow among Americans, and the demand for information and knowledge about trusts inevitably grows, it becomes equally important to acquaint the public with accurate facts about the Living Trust. With this book in hand, you'll quickly learn that with a properly prepared Living Trust you can have the security and peace of mind of knowing that your estate plan and intentions will remain YOUR plan and YOUR intentions—that it would not be altered by the court or by greedy relatives or unforeseen legal technicalities. *But equally important, you'll quickly learn that you have the legal right to, and can actually set up a trust YOURSELF, if you have the expertise to; and you'll just as quickly learn how exactly to do so—safely, and as competently as the professionals.*

Nor do you necessarily have to "do -it-yourself" for this book to be useful or necessary for you. In the end, even if you decide to have a lawyer or others in the estate planning field to do it for you, by doing some of the preliminary work yourself you would have been able to save the estate a substantial amount of money. And, anyway, with a well-grounded understanding of the definitive essentials which this book will provide you, you shall have been far better able to evaluate what estate-planning needs and services you need, and to make intelligent decisions on several critical questions of relevance: are you capable of doing your own estate plan and/or setting up your own trust? When do you need professional help, and what and what type of professional help—a lawyer, an accountant, bank trust officer, insurance underwriter, financial planner, etc.—do you need? And what is the professional competency of any such estate-planning help or advisors you use, if any?

The point is that the business of estate planning is too important to be left either to chance or entirely to lawyers and professionals. As amply emphasized in the book, estate planning is a continuous process, not a one-time chore. The important thing is to know all (or at least most) of your important options. This book very well sums up those options for you.

With this manual in hand, almost every American who wants to have a Living Trust can easily do so—competently, simply, and inexpensively. *To be sure, nowadays there is no shortage of books (and even computer programs) on "estate planning" and on Living Trusts. In deed, it can even be said, rather, that nowadays there is a proliferation and a super-abundance of it, rather than a shortage.* FINDING ONE, THOUGH, THAT IS AS COM-PLETE, COMPREHENSIVE, COMPETENT, AND UNDERSTANDABLE TO THE ORDINARY MAN OR WOMAN IN THE STREET AS THIS VOLUME, IS THE REAL PROBLEM!

As one respected estate planner so appropriately summed it up, "Most individuals do not plan to fail; they just fail to plan." You may, yourself, start, confidently and properly, to plan now—with *How To Properly Plan Your Total Estate With A Living Trust Without The Lawyers' Fees!*

Thank you very much,
The Publishers,
Do-It-Yourself Legal Publishers

HOW TO USE THIS MANUAL

A few words about the use of this guidebook. The "heart and soul" of this book—for a reader, especially, who is primarily concerned with actually creating and operating his or her own Living Trust or other similar estate planning instruments—are **Chapters 7 & 8.** These two chapters deal with what could aptly be described as the "nuts and bolts" of Living Trust creation and management—the actual process of practically doing it.

But, as you are quickly reminded by the manual (the Introduction), if you are to have a sound overall estate plan, the Living Trust should only be employed within a "complete" or "total" estate plan concept; as just ONE essential instrument among a handful of related but equally essential instruments which must, as well, be employed in one's estate plan to complement and supplement the Living Trust. In light of that, **Chapter 9** could be viewed as something of a "secondary" nuts and bolts chapter; it addresses the drafting and signing of the related instruments that should (MUST!) go with the Living Trust in any modern-day "total" estate planning scheme—*the Will, the Living Will, and the Durable Financial and Medical Power of Attorney.*

However, before one can effectively or prudently undertake the actual drafting of these instruments, one would need to have had certain basic knowledge and information about the essential law and requirements, about the major issues that need to be addressed, the necessary legal and technical procedures for going about it, etc.—matters which are addressed elsewhere in other chapters.

Thus, **Chapter 1** deals with the estate planning needs and objectives for which a Revocable Living Trust (and other related devices) are employed, and the estate planning needs and objectives which the Living Trust cannot fulfill for the estate plan maker. **Chapter 2** deals with the reasons why avoidance of probate is so vital an objective for the estate planner, and the many advantages of the Revocable **Chapter 3** Living Trust which make it such an attractive tool to employ as a probate avoidance device. addresses alternative probate avoidance mechanisms used in estate planning, and when and why they may be better substitutes in lieu of the Living Trust device. And **Chapters 4, 5 & 6** deal, respectively, with the major factors to consider and decide on regarding the terms and internal structure of a proposed trust, analysis of the other two types of Living Trust available, the A-B and A-B-C types, and when they may be appropriate for a given individual, and the task of data gathering on one's personal affairs and possessions as a basis and prelude for drafting the instruments. And, Appendix A spells out the essential requirements for a valid Trust in each of the 50 states and other jurisdictions. And so on and so forth.

*Granted, **Chapters 7 & 8** (and, similarly, **Chapter 9**) are the most pivotal segments, as these sections lay out a systematic, step-by-step procedure for properly drafting, executing and operating a valid Trust and other related instruments, and finally weave the whole process into a "total" or "complete" estate plan scheme.* But, as you will quickly discover in reading through or using the guidebook, for you to be able to properly and actually draw up the stated legal instruments under **Chapters 7, 8 & 9**, you need to have first mastered the background materials—materials which are contained elsewhere in the manual, in other passages alluded to above.

SO THE ADVICE IS THIS: first of all, to begin with, read and comprehend all the "background" chapters, most importantly, **Chapters 1 to 6 and 10 and 11,** and **Appendices A & C,** to name just a few. Then, finally, go to the chapters that tie it all together for you, first to **Chapters 7 & 8,** and SYSTEMATI- CALLY AND ORDERLY follow the procedures outlined therein to work out, and sign and operate a valid Trust. Then, to follow the book's prescription of the "total" estate approach, go next to **Chapter 9,** and, follow also the step-by-step procedures outlined therein, to crank out *the Will, Living Will, the Durable Financial and Medical Power of Attorney,* the essential supporting documents.

A lot of times, you would probably not need all or some of the information provided in a given chapter; some information may be irrelevant or inapplicable in your particular situation. It's all here, though, just in case your need it!

Introduction
THE LIVING TRUST AS A PRIMARY TOOL IN A "TOTAL" (COMPLETE) ESTATE PLAN SCHEME

A. The Purpose or Purposes of Estate Planning

In today's financial and social environment, the undertaking of "estate planning"—the planning for the efficient management of your estate (meaning the wealth and property you accumulated in your life) during your lifetime, as well as for its proper transfer or desposition, including providing for your loved ones, after your death — is almost universally viewed by experts as a vital component in any sound and overall financial planning and retirement planning. This phenomenon has assumed an increasingly special place especially in this era of longer life expectancies and medical breakthroughs.

For our purposes in this manual, suffice it simple to say that, for a variety of objective reasons, financial planners and professionals and legal advisors increasingly see the need for all persons, young and old alike, rich as well as poor, to "plan" their estates. For one thing, *good estate planning will, at the very least, provide you a framework by which to assess your estate and to also gain its optimum enjoyment during your lifetime. And, perhaps most importantly, estate planning, if done well and timely undertaken, will help bring one critical fact clearly home to you: the very need for you to plan your estate, and the stark reality that if you fail or neglect to do so, the government will do it for you any way, like it or not!*

B. Different Tools Are Used To Achieve Different Estate Planning Objectives

In point of fact, the term "*estate planning*" is a catch-all term for describing a range of objectives from which to choose, and the use of different tools and devices with which to accomplish them. *Among the most common estate planning objectives for most people, are the following:*

1. Avoidance of "probate" — which, in essence, really means avoidance of an often horrendous array of court costs and expenses, and the lawyers fees, involved in probating an estate [See Chapter 2 for more on this].
2. Minimizing death taxes [See Chapter 5 & 11 for more on this].
3. Arranging for proper distribution of your property, and for proper care, guidance and maintenance of your minor children and loved ones, if you should die.
4. Determination of what is to be done and choosing who is to make important legal, financial and medical decisions, or to handle your affairs, if you should become incapacitated [See Chapter 9].
5. Planning for your funeral and final settlement of your estate and affairs [See Chap. 10, for example].

C. The Estate Planning Tools & Devices Primarily Considered In This Manual

As mentioned above, in practice, the way the 'planning' process is basically done is that particular devices are used to attain particular estate planning objectives, in terms of one's specific circumstances, needs and objectives. For example, the Will (and the other related legal instruments, such as the Living Will and the Durable Power of Attorney and Medical Directive) are the primary tools employed by estate planners in attempting to accomplish the 3rd, 4th and 5th objectives listed above — namely the proper disposition of one's property and affairs after death, the proper care and maintenance of one's minor children or loved ones, and the like.

The subject matter with which this manual is primarily concerned — namely, the *Revocable* Living Trust — is primarily concerned with the 1st (and to much lesser extent, the 2nd) estate planning objective outlined above, namely, *avoidance of probate* — the goal of passing on property to one's heirs or beneficiaries without much waste, legal or administrative expenses or delays. To be sure, there are other tools in the estate planning arsenal that are also used for probate avoidance purposes. And, in fact, sometimes in given situations certain other tools, other than a trust, may even accomplish your probate avoidance goals better than a trust can, or can be used in combination with a trust.

These other probate avoidance (or reduction) devices include:

- Setting up joint ownership with the 'right of survivorship' provision in the document of ownership on a property or asset (e.g., savings accounts, securities, real estate, etc ...).
- Naming beneficiaries directly on the financial instruments, such as U.S. bonds, life insurance policies, and in employment related contracts or employee retirement fund plans.
- Making outright gifts of property to one's heirs while one is alive.
- The making of a Will.

[More detailed treatment of this subject is in Chapter 3]

D. The Fundamental Philosophy of Estate Planning In This Manual: Use Of The Trust in Combination With Other Tools in a "Total" or Complete Estate Plan Scheme

In this manual, the main focus is on the use of the principal probate avoidance device of all, the REVO-CABLE LIVING TRUST, in the estate planning process — the procedures of it's creation, use and ultimate termination. However, a fundamental theory of estate planning adopted in the manual (see especially Chapter 3) is the notion of 'total' or complete estate planning — an approach which rejects the exclusivity of any one probate avoidance or estate planning instrument, and holds, instead, that all available estate planning instruments complement and supplement each other. Thus, in accordance with this fundamental principle, other major probate avoidance devices used in estate planning are outlined as well in this manual (see esp. Chapters 3 & 9), and it is strongly emphasized that they be considered and used as well in a plan, either alone or in combination with the living trust, when and if necessary—in a 'total' estate plan approach.

Chapter 1

LET'S GET THE BACKGROUND INFORMATION
STRAIGHT, FIRST: THE TRUST BASICS

A. What Is A Trust?

How do you define or describe a "trust"? For this writer, one excellent definition of the term given by Charles Plotnick and Stephan R. Leimberg, authors on the subject, presents probably the most precise and descriptive explanation of the concept for the purposes of this manual:[1]

"A trust is a legal relationship that enables one party, the trustee, to hold money or other property (*trust principal*) transferred to the trust by a second party (*the grantor or settlor or trustor*) for the benefit of one or more third parties (the beneficiaries), according to the terms and conditions of a written document called a *trust agreement*. That document spells out the following: **(1)** how the assets of the trust are to be managed and invested, **(2)** who will receive income and assets from the trust, **(3)** how that money is to be paid out, and **(4)** when principal or income is to be paid (for example, at what ages or in what circumstances the beneficiaries will receive their shares).

The key is that you, the trustee—for investment, management and administration purposes—hold legal title to the property in the trust. But you may use the property—and the income it produces—only for the benefit of the beneficiaries (which may include the grantor)."

Plotnick and Leimberg added, in a rather more graphic further clarification of the term "trust," as it is employed in the estate-planning world:

"Picture in your mind a box. Let's call that box a *trust*. Into that box you can put cash, stocks, bonds, mutual funds, the deed to your home, or even life insurance. When you put property into the box, you are "funding" that trust. You can put almost any asset into a trust, at any time. For example, you can name the trust as the beneficiary of your life insurance, pension plan, IRA, or HR-10. Then, at your death, the trust would be funded."

To put it another way, a trust is a financial instrument by which you (the trust "creator" or "settlor" or "grantor") transfer property or money and appoint a person or institution (the "trustee") to administer it for the benefit of designated parties (the trust "beneficiaries). It is, in a word, a written agreement which has the legal effect of separating the ownership of the trust maker's property into two parts—with one part giving the legal title (or management) of the trust property to one person or institution, and the other part giving the beneficial ownership of the property to another. The person appointed to be the trustee (the administrator) of the trust can be anyone the trust-maker chooses or prefers—it could be himself, or a friend or relative, a bank, corporation, etc. Primarily, it is the designated trustee's duty to manage the trust assets and distribute its income to whoever is designated as the beneficiaries in the trust agreement, which may, and often does in-clude, the trust-maker himself, his spouse, children or other relatives, etc.

---

[1]Plotnick & Leimberg, *How To Settle An Estate*, pp. 247-8. Henry W. Abts III's definition is one of the 'better' ones that I've found as well. He defines it (a trust) as: "a legal entity that 'owns' (holds title to) your assets, but since you are the trustee, you maintain control over your assets." Abts, op. cit, p. 34.

B. The 'Living' Trust Versus The 'Testamentary' Trust

Broadly speaking, trusts are commonly classified into two main categories: either i) the *Living Trust* (also called inter vivos trust), which is one that is created and is in operation <u>during</u> the lifetime of the trust maker; or ii) the *Testamentary Trust* which is one created by Will and takes effect only <u>after</u> the death of the maker.

Then, within the living trusts category, there are again two basic types—the *irrevocable* Living Trust (a living trust which cannot be changed or cancelled by the maker), and the *revocable* Living Trust, which is a living trust that can be changed or cancelled by the maker during his lifetime.

In a revocable trust, withdrawal of any trust assets from the trust, or the complete cancellation of the trust, can be made at any time at the request of the trust-maker, except in certain limited special cases, e.g., where the trust-maker has surrendered the power of revocation to another person. In the typical revocable living trust, the trust maker (he's also known as the trust "creator" or "settlor" or "grantor") draws up the trust agreement transferring property to a named trustee, and giving to the person or bank that is named to act as the trustee the legal title, possession and management of the trust assets. The trust agreement usually provides for the trustee to pay the maker the income from the trust during his lifetime, and perhaps a part of the principal of the trust. The agreement would also give the maker the sole power to amend or revoke the trust or change the trustee at any time.

Under trust laws, once the maker of a trust dies, the trust becomes *irrevocable*: the terms of the trust at the time cannot be changed thereafter. Those terms would continue to operate for the benefit of other persons named in the trust. Hence, the effect becomes very much the same as though the property were being distributed under a Will. The trustee would, however, continue to retain control and management of the trust assets. And therefore, the trust assets do not have to pass through any estate administration process with the usual horrendous probate expenses and delays.

C. Trusts May Be Created For Just About Any Purpose

Actually, under the law you can set up a trust for just about any purpose at all, as long as it's legal. However, the most ostensible reason for which such trusts are set up, has to do with *estate planning* objectives—basically as a measure for seeing to it that your assets are managed, conserved and distributed as you want and to whom you want. More specifically, a trust can be structured to do the following, among other things:

- Reduce or avoid taxes (through, mainly, an irrevocable type of trust);
- Avoid the trouble, the court and legal expense, and delay of probate
- Ensure that your financial and personal affairs will be taken care of the way you want, if you become incapacitated
- Provide financial support for a dependent spouse or children both during your lifetime or after you die
- Provide financial support for a mentally or physically disabled dependent
- Ensure that your property is passed along bloodlines (for example, to your son but not to his wife)
- Protect your children from receiving an inheritance before they are old enough to manage it, or your property from going to any irresponsible beneficiary who won't manage it wisely.
  Ensure that your business is managed or otherwise disposed of the way you want
- Finance your children's education

D. The Many Advantages Of The Living Trust

To be sure, the Living Trust has quite a few significant advantages over a Will in estate planning, except, however, that—as is amply emphasized elsewhere in the text (see, for example, p. 23 & Chapter 9)—both

---

²It should be noted however, that trust creations do not necessarily come cost-free; there are costs associated with the administration of trusts, principally the trustee's fee and charges for managing the trust assets during and after the maker's lifetime.

instruments only complement each other and can be actually substituted for the other.

The advantages that a living trust has over a Will include the following:

1. Probate Avoidance

A Living Trust allows your estate to avoid probate. If, for example, your estate were to go through probate it would take months, perhaps even years to settle. On the other hand, with a living trust, since the trust is already in existence, no delay is necessary since the trustee, upon the trust maker's death, can promptly pay income or distribute property to trust beneficiaries, in accordance with the terms of the trust. (Note that, on the other hand, a "testamentary" type of trust—one that is established under the provisions of your Will—does not avoid probate. With a testamentary trust, the trust can come into being only if and after your will shall have cleared the probate court and the executor has been discharged.)

2. Flexibility: It Can Be Designed For Income and Inheritance

A living trust can be designed so that it will continue to pay the trust-maker while he or she is still alive. Assuming you still need income when you created the trust (as most of us will), you simply designate yourself as the primary beneficiary. After your death, the trustee will dispose or distribute the remaining income and/or assets of the trust to the other beneficiaries in accordance with your directives in the trust agreement.

3. It Can Provide Professional Management of Assets

The living trust provides you with a way to have your assets and investments managed by financial experts to the extent desired, or if you become too ill to do so or desire continuing professional management after your death; a person, for example, whose mental faculties or judgment are not so impaired as to justify being adjudicated an incompetent, would be well served by being relieved of the details of handling investments or business deals which age or ill-health may otherwise make burdensome.

4. A Trust Is Far Less Subject To Court Contest Or Challenge

Living trusts are more difficult for disgruntled heirs to challenge. In deed, while contested wills (especially poorly drawn up ones) are commonplace and cases abound where estates wind up not going to the beneficiaries designated in the will by the testator, living trusts are rarely contested, in contrast.[3] Analysts who have studied it, maintain that this attribute of the living trust is primarily due to its lack of public process—the fact of the exemption of a revocable trust from probate. Since, in probate, you are generally required to advertise the filing and presentation of the will for probate, and because the notice of probate must usually be published inviting anyone with a possible interest in the estate to file a claim, the process of probate inevitably invites public interest and contests regarding distribution of assets, since the standard custom in probate is that if an objection is filed the entire process stops until the objection is resolved.

Contrast that with the trust situation, on the other hand. Here, even if there is litigation, the trustee can continue the implementation of the terms of the trust even during the litigation, hence the factor of not being able to tie up the settlement process tends to reduce litigation and contests and discourages nuisance or questionable claims. In deed, so different are the procedures with respect to the use of inter vivos trust in terms of privacy, that parties likely to contest or protest often do not even learn of the death of the trust-maker until long afterwards when the transfer of the property shall have long been a thing of the past![4] Besides, the fact that the trust shall have been in operation during the life of the trust-maker, often makes the courts less likely to find much problems with it after the maker's death.

[3]Norman F. Dacey, the leading national authority on probate and living trusts, ventures this opinion: "I known of no instance of successful attack by a third party upon the legality or validity of a living will." Dacey in *How To Avoid Probate,* 1980 ed., p. 32.

[4]Dacey, the widely respected national probate authority, makes the point that "many patently unjustified Will contests are initiated by claimants who recognize the weakness of their cause but who figure that the original heirs, desperately in need of the money and wearying of the long legal delays, will agree to pay some amount of ransome in the interest of settling the claim. The inter vivos trust, [on the other hand], makes the assets available to the rightful heirs immediately, thus eliminating the unfair pressures." (Dacey, in *How To Avoid Probate.*)

5. Trust Property Is Less Subject To Attachment

The Living Trust is said to offer important "bonus" advantage—exemption from attachment. Providing the trusteeship is a valid one adequately supported by a written instrument, and that the title to the property is actually vested in the appointed trustee, property held in trust for another is not subject to attachment by persons having a claim against the person serving as trustee.

6. Trust Allows For Quicker, Almost Immediate Payment Of Inheritance To Beneficiaries

During the probate process, which, as a rule generally is a long drawn-out process, the court will usually allow a limited payment of support to a widow (or widower), but not to the children and other beneficiaries, often working hardship upon the beneficiaries. Not so, though, when you have a living trust. In that case, all that the trustee operating at the time needs is basically a certification of the trust-maker's death and he can fully activate the trust's income provisions and flow of funds for the needs of the heirs.

The assurance that succeeding beneficiaries can receive trust income and principal immediately after the trust-maker's death (except on rare occasions when tax considerations or the need to obtain releases cause delays), is an important advantage of the living trust to a family, particularly in a situation where there is a business to be run, or where a business needs to be liquidated on favorable terms. In the probate of an estate, an inventory of your assets and financial liabilities is usually a matter of public record, and hence one's business competitors would easily be handed valuable business information and closely guarded trade secrets from such records; and such a factor can adversely affect efforts to sell the business on fair terms or to keep up with the competition, if the business is maintained.

With the living trust mechanism, on the other hand, all of these disadvantages are eliminated. Rather, as one respected analyst summed it up, the living trust enables the trustee to "take action swiftly, without waiting for the ponderous machinery of probate to grind out an approval...unlike a will, its terms are not disclosed to a probate court, and its assets and the identity of the persons to receive them are closely guarded secrets."[5]

7. It Maintains Confidentiality And Privacy Of Affairs And Records

A living trust has elements of privacy and confidentiality not afforded by a will. With a living trust, you are able to keep your assets confidential because the public does not have access to the trust documents or trust assets as it does to the probate court records. Probate records, on the other hand, are public records which are open to public examination. *In deed, it has been noted by experts that many people who use living trusts do so mainly to be able to avoid probate in order to keep their family's financial information private.*

8. Ability To Change Provisions As Often As Desired

If the living trust is the "revocable" type (meaning one where the terms can be changed by you as the creator), you can cancel or change the terms of the trust at any time.

9. Centralization Of Management

A living trust can be used to centralize management and establish the location of the assets in cases where the trust-maker travels a lot or has no permanent home.

10. Virtually Any State Can Be Your "Home" State

The settlor (trust-maker), no matter where he/she lives, can ordinarily choose the state whose laws will regulate the trust (providing that the state has some material connection with the trust, such as choosing a trustee in that state.) A will, however, must be probated in the state and county of the deceased's domicile at the time of death, and also in every state and county in which the deceased owned real property.

11. Ability To Test Out Your Trust Provisions Or Management While You're Alive

A living trust has been described as an "opportunity to see one's will in action," and as a "testing ground." By this, it's meant that where someone other than the trust-maker is named as the trustee, it can provide the

---

[5]Dacey, ibid p. 32.

trust-maker and his family the opportunity to observe how that person manages the assets, and to therefore make a decision on whether they wish that person to continue to manage the assets after the settlor's death, or they can replace him or her. Also, by the fact that the trust can be created in a manner that it can be function- ing while the settlor is still alive, the settlor can have a "dress rehearsal" of his or her estate planning.

12. Tremendous Savings In Administrative And Probate Costs And Expenses

Finally, *perhaps the greatest advantage of the living trust is saving of expenses.* As stated in Item #1 above, the living trust mechanism allows your estate to continue to avoid probate. Hence, the trust assets do not become part of the decedent's "Probate Estate" and are therefore not included in figuring the executor's commission or the attorney's fees. In terms of putting a specific dollar figure on it, informed estimates[6] of the cost of administra- tive expenditure on estates, has been put at 20% on small estates of $10,000 to $20,000, 10% on medium-sized estates of, say, $100,000, and a somewhat smaller percentage for larger estates. The most recent nationwide survey of probate and administrative costs available to the author was published by the Estate Research Institute (See Table 1-A below). In viewing that table, note, however, that the fees are based on the *"gross estate"*—that is, on the TOTAL value of the estate, with the debts and mortgages owed to other parties in- cluded.[7] Furthermore, there's ample credible evidence and documentations that the costs of probate adminis- tration, in practice and in reality, is far more than these "official" estimates.[8] In any event, this is the propor- tion of your estate, at the very least, which the living trust device can save you—the legally sanctioned but private form of "tax," or tribute that is otherwise imposed upon you, the private citizen, by the legal profession!

TABLE 1-A
PROBATE AND ADMINISTRATIVE COSTS

Gross Estate	Probate and Administrative Expenses
$ 50,000	8.6%
100,000	8.2
200,000	7.7
300,000	7.4
400,000	7.2
500,000	7.0
600,000	6.8
700,000	6.7
800,000	6.6
900,000	6.5
1,000,000	6.4
1,500,000	6.1
2,000,000	6.0
2,500,000	5.9
5,000,000	5.8
10,000,000	5.7

[6] Dacey, ibid, 14,32-33.

[7] For example, say your house is valued at $200,000 but has a mortgage of $150,000 on it, the gross value of your house estate, as far as lawyers are concerned, for imposing their fees, is not $50,000 (200,000-150,000), but the entire $200,000! That's what they'll figure their percentage charge on.

[8] For example, one of the leading county bar associations which surveyed its membership of over 23,000 attorneys about probate costs, was said to have found that i) the cost ranged from 8 to 10 percent of the gross estate; ii) lawyers, as a rule, do not simply charge the so-called "statutory" fee (i.e., the fees established by the legislature as the minimum rate to charge), but rather, they routinely charge both "statutory" fees and "extraordinary" fees added on by the lawyers; iii) two nationwide studies, as well as private interviews by a probate expert with numerous estate planners, probate attorneys, and trust officials, show that the actual cost of probate is more like 8 to 10 percent of the gross estate before any liabilities are subtracted; and iv) in any event, objective estate authorities think that even if the probate fee is only as much as 5 percent of the gross estate, such a probate cost is excessive. (For the data on these, see *"The Living Trust,"* by Henry W. Abts III, Contemporary Books, Chicago: 1989, pp. 6-7).

E. Some Common Myths About Trusts

The following are some of the most common myths and misconceptions which often prevent many from making a trust, or make them put it off till it's too late.

1. That Only Wealthy People (Or Persons With Considerable Property) Need Have A Trust

This is not true. At least not for several decades now has that notion not been true in America—since about the mid 1960's when, largely thanks to Norman F. Dacey and his 1965 all-time best-selling *"How To Avoid Probate,"* the legal profession, in particular, and the American public, in general, came to learn or understand that trusts offer equal advantages to just about anybody who desires to pass his or her assets on to their heirs with as little delay and legal expenses as possible!

Quite to the contrary, the fact is that you need not be wealthy or even well-off to have a trust; if you only have a modest estate, you can benefit just as well from setting up a trust.

2. That, With A Trust, You Lose Control Of Your Property

Not quite so. True, you will have to formally transfer title of the estate property to the trust, and true, this may cause additional problems if you later decide to sell or otherwise dispose of the property prior to your death. But, in the first place, in establishing a trust you can withhold from the trust any property you may wish to sell or dispose of otherwise. But, even more importantly, for the type of trust about which we are primarily concerned with in this manual, namely, the "revocable" trust, there is no real problem of loss of control of the property put into the trust. For, in a revocable trust, you may modify the trust by transferring the trust property back to yourself. And you can then sell it or dispose of it any other way.

3. That If You Have A Trust You Can Totally Avoid Taxes—That You Won't Have To Pay Any Taxes

This is not quite so. A truer statement of the fact on that matter is that whether you will be liable to pay taxes or not will depend on three basic factors: the size of your estate, the type of trust you have, and how much control over that trust's property you still retain, if any. A "revocable" trust—one which you can change or cancel at any time—has, for example, no real tax advantages whatsoever. And, *in deed, tax-savings has never really been the primary purpose for which living trust-makers make the revocable trust; rather, it has been for other purposes, principally for probate avoidance!* In a revocable trust, you still retain control over the trust assets, and hence, they are still considered part of your estate for federal tax purposes. Also, because it is set up so that you receive income from it during your lifetime, you'll have to pay the "income" type of taxes on any money you receive from it. [See Chapter 5 and Appendix C for more details on this].

4. That You Can Avoid Probate With Any Kind Of Trust Whatsoever

Not so—at least for certain kinds of trusts. To put it briefly, it depends on the type of trust you have. If you have a "testamentary" trust (i.e., a trust established under the provisions of your will), your estate will not avoid probate; as explained elsewhere in this manual (p. 5), that kind of trust comes into being only if and after your will shall have gone through the probate court process. If you have a "living" trust type of trust, however, sure you can avoid probate (see pp. 11-14).

5. That You Can Use A Trust To Avoid Paying Your Legitimate Debts

False. You can't. A trust may not be used to intentionally deprive a spouse or creditors of sums to which they are rightfully entitled, and the court can compel the trust creator to make payment if the creator sues and prevails on a legitimate debt.

6. That Everyone Should Have A Trust

Then there is the myth, propagated in these times by many estate-planning professionals: that anyone and everyone should have a trust. Not true. In truth, much as having a trust may be an essential "must" for the vast majority of the American population, nevertheless, there is still a sizable number of people who do not necessarily have to have it, and will lose nothing whatsoever by not having one. Consider that, as has been amply emphasized in several parts of this manual, the prime and most common reason for getting a trust if for probate avoidance purposes. Hence, you may not necessarily need a trust if you fall under any of the following categories, for example:

•If you qualify for "simplified" or "summary" probate procedures under your state's small-estate rules, or are exempt from undergoing probate because you have a net estate that is worth less than the dollar limit set under your state's probate procedures. (See Appendix C, but generally the dollar limits range from $10,000 to $60,000 in most states)

•If you have your major assets in other forms of probate avoidance devices which has the primary affect of getting the property directly to the inheritor—jointly-held property, U.S. bonds, life insurance policies, and the like, as outlined in Chapter 3.

7. That If You Have A Trust, You Don't Need A Will

Finally, there is the belief held by some that if you have a trust, then you don't need a will. False! In point of fact, you should still have a will—that is, one that is well drafted and properly coordinated with the trust provisions—even if you have a trust, and even if you have put all your assets into a trust. As more fully elaborated elsewhere in the manual (see p. 23), a will is uniquely suited to serve certain needs and purposes which the trust, by itself, cannot serve for you, and one instrument does not substitute for or displace the other. [See pp. 22-3 & Chapter 9 for more on this].

Chapter 2

THE PRIMARY ESTATE PLANNING REASONS WHY YOU SHOULD HAVE A REVOCABLE LIVING TRUST: TO AVOID PROBATE

A. Should You—Must You—Have A Revocable Living Trust, And Why?

Why should you (or must you, by most expert opinion) have a (revocable) living trust? One way of answering this is to simply say that you should because having one yields you all those estate planning "advantages" enumerated in Section D of the preceding chapter (see pp. 5-8). However, to sum it up in one word, the question can be more directly answered this way: *the reason it's necessary for you to have a LIVING TRUST is because, over and above everything else, it enables you or your estate to legally AVOID PROBATE; it spares you (your estate) the horrendous troubles of having to go through "one of the most agonizing and expensive experiences in which an individual can participate"* — *the words of a veteran California estate planning specialist in describing the probate process!*

The point is that the term *"probate avoidance"* most singularly captures the very heart and soul of the central rationale for the employment of the revocable living trust in the modern-day estate planning world. Much is frequently made by contemporary estate planning professionals about the necessity of "avoiding" probate. *In deed, ever since Norman F. Dacey first published his now-famous, pioneering estate-planning classic, "How To Avoid Probate!," and first exposed what he called "the ugly side of probate" to a wide national consciousness, America's probate lawyers and estate planning practitioners have come to the belated, often grudging concession that probate "avoidance" is a legitimate cardinal cornerstone of any credible estate planning scheme. And, in that context, almost every credible practioner in the field now agrees that the Revocable Living Trust — sometimes called the 'Dacey' Trust or the inter vivos trust, among other names — is essentially the major tool for use in attaining that goal.*

B. Why Avoid Probate?

But why the obsession with 'avoiding' probate? Why is it so necessary, even critical, to avoid probate? What is it that is so implicitly (or actually) dreadful and horrible about probate?

Theresa Meehan Rudy and her co-authors, recent researchers on the subject who are among the latest in a string of investigators to examine that issue, came away with this answer from their study:[1]

> "Probate sounds simple enough, and in practice it should be. Why, then, do people talk about avoiding it like the plague? Two reasons: time and money. Probate can use too much of both. The process can take up to a year or more, and legal fees can run as high as 10 percent of the estate's value, regardless of how much time or work was needed. If a lawyer has been named PR [the personal representative of the estate] in the will or by the court, there may be no way of avoiding most of these fees.
>
> Sometimes you don't even have to die before the probate system closes in on your property. Ethel F. Donahue, an 88-year-old Connecticut resident with considerable assets — $38 million — suffered several small strokes in 1979. Judge James H. Kinsella of Hartford…named two close attorney friends to supervise her estate, along with a third attorney.

[1] Theresa Meehan Rudy, Kay Ostberg & Jean Dineo, *"How To Use Trusts To Avoid Probate & Taxes"* (Random House, N.Y. 1991) p. 8-9.

The three lawyers wrangled over control of the estate, the largest ever handled by the court. By the time the wrangling stopped, they had amassed more than $500,000 in fees — all without the knowledge of Donahue, her friends or her relatives…Newspaper headlines like 'Legal Fees Eat Up Half Of Estate' or 'Probate Fees Legalized Racket' are scary but not uncommon [or untrue]."

Another recent analyst, Henry W. Abts III, a probate affairs author, lecturer and co-founder of The Estate Plan, which has created thousands of living trusts across the nation, was even more dramatic but direct and to the point on the same question:[2]

"In the United States today, probate is one of the most agonizing and expensive experiences in which an individual can participate. [Probate] …places an incredibly painful burden upon that individual [who must take part in the process]. I would not wish that experience on my worst enemy…

Everyone should know that the process of settling an estate [through the probate process] can be incredibly costly, time consuming, and frustrating. I have watched grown men cry over the sheer frustration of probate. I have watched stock values deteriorate while the legal process moved forward with laborious and painful slowness. I have watched small businesses, built through years of hard work, falter and die in the probate process. I have watched valuable businesses entirely consumed by legal fees. The tragedy is that none of this frustrating process is necessary — with proper estate planning …"

Abts sums up his first hand , almost clinical diagnosis of human "trauma" and human "agony" he personally observed which is involved in probate:[3]

"Yet, regardless of the amount of money involved in setting up a Trust, it is insignificant in relation to the human trauma of going through the probate process…

I have seen once thriving businesses shrivel up and die as they were held in limbo by the probate process. I have watched large stock portfolios disintegrate to the point of being almost worthless. I have seen savings accounts remain locked in at 4 percent interest when the market rate (in 1979) was 16 to 20 percent. I have witnessed homes literally being given away in distress sales after standing unattended for two or more years. I have observed liquid assets being drained away by legal fees. Everything stands still — nothing can be sold — as the process of probate drones slowly on toward establishing clear title.

I watched as a widow was required to pay $6,000 for a bond in order to act as executor of her (and her deceased husband's) jewelry business. I watched as a son, sole heir, almost had apoplexy as the court required him to purchase a bond in order to act as executor of his parents' estate.

Unfortunately, all of the mental trauma associated with probate happens during the worst period of an individual's life — the loss of a beloved companion or parent.

For example, I remember a mother of seven young children who had recently lost her spouse. She not only had to be both mother and father, but she also had to return to college in order to complete her education, so that she could provide for her family. By the day's end, the young women was exhausted, lonely, and very frustrated over the legal paperwork of probate and over delay after frustrating delay. Too often, I found the young mother in tears. As if the loss of the woman's beloved companion were not enough, she continuously had to try to cope with an unreasonable legal system…"

C. Now The Good News: You Can Easily Avoid The Dreaded Agony Of Probate By Having A Living Trust

Now, does this "probate system" described above, sound dreary and abhorable enough for you to want to — for you even to do everything to — "avoid" it? Do you begin to comprehend why you need to have a living trust — the only major tool agreed by all to be the most effective for doing just that!?

The good news is that probate is not inevitable; that you don't necessarily have to go through one bit of the agony of probate. Simply put, you easily can avoid it! How? It's simple: SIMPLY GET YOURSELF A GOOD (REVOCABLE) LIVING TRUST!

[2] Abts, *The Living Trust*, Contemporary Books (Chicago: 1989) pp. 1-2.

[3] Ibid. pp. 2 & 10.

FIGURE 2-A
SCHEMATIC ILLUSTRATION OF HOW HAVING YOUR PROPERTY IN LIVING TRUST AVOIDS PROBATE

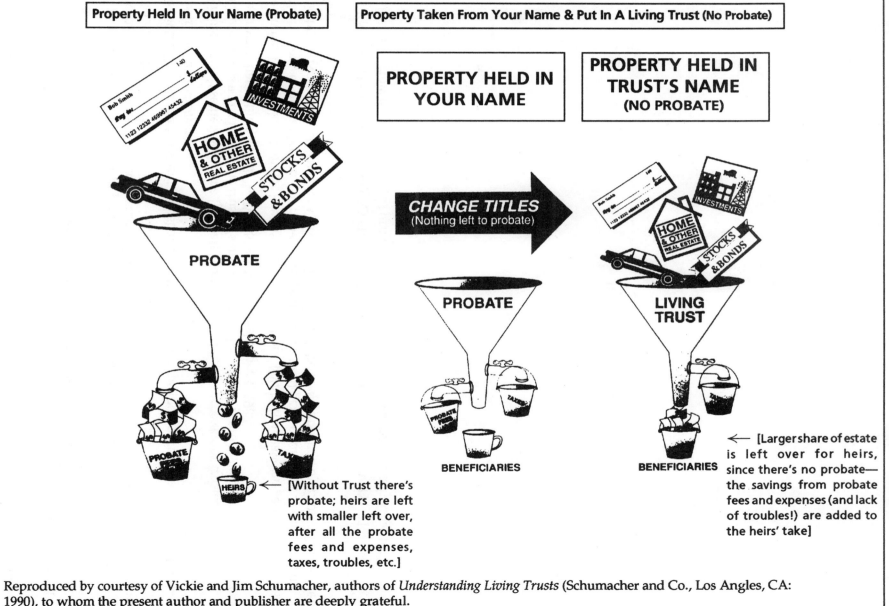

Property Held In Your Name (Probate)

Property Taken From Your Name & Put In A Living Trust (No Probate)

PROPERTY HELD IN YOUR NAME

PROPERTY HELD IN TRUST'S NAME (NO PROBATE)

CHANGE TITLES (Nothing left to probate)

PROBATE

PROBATE

LIVING TRUST

BENEFICIARIES

BENEFICIARIES

[Without Trust there's probate; heirs are left with smaller left over, after all the probate fees and expenses, taxes, troubles, etc.]

[Larger share of estate is left over for heirs, since there's no probate— the savings from probate fees and expenses (and lack of troubles!) are added to the heirs' take]

Reproduced by courtesy of Vickie and Jim Schumacher, authors of *Understanding Living Trusts* (Schumacher and Co., Los Angles, CA: 1990), to whom the present author and publisher are deeply grateful.

Virtually every experienced, respected estate planner or expert in the field agrees; everyone now concurs that the revocable living trust is the principal solution to avoiding the probate process. *The following statements from across the entire spectrum of estate planners, illustrate the point:*

- "Probate is essentially unavoidable unless a person has a living trust; it is the single most important reason for having a living trust" — Henry W. Abts III in *The Living Trust*, published by Contemporary Books.

- "[T] he most viable alternative [for probate avoidance that's] presently available, is the use of the revocable living trust" — George Turner in *Revocable Trusts*, written by estate attorneys and published by McGraw-Hill.

- "The Living Trust is the finest gift a husband [or wife] can give his [her] wife [husband]" — Max B. Lewis in the *Readers Digest*.

- "A Living Trust is settled without a [probate] court proceeding; a successor or trustee simply distributes assets according to the trustor's instructions. The process is much quicker, cheaper and more private that settling a Will" — *Wall Street Journal*, February 4, 1987.

- "The Living Trust is like the magic key to probate exemption. [With it] no lawyers, executors, administrators, or probate court. No two-to-five-year delay, no 10 percent or more in expenses, no publicity" — Norman F. Dacey in his Classic, *How To Avoid Probate!*, published by Crown Books, New York.

NOW YOU KNOW THAT YOU'D NEED TO HAVE A GOOD LIVING TRUST AND WHY! The next question of relevance: How do you get one? Turn to the next chapter(s) for that, particularly Chapter 7.

Chapter 3

OTHER PROBATE AVOIDANCE METHODS OF TRANSFER USED IN ESTATE PLANNING & WHEN THEY MAY JUST BE THE PROPER TOOL FOR YOU

A. The Trust Is By No Means The Only Method Of Probate Avoidance Transfer Available

With the vast popularity, among today's estate planners, of the revocable living trust as the premier tool for probate avoidance and its great appeal and wide acceptance within the professional ranks, it is somewhat easy to assume that the trust is just about the ONLY probate avoidance method for transfer of property that is available. In truth, however, the trust is far from being the only method of probate avoidance available; there are, rather, other estate planning devices that can be and are equally used for the same objective, depending on the estate planning needs and circumstances of a particular individual.

Deciding which probate avoidance method or combination of methods is best for you, is a major part of estate planning. Hence, in this chapter, we shall discuss the other probate avoidance methods available in estate planning, with particular focus placed on situations where and when the use of the living trust may not be the most advantageous or suitable, or the categories of people for which the other methods may be the more suitable estate planning strategy.

B. Major Other Methods For Avoiding Probate

The following are among the other major probate avoidance (or reduction) methods used and usable:

1. Jointly held property

Where any property or assets — e.g., savings accounts, stocks, bonds, real estate, etc. — are owned by two or more persons as joint tenants with the *"right of survivorship"* clause properly entered in the document or instrument of ownership, such as a deed or stock certificate, then that property or asset will generally pass DIRECTLY to the surviving partner simply 'by the operation of the law.' That is, upon the death of one party, that property or asset automatically passes to the remaining party that survives, without probate or court intervention of any kind.

The way joint tenancy works is rather simple. While the joint owners are alive, each owner holds equal interest in the entire property or asset — in the checking or savings account, the residence, the stock, the bonds, or what have you. Then, when one of them dies, that owner's share automatically "passes" (transfers) to the surviving joint owner (or joint owners) without going through probate.

By and large, there's nothing complicated about creating a joint tenancy: simply be sure to write a statement such as *"Joint tenants with right of survivorship"* after your names on the legal document of ownership for the property or asset — e.g., on the bank pass book, the real estate deed, the stock certificate or bond certificate, etc. The vast majority of states in the nation permit joint tenancy; in deed, so far as can be determined by the writer, only in just about three states, Alaska, Tennessee and Texas, is the joint tenancy legally restricted, and even in those states the method is only prohibited if and when the property involved is not between a married couple. (See Appendix A for the particular provisions regarding approved forms of property ownership for a given state). [Under the laws of most states, where the title of ownership does not specifically state that the property is held by the parties as "joint tenants with the right of survivorship," the property is presumed to be held as *'tenants-in-common,'* meaning that each party owns specific undivided share in the property, and upon the death of one of the parties, only that party's underlined proportional share automatically passes to his own heirs or divisees, and NOT to the other survivors.] The term 'tenancy by the entirety' is the term preferred in certain states for joint tenancy, but is reserved specifically for married couples.[1]

One distinct advantage and attractiveness of having property in joint names is its mechanism of immediate, automatic transfer of title to the survivor. Most estate-planning professionals agree that joint tenancy is an excellent arrangement for spouses or for persons who get along or can totally agree on the disposal of the property after they die.

However, there are some important disadvantages to joint ownership arrangements. For example, both partners may die in a common accident thereby throwing the property up for grabs — unless, of course, they also have drafted a good Will (or a good trust) as well. Secondly, joint ownership arrangements may be a problem where the family relationship ceases to be harmonious, e.g., through a divorce. In sum, the point is that for a joint ownership method of passing property or avoiding probate to work, the joint partners must be persons who are generally in agreement and have the same ideas about how long their relationship as joint owners will last, or about who should inherit the property. But, where and when such elements are lacking, a joint ownership arrangement can throw a wrench into your estate plan. Also, another major disadvantage of this method as a probate avoidance device often cited by analysts, is that while it's true that you'll be able to avoid probate by use of a joint tenancy arrangement, that advantage ceases to be true, though, when the last surviving joint tenant dies — that is, when the last survivor dies, the property will then have to go through probate at that stage.

2. United State Bonds

When U.S. savings bonds are held in the names of two persons as co-owners, the surviving co-owner becomes the sole owner on the death of the other. And when the bond is held in the name of one person and is payable on death of another person, the person named as beneficiary becomes the sole owner upon the death of the person in whose name it's held. In each instance, the bond will pass directly to the parties, and no probate is required.

3. Life Insurance

Life insurance proceeds are always paid directly to the person(s) named as the beneficiary in the policy, without probate or court intervention. However, you should be careful to know exactly what you are doing because, if and when you (the insured person) were to designate yourself as the beneficiary of the proceeds, or if you designate your "estate" or your personal representative, then they will be treated as part of your (the decedent's) estate and be subject to distribution as such.

NOTE: One unusual virtue of insurance, is that when the proceeds are payable to the estate of the insured, they are exempt from the claims of his creditors; and when the proceeds are payable to the spouse of the insured, they are exempt from the claims of the spouse's creditors.

4. Employment Benefits, Pension Funds & Death Benefit Plans

Various types of employment-related benefits are almost always paid directly to the person designated as the beneficiary in the employment contract. Examples of employment-related benefits would include the following: any wages, vacation pay or fringe benefits to which the decedent is entitled; life, heath or accident

---

[1]This special form of property ownership is available only in the following states: Alaska, Arkansas, Delaware, District of Columbia, Florida, Hawaii, Indiana (with respect only to real property), Kentucky, Maryland, Massachusetts, Michigan (real estate only), Mississippi, Missouri, New Jersey (real estate only), New York (real estate only), North Carolina (real estate only), Ohio, Oklahoma, Oregon (real estate only), Pennsylvania, Tennessee, Vermont, Virginia (real estate only), and Wyoming (real estate only).

insurance plans; retirement, pension or profit-sharing plans; stock option plans; deferred compensation or union benefits; social security, and the like. [If and when, however, the employee's contract were to direct that the benefits are to be paid to his "estate" or "personal representative" as the beneficiary, then in such an instance upon the employee's death, the proceeds will be treated as part of his estate and will be subject to probate.]

For example, you can designate in your Individual Retirement Account (IRA) (a special savings plan under which you can designate your beneficiary on the account registration document) as a specific beneficiary; when you die, any funds remaining in the IRA will pass directly to the beneficiary (or substitute beneficiaries) you designated, thereby avoiding going through probate.

5. Pay-On-Death Bank Accounts (The Totten Trust)

This is a property ownership arrangement whereby a bank account is held in trust for a designated beneficiary. It's called by other names, such as a "Totten" trust or "Bank" trust account.

There's nothing complicated about setting up this account: simply ask your bank officer for a designation of your bank account as a pay-on-death account, and they'll usually have you fill out a few simple forms to accomplish that. In deed, any type of bank account — savings, checking, money market, certificate of deposit, etc. — may be designated as a totten trust account.

Most estate planning professionals would agree that this is a simple and uncomplicated method by which to provide that the funds in a bank account be paid immediately and directly to one's beneficiary upon the death of the depositor, allowing the assets to be transferred without delay and without probate. Furthermore, an advantage of this type of bank account over a regular joint bank account, is that with the totten trust account, your beneficiary does not have any involvement with or control over the account during your life.

6. Life-Time Gift Making

This is a device for primarily reducing the size of your taxable or probate estate. You simply give away some of your money or some of your other assets to your intended heirs while you are still alive. This is a common strategy for those who not only know years before they die whom their intended beneficiaries are, but probably have more wealth than they can literally handle.

Under the current 1981 annual gift tax exclusion law, aside from the unlimited gifts you can make to your spouse, you are allowed to make gifts during your lifetime, of up to $10,000 in value per year ($20,000 when the gift giving is jointly made by a married couple) to each recipient, to as many persons as you wish to give, and such gifts will be tax-free in your (the giver's) estate. (By "gifts" here, is meant anything of value — cash, jewelry, fine art, stocks or bonds, real estate, a trust, bank accounts, or what have you.) This method has some problems, though, as a probate avoidance device. For one thing, under the law, for such a gift to qualify, once you give away the property or asset, it's gone and final, the recipient must have immediate right to the gift; you cannot have any strings attached, the gift is gone and final and is irrevocable. In other words, gifts of items or property which the recipient cannot use or enjoy immediately, or over which you still retain some rights or power, such as the right to revoke a trust, do not qualify. To be a true gift which qualifies under the tax code for this purpose, the gift must be absolute and <u>irrevocable</u> once made. It's gone, once made, and you cannot claim or recover it.

So, ultimately, there's really one underlying consideration you must think about in this regard. Can you afford to give away something, in the first place? Would you have enough to cope with, for example, if after you've transferred large chunks of your estate to others you're struck by a sudden, unanticipated change in your economic status, or in your health?

Furthermore, if a titled property is among the property you are giving away, you could potentially be handing your recipients a substantial income tax problem. Why? Because under the Internal Revenue Code rules the property given away under such circumstances as a gift, would not be valued on a *"stepped-up"* basis — that is, the values that is needed to determine the gain or loss on the property for purposes of income tax calculation, or simply what you *paid* for the property versus what you *received* for it when it's sold, will be based on what the property is worth as of the date of the giver's death, rather than what the giver paid for it when he bought it. To put it differently, the rule is that for property received as a gift during your lifetime, your basis remains the same, (i.e., it is what you paid for it), while for property received as an inheritance, say through a Will or trust, the property acquires a new basis — a *"stepped-up"* basis — and is revalued for the recipients as of the date of your death.

Translated in concrete terms, here's what this can mean to your children or other recipients. Let's say the cost of a piece of real estate you purchased 20 years ago is $100,000, and that it's worth $200,000 at the time of your death. If your children or other beneficiaries were to receive this property as an inheritance upon your death, the basis for the property would be $200,000, meaning that if they were to sell it, they would pay no income tax on it — except to the extent that they can sell it for over $200,000. If, instead, you transferred that property to the children or other recipients as a "gift" while you were alive, the basis in such a case would be $100,000 (what you paid for it). Assuming that the recipients sell the property for $200,000, they will have to pay income taxes on $100,000 gain — $200,000 minus $100,000! [NOTE, however, that in all events the recipients of the lifetime gift, to the extent that the gifts remain under the allowable annual limits, will not be liable for either federal estate taxes or gift taxes on such gifts — see pp. 185-186, and Appendix C, for more on this].

C. The Living Trust Device May Not Suit Everyone Or Every Situation

Of course, as an estate planning device, the living trust comes 'highly recommended' by most expert opinions! But does that mean that this method is for everyone and every situation? To hear the present-day estate planning professionals talk about it, the LIVING TRUST is simply the next thing to perfection since the creation, the only tool with virtually no disadvantages in an otherwise imperfect estate planning world in which every other tool employed in the industry for transfer of property is riddled with one serious 'disadvantage' or the other!

Dacey, the premier probate avoidance authority in the nation, called the Living Trust mechanism, "a magic key to probate exemption, a legal wonder drug which will give you permanent immunity from the probate market."[2]

But even this rather lofty characterization by Dacey is modest by today's standards. In deed, today, most experts, ranging probably from persons just a shade below Dacey, down to the least knowledgeable store front probate lawyer who prospects for clients in newspaper advertisements and at public seminars, now swear by a kind of frenzied "new theology" of probate avoidance that seems to hold that the living trust device is no more just an effective tool for probate avoidance, but is actually the ONLY viable or prudent tool to use for probate avoidance in all circumstances. *To put it simply, the impression is universal and almost total among today's estate planning professionals and experts, that the living trust should be used by all people in all situations; that is it not ONLY the prudent tool for probate avoidance for everyone to use, but that everyone needs to use it.*

This reaction by a team of two analysts is fairly typical. After systematically reviewing each of the other major devices commonly employed for probate avoidance, from the use of a Will, to joint tenancy, gift-making and others, Vickie and Jim Schumacher soundly faulted each method and concluded with these words: "Now you know about the risks involved with these methods...[as tools] to try and avoid probate. [In contrast], a living trust has none of these risks. It completely avoids all probate and lets your plan stay your plan — it won't be altered by the court, unforeseen legal technicalities, or greedy relatives."[3]

And Henry W. Abts, another professional estate planner and author, in assessing joint tenancy as a probate avoidance mechanism, promptly pronounced it a "poor alternative" to the living trust, and concluded: "In contrast, a living trust is the best of both worlds, [in that it]...is so much simpler, affords greater security, and provides a better solution to proper estate planning,"[4] and added: "Everyone needs a good living trust...the answer to sound estate planning and peace of mind for you and your heir is very simple: a living trust instead of the typical Will."[5]

---

[2]Norman F. Dacey, How To Avoid Probate!, 1980 ed., p. 31.

[3]Vickie & Jim Schumacher, "Understanding Living Trusts," p. 22.

[4]Henry W. Abts III, op. cit., p. 23.

[5]Ibid., p. XVII.

But, to what extent, if any, is this 'new theology' espoused by these modern-day estate planning professionals actually valid? To put it more specifically, to what extent, if any, is the thesis valid that the living trust device is the only viable or prudent tool for probate avoidance worthy of use? How true, if at all, is the view that the living trust should be used by all people in all situations, or that everyone needs or must have a living trust?

These questions are not matters merely of intellectual or academic interest to you as an estate planner. Quite to the contrary, they are substantive and relevant questions which go directly to the very heart of being able to devise a sound overall plan. For you as an estate planner, having an informed answer to such questions will be directly relevant, for example, in being able to make a sensible and rational decision as to when, how, or whether to use a living trust, or when, how and whether, on the other hand, to use other probate avoidance methods, or a combination of them thereof.

And now, back to the above questions. As for an answer to these questions, this much can be said outright: there is no disputing the fact the (revocable) living trust is, in the assessment of a wide spectrum of respected expert opinion on the subject, probably the single most dominant and effective device for transferring property to one's heirs while avoiding probate. And, in fact, for most people, it may well be the "best" device in the trade, for achieving that objective.

In my studied opinion, that is precisely where the consensus ends, however, on this question. Beyond that point, estate planning professionals and experts part company and honest differences of opinion develop, particularly on the central claim of the die-hard living trust enthusiasts who would maintain that the living trust is the only device for probate avoidance that everyone should use in every instance, or that everyone necessarily needs a trust and must have one. Or, that every other traditional method of property transfer and probate avoidance — the Will, joint tenancy, pay-on-death bank accounts, lifetime gift-making, etc.—is totally ill-advised and could not serve any useful purposes to an estate planner under any circumstances. Many analysts, no less respectable or knowledgeable in estate planning, strongly contend that, *notwithstanding the pervasive impression to the contrary, there are many situations when, and certain categories of people for which, one or more of the other traditional methods of probate avoidance may be a better tool to use than the living trust, depending on the given circumstances, needs and objectives of an individual.*

One analyst, Denis Clifford, a lawyer and probate author, noting the sweeping popularity of, and the advocacy for, the use of trusts among the authorities in the field, pointedly summed up the position of this school of thought this way:

> "Given the advantages of avoiding probate that a living trust confers, shouldn't every prudent person use one for their property? Despite my enthusiasm for living trusts, my answer is 'not necessarily.' The reason for (my) saying this is twofold: First, some people don't really need to plan to avoid probate now, and, second, there are other probate avoidance methods which may fit a particular estate planning situation better.
>
> Good estate planning isn't mechanical. To make sensible decisions about using a trust, you need to understand what it can and cannot accomplish , and how it can be used with other estate planning methods in devising your overall plan...the sweeping claims [often made by probate professionals and lawyers in advertisements and seminars that living trusts should be used by all people in all situations] are too extreme. Generally, there are a number of categories of people who may [rightly] conclude that creating a living trust is not their best estate planning strategy, at least not right now."[6]

Another voice, a team of recent analysts on the subject, noting that there is in the estate planning field, "a recently propagated myth" that everyone should have a trust, adds that "though trusts can offer substantial benefits, some people go through life never needing one; others don't need one until late in life, after they accumulate a substantial amount of property."[7]

[6]Denis Clifford, in Plan Your Esate With Living Trusts, p. 9/2.

[7]Theresa Mechan Rudy, Kay Ostberg & Jean Dimeo, in How To Use Trusts To Avoid Probate & Taxes, (Random House, New York: 1992) p.6.

Oddly enough, in deed not even Norman Dacey himself, the nation's foremost authority on the use of the Living Trust for probate avoidance who is the person most singularly responsible in America for the modern-day living trust "revolution," subscribes to this extremist orthodoxy of estate planning to which his modern-day pupils have taken. At the very most, Dacey only saw the inter vivos (or living) trust as "a magic key," a "legal wonder drug" for probate avoidance. He never claimed it was the cure-all drug, the only drug worthy of use by all people at all times under all situations! Dacey, for example, has been realistic — and smart enough (isn't he always?) — to recognize and concede that even with the best drafted living trust in the world, "you'll still need a Will." As he summed it up: "[a good living trust will] make it possible for you to eliminate completely the necessity for probating your estate. That doesn't mean, however, that you shouldn't have a Will. [Unless, for example, you also have a Will], it is not possible to anticipate and thus to exempt from probate every last asset [or circumstance just with a living trust]."[8]

In sum, the point is that all persons and all situations differ, and because each individual's situation, needs, and estate planning goals are often different, the method most suited or actually employed by each for probate avoidance may often differ as well. For some, in deed, probably for most, the optimal tool may be solely the trust, while for others, it may be other tools, or other tools used in combination with a trust.

D. Some Specific Situations When The Living Trust May Not Necessarily Be The Best Or The Only Method

The following are examples of categories of people or situations for which devices other than the living trust may be more suitable for purposes of passing on property to one's intended heirs, or who at least may not necessarily need a living trust and will lose absolutely nothing for not having one:

1. Simplified Small Estate Category Of People

Do you fall under the category of people who qualify under your state's "simplified" probate procedures or are exempt from probate because your estate is worth less than the dollar limit set under the state's probate law? If you do, then you do not necessarily need a living trust, and will lose absolutely nothing by not having one.

Simply stated, the rule works this way: if you leave an estate with assets worth NO MORE THAN a given value specified under the law, your estate will qualify as a "small" estate, and it is allowed to be excused from formal probate and be settled in a "summary" fashion without having to go through a formal probate court administration.

The permissible maximum dollar value for an estate to become eligible differs from state to state. For example, you qualify for a small estate in the state of California, if the "gross" value of the property, real or personal (i.e., the value of the property not counting any money owed on it), is no more than $60,000 as of the date of death. And, for the state of New York, you'll qualify for a small estate treatment if you left within the state personal property with a "gross" value of no more than $10,000.

BUT HERE'S THE FACTOR THAT MAKES A BIG DIFFERENCE HERE: these specific dollar figures designated under the law are, in fact, greatly misleading, because the law allows that to calculate the value of the decedent's (your) estate for the purposes of determining whether or not an estate falls under a "small" estate category, certain major assets owned by the decedent may be excluded and not be counted. In general, only the decedent's so-called "non-probate" assets, meaning his(her) solely-owned assets, are counted, and any assets he holds in some form of joint ownership with someone else or in trust, may not be counted among his assets in determining the minimum value set for qualifications as a small estate, since such property are said to pass directly to their inheritors 'by operation of the law' anyway, and need not go through probate. Thus, property such as the following would generally not be counted: the decedent's interests in jointly held bank accounts or in jointly-owned personal property or assets of other types; jointly-held trust accounts or U.S. savings bonds; or jointly-held real property, regardless of it's value. Further, community property states allow

[8]Dacey op. cit. p.555.

one half of the value of the community property to be deducted from the probate estate when the decedent is a spouse.

IN OTHER WORDS, IN EFFECT, YOU MAY REALLY HAVE A PRETTY LARGE ESTATE BUT STILL QUALIFY AS A "SMALL" ESTATE FULLY ELIGIBLE TO USE THE FAR MORE SIMPLIFIED "SUMMARY" PROCEDURES TO TRANSFER (OR COLLECT) THE LESSER ASSETS. (And this will be even more so especially if you take your time to consciously 'plan' your estate well! Take a look, for instance, at the state of California for an illustration. In calculating whether or not the "gross value" of all property owned by the decedent at death is below the $60,000 figure, you may ignore and NOT count the following property.[9]

- Any and all jointly-held property owned by the decedent within California
- Any and all real property owned by the decedent outside California
- Any and all property, whether owned as community, quasi-community, or separate property, which passes directly to the surviving spouse — e.g., through a trust in which the decedent had a life estate terminating on his death, joint tenancy, etc...
- Any and all property that pass directly to a named beneficiary — e.g., U.S. bonds, life insurance benefits, corporate stocks and bonds, employment-related benefits, pension funds and death benefits and other similar assets, such as the ones listed above in Section B of this chapter
- Any pay-on-death or totten trust kind of bank account owned by the decedent (see item #5 of Section B above for more on this kind of account)
- Any manufactured home, mobile home, commercial coach, floating home, or truck camper registered under the Health and Safety Code in the decedent's name
- Any motor vehicle, mobile home or commercial coach registered under the Vehicle Code in the decedent's name
- Amounts due the decedent for services in the armed forces; amount due the decedent for uncollected wages or retirement benefits up to the amount of $5,000.

As you can see from the above list, *the point is that a great number of people, far more than is ordinarily imagined , may potentially qualify to use the summary probate proceedings to transfer property and need not undergo the regular probate proceedings; you could even have a pretty large estate but still qualify to use the simplified, summary procedure.* And, if you are among the vast number of people who do not necessarily need to have a living trust — and who will lose absolutely nothing, procedurally or financially, if they don't have one. With this summary form of probate, your property may be transferred to beneficiaries by very simple transfer procedures; anyone entitled to inherit from you, whether as a beneficiary under the Will or a trust or as heir under interstate succession laws, may obtain title to or possession of the property through these far simpler transfer procedures, some of which may be as simple as the persons entitled to the property merely submitting the decedent's death certificate and a sworn affidavit of claim to the probate court, and/or to the person or institution having custody or control of the property, such as a bank.

2. When You Already Have Your Property In Other Probate Avoidance Forms That Are Just As Effective

Of course, as recounted elsewhere in the manual (see, for example, Section C above of this chapter), living trust absolutists in the estate planning trade who preach the exclusive use of the living trust mechanism for probate avoidance, are quick to point to a litany of supposed "disadvantages" that supposedly plague virtually every "traditional" method of holding and transferring property among Americans — from joint tenancy, to pay-on-death accounts, life insurance, gift making, etc. And which thereby make such methods, they would say, a "poor alternative" to the living trust.[10]

---

[9]See California Probate Code §13050.

[10]Henry W, Abts III, op. cit., p.23.

But, such rather simplistic generalizations aside, the reality is that there is a sizable category of Americans who can just as prudently, and in many cases less expensively, transfer assets by these other traditional probate avoidance methods, nevertheless, depending on their particular circumstances and special needs and objectives. *The point is that there are situations for which other devices may be the simpler, less expensive and more convenient, but just as effective a method to use than employing a living trust.*

Joint tenancy, for example, will be an excellent arrangement for spouses whose marriage is fairly secure — even if it may not be quite as solid a method for holding property for spouses having a shaky relationship or facing divorce, or for non-marital co-owners who do not get along. Its prime attraction is simplicity, as it is much simpler and mostly far less expensive to establish than the trust. A joint bank account, for instance, would give your beneficiary an immediate and probate-free access to your money in the event of your death, thus affording the beneficiary the kind of prompt, flexible and easy access to funds that even a living trust cannot provide. Furthermore, financial institutions are more commonly familiar with joint tenancy form of ownership and readily accept it. And, as we have seen from the discussion in Item 1 above, even if an estate has a substantial amount of assets that is held in joint tenancy form, or is one that consists largely of assets that pass directly to the surviving spouse, it may well qualify for the more simplified "summary" method of transferring one's property, thus enabling the decedent to have his estate essentially settled without any formal probate proceedings.

Again, the point, simply, is that there are instances and circumstances when property held in other methods of holding property may be the prudent and proper way to go for an individual estate planner.

3. When You May Be Just Too Young, Or Own So Little Property To Need A Trust

There is another category of people who may not really have to have a trust, simply because they do not need one because their circumstances do not legitimately warrant one: the vast number of people out there in the nation who are, for example, young and healthy and in no immediate risk of dying, or simply people, young and old, who merely own very little or no property. For such people, there simply isn't any point to even bother about creating a living trust or about avoiding probate! Rather, for them, a more modest estate plan may be all they need, a plan which may be more adequately met by lesser instruments of estate planning, such as, say, a Will, a durable power of attorney for heath care, and a Living Will.

Take a healthy, responsible, unmarried young person, a student, who is in no immediate danger or likelihood of death, or an older person or a parent who literally and practically owns nothing. For persons in such a situation, the primary objective would usually be to make sure that whatever little property they own will go to who they would want it to go to, and to be sure that they make provision for loved ones or relatives who would care for them in the event of incapacitation, serious medical emergency, or death. Hence, a more modest set of estate planning instruments, such as a Will, and other related instruments, any be more adequately suited to such a person. Additionally, such a person may supplement his or her estate plan with a life insurance, or a pay-on-death bank account, and similar such more traditional instruments that are less involved and simpler to create or operate than the living trust.

Absolutists who would insist on or have you believe that **EVERYONE** should have only a trust, and never consider any other estate planning device, probably haven't thought of this type of people, the too-young or have-nothings, of which there are by no means not just a few in the United States.

In deed, in all frankness, I can only think of one apparent explanation accounting for this extremist position by the proponents of the everyone-must-have-a-trust theology: the general fascination and mass hysteria of the legal and estate planning profession of today with this new "legal wonder drug" of the probate world, the INTER VIVOS TRUST! For, in the frenzied race of the modern-day estate planning professionals to embrace the living trust tool as the "in" tool of the trade, they have unwittingly mistaken the technique for the rationale for which the technique is used, in the first place, or the goal of the exercise. For, when you consider that the undisputed primary purpose for setting up a living trust is for one reason and one reason only, namely, to avoid probate, then how could these professionals advocate the creation of one by a young man or woman who is just too young to own anything or to worry about dying? Or, by a man or woman, young or old, who owns absolutely nothing!?

The point is that for this type of people, a Will, for example, will be a more appropriate tool to employ; it will be simpler to prepare than creating a living trust. But, given the limited needs and goals of the person in this situation, the Will will just as well suffice in distributing his limited estate, while the proceeds from his life insurance will suffice to make some provisions to take care of some loved ones left behind in an estate that otherwise would likely have little or no property.

4. When A Will, And Not A Trust, May Be All You Really Need Because Of Your Special Situation

Finally, suppose your primary estate planning need and goal is simply making certain that you do have a guardian appointed who will step in and care for your minor children in the event of death or incapacitation, and not much else? Or, let's say you legitimately need to have a living trust and you do actually have one created, but that you still need to have a guardian named because you have minor children?

In that kind of situation you'll be talking about an objective, often the most crucial one for a person with little ones, for which there is no other tool to accomplish it within the estate planning field except by employing that most commonly used and oldest of the "traditional" estate planning devices — the good, old WILL! As versatile and all-powerful as the living trust is supposed to be, a living trust just won't be able to help you on this because, by law, such a provision is simply not allowed to be made in a living trust.

In short, if you are in a situation wherein you need to provide for a guardian for your children's care and upbringing, the ONLY way you can legally go, both from the standpoint of sound estate planning and what is legally practicable — will be through having a properly drawn Will drafted, naming a guardian (and successor guardians) "of the person"[1] for the children — that is, one who will be primarily responsible for the actual care, custody, upbringing and guidance of such children in the event of your death or incapacitation until they are of certain specified age of maturity to handle their own affairs.

THE BACK-UP ROLE OF A WILL

What kind of Will are we talking about here? The kind of Will we have in mind here is often referred to as a "back-up" (or "Pour-over") Will because it can be used side-by-side with a living trust (or other estate planning instruments) as a back-up to a trust to provide for any remaining matters not covered or incapable of being covered by a trust. You'll simply provide in such a Will that any assets remaining in your estate at your death which are not expressly covered by your living trust, shall be transferred to the trust, or that they be otherwise disposed of as may be provided for in that Will. [See a sample Back-up Will on p. 148-151].

In this regard, as a back-up instrument, there are several advantages a Will can bring to bear as an estate planning tool which, in and of themselves, make a Will a prudent device to use any way over and beyond the trust (or any other probate avoidance device), and which, in many instances, may essentially be accomplished only through the use of a Will. For example, only virtually through the use of a Will can these be accomplished, among others:

● Providing for expressed disinheritance of a child or other relative whom you might feel is undeserving of inheritance, or who has no need for the inheritance.

● Providing that assets possibly neglected, forgotten about, or otherwise not covered in your trust (e.g., a last-minute inheritance or property you might receive shortly before death, or an expected settlement award from a lawsuit that is still pending, or money won in a lottery, etc.) will get into the trust, or in any case will not wind up getting into the hands of some unintended heirs as intestate property.

● Providing for debts that are owed you to be forgiven, or for donation of your body organs, disposition of your body, and a desired specific funeral prescription.

● Providing overall for planned, orderly, organized disposition of your property and the overall settling of your affairs.

---

[1]Note that there are two basic types of guardians of interest for our own purposes here — a guardian "of the person," and a guardian "of the property". A guardian of the person refers to a guardian whose function is primarily concerned with the care, custody and upbringing of the minor, while a guardian of the property is similar to a trustee appointed in a trust situation, in that it refers to a guardian whose function is primarily concerned with managing the money or property left for the children until they are of age. Generally, when experts speak of the type of guardian appointed through a Will they essentially have in mind the "guardian of the person" type, since it is commonly believed among estate planners that where a need actually exists for a minor's inheritance to be administered, the role of the guardian of the property type of guardian is better played through the setting up of a trust and appointing a trustee to administer the inheritance property. There is no law that says, however, that the same person can't act as both a guardian and a trustee, and in practice both roles are acted by the same person or persons.

[See chapter 9 for further discussion of back-up or pour-over Will, and the actual procedures for drawing up each document.]

E. The Concept Of 'Total' Estate Planning Approach

In this writer's considered estimation, the underlying causative factor why the Living Trust absolutists who argue for the exclusive use of the revocable Living Trust as the sole probate avoidance technique have missed the mark so widely, is rooted in one fundamental thing; failure on their part to take the 'total' approach in their view of estate plan-making! That is, their failure to recognize that to be ultimately able to determine which estate planning method or option, or a combination thereof, is best for you, you necessarily have to first consider ALL the methods or options available. Taking a 'total' approach is essential because, as an estate planner, it enables you to take advantage of not just one, but the whole range of options, and to zero in on the method or methods which may better fit your particular estate planning goal and situation, or best work for you.

The failure, on the part of the advocates of the Living Trust exclusivity to take the 'total' approach primarily strikes at the heart of their case, in that they operate from a professional perspective and mindset that is ultimately flawed, or at the very least, suspect. For, in point of fact, a lot of what are said to be "drawbacks" and "disadvantages" of particular traditional probate avoidance devices by critics and Living Trust absolutists, are not really faults in an intrinsic or structural sense, but actually one minor inadequacy or the other that a particular instrument may possess, but which frequently can be easily cured simply by using one other additional estate planning instrument or another in combination with the original instrument — that is, simply by employing the 'total' plan approach. Thus, elements in each traditional probate avoidance tool — the Will, joint tenancy, gift-making, etc. — which are often pointed to by critics as constituting a disadvantage or drawback of the particular tool, are simply matters which can easily be corrected for, if only one other additional tool (or more) is employed in combination.

Take, for example, the joint tenancy method of avoiding probate. Among the major "disadvantages" and "drawbacks" that are said by its detractors to plague this tool, are the following; that it doesn't avoid probate in the event that both spouses (or both joint owners) die simultaneously (an event which is statistically very unlikely, in the first place); that where the joint tenants are not spouses and the estate is large enough to be taxable, it can result in "double taxation," the first, for income taxes on the estate of the first joint tenant to die, and the second, as a gift tax to the inheritors on the property passed on to the surviving joint tenant; that there is a problem if one party becomes incapacitated or incompetent; and that when the last survivor among the joint tenants dies, the property will then have to go through probate at that stage.

Each of the above mentioned 'shortcomings' can be directly and easily cured, however, by using one or more other additional estate avoidance or planning devices to supplement the joint tenancy arrangement. With a properly drafted back-up Will, for example, you can easily provide for the transfer of your interest in the jointly-held property in the highly unlikely event that a joint simultaneous death occurs. If you simply make it a point to keep good records sufficient to show that the surviving joint tenant or tenants, and not just the decedent, made payments or other contributions towards the purchase or maintenance of their joint property, the risk of counting 100% of the jointly-held property as part of the first decedent's taxable estate will be averted, and the value of the property will be apportioned proportionately among the joint owners. The potential problem of one of the joint owners becoming incompetent can be easily taken care of by having a good Durable Power of Attorney drawn up, appointing a proxy or agent to act in such an event, among other functions. And, the risk of having the property go through probate when the last surviving joint tenant dies, can be adequately addressed by the last joint owner entering into yet another joint tenancy arrangement with his or her intended beneficiary.

Or, let's take a Will, for another example. Proponents of the new you-must-have-the-living-trust-or-nothing-else theology of estate planning would have you believe that this instrument is riddled with a long string of "disadvantages" and "drawbacks" as an estate planning tool. Yet, in some significant ways, even for people who legitimately need and do actually have a living trust, especially those among them with minor children, there is a certain amount of imperative to employ a 'total' estate plan approach — an imperative to have a "back-up" Will, for example, to complement the living trust!

We could, of course, go on and on with other possible examples and scenarios. But the point should be somewhat clear by now. *The point is that contrary to the living trust absolutists' notion of the one-tool-for-everything-and-everybody, all estate planning and probate avoidance devices complement and supplement one another, and no one device, however good or popular, is so worthy or efficient as to warrant that it be the sole and exclusive instrument employed; that in the final analysis, for optimum estate plan or probate avoidance scheme to be had, it is imperative that all available options and methods, and not just one or a limited number, be considered and employed, when and if necessary — in a 'total' estate plan approach.*

F. A Prudent General Principle Of Estate Planning: Employ Particular Probate Avoidance Tool Or Tools Depending On Each Individual's Needs & Situations

By way of summing up this rather pivotal chapter, the underlying central lesson to take away from the discussions in the preceding sections on the differing probate avoidance tools available and their differing capabilities, cannot be mistaken from the standpoint of sound estate planning. It is simply this: that EACH INDIVIDUAL'S SITUATION, NEEDS AND GOALS ARE UNIQUE AND DIFFERENT; and a probate avoidance plan or strategy, or the planning tools employed to implement that, should differ from individual to individual and from situation to situation.

What this says is of profound implication in terms of formulating a philosophy of estate planning, for it goes to the very heart of the central principle by which you — any estate plan-maker — should be guided as you go about the very serious task of making informed, prudent choices from among the array of probate avoidance devices available in an attempt to formulate the best possible estate plan for yourself. What that says to you, in a word, is that *as an estate plan-maker or strategist designing a probate avoidance plan, you should not close your mind or eyes to any options or be rigidly married to any one tool or a limited number of tools, but leave yourself open to employing different tools and strategies carefully tailored to the facts, circumstances, and estate planning needs and goals of each individual.*

What is central to understand is that, as any experienced estate planner will quickly tell you, good estate planning is a PROCESS — in deed, a continuous process. And not simply a one-time undertaking. It isn't, as stated earlier, simply mechanical. In fact, as important as that aspect of it might be, it's much more than simply planning for the transfer of property on your (or one's) death; it is also planning for your estate in the best possible way and manner as to ensure effective enjoyment of it during your lifetime.

The point is that, from the overall standpoint of making an estate "plan" (or for that matter, any kind of plan whatsoever), it makes little strategic sense for one to limit or commit oneself merely to any one particular method (or selected methods) of operation, whatever the purported efficacy of that method. To be able to make a sensible and rational decision regarding your estate plan, or about using a living trust or any estate planning tool at all, while being able to judge their merits or competence, you need to understand <u>EACH</u> estate planning technique — what it is, what it can and cannot accomplish, and how it can be used, either alone or in combination with other estate planning techniques—in formulating an overall plan. You need, in short, to follow a 'total' planning approach. Sure, the Will, joint tenancy arrangements, and other "traditional" devices of estate planning or probate avoidance, may have certain drawbacks and disadvantages in given situations; and, to be sure, none of these other methods may actually have the overall breath and flexibility of a living trust in terms of the types of assets it can cover and what it can be used for. But they can be easier, more handy and less expensive to employ than the trust in particular situations, and yet be just as effective in accomplishing the desired goals for the estate plan owner. Furthermore, the important thing is for the planner to have looked at **ALL** the reasonable and available options and tools. It may still turn out that most people will still choose to go with a living trust as their "best" or most primary device by which to transfer their property or to avoid probate. But, at least, they would be doing so after they shall have had the benefit of considering the whole range of options! *In short, as a strategy of estate planning and estate plan-making, the best approach is to adopt a "total" estate plan approach — to, in a word, consider and understand all estate avoidance methods, and then to decide which particular one or ones will be best for you. To put it another way, it is the facts of a given case — the circumstances of the individual involved, his particular estate planning needs and goals — that should, in turn, largely dictate the estate planning method or methods you should choose to attempt to accomplish the desired estate planning objective!*

Chapter 4

Major Factors You'll Have To Consider & Decide On In Establishing A Living Trust

So you're seriously thinking of establishing a revocable living trust to avoid or minimize probate (or for some other reasons)? Then, here are the major factors you'll have to consider and decide on regarding the terms and provisions of the trust you may have to set up.

A. Basic Trust Terminology

As an aid to understanding how a living trust works, we shall attempt here to define certain basic trust terms and terminology as well as the roles of the key persons involved in the trust.

1. The Grantor

When you set up your trust and transfer property into the trust, you become known as the "grantor" of the trust. The grantor is also known by various other names—the "creator," "settlor," "trustor," "donor," "transferror," "assignor," etc.

Basically, as a grantor all you need to be able to create a trust are two things: you are to have the property to put into it, and you have to have the legal authority to, and be "legally competent" to give ("convey") the property to someone else. (Persons who are minors, for example, or are mentally unstable or bankrupt are not legally "competent" and may not act as grantors or even trustees.)

2. The Trust Res

The Trust Res is the property or the property interest held by the trustee under the trust.

3. Per Capita

Trusts are often prepared by lawyers and trust banks from pre-printed forms. If you use a pre-printed trust form, in all likelihood you will probably see either the words *"per stirpes"* or *"per capita"* in the beneficiary clause of the trust which specifies how the assets are to be distributed. These words are important because they describe how your assets are to be distributed to your descendants if any of your immediate relatives die BEFORE you do—in other words, if one of your children dies before you, how his or his own children (your grandchildren) are to inherit. If the phrase *"per capita"* is used, it means that the property or gift involved should be distributed in equal shares to all the beneficiaries involved, regardless of generation. Under this distribution plan, if one of your beneficiaries (your children) dies before you do, all of your remaining surviving descendant beneficiaries (meaning, actually, all of your remaining living descendants, e.g., children, grandchildren, great-grandchildren, etc.) will get equal shares of the estate, regardless of generation. Thus, for example, if there are 10 descendants still living, each would get one-tenth of your estate. [Notice, however, that if you want only your *surviving children* to inherit your estate, and not their own living descendants as well, you will have to stipulate something like this in the trust: *that your estate be distributed "in equal shares to my children surviving at my death, per capita."*

4. Per Stirpes

The term "per stirpes" is the opposite of per capita. When the phrase *"per stirpes"* is used, it means that if any of the named beneficiaries (say, your children) should die before he could receive the gift, then the amount that he (i.e., your child) would have received had he or she lived, will be passed on to that beneficiary's direct descendants (i.e., to that child's children) as a class or family; that that child's children will be entitled to that portion to which their parent would have been entitled if he had lived long enough to be able to get the inheritance. In other words, under a per stirpes distribution provision, if one of your beneficiaries dies before you, the amount that that beneficiary would have received had he or she lived, will be passed on to all his direct descendants for them to share as a group.

Thus, let's say you have 5 living children, and stipulate in your trust that your estate be distributed "to all my children surviving me, per stirpes," and that one of your children dies before you, before he could be entitled to the inheritance, but leaves behind a family of 3 children. This would mean that your estate would be divided into 5 parts, with each of the other four remaining surviving children directly receiving his or her one-fifth of the estate, and the one-fifth which had been bequeathed to the dead child under the trust going to his (the dead child's) 3 children as a group.

ILLUSTRATIONS: Assume these facts in each case: John, the trust-maker has two children, Edward and Joe. Edward dies before his father John, but Edward has two children, Jane and Mike, while Jane, in turn, has two children, Dave and Mary. Jane, the trust-maker's granddaughter (who has two children, Dave and Mary), also dies before her grandfather, John, the trust-maker.

Figure 4A: Under the *per capita* stipulation, when John dies, his estate will simply be equally divided among all his then surviving descendants, irrespective of generation—that is, son Joe, grandson Mike and great-grandchildren Dave and Mary, who will each receive one-fourth (25%) of his estate.

Figure 4B: Under the *per stirpes* stipulation, on the other hand, upon John's death, Joe will receive 50% of his father's (John's) estate; the other 50% of John's estate which would have gone to son Edward, who is deceased, would now go to his (Edward's) children (Jane and Mike). Mike gets his one-half of the father's 50% of the estate or 25%, but since Jane (Mike's sister) is again deceased, her (Jane's) share (i.e., 1/4 of the estate) will be split between her two living children, Dave and Mary, giving each 1/8 or 12.5% of John's estate.

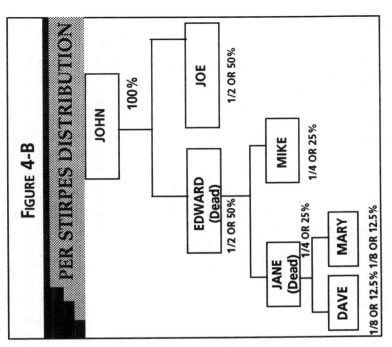

FIGURE 4-B

PER STIRPES DISTRIBUTION

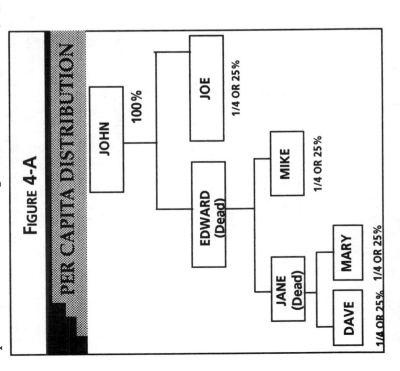

FIGURE 4-A

PER CAPITA DISTRIBUTION

5. Blood Or Adopted (Child)

Under the law, when the term 'child' or 'children' is used in a trust, it is deemed to mean children by blood or by legal adoption.

6. Issue

Refers to your immediate descendants—your children, children's children, children's children's children, and so on, by blood. In other words, your biological children and their offspring. For the term to be taken as referring to your adopted children and their offspring, it has to be defined to say that specifically in the trust.

B. The Essential Elements & Formalities Of A Living Trust

To create a (revocable) Living Trust which will meet the test of validity and legality under any jurisdiction, it's important that we first be clear on the necessary *"elements"* that such an instrument must possess. *They are, for our purposes in this manual, the following:*

1. The Creator's Intent For Creating The Trust

There must be a clear statement on your part—in writing, orally or by conduct—objectively expressing your intent to create a living trust. Essentially, this is taken care of by writing up an appropriate *"Trust Agreement"* or *"Declaration of Trust"* (see pp. 74-b for samples).

2. Picking Out Specific Property Or Asset(s) To Put In The Trust

You must designate specific assets—real or personal property or asset, or both—that are to be transferred to and placed in the trust as the trust property or *"principal"* (also called the *"corpus"*). In most states, you must make a present transfer of an interest in the designated property to the trust, and clearly describe the assets (mortgages, titles to a house, land, bank accounts, stocks and bonds, cash, insurance proceeds, the family business, rights to a patent, copyright or trademarks, etc.) as specifically as possible.

The trust must be funded with assets of substantial value; if the assets of the trust are of only of nominal value, then the trust is deemed to be *"unfunded."* And, hence, in furtherance of this requirement, the trust maker must be sure to formally and actually transfer assets to the fund. That is, once a particular property or asset is transferred to the trust as trust property, that trust property must be segregated and handled separately from the settlors or the trustee's other property; or, if the records and the asset of the trust are not maintained, a court may decide that the trust is a sham and thus invalid.
[See Section D of Chapter 7 (pp. 67-73) for details about the actual operational procedures of transferring property into a trust].

3. Having A Valid Purpose For A Trust

The purpose for which the trust is created must be a valid purpose. That is, it must be a purpose that is not illegal or immoral.

4. Choosing & Naming A Trustee

You must designated a trustee for the trust. The trustee you designate can be either a bank or an individual (if you choose an individual, it will be critically important that the person you select be trustworthy and responsible and likely to live long enough to carry out the trustee's duties under the trust, particularly where there are young children involved as beneficiaries.)

Among the trustee's duties, he (or she) is to maintain records of all trust activities and operate the trust as a legitimate independent entity totally separate and apart from the settlor's (trust-maker's) personal affairs and/or the trustee's. [See Section C below for more on the nature, character, and selection process of the trustee].

5. Name More Than One Beneficiary

We'll assume that you'll name yourself, the grantor (i.e., the trust-maker), as the primary beneficiary of the trust. You should note, however, that if the only person you name as the beneficiary is yourself, then that won't be sufficient. Under the law, for the trust you set up to be deemed legally valid, you must name at least one other beneficiary *other than yourself*. If you are the sole trustee and the only beneficiary, the courts consider that all claims to the title of the trust assets "merge"—i.e., that they belong to the same person; therefore, there is no trust, since for there to be a trust, *legal title* to the assets are deemed held by the trustee, while *equitable title* is with the beneficiary or beneficiaries.

NOTE: For our purposes in this manual, though, we shall opt for the simplified approach and follow Dacey's prescription and adopt the *"one party trust"*—basically a two-person trust wherein you name yourself as the trustee and name a second person, probably your spouse or child, as the beneficiary who also double as your successor trustee. We opt for this approach because, in my view, *Dacey's studied position seems valid that for the needs of the overwhelming majority of Americans, the one-party trust will suffice, because "while the withholding of assets from heirs who may be immature or profligate is oftentimes wise and prudent [as to necessitate appointing an outsider or a bank to serve as the trustee], the great majority of Americans are concerned simply with getting their estates to their families promptly and with the least possible wear and tear."*

6. Identify The Trust With A Federal I.D. Number, If Necessary

If the income exceeds a base amount, a federal employer identification number must be obtained (for the trust) from the IRS for the trust. For a revocable trust, the settlor's income from the trust must be reported by him on his or her personal income tax return but without having to report the trust income separately.

C. The Trust Team

To create a living trust, you'll need to assemble your "trust team"—persons who constitute the essential elements in the creation, operation and eventual termination of the trust. This will include the following: You, the grantor (or grantors), of course, the trustee, the back-up trustee, and his/her alternates, the beneficiaries, children's trustee (where minor children, and probably a children's trust, are involved).

We shall consider below each of the above-mentioned members of the "team" and their roles in some details, as an aid in shedding some light on how a living trust works.

1. The Trustee

In the trust agreement (the "declaration of trust") establishing the trust, you (the trust settlor or grantor) will name a TRUSTEE to hold the "legal title" to the assets in your trust and manage them—in accordance with the specific provisions of the trust agreement. To put in another way, as a grantor you will give the trustee a "legal interest" in the property (meaning, the right to control the property or invest and distribute the property as directed by the trust), while giving the trust beneficiary an "equitable" or "beneficiary" interest in the property (i.e., the right to enjoy and use the trust property), as directed by the trust agreement.

The person or entity you choose to appoint to act as your trustee can be anyone you wish. It could be a corporation, a government agency or an individual, including yourself or your spouse or family members. *As a rule, however, the common practice for grantors of living trusts, especially when the trust is of medium size and the trust provisions are fairly simple, is to simply name themselves (and/or their spouses or close relatives) as trustee so they can maintain complete control over the trust assets.* This way, nothing shall have changed in terms of effective control after the trust is created—you remain in control, in continued management of your financial affairs, same as before. If you appoint yourself as your own trustee, as is often the case with most living trust makers, a prime advantage of this is that you may continue to handle the affairs of the trust for as long as you are alive and are not incapacitated or incompetent. And, if you appoint your spouse a co-trustee, you will be giving each of you the legal authority to act as trustee. Thus, this way either one of you can automatically act for the other, much as you would in a joint checking account, and if and when one of you should die or become incapacitated or incompetent, the other automatically has control of the trust property—with no court authorization needed.

Then, of course, if you and your spouse also own property separately (say, for example, an inheritance or property you owned before your previous marriage), you may want to consider having each spouse establish an individual trust for his or her separate property, in addition to the common trust for the shared property owned together. The primary effect of this would be that it would keep such property separate, even in a community property state or otherwise.

DESIGNATING SOMEONE ELSE OTHER THAN YOUR SPOUSE TO SERVE AS TRUSTEE

Of course, you don't necessarily have to be your own trustee. As stated earlier, you can name anyone (or any institution) you want to serve as your trustee, or to serve as a co-trustee with you. If, for example, you prefer to or don't feel that your spouse can quite competently handle all the financial and management responsibilities of being a trustee or a co-trustee, you can name someone else other than yourself. *You may, for example, choose an adult son or daughter, or some other relatives, friends, or a corporate trustee. In those instances, however, when you do decide to use someone else (even your spouse) as your initial trustee, or a co-trustee, you had better be sure to take further precautions and put in place more detailed controls on the trustee's power to act alone.* You may, for example, require both signatures (yours and his) to buy, or sell or otherwise dispose of the trust property. In any event, whoever you pick for this role, you had better made absolutely certain that there's no question he's the kind of person you can trust with your property. Otherwise, if you have any lingering doubts at all, don't ever pick him (or her) at all!

2. The Back-Up Or Successor Trustee

Next, in addition to naming yourself (or some other party) as the initial trustee, you will need to designate someone, a trusted and reliable person or entity, to take over if the original trustee (or his co-trustee) were to die or for whatever reason is unable to manage the trust—called a successor or "back-up" trustee. In a living trust situation, typically the spouses are designated co-trustees. And in such a case, the SUCCESSOR TRUSTEE is named to take over in the event that something were to happen to both you and your co-trustee. In a marital trust situation, the successor trustee takes over only after both spouses die.

The job of back-up trustee is probably the most sensitive or critical function of all among all the persons within your 'trust team.' In deed, the back-up or successor trustee is probably the most important single officer in your entire "probate" team, in that he's the one who makes sure that the trust is implemented if you (and/or your spouse, in a marital trust) were to die or become incapacitated, the one who distributes the trust assets to your beneficiaries, or takes over the control and management of the trust (payment of the bills, selling of property, financial transactions and decisions, etc.) in the event of your incapacitation. His role is akin to the role typically assigned to the executor of an estate and may often be one and the same in many estates, since most people typically name in their wills the same persons or institutions they appoint as trustee or successor trustee to serve as the executor or personal representative of their overall estates.

THE IDEAL QUALITIES TO LOOK FOR IN A GOOD BACK-UP TRUSTEE

CONSEQUENTLY, IT IS MOST IMPORTANT THAT YOU BE EXTREMELY CAREFUL IN CHOOSING WHO YOUR BACK-UP TRUSTEE(S) IS TO BE. What are the ideal personal qualities or attributes that an ideal successor trustee (or an estate executor or administrator) should possess? Aside from being persons of unquestioned integrity upon whom you can completely rely, the persons you choose should preferably be persons you know and trust whose judgment you respect and who you know will respect your wishes. In addition, the person should be the type who has the level of financial and business experience and temperament, and can afford to devote the amount of time that will be necessary, to be able to handle the trust responsibilities, bearing in mind the size or complexity of the trust and the trust provisions thereof. (As a rule, most family-oriented trust-makers choose a principal beneficiary of the trust, such as a spouse or their adult children, or other relatives or trusted friends, to serve as the back-up trustee).

Charles Plotnick, a long-time Philadelphia estate attorney, and Stephan Leimberg, a professor of estate planning at Bryn Mawr, Pennsylvania, attempted an informed examination of the major characteristics and qualifications which a good estate executor or personal representative should possess. They found that the

Chapter 4: Factors To Consider In Establishing A Living Trust

essential attributes and considerations are many and varies: they range from "competence" for the kinds of tasks involved, to the person's ability to appreciate and concentrate on "the best interests" of the estate's beneficiaries, possessing personal knowledge of the beneficiaries' needs and the subject matter of the estate, experience in handling the inner workings or operations of the decedent's business, especially when the business is a specialized one, having management or investment knowledge of the kind that would put one in "a better position to step in and take control of the decedent's affairs," the objectivity and impartiality of the person, having and being able to devote the amount of time necessary for discharging the duties and responsibilities of a personal representative, and the physical proximity of the person to the estate assets and the beneficiaries. How-ever, concluded the Plotnick and Leimberg team, *of all the essential characteristics making for a good estate manager, in the final analysis the most fundamental one for a manager to possess is the "human factor"—the proposed person's "competence in a general sense."* By this, they mean essentially the person's ability to learn fast and to learn and grow on and with the job, his ability to work with and to get along with people, especially the estate beneficiaries.

Plotnick and Leimberg summed up their findings on the composite characteristics of a good estate executor or manager [or trustee] this way:

"Knowledge of financial matters is not necessarily the most important qualification of an [estate or trust] executor. [This is so since] it is always possible for an executor, if lacking knowledge in certain areas, to learn more about the subject. Selection of a person (or persons) who can firmly adhere to sound values is also important. Likewise, personal integrity and devotion to duty should be valued attributes, although these are often difficult to measure objectively. That is why, in the final analysis, the human factor [the amount of personal effort and attention the party can bring to the task] plays such an important part in the evaluation of the executor's functions...

No list of standards, therefore, can be complete unless due consideration is given to the personal image of the executor as an incorruptible and caring individual in regard to the psychological as well as financial needs of the beneficiaries. Although it would seem obvious that an executor's "competence" must be paramount on any list of qualifications, this factor is often overlooked because of the sometimes emotional nature of the appointment.

[Take this scenario, for an example]: Nancy, a dynamic an worldly business owner who ran an empire of interlocking businesses requiring the greatest amount of expertise, named her husband as her executor. Unfortunately, her husband could barely balance the family's checkbook. The results of Nancy's decision (based on emotion rather than logic) were disastrous. And the negative impact of her decision fell mainly on the spouse whom she had intended to protect.

Competence in a general sense is not necessarily measured by an awareness of all of the decedent's personal affairs or the intricacy of the decedent's business. *A competent executor is one who can analyze the affairs as quickly as possible under the circumstances, determine what facets of the estate can be handled within the bounds of his or her knowledge and capabilities, and then secure professional assistance in those areas in which it is needed...*

[In sum], executors [should not be persons] who preform their duties in an objective vacuum, without giving due consideration to the interests of the beneficiaries, [for when they do, they would] often find that they have put out the fire only after the building has been destroyed... [Rather, the ideal candidate for the job is one who can recognize that] the executor's ultimate responsibility is to handle the estate and preserve and transfer its assets [to beneficiaries] in the most efficient manner possible under all attending circum-stances." [Emphasis added by the writer]

TRANSLATION: True, the other rather more "obvious" qualities and qualifications for a good estate executor (e.g., having the appropriate business sense, and the required ability and amount of time to devote to the responsibility, and similar personal qualities and attributes mentioned above) are important and relevant attributes; but, above all, THE MOST FUNDAMENTAL AND IDEAL PERSONAL QUALITY REQUIRED OF AN EXECUTOR IS HIS OR HER "COMPETENCE"—HIS/HER ABILITY TO ACT AND DECIDE ON MAT-TERS BASED ON LOGIC AND RATIONALITY AS TO WHAT WOULD BE IN THE BEST INTEREST OF THE ESTATE'S BENEFICIARIES, RATHER THAN ON EMOTION; HIS/HER ABILITY TO BE TRULY DEDI-CATED, OBJECTIVE, AND REALISTIC WHILE ALSO BEING CARING AND UNSELFISH, ONCE YOU (I.E., THE TESTATOR OR TRUST-MAKER) ARE GONE!

¹Plotnick and Leimberg, *How To Settle An Estate*, pp. 12-14.

3. Alternate Back-Up Trustee

O.K. So you've got the point. Picking the right person to serve as your trust successor trustee is one of the most important decisions you'll have to make! There's one more thing you've got to do after you've named a back-up trustee: you should still name an "alternate" back-up trustee (same thing as alternate successor trustee), who is to act in case the back-up trustee dies before you do, or for any reason cannot serve. These persons who you appoint as your back-up and alternate back-up trustee do not necessarily have to live in the same state as you (although it would be more convenient if they were to, or live closely to you)

NOTE: If you have a back-up will (see p. 23 & Chap. 9), the person you appoint to serve as the executor of the will should also be the same person you name as your successor trustee, in the interest of harmony and orderliness.

A FINAL POINT ON PICKING A TRUSTEE OR BACK-UP TRUSTEE

And, finally, before we leave this gravely important issue of ensuring that you pick the right person for the job of the back-up trustee (or trustee, in general), there's one very essential element we shall mention. Namely, *whoever you ultimately settle on picking, it is critically essential that you first be absolutely satisfied that he/or she completely agrees to take the job—and all the responsibilities, obligations, and devotion of time and efforts that go with that.* That means that you shall have interviewed your prospective back-up trustee and exhaustively discussed the matter with him, not only to be sure that he (she) knows what is involved or can handle the responsibilities of the task, but even more importantly, in order to be sure that he (she) would actually want to do the job, in the first place.

The point is that you simply can't "assume" that someone—anyone—you have in mind would want the job or would do the job; or that he or she will do a good job of it. Worse of all, you simply can't name someone in the trust document as your trustee or back-up trustee, unknown to him and without prior discussions and his or her consent, and just "assume" that he would do the job when the time comes, much less do it well, whoever he or she may be! In this connection, it is probably very much advisable that you have such a person (or persons) thoroughly review, with you, the sections in this guidebook dealing with the duties and responsibilities of a back-up trustee (see, for example, p. 29-32 & Chaps. 8 and 10) in advance of your discussion with him (or her) about the prospective appointment. In deed, you may also want to give each prospective back-up trustee you have in mind a copy of this manual so as to thoroughly familiarize them not only with their own responsibilities as a trustee, but with the whole matter of the living trust and how it works, and the whole matter of the settling of an estate.

4. Beneficiaries And Alternate Beneficiaries

As one essential "element" for your trust drafting, you will need to name the people and/or organizations you wish to receive your trust assets when you die—your BENEFICIARIES. This can be any person or persons, or any institution(s) you wish, but most people in living trust situations generally name their relatives as the major beneficiaries.

THE SPOUSE

A cardinal principle in estate-planning is that the primary purpose of a Living Trust is to provide for the surviving spouse, and upon the death of both parents (or a parent, if single), the purpose of the trust is generally to provide for the welfare of any minor children, any minor children of a deceased child.

Typically, in a marital trust situation, the surviving spouse is the *"primary"* beneficiary of the trust (as well as the surviving trustee); and the children or other named heirs are the *"contingent"* beneficiaries, meaning that this category of heirs is going to inherit property ONLY IF they are living when the surviving spouse (the second one to die) dies and assets are still left in the trust which are to be distributed to them. To put it another way, in a marital trust situation, upon the death of the first spouse, the surviving spouse is the beneficiary of the trust, and if perchance the children are not living upon the death of the surviving spouse, or there are no assets remaining in the trust at the time, the children are not considered to be beneficiaries.

A beneficiary may be an *income beneficiary,* meaning that he's to receive the earnings from the trust (e.g., interest from a savings account or rents from a real property), or he may be a *principal* beneficiary, to receive the actual trust assets, such as the original principal in the savings account or the actual real property. Or, a beneficiary may be both an income and a principal beneficiary, depending on the stipulations of the trust or the discretion of the trustee.

After naming the "alternate" beneficiary (or beneficiaries)—parties who are to receive the trust property in case your primary beneficiary does not survive you—you are then to name, finally, a *residuary beneficiary,* who takes whatever is left of the trust property when the trust ultimately ends. Alternate beneficiaries are, by their very nature, "contingent beneficiaries"—meaning that their being able to inherit will be contingent (dependent) on the primary beneficiaries not being alive or otherwise able to inherit.

CAUTION: In this connection, while we are on the matter of naming and picking and choosing your beneficiaries, there's one thing you must be careful never to do. And here it is: Never, never name or designate "MY ESTATE" as your beneficiary in the trust. NEVER! Surprisingly, for some strange reason, many people—persons who are obviously not too knowledgeable about estate planning—are known to do this. But nothing could be more ill-advised or improper than to do this, for *if you name your estate as your beneficiary, you are, in effect, expressly asking that your estate (your property and affairs) should go through probate—the very thing you had all along wanted to avoid in the first place by creating a trust!* Why? Because, consider this: who, after all, is your "estate"? It's YOU. Hence, it will be the probate court that will, in that instance, take charge of your assets and undertake the distribution—through the much-dreaded, costly probate process!

5. The Children's Trust, If Appropriate

If you have minor children, it will often be advisable to set up a children's trust within your living trust—a "sub-trust" of the living trust. This way, if you or your spouse were to become disabled or to die, the specific assets designated in the children's trust can be used to educate and support the children—until they reach a certain specified age—without court involvement.

BUT IS THE CHILDREN'S TRUST APPROPRIATE OR ADVISABLE FOR YOU?

Be cautioned of this, though: Experts calculate that a formal children's trust may be advisable only if and when the value of the property being left a minor is substantial—generally more than $25,000 to $50,000. Why? Because, according to these experts, only in such a situation will the cost of managing the estate be outweighed by the advantages a children's trust offers, or the income produced by the trust be large enough to justify tying up the principal.[2] The prime advantage of a children's trust is that it allows you to name a person you trust to specifically manage property for your children's benefits with a minimum of red tape, without expecting the property to go through probate before it is eventually turned over to the children.

Typically, the children's trust is established as a "sub-trust" of your living trust at the same time and in the same founding documents as the living trust, giving your successor trustee flexible powers to spend any of the child(ren's) trust income or property for the health, education, and living needs of the child. And, upon the

[2]This view is expressed by Dennis Clifford, *Plan Your Estate With A Living Trust* (Nolo Press, 1992) at p. 6/9. Clifford advises the use of another method, the Uniform Transfers To Minors Act (UTMA), to leave property to the minor when small estates are involved, or to leave the property directly to your spouse or co-parent if you are in a state which has no UTMA provision—CT, DE, LA, MI, MISS, NEB, NY, PA, TN, TX, VT.

Or, alternatively, as a last resort, to consider leaving the smaller gift to the children through a will, with a property guardian duly appointed.

Basically, here's how the UTMA works for leaving property to your minor children. You make a gift, in your Will or Living Trust, designating the property given, the minor to whom it is given, and a "guardian" you appoint who is to manage the property, and stipulate in the will or trust that the custodian [and a successor custodian, if you name any] is to act "under the [*name of your state*] Uniform Transfers to Minors Act" (for a reasonable compensation from the gift property). Thereupon, the custodian supervises and manages the property and uses the property as he or she decides is in the child's best interest, and normally without bond or court supervision. And upon the child reaching the age of termination specified in the Act, the custodian turns over to him the balance of the gift still remaining, with a final accounting of all the funds distributed, and the gift ends. The age stipulated under the law at which the gift (whatever is still left in the account at the time) can be released to the minor, ranges from 18 to 21 for different states, except for California and Alaska where the age can be extended at your option to 25.

Of all the UTMA states, only the following five authorize the release of the assets when the child reaches the age of 18-21: Arkansas, Maine, New Jersey, North Carolina, and Virginia; the following authorize release at the age of 18: DC, KY, NV, OK, RI, and SD, and the rest of the states listed (except for AK and CA) designate the age of 21 as the age of release.

attainment of a specified age of maturity by the child, the trustee turns over the remaining trust assets to the child(ren). In essence, upon your death, the trust does not automatically terminate since each child to whom you leave property in the living trust does not receive the property, but has it held in a separate sub-trust of the living trust—the children's trust.

As for the children's trustee, for convenience and the greatest level of flexibility, all children's trusts should be managed by the same trustee, generally the same person appointed as your successor trustee for the living trust. The key to a good children's trust is to allow the trustee some flexibility in how to use the trust assets, and sufficient discretion to provide for each child's individual needs as they arise, just as you would as a parent.

CLUE: Put yourself in the shoes of your child's trustee as well as your children's guardian (who should be, and often are, one and the same person); and suddenly you have additional children to raise. What sort of authority, physical facilities and financial resources might you need to adequately carry the extra workload!?

To summarize, a trust for a child should contain at least this information:

• How long the trust is to pay income from the trust to the child

• At what age the child should receive the remaining trust assets

• Under what conditions the trustee may use the assets (as opposed to the income) to pay for the child's education, maintenance and welfare

• The name of a successor trustee to manage the trust in the event the original trustee dies or is unwilling or unable to serve [should, as much as possible, be the same persons as the children's guardian named to care for the child if you die before he or she becomes an adult]

• What is to happen to the assets if the child dies before the trust expires

• A spendthrift provision instructing the trustee as to when and how much income should be paid to beneficiaries who are too young to make financial decisions for themselves

• Provision instructing the trustee to turn over the assets to the child when the child reaches a specified responsible age (typically 25, 30 or 35 years old), or attains certain specified goal (e.g., attainment of college degree)

• Finally, remember to make it a point to review the trust for needed revision whenever a child is born in the family, or is adopted or dies, so as to be sure the trust document still continues to reflect your family needs at all times.

6. Appointment Of A Children's Guardian

If you have minor children, it may be highly advisable that your living trust should contain a children's trust. On the other hand, you will also need to appoint in your pour-over will a guardian for the minor children, as well as for any physically or mentally handicapped persons regardless of age.[3] So, who are you to appoint to serve as the guardian of the children's trust and the alternative guardians? (Persons chosen must be adults, close family members, close friends, etc., who you know and trust will respect your goals and values and will raise your children the way you would want.) Remember, also, to name an alternate guardian to act in the event the primary guardian is unable or unwilling to act for any reason.

---

[3] The guardian is primarily concerned with the raising and upbringing of the children when both parents are no longer living, until they reach majority age, but not concerned with the management of their inheritance. It is the trustee of the children's trust that is responsible for the property management's aspect of the child's life. Many parents, however, name the same person to serve in both capacities, making it convenient for one person to play both roles, although a children's trustee can be a different individual, or a corporate entity, or, if you wish, you can name more than one person to act together as co-guardians.

D. Allocation & Distribution Of Assets: Some Factors To Consider

Note that one unique feature of the Living Trust is that, unlike a Will, the living trust gives each spouse an *independent* right to determine to whom he or she wants his or her own assets given, in what proportion, and when. For a couple with an A-B type of trust, for example [see Chapter 5], at the death of the first spouse, the decedent's trust (Trust B) becomes IRREVOCABLE at that point—that is, the provisions as to the beneficiaries, what they are to be entitled to, when and how the distribution as to the decedent's share of the assets is to be made, etc., become permanently fixed as written. However, as to the surviving spouse's own share of the assets in the survivor's trust (Trust A), the surviving spouse may continue to change its terms and provisions as he or she may desire.

FACTORS TO CONSIDER

Of course, you can leave your assets to anyone or any organizations you may wish, and on the surface the issue of deciding who will be your beneficiaries may probably seem like a "cut-and-dried" matter to you not worthy of being given much thought. There are, however, certain things and certain information you need to keep in mind as you go about making the decision as to who and who you want the inheritances to go to, and when, in what amounts and in what forms. Here are some of such concerns and options you may have to consider in making such decisions:

1. When, Exactly, Is The Specified Inheritance To Be Distributed?

The most commonly used timing provisions for asset distribution are: outright, at a specified age, income only, and deferred distribution. The most common type of distribution asked for by estate plan makers, for minor children and adult beneficiaries alike, is deferred distribution whereby the assets are not automatically distributed to the heirs, but are, in stead, delayed for a specified period or until the heir attains a specified age. For persons with minor children (those below the age of 18), or children who are irresponsible or spendthrifts, this approach is often most advisable.[4]

You could provide, for example, that upon your youngest child reaching the age of 25 and if both you and your spouse are by then dead, each child would immediately receive 1/3 of his or her inheritance; one-third would be distributed to him or her 5 years later, and the final one-third in another 5 years. [Use percentages instead of amounts]

2. In What Form Is The Distribution To Be Made?

Should the trustee distribute the trust assets in kind, or liquidate the assets and distribute cash? [As much as possible, the distribution in kind is to be preferred to liquidation, since it's easier to make the distribution that way. For example, real estate can be distributed by simply rewriting the deed in the name of the beneficiary, (or beneficiaries) or shares of corporate stock distributed by rewriting the stock certificate in the name of the beneficiary].

3. Allocation To Children

Assuming you have children and are married, the following will be some of the major items and options you may have to decide on:

• To whom would you want your assets to go upon the death of you and your spouse (Generally to the children).

• Gifts to parties other than your children. What kinds and types of special bequests, if any, do you wish to make to other parties you may have in mind—your grandchildren, brothers and sisters, church, favorite charities, etc.?

---

[4] According to experts, the advantages of this deferred distribution approach are the following: firstly, it enables parents to give their children more than one opportunity to invest or use their inheritance wisely; if an individual gets the first sum of money and wastes it, he or she still gets another chance to make things right; and secondly, all people mature with age and many individuals need to learn by experience. Said one expert of this method: "Being a registered investment adviser, I have learned from observing many 'mature' people that age is no guarantee of wisdom...I feel strongly about deferred distribution—and providing a second chance—that I have used deferred distribution in my own family's living trust for my children..." Abts III, in *The Living Trust*, p. 210.

• **Allocation In Equal Shares?** Do you wish to allocate the assets equally to each of the children, or to allocate them to each child in different proportions?

4. Distribution Of Income Or Assets?

As to distribution, do you bequeath to your heirs just the *income* derived from assets in the estate, rather than directly giving them the *assets*? (In a situation where, for example, you feel that your children or certain ones among them are immature and/or spendthrifts, you may determine to retain the assets in the trust and pay "income only" to the particular children, either at certain specified times or for a variety of specific needs and circumstances—say, for support and maintenance, medical care, or educational assistance or career development. Income, or a combination of income and distribution, may be more preferable in large estates, particularly ones with sizable real estate holdings where the estate planner may desire to retain the holdings to provide future income to the children. For the children who you feel are quite mature and competent to manage their inheritance outright, you could provide for distribution of the assets to them. In short, you may tailor the distribution to vary from one individual to another, as applicable, as well as for each asset, where appropriate).

5. Per Capita Or Per Stirpes Distribution?

What is to happen to a child's share of your estate (his/her inheritance) if he or she fails to survive you? (Typically, it will pass to the children of that deceased child, that is, your grand-children by him or her).

6. Possibility Of Divorce & Inheritance In The Midst Of Divorce

What happens to your assets if your children were to some day get divorced? (Possible outcome: leave your assets in trust, with the children receiving the income only, thereby excluding the trust assets from being considered the children's property and hence being subject to division between the divorcing spouses; or create separate living trusts for each of your children with separate Property Agreements that designate any "parental assets" passed on to the children as their separate property).

7. Providing For Loans For Older Children

What if you want to keep the trust assets intact until your youngest child reaches a certain age, but, at the same time you want to provide for all your children but do not want to penalize your older children who may need funds to help purchase a home, or start a business, and the like, while they are waiting for the younger ones to get of age? [You may consider providing some guideline as to the amount to be given as an advance or loan to one or more children from their inheritance, which will, upon your death, be considered part of the overall estate and be deducted from the child's share of his or her eventual entitlement in the estate.]

8. Providing For Special Needs Children

Do you have a mentally, physically or developmentally disabled child who may be entitled to government benefits or assistance, such as supplemental security income (SSI) or Medicare, now or in the future? (Solution: To avoid jeopardizing government benefits that are often crucial to the very survival of such an individual, here's what you do.[5] Never include such a child to directly receive the trust asset or income as a distribution; instead, using appropriate and carefully worded language, authorize and direct the successor trustee to provide funds to SUPPLEMENT the regular government benefits—that is, to provide only benefits ABOVE and BEYOND the benefits the child receives from any local, state and federal government or private agency, and which do not duplicate any government-provided services. Thus, the trick is for the trustee to be able to

[5]Rather than make these specified provisions in a Living Trust, a variation of the designated option may be used, which is to create a separate trust (a 'special needs trust') for the disabled child at the same time as the living trust is established, specifically making the same provisions. In drafting the trust instruments establishing this trust, it is extremely essential that the papers be properly drafted to avoid any semblance whatsoever of any trust income whatsoever going directly to the handicapped child, or of his owning any part of the trust assets. Otherwise, upon the death of the grantor, the government may disqualify the child from receiving the government benefits, which may probably be crucial to his survival, or directly step in and grab the entire inheritance you shall have left to the child. A general principle in ensuring that the trust is properly set up, is to be absolutely sure to give the trustee complete control over the trust assets and any income they generate—the child should not be able to receive any distributions whatsoever, as principal or income, from the trust; the trustee, and not the child, is the party who directly makes all required purchases for the child's needs, which should be in the nature only of goods and services that government benefits do not provide—e.g., furnitures, stereo or t.v. set, travelling expenses, etc.

directly pay of child's regular expenses (rent, board, education, medical and psychiatric care, transportation, entertainment and the like)—without making any DIRECT PAYMENTS to the child

9. Gifts To Charities

Are there any charities, churches, foundations or other organizations you wish to leave something for? (If so, take a few moments to sort out these organizations and causes that are special to you, and designate them; you can make your gift as specific or general as you like to, and as large or small, but be sure to specify the legal name and correct street address of the organization you have in mind and an alternative charity beneficiary. Always state the charitable contributions as a percentage of the estate, and never as a dollar amount, to protect your heirs from the potential risks involved from the fact that there's the possibility that the value of the estate could shrink by the time of the first spouse's death.

10. What Kind Of Living Trust To Create

Were you and your spouse previously married with children from your previous marriages? If so, what kind of trust is most advisable to establish from the standpoint of allocating assets fairly? (Consider an A-B Trust, it allows the spouses to combine their assets thereby enabling them to upgrade their standard of living, and since the A-B trust also retains the combined assets, the surviving spouse may maintain the same standard of living as when both spouses were alive. Then, upon the death of the surviving spouse, the assets in the A trust go to the children of the surviving spouse and the assets of the B Trust go to the children of the first spouse to have died.) [See Chapter 5 for more on the three basic types of Living Trust available.]

11. Disinheriting Someone

Are there any child or child of a decedent child you specifically do not want to leave any gifts or bequests for? If so, all you need to do is simply exclude that person or persons as beneficiaries in the trust; no statement needs to be made in the trust document to the effect that the person is excluded. However, to avoid any possibility of any implication that a child was forgotten in error, it's very important that you do this: specifically name each and every one of your children, whether or not he or she is to be named a beneficiary of the trust in the separate back-up or pour-over will you draw up, and leave each of them just $1, in addition to any other bequests also given them. (See pp. 148-151 of the manual for sample of a back-up will)[6]

12. Pets As Beneficiaries

Do you wish to provide for a friend or relative to care for a pet you might own? [You can provide for same in your living trust (or will) with some money set aside therein for the pet's care and maintenance, providing you thoroughly discussed it with the chosen person or veterinarian who you designate to look after the pet and that he is totally agreeable. But, in any event, never name your pet as beneficiary or leave a donation or gift to a pet, through a will or a trust, for the law says that animals are property, and one piece of property (your pet) simply can't own another piece of property (the gift)!!]

---

[5]Note, however, that when it comes to your spouse, no total disinheritance is legally permissible except in the 8 states that fall under the community property distribution system. In community property states, each spouse has no legal rights to receive any of the other spouse's assets, or his or the other spouse's property.

[6]In all other states, under the dower and curtesy laws of the states, a spouse is allowed to claim a substantial portion (generally 25% to 33 1/3%) of your estate regardless of your wishes, unless a spouse has legally waived those rights in a valid written marital property settlement agreement. [see Appendix A for details of each state's provisions on this.]

FIGURE 4-C
GENERAL SUCCESSION OF HEIRS IN INTESTATE DISTRIBUTION SITUATION:
DISTRIBUTION BASED ON FAMILY RELATIONSHIPS

The following illustrates the *general* order of priority by which one's assets will be distributed to his or her relatives when there is no surviving spouse or children. (For the specific pattern of succession distribution and the related percentages, refer to the probate code of the given state).

Explanation: ① First, distribution would be to the parents (if living); if not living then distribution would be to the brother and sisters ②; if neither the parents nor the brothers or sisters are living, then it will go to the nieces and nephews, if any are living ③; and so on.

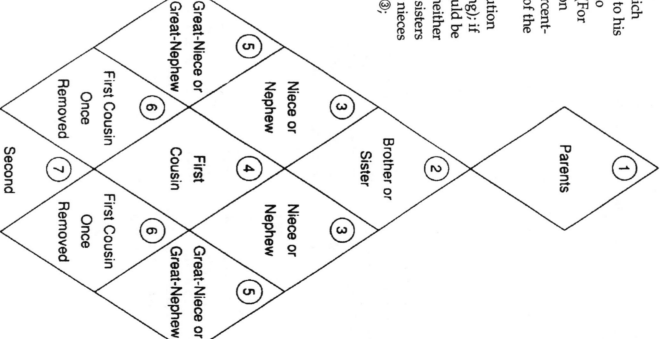

Chapter 5

The 'A-B' or 'A-B-C' Types Of Living Trust: How To Reduce Your Federal Estate Taxes If You Are In A "Large" Estate Bracket

A. Tax Reduction or Minimization As An Estate Planning Objective

The central theme of this book is, of course, PROBATE AVOIDANCE. We're all agreed, it's a major dimension of estate planning. But, there's an aspect of estate planning which we haven't talked about much but which is just as important. It's estate tax reduction and tax planning — planning for minimizing of the taxes that are paid at death, the so-called "death taxes," for short.

In an earlier section of the book (see, especially, Chapter 2), we had explained that the living trust is used primarily for probate avoidance purposes, and that the tool isn't of much value as a tax-saving or tax-planning tool. Well, that is basically right. What we should add, though, is that there is actually a special type of living trust which, with the right category of people who have bigger-sized estates, can provide substantial savings on just one type of tax — the *Estate or "Death"* Taxes. They are the "A-B," and the "A-B-C" types of Revocable Living Trust.

In this chapter, we shall deal with the A-B Living Trust and the A-B-C Living Trust—when they may be best used, how they are created and used, and it's value and benefits as a tax planning and estate planning device.

B. 'Income' Taxes As Compared To 'Death' Or 'Estate' Taxes

As a helpful background material for better clarification and comprehension of what this is all about, let's first explain *the two basic kinds of taxes that are paid at one's death — the income taxes and death or estate taxes.*

1. Income Taxes

Income taxes are, as the name implies, taxes that are assessed or payable on your INCOME — on any income you might have earned or received during any period in your lifetime, before death. For example, even after you die, your estate may still be required to file a final federal income tax return (and pay taxes due on it, if any) for any earnings you might have had, if any, for that portion of the final year in which you lived. And, depending on your state of residence (see Appendix A of the manual), you may also have to pay state income tax as well.

On this type of tax, namely, the income tax, let us make this absolutely clear to you: your living trust will have no effect whatsoever for you; it will neither lower nor eliminate this type of tax (income tax) for you.

2. Estate & Inheritance Taxes (Death Taxes)

Then, there is the other type of tax we are concerned with — the federal ESTATE tax and the state INHERITANCE tax — the DEATH TAXES, for short. With respect to the federal government, this is the type of tax the federal government (the IRS) levies on your estate when you die — if the net value of your estate is more than $600,000, payable by your estate before it is distributed to your beneficiaries. The "inheritance" tax is a state imposed tax levied on the "right" to inherit, paid by the estate before any assets are distributed to the heirs.

HERE IS THE POINT OF SIGNIFICANCE HERE, THOUGH: *On this type of tax, there is better news for you. This type of tax can be reduced, or even eliminated, with the use of a living trust, the type called the "A-B" Living Trust, or the "A-B-C" Living Trust.* [See Chapter 11 and Appendix C for more on estate taxation procedures] We shall get to the actual procedures involved in the "A-B" Living Trust and "A-B-C" Living Trust in a moment. But before we do, let's further review a few more background concepts.

C. What Is Your Net Estate Worth?

As we can see from the discussion above, the SIZE of an estate is of great importance in determining whether the estate will be subject to (federal) death taxes at all, or be exempt from it, since you are subject of this tax ONLY IF the "net" value of your estate is MORE THAN $600,000. Hence, *an important related question to determine is this: is your 'net estate'[1] (meaning the value of your total assets, minus your total debts) large enough to make you subject to estate taxes, in the first place — i.e., an estate worth up to $600,000, if single, or the same amount for both spouses, if married?*

The determination of the size of your net estate is somewhat simple to make. In essence, here's what you do: simply add up the present market value of all your assets (everything you own) , subtracted from that, any debts and mortgages you owe, and add to that the value of life insurance on both spouses, if any (see Figure 5-A below for a synoptic illustrative example). [For a more comprehensive calculation of your net estate, refer to the "Estate Information Organizer Worksheet" (pp. 55-62), and use the Financial Information section thereof (pp. 58-60) to work out your net worth].

FIGURE 5-A
YOUR GROSS ESTATE AND NET ESTATE

GROSS ESTATE

Checking and savings accounts	$ 5,000
Stocks and bonds	40,000
Home	550,000
Value of your business	100,000
Total *gross estate*	$695,000

NET ESTATE

Checking and savings accounts		$ 5,000
Stocks and bonds		40,000
Home	$550,000	
Less: Mortgage	(150,000)	
Net value of home	$400,000	400,000
Value of your business		100,000
Total net estate without life insurance		$545,000
Plus: Life insurance on both spouses (if any)		100,000
Net estate, plus life insurance..........		$645,000

---

[1]To be sure, in certain circumstances the value of your "gross" estate (i.e., all your assets without your liabilities being taken out), as differentiated from your "net" estate or the net value of your estate, could be just as important for some estate planning purposes; it is on the gross value of the estate, for example, that the probate fees are calculated. However, for our purposes here, we are more specifically concerned with the "net" estate value, the value on which the estate and death taxes are calculated.

Alright. Let's just say that your calculations on your net worth pretty much indicates that the value of your net estate is large enough for estate tax purposes, that it is worth at least $600,000 — meaning, in other words, that your estate will likely by subject to some federal estate and/or state death taxes. So, you'll be one for whom some planning for estate tax minimization will be appropriate.

Or, let's say that your calculations indicate that, at least on the surface, your estate isn't exactly large enough to be subject to (federal) estate taxes as of today, but that you feel it will get to be big enough in a few months or years to be potentially taxable. For, consider this for a moment. Consider the very real possibility that inflation could double, triple, or even quadruple an estate fairly quickly; a substantial life insurance policy you may not have today but may become secure in a few years, can add tremendously to the value of your estate; a home or other real estate you own as your major asset today can easily appreciate drastically in value in a matter of a few years, especially in certain parts of the country. In deed, as the chart below clearly illustrates (see Figure 5-B), with a modest inflation rate of only 5 percent per year, an estate with only $300,000 today will hit the magic figure of $600,000 in only 14 years, subjecting it to an estate tax bite just as well; and at the same 5 percent growth or inflation rate per year, an estate worth $500,000 would be worth an excess of $600,000 in just 4 years! Furthermore, people are living longer and longer in contemporary times in America, wives more so than their male counterparts. The point is that the $600,000 figure you think is too far out for you (or you and your spouse) today, may not be as far out as you might think; and that whatever the current net value of your estate, real or apparent, you may need a good estate tax planning just as well, and benefit from at least having an estate tax minimization strategy.

FIGURE 5-B
EFFECTS OF INFLATION ON AN ESTATE'S VALUE

Inflation Rate	Years To Double	Years To Quadruple
5%	14	28
6	12	24
7	10	20
8	9	18
9	8	16
10	7	14
11	6.5	13
12	6	12

D. The Marital Deduction Provision

To try to understand how this system works, let's start by explaining what is known as: The MARITAL DEDUCTION. The "marital deduction" is, in a word, a provision under the tax laws that allows a reduction in estate taxes when you die, if you are married. Based on the concept that a married couple is one economic "unit," and that the estate tax should therefore be postponed until the death of the second spouse, the marital deduction works this way: upon your death (the death of the first spouse to die), you can leave any amount of assets you own, even to the extent of 100 percent of it, if you wish, to your spouse and it will not be taxed at your death, thus allowing the family the use of the funds during the life of the surviving spouse. However, upon the death of your spouse (the second spouse to die), at that point the FULL amount of the estate — both yours and your spouse's — will now be taxed (estate tax).

BUT, HERE'S THE POINT OF DIFFERENCE. Ordinarily the estate — every estate — is entitled to claim a "tax exemption" on the amount of $600,000, so the first $600,000 value of the surviving spouse's estate is not taxed, and can go to your designated beneficiaries tax free. However, you and your spouse didn't actually have to have just a $600,000 exemption; rather, you are entitled to, and could have used <u>each</u> used a $600,000 exemption, for a combined total of $1.2 million exemption from estate tax — IF ONLY YOU HAD PLANNED AHEAD! You hadn't planned ahead, so you, in effect, "wasted" your own $600,000 exemption, and all you could take advantage of is ONE exemption, rather than TWO — the second spouse's exemption.

So, the important question is: since the trouble stems from your not having planned ahead, how do you correct for it? The short answer is *that that's where the A-B and the A-B-C types of living trust come in. Simply put, in the case of the A-B trust, for example, the Trust "B" part of this will use the surviving spouse's $600,000 exemption to which the first spouse to die is entitled, while the Trust **A** part will use the surviving spouse's $600,000 exemption later, when he or she dies—thereby enabling you to pass $1.2 million (rather than just $600,000) to the beneficiaries, tax-free!*

Now you have the general idea. Let's get into the details.

E. An Estate Tax-Saving Solution: The A-B Living Trust

To put it simply, assuming you are in a situation where you'll be subject to (federal) estate taxes, one estate-planning tool available for avoiding paying too high or unnecessary estate taxes is the use of a special form of the living trust: the A-B TRUST. The A-B trust is a kind of *"marital life estate"* trust in that it is primarily meant for and mostly used by married couples, although it can be used as well by any couple, whether married or unmarried. Trust specialists call this kind of trust by any number of names: *"Bypass Trust," "Family Trust," "Spousal Life Estate Trust," "Qualified Terminal Interest Trust"* (Q-TIP, for short), *or "A-B Trust."* But don't let the names confuse you. They are all referring to the same basic type of trust.

F. What is an A-B Trust?

An A-B (living) trust is a particular form of living trust which is usable by any two individuals, married or unmarried, whereby when the first party dies, this trust automatically splits into two separate parts of the same trust, with one part, referred to as the "A" Trust, pertaining to the surviving party or spouse, and the other part, the "B" Trust, pertaining to the deceased party or spouse. [For an easier way to recognize which is which, simply use this word association approach: simply think of the "A" trust as the one for the party(spouse) "Above" the ground (still alive), and the "B" trust as the one for the spouse who is "Below" the ground, or the deceased].

Thus, with the couple's assets placed into an A-B trust, upon the death of one individual, one-half of the assets will flow down into a separate division of the same trust, the B (or decedent's) trust, and the other half of the assets will flow down into the second division of the trust, the A (or the survivor's) trust. Thus, the trick here is that both spouses (or parties) shall have preserved both federal estate tax equivalent exemptions ($600,000 each) and would have thus avoided liability for any estate taxes for that amount of estate value. For example, say the value of the assets in the common trust is no more than $1.2 million, each part of the trust will be entitled to a $600,000 exemption — Trust B gets the deceased party's exemption of $600,000, and Trust A will use the surviving spouse's $600,000 exemption later, when he or she dies, at which point the assets in both trusts are also distributed to the beneficiaries designated. THUS, IN THIS PARTICULAR EXAMPLE (A TWO-PERSON ESTATE WORTH NO MORE THAN $1.2 MILLION) THE ENTIRE ESTATE SHALL HAVE ESCAPED ESTATE TAXES!

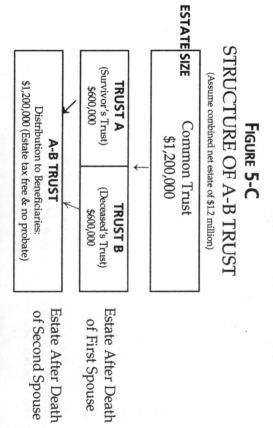

FIGURE 5-C
STRUCTURE OF A-B TRUST
(Assume combined net estate of $1.2 million)

ESTATE SIZE		
Common Trust $1,200,000		
TRUST A (Survivor's Trust) $600,000	**TRUST B** (Deceased's Trust) $600,000	Estate After Death of First Spouse
A-B TRUST Distribution to Beneficiaries: $1,200,000 (Estate tax free & no probate)		Estate After Death of Second Spouse

G. Here's How The A-B Trust Works In Practice

1. A couple (usually married couple) establishes a bypass Living A-B type Trust, stipulating, among other things, that upon the death of one spouse, the designated trustee of the trust (usually the living spouse), will divide the estate into two separate parts — Trust "A" and Trust "B".

2. Thereafter, upon the death of one spouse (call him "B" or the Deceased), at that point the living trust automatically divides into two separate parts of the same trust — Trust "A," for the share of the trust attributable to the surviving spouse, and Trust "B", for the share of the trust attributable to the deceased spouse.

3. The usual practice, if the estate value of the trust is $1,200,000 or less, would be for just one-half of the total trust assets to be placed in Trust A, and one-half in Trust B. If, however, the common trust is OVER $1,200,000 in value, then usually only $600,000 worth of the trust is placed in Trust B, since that's the maximum amount of the federal estate tax exemption — the rest will then go into Trust A (the survivor's trust owned and controlled by her) in order to use the marital deduction mechanism so as to avoid paying any estate taxes at that time. (In other words, in such instances, only $600,000 of the estate will be placed in Trust B (the deceased's trust), since this is the maximum amount of the federal estate tax exemption allowed one spouse, which will mean, in effect, that Trust A (the survivor's trust) will usually contain the survivor's share of the assets plus that portion of the deceased spouse's assets that is in excess of $600,000, if any[2]).

4. Upon the death of one spouse, once the common trust divides into part A (the survivor's trust) and part B (the deceased's trust), and the assets go into the bypass trust (Trust B), the surviving spouse, as the trustee of Trust B, would be entitled to withdraw only the income from trust B for life, and maybe some 5% of the trust asset, but she may not "invade" (i.e., she cannot touch) the principal constituting trust B, unless, upon permission, the co-trustee (one is usually advisable in this kind of trust) agrees that she needs the money for a medical emergency or basic survival.

5. At the death of the first spouse to die, his part of the trust (Trust B) will be subject to an estate tax for that $600,000 asset value in trust B. But, no federal estate tax will be due on it because the $600,000 value placed in trust qualifies for the federal estate tax exemption; and in most states there also would be no state inheritance tax assessed to it. Trust A, on the other hand, is taxed when the second spouse dies.

6. Upon the death of the first spouse, all the provisions concerning his part of the trust (Trust B) or assets apportioned to it, become fixed and irrevocable at that point — no changes can be made to them, thereby giving the first spouse to die a solid way of controlling the eventual inheritors at least of the assets in Trust B.

7. In the meantime, upon the death of the first spouse, the surviving spouse will have complete control over Trust A (the survivor's trust), and can do whatever she wants with the assets, while continuing to receive essentially only the income from Trust B for the rest of her life; the Trust A part will continue to operate as a revocable (changeable) living trust controlled by the surviving spouse, until her own (the surviving spouse's) death.

8. Then, upon the death of the surviving spouse (the second spouse to die), the assets of her share of the trust, Trust A, up to a maximum of $600,000 in value, will also escape estate tax in this way: because she now gets her own personal $600,000 federal estate tax exemption! In sum, as Figure 5-D clearly shows, an entire $1,200,000 estate passes to the heirs tax-free!

---

[2]This is another way of simply saying that under the A-B bypass trust scheme, everything else — except for $600,000 — will have to be placed in the surviving partner's trust (Trust A). Now, note, however, that there is necessarily no law that says you can't put more than $600,000 in Trust B. You certainly can do so, if you desire. For one thing, doing that will give you (assuming you are the spouse who dies first) control over who receives that much estate in Trust B. But it's just that if you were to do that, you'll be losing out on one tax-saving aspect: estate taxes would have to be paid on the excess over and above the $600,000 limit at the time of your death.

Simplified in a nutshell, here is how the probate tax-saving arithmetic will work out using an A-B living trust, (assuming a $1,500,000 net estate):

FIGURE 5-D

THE LIVING TRUST ESTATE TAX 'ADVANTAGE' ON A $1,500,000 ESTATE

Trust A (Surviving Spouse)		Trust B (Deceased Spouse)	
2nd spouse's half of the trust	$750,000	1st spouse's half of the trust	$750,000
Add: excess over $600,000 from deceased's estate via marital deduction	+150,000	Less: excess over $600,000 transferred to Trust A via marital deduction	−150,000
Balance	$900,000	Balance	$600,000
Subtract: 2nd spouse's federal estate tax exemption	−600,000	Subtract: 1st spouse's federal estate tax exemption	−600,000
Taxable estate	$300,000*	Taxable estate	$ 0

*INTERPRETATION: in this estate of $1.5 million in value, only $300,000 of that will be subject to federal estate taxation! Plus, there will be no probate costs!

9. Upon the death of the second spouse, the assets in Trusts A & B[3] are combined by a successor trustee and distribution is made to the beneficiaries according to directions contained in the original Declaration Trust establishing the trust — tax-free (at least up to $1.2 million), and without probate.

H. Summary Of The Advantages Of A-B Living Trust

The following are among the major advantages attributed by estate planners to the A-B Living Trust:

1. Estate tax savings. It saves the estate unnecessary estate taxes, principally by the device of allowing each spouse (or member of an unmarried couple) to use the $600,000 federal estate tax exemption. Through the magic of the A-B living trust mechanism, each trust (trust A and Trust B) is considered, for federal estate tax purposes, a "separate" estate of each of the spouses, thereby making EACH trust eligible for a $600,000 federal tax exemption. This means, in effect, that you are able to enjoy the benefits of TWICE the federal tax exemption, or $1,200,000, as compared to the one exemption or $600,000 that you would otherwise have been entitled to if merely using the standard living trust.

2. No probate fees or expenses. With the use of the A-B trust, you'll be able to get another major savings — there will be no probate costs and fees for your estate to pay.

3. Assures control of one's property and that one's wishes as to inheritance will be fulfilled. Use of the A-B living trust ensures that the assets attributed to the first spouse to die would eventually flow down to his or her intended heirs because, under the principle of irrevocability governing the instrument, once the first spouse dies and the trust assets automatically split into two, no changes can be made thereafter to the provisions regarding trust B (the decedent spouse's trust). Thus, each spouse can be assured that at least the assets he or she agreed to or stipulated in the trust document will go to the heirs he or she designated, whether he or she is living or dead.

Typically, upon the death of a spouse, though, the decedent spouse's share of the estate flowing into his or her trust (Trust B) is subject to the use of the surviving spouse for her lifetime, but upon the death of the surviving spouse, however, those assets will be distributed by a successor trustee to the parties designated as beneficiaries in the original document creating the trust. As a rule, a standard provision in the trust document is a strong prohibition against changing the beneficiaries of trust B. Furthermore, to assure that the assets that you leave behind will eventually get to your beneficiary, such a trust can be used to impose controls on the

---

[3]NOTE: Note that trusts A and B are not really separate trusts and are actually not viewed as such in actual practice; rather, they are merely two parts or divisions of the same trust.

property in the trust, and can be more specifically designed to minimize the chances that the surviving spouse will squander or waste that property and to assure that the property will be safeguarded to eventually go to your designated heirs. Frequently, for example, an occasion may arise where a spouse in a second marriage wants to assure that his or her own separate property eventually reaches his children by his previous marriage without being consumed or diverted by the present surviving spouse. In such a situation, any number of controls could be imposed on the surviving spouse by use of properly worded language in the Declaration of the Trust creating the trust. For example, you could strictly prohibit sale or other disposition of any property in the trust estate, or name someone to serve as co-trustee with your spouse, you could name someone else other than the surviving spouse (e.g., your trusted child or children) as a successor trustee, charged with managing the trust estate and with some requirement imposed for periodic reports and accounting to be made to the final beneficiaries by the successor trustee.

4. Protection of Assets In the Event of Catastrophic Illness. Under the rules governing trusts, provision can be made in an A-B trust to protect assets in Trust B (the decedent's trust) in the event of catastrophic illness or injury of the surviving spouse — something that cannot be provided for in the regular trust, since such a trust cannot be divided. In drafting the catastrophic illness clause in the trust, the aim of the provision is to assure that only the assets in Trust A (the surviving party's trust) will need to be "spent down" to qualify for a critical government assistance. Being able to make such a provision could come in handy for anyone. For, under many government regulations, persons who face catastrophic illness (i.e.,an illness that is very expensive relative to the size of one's estate) would often have to spend down their assets until their life savings or assets are practically exhausted.

Thus, proper provisions can be written into the A-B trust providing that in the event of a catastrophic illness, one-half of the couple's total assets are immediately preserved for the benefit of the other spouse, thereby effectively ensuring that only that share of the estate belonging to a given spouse with the catastrophic illness need to be consumed; and upon exhaustion of that spouse's asset share — and without having to invade the other spouse's half of the assets — he or she can then be eligible to receive medical assistance from the government.

5. May be used to make provision for income and maintenance of surviving spouse. The A-B Trust device can be used to leave property for the use of the surviving spouse (or mate) during his lifetime — but with the flexibility of having her do so with or without becoming the legal owner of the property. Thus, the trust can be tailored so that the surviving spouse has complete control over the trust A assets, but can be limited to receiving only the income (except in extraordinary circumstances) from Trust B.

6. Any appreciation in value of assets in Trust B is estate tax-free. Under the rules, it is at the time of the death of the first spouse to die that the assets placed in Trust B are valued for tax purposes. And, only then! Thereafter, the value assessed on the assets is said to have been "locked in" for estate tax purposes — meaning that that value is the value that will be permanently and exclusively assigned to the items for estate tax purposes in the future. Hence, the value of your trust B assets may multiply and appreciate literally a hundred fold over between the time the first spouse dies and the time the second one dies, and the assets in trust B will still be distributed to your beneficiaries estate tax-free, still based on the original valuation!

I. The Estate Tax Savings Realizable By Use Of The A-B Living Trust, As Compared To Use Of A Will Or A Regular "A" Type Of Trust

What would you have to lose in terms of estate taxes, if anything, if you don't use the A-B type of trust in your estate planning programs? Or, to put it another way, how much better off are you, if any, if you were merely to employ a Will or a regular "A" type of trust, instead of the A-B type of trust? A clear and direct way of demonstrating how much better you'll fare in terms of estate tax savings by use of the A-B trust, is to make a comparison of what would be your estate tax position when you use an A-B trust, as against your position if you were simply to use the more regular method, namely, the regular living trust (the "A" trust) or a Will to pass on your estate to your heirs, or use no estate planning device at all and just rely on the marital deduction.

Here is the comparative analysis:

FIGURE 5-E
COMPARISON OF DEATH (PROBATE COSTS & ESTATE) TAXES:
The Will Versus The "A" Living Trust, & The "A-B" Living Trust

Estate Size		Probate Costs & Estate Taxes			Savings in Comparison To The Will	
		Will	A Trust	A-B Trust	A Trust	A-B Trust
1. $100,000	Death costs (probate fees) on 1st spouse*	$ 4,000	-0-	-0-		
	Death costs on 2nd Spouse*	$ 8,000	-0-	-0-		
	Estate taxes**	$ 0	-0-	-0-	$12,000	$12,000
		$12,000				
2. $300,000	Death costs (probate fees) on 1st spouse*	$12,000	-0-	-0-		
	Death costs on 2nd Spouse*	$23,000	-0-	-0-		
	Estate taxes**	$ 0	-0-	-0-	$35,000	$35,000
		$35,000				
3. $600,000	Death costs (probate fees) on 1st spouse*	$24,000	-0-	-0-		
	Death costs on 2nd Spouse*	$46,000	-0-	-0-		
	Estate taxes**	$ 0	-0-	-0-	$70,000	$70,000
		$70,000				
4. $800,000	Death costs (probate fees) on 1st spouse*	$ 32,000	$ 0	$ 0		
	Death costs on 2nd Spouse*	$ 61,000	$ 0	$ 0		
	Estate taxes**	$ 40,000	$74,000	-0-	$59,000	$133,000
		$133,000	$74,000			
5. $1,200,000	Death costs (probate fees) on 1st spouse*	$ 48,000	$ 0	$ 0		
	Death costs on 2nd Spouse*	$200,000	$ 0	$ 0		
	Estate taxes**	$ 70,000	$259,000	-0-	$59,000	$318,000
		$318,000				
6. $1,500,000	Death costs (probate fees) on 1st spouse*	$ 60,000	$ 0	$ 0		
	Death costs on 2nd Spouse*	$115,000	$ 0	$ 0		
	Estate taxes**	$285,000	$285,000	$60,000	$175,000	$400,000
		$460,000	$285,000	$60,000		

*For the Will case, the 8% probate cost is levied twice—first on the first decedent spouse's one-half of the estate (on 50% of the original estate), and then later, it (8%) is again levied on the second decedent's estate. (The 2nd decedent's estate amounts to her first 50% of the estate, added to the half inherited from her spouse, with the 8% probate cost on it subtracted [i.e., 50% + (50% minus 8% of 50%)].

**Estates do not begin to incur estate taxes until they are worth in excess of $600,000.

NOTE: Assume in each case, a married couple, a probate cost of 8%, and a federal estate tax equivalent of exemption of $600,000. For simplicity, assume in each example that upon the death of the first spouse the estate is divided equally between both spouses, with one-half being attributed to the spouse who died, and 50% attributed to the spouse surviving. In other words, in the Will case, the probate costs are incurred on two occasions—the first, when the first spouse's one-half of the estate is probated, and secondly, when the second spouse's estate is probated.

Source: Figures, as extrapolated by the writer from the illustrative charts and calculations cited in *"The Living Trust"* by Henry W. Abts III (Contemporary Books: Chicago, 1989), to whose author and publisher the present writer is deeply indebted.

J. Some Disadvantages Of The A-B Trust

Despite the many advantages of the A-B trust outlined in the preceding Sections which obviously make it an attractive tool at the hands of an estate planner, use of the A-B trust has some disadvantages and drawbacks which are worthy of note, nevertheless. And, for purposes of a sound and rational planning, it is only proper that you have a more balanced and complete assessment of the pros and as well as the cons of using the device before deciding on the appropriateness and advisability of its employment. In addition, recall, also, that, as was pointed out above (see p. 44), once one spouse dies the provisions of the A-B trust are irrevocable with respect to that deceased party's assets (the "B" part), and it shall have been too late by then for you and your spouse to decide that the trust isn't the proper option for you.

Summed up in a word, essentially the major drawbacks of the A-B bypass trust cited by analysts, revolve primarily around the issue of alleged lack of practicability and flexibility of the device, and alleged lack of complete control of the trust assets by the surviving spouse upon the death of the first spouse to die.

The stated major drawbacks include the following:

1. Lack of Flexibility or Complete Control of Trust Assets

With an A-B Trust, when one spouse dies the surviving spouse has only limited access to the totality of the trust assets; the trust property (or at least a substantial part of it) is left for the use of the surviving spouse during his(her) lifetime, but he doesn't have legal ownership of the property, and can't spend the property as freely and unrestricted as he may need to. Primarily for this reason, say analysts, this sort of trust may be ideal for older or elderly couples with substantial assets, but may not be quite as practical for young couples, for, as one analyst put it, "a young surviving spouse, especially one with family responsibilities, is likely to need access to the full marital estate."[4]

This reaction by one analyst, sums up the salient points of this kind of complaint rather comprehensively: *"This is why this sort of trust is not recommended unless both spouses are old. If both spouses are in their 50's, even if one dies unexpectedly the other will likely live 20-30 years or more. Spouses usually feel that having property tied up, and limited by, a marital life estate trust for so long isn't a good idea, even if some estate taxes are saved in the long run. Similarly, these trusts aren't desired if the spouse is considerably younger than the other and presumably will live much longer than the older spouse."[5]*

It should be pointed out, however, that this point has been strongly disputed by many reputed and knowledgeable experts, who contend that such a concern about the surviving spouse not having control of the assets in the decedent spouse's Trust B, is ill-founded and really an over-exaggeration borne out of confusion among the critics on the actual right of the parties in an A-B trust. Actually, these experts say, the surviving spouse, largely acting in the capacity of the trustee of the decedent's trust B, retains the key beneficiary rights in trust B which, they contend, give the surviving spouse the right to effectively use the assets in trust B without restriction.

One such expert, Henry W. Abts III, a professional living trust specialist who has actually created more than 2000 living trusts, takes this later position. Abts notes that the surviving spouse, as the designated trustee in most living trusts, has these three basic "beneficial rights": they have the right to all the income in trust B, the right to use any or all of the principal in trust B as is necessary to maintain the same standard of living, largely as determined by her, including any medical needs, and thirdly, the right to spend, each year, the greater of 5% or $5,000 of the assets in trust B, regardless of how frivolous the purpose. These three rights, Abts says, "in effect give the surviving spouse the right to use the funds in trust B without restriction."[6]

Abts takes the position that the specific wording in the living trust document which seemingly restricts the rights of the surviving spouse with respect to trust B assets, is actually "used [in order] to satisfy the Internal Revenue Service Code in order to insulate the assets in the decedent's trust B from further estate taxes,"[6] and

---

[4] Theresa Meehan Rudy, et al, *How To Use Trusts To Avoid Probate & Taxes*, p. 117.

[5] Denis Clifford, "Plan Your Estate With A Living Trust (Nolo Press: 1992), p.16/4.

[6] Abts, op. cit., p. 65.

that, in actuality, so long as the surviving spouse, as trustee, does not abuse her fiduciary responsibility to protect the rights of the beneficiaries to the decedent's trust B (say, for example, by removing substantial sum from trust B and losing it, gambling, or by adding it to the survivor's trust A, so that such additional assets would eventually pass to her own children rather than the decedent's children), the trustee can do virtually any prudent thing she wishes with respect to the assets in trust B.

Abts adds that, in any event, the creators of a trust can themselves always draft the trust documents to give as broad or as narrow a spectrum of powers to the surviving spouse as is desired or required in a particular situation. Abts sums up this argument this way:[7]

"If trust B assets are used properly [by the surviving spouse as trustee], there is no practical restriction on the use of the assets in the decedent's trust B by the surviving spouse. For example, the beneficial right of the surviving spouse to invade the principal (as may be necessary to maintain the "standard of living") is not considered to be an abuse of fiduciary responsibility. Who determines what is the standard of living? The surviving trustee. Who is the surviving trustee? The surviving spouse. Thus, *the surviving spouse has substantial latitude in using the funds in the decedent's trust B, but again the latitude must not be abusive. In effect, the surviving spouse has the right to use the funds in trust B almost without restriction.*

Could the trust B assets be entirely consumed for medical needs? Yes, most definitely. If, for example, the surviving spouse contracted cancer and incurred enormous medical bills, all of the assets in trust B could be consumed to meet those medical expenses. That is as it should be and as the decedent spouse would have wanted …

In effect, the creators of the trust have the latitude to make the powers of the decedent's B trust as broad or as narrow as desired for the surviving trustee. Although various restrictions may be imposed upon the surviving spouse as trustee, remember that the situation is a two way street. Restrictions imposed by one spouse are usually imposed as well by the other spouse — and either spouse could end up as the restricted surviving spouse, depending on which spouse is the first to die. Such restrictions could limit the rights of the surviving spouse to income only, with no rights to residual assets even for medical needs; could impose a co-trustee on the surviving spouse; or could distribute some or all of the assets upon the death of the first spouse." [Emphasis added by the present author]

2. Problems Associated With Income Taxes and Estate Taxes

The second major drawback associated with the A-B type of trust has to do with its effect on the "income" type of tax relative to the estate beneficiaries. With respect to the marital life estate trusts, in general, though the A-B (or, for that matter, an A or A-B-C trust) may save the estate some *estate* or *death* taxes, it's not so with respect to *income* taxes. On the contrary, income taxes are owed on whatever income that is receivable from the trusts, and are paid and payable either by the trust, or if distributed, by the beneficiaries. Thus, the surviving spouse (or mate) who receives income from the trust may face substantial income taxes which may even threaten the very existence of the estate.

Secondly, as a rule, if any estate taxes are assessed on the estate when the first spouse dies, it is generally required to be paid within 9 months after death. Thus, substantial cash must often have to be raised at a very short notice and quickly, often compelling the surviving spouse to dispose under pressure and at a loss, a major non-liquid trust assets, such as real estate, especially if the estate lacks liquid assets, such as cash or securities. And, frequently, when such property is disposed of, it is at a substantial loss.

3. Complexity: It Requires Major Considerations and Determinations

The third drawback cited by some critics about the marital life estate bypass trust, is that it involves some complexity, as it often comes in many variations and with many considerations and many technical IRS requirements must be met in order to obtain the required estate tax benefits. Some of the somewhat complex consideration that can arise include:

• What amount of managerial control is to be imposed on the property that is to be left in the decedent's trust B (especially in a situation where there's legitimate reason to worry about the competence of one spouse to sensibly manage the trust property or investment, or where there are worries about ensuring that the property eventually flows down to one's children by a previous marriage)?

[7] Abts, Ibid pp. 66-7.

- Do you want your spouse (the surviving one) to be the trustee of the Trust (which is generally the case), but with a co-trustee, such as a child, also named to act with the spouse?

- Should the surviving spouse, as trustee, be given the power to be able to "invade" the Trust B principal for the surviving spouse's use in the event of some emergency, and if so, under what circumstances and to what extent—to the extent of 25%, 50% or even 100%, or what?

  Or, should the said surviving spouse be only entitled to the income from the trust B property, or merely have a "*usufruct interest*" for life in the property (meaning the legal right to use and enjoy the property, as in the right to live in the house but not to rent it)?

- Which specific marital property will be placed in the Trust B upon the death of the first spouse to die, and which ones will be transferred to Trust A? (Pointers: The governing principle is to place in the B Trust (and C Trust, if applicable) assets that would likely appreciate the most in value over the next few years; since the assets in Trust B are only valued for tax purposes when the first spouse dies and the value "locked in" thereafter at that value, a rapidly appreciating asset will profit from your estate more if contained in trust B in that upon the death of the second spouse later, the higher value will go to your beneficiaries—estate tax-free) [see pp. 168-9 for more on this].

- Should the surviving spouse be given the so-called "5 and 5" power — the right to spend, each year and for any reason whatsoever, $5,000 or 5% of the principal in trust B, whichever is greater.?[8]

- Under the IRS rules, the surviving spouse of the trust-maker must keep and maintain two sets of books and records for the trust — one, for the decedent spouse's trust B, and the other, for the survivor spouse's trust A — in that the property in "each" trust is legally considered a "separate" property from the other. However, while the property of each trust must be formally identified and a separate set of records maintained, a separate Form 1041 need not be filed for trust tax returns. Rather, all you do is simply retain your assets under the same personal social security number you use on your Form 1040, the U.S. Individual Income Tax Return, and continue to report all trust income flow, as in the past, on the Form 1040 personal income tax return — whether you are a single person, or married and filing a joint return, or filing as head of household. Thus, use your own social security number as the identification number for the trust, if you are single; and use your spouse's social security number, if you are married. (The legal right not to have to file Form 1041 [the trust tax return form] for a revocable living trust derives from a law passed by Congress in 1981, by which the "Grantor" trust, as the living trust is specifically called under the IRS rules and procedures, is no longer required to file Form 1041, which rule is reflected in Section 1.671 — 3 (a)(1) of the IRS Regulations.) [9]

4. Concern About Effect on the Living Trust in Case of Divorce

Finally, there is a concern voiced by many people who are interested in the A-B living trust about what effect a divorce will have on the living trust. Actually, in the event of divorce by a married couple who have an A-B living trust, the trust cannot usually be split in half, as it is simply impracticable to do so. Hence, the common solution is for one spouse to retain the trust (meaning essentially that he/she would retain his or her assets in the name of the trust), while the other spouse would remove his or her assets from the trust and formally revoke, in writing, his or her interest in the trust. Such withdrawal of one's assets from and revocation of interest in a trust is easily accomplished by the signing of a "*Spouse's Disclaimer Of Trust Asset Or Interest*" form by the party who is not retaining the trust. (see sample Form LT-8 on p. 116).

K. The A-B-C Trust

Well, we just had the type of trust called the "A-B" Trust in the preceding section. Now, let's just add the "C" part to that to have the last type of the living trust that exists — *the "A-B-C" Trust*.

---

[8]Note that this right is not "cumulative" — i.e., the money must be taken in each particular year, or it's lost forever.

[9]Interpretation of the law, as given by Abts, Ibid. pp. 69-70.

What is the A-B-C trust? First of all, unless you are legally married and you and your spouse have a combined net estate of MORE THAN $1,200,000, you shouldn't even bother about this type of trust, for it's just not for you. (Under the law, the A-B-C trust can be used only by married couples, and not by a mate in a non-martial relationship). But briefly defined, the A-B-C trust (also called the "*Q-TIP*" Trust, the IRS jargon for "*Qualified Terminal Interest Property*"),[10] is the final variant of the living trust *whose specific purpose and advantage is one thing and one thing alone: namely, to enable the surviving spouse to postpone payment of any estate taxes that would have otherwise been due on the first spouse's property when the first spouse dies, until the death of the second spouse — regardless of the size of the estate.*

Basically, the A-B-C trust device — more specifically, the "C" part of it — is simply a way to POSTPONE paying estate taxes if your estate is more than $1.2 million in value.

Let's look at it this way, for a simpler understanding of the concept involved. Assume for a moment, that you have a combined estate worth IN EXCESS of $1.2 million in net value. And that you already have the A-B trust, so you should have already taken advantage of the two estate tax exemptions of $600,000 each — or up to the $1.2 million maximum limit of exemptions allowed. But you have an estate worth in excess of $1.2 million, remember? So what you do is create (or add) a "C" part of the trust so that you can place that excess over the $1.2 million in the "C" trust and at least be able to delay payment of the taxes due on that part of the estate — the excess over $1.2 million that is segregated in the C trust — until the second spouse dies. Let us be clear on one fact, though: that portion of the estate placed in trust C, you should know, is not exactly exempt from estate taxes, since you've already taken the maximum allowed exemption with your A-B trust. Rather, all you get from using the "C" trust mechanism, is a <u>delay</u> — postponement of the estate taxes that are otherwise due when the first spouse dies, until the second spouse dies. But in the end, you or your estate (the surviving spouse) will still have to pay whatever estate taxes are due on it.

ILLUSTRATION: Assume that a couple has a combined net estate worth $1,500,000. Upon the death of the first spouse to die, the estate would be divided into half, one-half of the estate $750,000, will go into trust A (the survivor's trust), and the other half, $750,000, will flow into trust B, (the decedent's trust). But the amount in trust B, the $750,000, is in excess of the $600,000 federal equivalent exemption allowed, and hence an estate tax would be due on that excess amount — that is on $150,000 ($750,000 - $600,000). If all you have is an A-B trust, then trust B will have to pay there and then the estate tax payable on that excess of $150,000 in the decedent's trust B estate, say it is assessed at $60,000, and the balance of the excess estate (i.e., $150,000 - $60,000, or $90,000) will then be added to trust B and would therefore be sheltered from any further estate taxation.

Remember, what we've just described is the scenario you'd have — what will happen — if all you have is an A-B trust, and nothing else. But, what if what you have is an A-B-C trust, instead, and not just an A-B trust? Then, here's what would happen. Rather than having to bring down the decedent spouse's entire one-half of the estate ($750,000) into trust B and have it yield an "excess" over the $600,000 equivalent exemption with the resultant estate tax of $60,000, only $600,000 of the decedent's $750,000 estate would be put into the decedent's trust B. That would then leave the excess of $150,000 (i.e., $750,000 - $600,000) remaining in the decedent's $750,000 share of the estate. That excess of $150,000 is what goes into the "C" trust through the A-B-C trust mechanism, you wouldn't have to pay the $60,000 estate tax at once upon the decedent's death; rather, no (federal) estate tax would be payable — until the death of the second spouse.[11]

[10]The Q-TIP actually refers to the "C" part of the trust, and the rationale for this jargon is defined as follows: since the surviving spouse must receive the income from trust C and may have access to its principal under certain limited circumstances, it is said to be his or her "qualified interest" in the property; and the interest is "terminal" because it ends upon the death of the surviving spouse.

[11]And, very importantly, note that any estate tax which would be computed on the assets remaining in trust A and C upon the death of the surviving spouse, is computed on what is left in the trust as of the time of the surviving spouse's death — and not on what was put into it. That is to say, that the tax is not a "deferred" tax (as $60,000 would be, for example, in our illustrative example), but is simply a tax levied on any assets found remaining in trust A and trust C as of the time of the death of the second spouse. Thus, if in our illustrative example the combined value of the assets in trust A and trust C were less than $600,000, then no federal estate tax at all will be due of that estate upon the death of the second spouse.

FIGURE 5-F
STRUCTURE OF A-B-C TRUST
(For estate worth over $1,200,000)

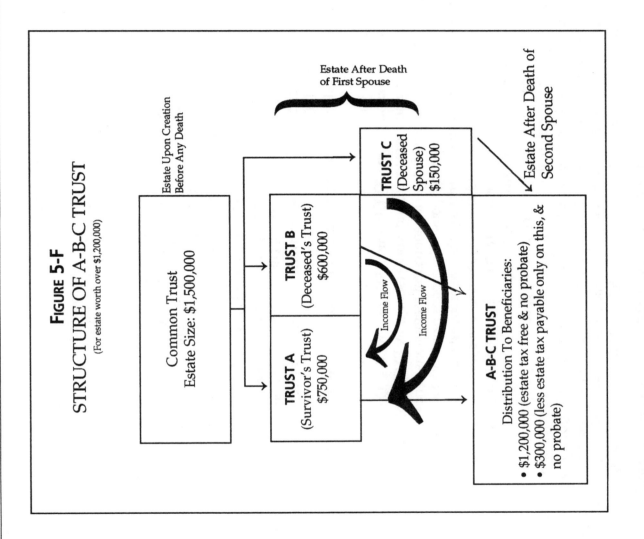

Estate Upon Creation
Before Any Death

Common Trust
Estate Size: $1,500,000

Estate After Death
of First Spouse

TRUST A
(Survivor's Trust)
$750,000

TRUST B
(Deceased's Trust)
$600,000

TRUST C
(Deceased
Spouse)
$150,000

Income Flow

Income Flow

Estate After Death of
Second Spouse

A-B-C TRUST
Distribution To Beneficiaries:
• $1,200,000 (estate tax free & no probate)
• $300,000 (less estate tax payable only on this, &
no probate)

L. The Three Types of Living Trusts: Who Should Use The "A," The "A-B", or "A-B-C" Trust?

As we have elaborated in the preceding passages of this chapter, there are three basic forms which the living trust can take: an "A" living trust (meaning the regular trust); an "A-B" living trust; and an "A-B-C" living trust. A very important and relevant question for you, as an estate plan-maker, is: which of these trust types is the proper type of trust for you, and which should you use? The answer, in a word, is that it is the one that best fits your own particular situation — the one, basically, that best suits your marital status, the net worth of your estate, and the distribution that you desire for your heirs.

Here are a summary of the basic factors by which to quickly determine which type is the proper one for your use:

1. The "A" Trust

The A trust (meaning the regular trust) can be used for single persons or married couples, but is more advisable, from the standpoint of better estate planning and estate tax savings, to be used when only one person is involved. (Basically, under the A trust, for estates valued less than $600,000, the entire estate will flow down to the heirs; because it is small, the entire estate also will incur no estate tax or probate fees; for estates valued more than $600,000, however, taxes will be due).

Pointers: • Use the A trust if you are a single person.

• If you are a couple (married or unmarried), use the A trust only if your estate (basically your total net worth and life insurance) is valued at less than $600,000, but note that you cannot employ the Catastrophic Illness provision (see p. 45) with an A trust.

2. The "A-B" Trust

The A-B trust is used when two individuals, whether married or unmarried, are involved in the trust. (Basically, under the A-B trust, upon the death of one individual, one-half of the assets will flow down into the B (or the decedent's) trust, and the other half will flow down into the A (or survivor's trust), thus leaving the entire estate available to be used by the surviving spouse while at the same relieving the estate of any federal estate taxes for everything under $1,200,000).

Pointers: • If a husband and wife (or couple), you should always consider using an A-B trust anyway, as opposed to simply an A trust, even if your estate's value is less than $600,000 (see p. 41 for the rationale).

• If you are a couple, from the standpoint of estate tax savings, the A-B trust is particularly suitable for you if your estate (i.e., your total net worth plus life insurance) is more than $600,000 but LESS THAN $1,200,000.

• You can employ the catastrophic illness provision (p. 45) as well in A-B trust.

3. The "A-B-C" Trust

The A-B-C trust (also known as the "Q-TIP" trust, IRS jargon for the "Qualified Terminal Interest Property"), is used for a couple who must be married, and whose estate is IN EXCESS of $1.2 million, thereby giving the parties the benefit of two (not one) federal tax equivalent exemptions. The primary purpose and advantage of an A-B-C trust is to enable the surviving spouse to postpone payment of any estate taxes assessed on the property of the first spouse to die, regardless of the size of the estate, until the death of the second spouse. (This is achieved through this basic mechanism: of the decedent spouse's portion of the estate, $600,000 will flow into B [the decedent's trust, which is already shielded from taxation], and whatever excess left over the first $600,000 of the decedent's estate share will, in turn, "over flow" into trust C, thereby shielding that sum as well from estate taxation — until the death of the second spouse).

Who uses the Q-TIP trusts? Actually, any couple having a net estate value that is in excess of $1.2 million may — and should — use this device. In reality, however, it is the wealthy people who have children from a previous marriage that most often use it. They use the income generated by the trust to support a surviving spouse for life, and, upon the death of the spouse, pass the remaining assets to whomever the grantor designates as the ultimate beneficiaries who are often their children from a previous marriage.

Pointers: • Use the A-B-C trust if you are a married couple with an estate (one having a total net worth plus life insurance) that exceeds a value of $1.2 million.

• You can employ the Catastrophic Illness Provision as well in an A-B-C trust. (See p. 45 for explanation of the use of this provision. Note, however, that the income from Trust C will have to be included in the spouse's assets in making the application for benefits).

M. Here's How The A-B-C Trust Works In Practice

1. A couple (only a married couple) having a net estate worth in excess of $1.2 million, establishes a bypass A-B-C type living trust stipulating, among other things, that upon the death of one spouse, the designated trustee of the trust (usually the surviving spouse), will divide the estate into three separate parts — Trust "A," Trust "B", and Trust "C." (Assume, in this instance, a net combined estate worth $1.5 million).

2. Thereafter, upon the death of one spouse (call him "B" or the deceased), at that point the living trust is divided into two equal parts. Since the common trust is IN EXCESS of $1,200,000 in value, one-half part belonging to the surviving spouse, goes into Trust A (the survivor's trust); the other one-half part ($750,000) belonging to the deceased spouse is put into Trust B (the deceased's trust), to the extent of $600,000 in value, and anything over $600,000 (it is $150,000 in this case) is put in Trust C (the deceased's trust). (In other words, only $600,000 worth of assets in the one-half share belonging to the deceased spouse, is placed in trust B [since that is the amount of the maximum amount of the federal estate tax exemption allowed one spouse], and the excess over $600,000 is placed in trust C).[12]

3. Upon the death of one spouse, once the common trust divides into part "A" (the survivor's trust), and parts "B" and "C" (the decedent's trusts), the surviving spouse, who serves as well as the trustee of trust B and trust C, would be entitled to withdraw only the income of trust B and trust C, and maybe some 5% of the trust assets, but she may not "invade" (i.e., she cannot touch) the principal of the B and C trusts, unless, upon permission, the co-trustee (one is usually advisable in this kind of trust) agrees that she needs money for a medical emergency or basic survival.

4. That part of the trust which constitutes the estate of the first spouse to die (trust B and trust C) will be subject to an estate tax for the amount in his part of the estate — a combined amount of $750,000 in our illustrative example. However, since one of decedent's two trusts, trust B, contains only $600,000 of that, no estate tax would be due on that (trust B) since that amount is exactly the federal estate tax equivalent exemption.[13] The overflow or excess (any amount over $600,000) still remaining in the decedent's share of the estate, is $150,000 (i.e., $750,000 - $600,000), and that "overflow" amount would otherwise have been subject to immediate federal tax, but is placed in the decedent's second trust, trust C, and hence, no federal estate tax will be due on it at this time — until the death of the second spouse.

5. Trust A (the surviving spouse's trust), is as well taxed when he or she, the second spouse, dies.

6. Upon the death of the first spouse, all the provisions concerning his share of the trust (trust B and trust C) or the assets apportioned to it, become fixed and irrevocable at that point as to those shares — no changes can be made to them, thereby giving the said first spouse to die a solid mechanism of controlling the eventual inheritors at least of the assets in trusts B and C.

7. In the meantime, upon the death of the first spouse, the surviving spouse will have complete control over trust A (the survivor's trust) and can do whatever she wants with its assets while continuing to receive essentially only the income (and principal if needed for certain living expenses) from trusts B and C for the rest of her life; the trust A part will continue to operate as a revocable (changeable) living trust controlled by the surviving spouse, until her own (the surviving spouse's) death.

8. Then, upon the death of the surviving (the second) spouse, the assets in her share of the trust, trust A, will be subject to estate taxation at that point; any estate tax computed on the assets in trust A (as well as in trust C), will be based not on what was put into the trust, but what is left remaining in the trust (in trust A and trust C) at the time of the surviving spouse's death. Thus, if, for example, the combined value of the assets found at that time in trust A and trust C were less than $600,000, then no federal estate tax would be payable on them.

---

[12]Now, note that there is necessarily no law that says you can't put more than $600,000 in trust B. You certainly can do so, if you desire. For one thing, following that path will give you (assuming you are the spouse that dies first) control over who receives that much of the estate in trust B. But it is just that if you were to do that, you'll be losing out on one tax-saving aspect: estate taxes would have to be paid on that excess over and above the $600,000 limit at the time of your death.

[13]Note that for federal estate tax porposes, the value of the assets in trust B, as assessed as of the time of the death of the first spouse, is "locked in" once made, and will be the value exclusively assigned to the trust B assets for tax purposes; no re-evaluation will be in the future be made for tax purposes on account of any appreciation made by the assets.

(Thus, using our illustrative example of $1.5 million estate wherein trust C contains $150,000 and trust A contains $750,000, the total taxable estate would be $150,000 + $750,000 or $900,0000; and upon subtracting the second spouse's $600,00 federal equivalent exemption from that, the balance of $300,000 would be the figure subject to federal estate taxation, yielding a tax of approximately $115,000 (39% of $300,000) on the original estate of $1.5 million.

9. Upon the death of the second spouse(the second spouse to die), the assets in all three trusts[14] are combined by a successor trustee and distribution is made to the beneficiaries according to directions contained in the original Declaration of Trust establishing the trust — tax-free (at least up to $1.2 million,), and without probate.

IMPORTANT: Note, however, that to ensure that your trust qualifies for the right to use the "unlimited marital tax deduction" provision to minimize estate taxes and/or at least postpone it until the death of the surviving spouse, under the IRS rules a Q-TIP trust must include certain provisions . Most importantly, the surviving spouse must have a right to ALL of the income earned on the trust assets each year, and for his/her lifetime; in deed he or she and no one else, must be its only income beneficiary (the surviving spouse need not be given the right to use the principal), and the income right to the spouse may not be terminated at any time during the life of the surviving spouse. (*In other words, the essence is that the assets be preserved for those eventual heirs, but that the spouse use any income derived from it.*

Note, also, that what this means is that where a spouse desires to pass a substantial share of his/her assets *directly* to his heirs (e.g., to his/her children by a previous marriage), the assets would not qualify for inclusion in Q-TIP trust, since there would be one key ingredient missing: the surviving spouse would not have the right to the income from these assets. Such property would, therefore, be subject to federal estate taxes upon the spouse's death).

The second important condition is that no one must be given the authority to give any part of the trust income or principal to anyone else other than the surviving spouse during his or her lifetime. (This is meant to ensure that the assets, which were passed on, tax-free, to the surviving spouse, will be included in the spouse's estate for federal estate tax purposes when that spouse dies, so as to guarantee that taxes will be paid on any of the couple's assets that are left at the second spouse's death). The surviving spouse may, however, be given the power to name or change during his or her remaining life, by his or her own will, the beneficiaries of trust C (and of trust C only).

N. Summary of the Advantages of A-B-C Trust

For these, see Section H on pp. 44-5 above, dealing with the advantages of an A-B Trust. Those same advantages also apply in the case of A-B-C Trust.

[14]Note that trusts "A", and "B", and "C" are not really separate trusts, and are actually not viewed as such in actual practice; rather, they are merely three parts or divisions of the same trust.

Chapter 6

THE ESTATE INFORMATION ORGANIZER WORKSHEET

Form LT-101

The Estate Information Organizer Worksheet

This WORKSHEET is meant to serve two prime purposes. First, it should be used for the purpose of gathering vital information as a vital aid in the drafting of your Trust (or Will) documents, and in your overall estate planning undertaking. And, secondly, it is to serve as a personal affairs record of essential basic information to assist your Trustee or Successor Trustee, or the Executor of your will or overall Estate Representative, in having all of the information he or she should need to better carry out his fiduciary duties and, in the end, the work of settling the estate.

This worksheet is a key and indispensable component for having your estate ORGANIZED, without which your estate and loved ones will not really be able to "avoid probate" or its horrors even with a good Living Trust, nor your trustee or executor be readily able to settle your estate. *Complete the whole worksheet in full; if an issue does not apply, do not leave it blank, enter 'N/A' (Not Applicable). Frequently, update the worksheet to keep it current—ALWAYS. Keep a (latest) copy alongside your Will and Living Trust instruments.*

FAMILY INFORMATION

1. Your legal name (in full): _____

2. Other names by which known: _____

3. Date of birth _____ Place of birth _____

4. Social Security Number: _____

5. Spouse's name: _____

6. Spouse's date of birth _____ Spouse's place of birth _____

7. Spouse's Social Security Number: _____

8. Your Home address: _____

9. Your Business address: _____

10. Place and date of present marriage: _____

11. Prior marriages: (date and place of marriage and how it was terminated:) _____

12. Name(s) of former spouse(s): _____

CHILDREN (by birth or adoption by present or past marriage:)

13. Name   Date of birth   Present Address

Grandchildren:

14. Name   Date of birth

OTHER RELATIVES

15. **Parents:**   Of Yours   Of Your Spouse's

Father's name and date of birth:

City & Country (State) of birth:

Address:

     Living ☐   Deceased ☐   Living ☐   Deceased ☐

Mother's name and date of birth:

City & Country (State) of birth:

Address:

     Living ☐   Deceased ☐   Living ☐   Deceased ☐

16. Other relatives (included in Trust & Will). [Your brothers, sisters, grandparents, aunts, uncles, nieces, nephews, etc.] (Names & Addresses)

17. Special medical or financial needs or conditions of self, spouse and dependents, if any:

18. Keeping or Selling of Assets

If necessary to pay for my care (or my spouse's care), I want certain assets to be sold first, as follows:

INSURANCE

19. List all insurance policies, pensions, life, retirement & death benefits:

Type of policy & Company   Policy number

20. Accounts & Notes Receivable:

BUSINESS INTERESTS AND AGREEMENTS

21. List all business interests and affiliations you're currently involved with and any business agreements that you are a party to:

_____

STOCKS, BONDS, CD'S, SECURITIES, ETC.

22. Description & Location   Date acquired   Original Cost

23. RECORDS & DOCUMENTS [Indicate the EXACT locations of the following records]:

Birth Certificate Family records: _____

Military records: _____

Will, Living Will, etc. (originals): _____

Appointment of Guardian/Conservator papers: _____

Corporation/Partnership records: _____

Trust documents: _____

Stock certificates, bonds, etc.: _____

Retirement and pension records: _____

Safe deposit box and key: _____

Bank book and savings passbook(s): _____

Life Insurance policies, etc.: _____

Accident & other Insurance policies: _____

Property/Real estate deeds and titles: _____

Powers of attorney: _____

Prior federal tax returns: _____

Financial Statement (Summary of Net Worth): _____

Business Agreements (e.g., buy-sell agreement, etc.): _____

Deferred Compensation Benefits records: _____

Automobile titles: _____

Gift tax records: _____

Medical records: _____

Cemetary deeds: _____

Funeral home information: _____

Your Social Security Card: _____

Spouse's Social Security Card: _____

Promissory notes: _____

Marriage License & Certificates: _____

Divorce Papers from Prior Marriages: _____

Property Settlement Agreements: _____

Postnuptial/Antenuptial agreements: _____

Credit card records: _____

Club, union, civic or fraternal organizations: _____

Safe Deposit box(es): Location & under what name registered _____

Key(s) to each of the safe deposit box(es): _____

58

A. List Your Assets

24. REAL ESTATE (land, home, business property, condos, co-ops, etc.)

Description & address　　　　How ownership is held　　　　Market Value　Equity

25. CASH OR EQUIVALENT FUNDS (checking accounts, savings accounts, money market accounts, certificates of deposit, etc.)

Type　　　　Bank　　　　Account number　　　　Balance

26. INVESTMENTS (stocks, bonds, mutual fund shares, CD's, other securities etc.)

Type　　　　Company　　　　Number of shares　　　　Market Value

27. PERSONAL PROPERTY—whatever you own [furnitures, clothes, etc. that are not major (you need not list individual items unless of significance)]

Description　　　　　　　　　　　　　　　　　　　　　　Approx. Value

28. AUTOMOBILES

List all interests in automobiles

Type　　　　License number

29. RETIREMENT PLANS (IRA's, profit sharing, pension plans, Keoghs, etc.)

Type　　　　Name of plan　　　　Beneficiary　　　　Current Value

30. LIFE INSURANCE (also note the policy number and type of insurance coverage, such as "whole" or "term")

Insured　　　Company　　　Insurance Co.
1st Beneficiary　　　2nd Beneficiary　　　Beneficiary
　　　　Death Benefit

31. ACCOUNTS/NOTES RECEIVABLE & DEBTS OWED YOU *(include name, address and phone number)*

Who owes you (Names & Address)   Amount owed

_____

_____

32. SPECIAL ITEMS OF VALUE *(items of substantial value, e.g., coin collections, antiques, jewelry, art, etc.)*

Description   Approx. Value

_____

_____

33. DEFERRED COMPENSATION *(income earned but not received)*

Employer/Company   Amount Due

_____

_____

B. List Your Liabilities

Type	Company/Person owed	Amount owed	When due	Secured by

34. Mortgages _____

35. Installment loans _____

(credit cards, etc.)

36. Education loans _____

37. Personal loans _____

_____

38. Taxes owed _____

39. Other debts _____

C. Figuring Your Net Worth

	Husband	Wife	Joint
		AMOUNTS	

ASSETS

Real Estate
Cash or equivalent funds
Investments
Personal property
Automobiles
Retirement plans
Life insurance
Accounts rec/debts owed you
Special items of value
Deferred Compensation receivable
TOTAL ASSETS .... (A)

LIABILITIES

Mortgages
Installment loans
Education loans
Personal loans
Taxes owed
Other debts
TOTAL LIABILTIES .... (B)

NET ESTATE
(assets minus liabilities)

(A) — (B)

OTHER VITAL ESTATE DATA

A. MAJOR ASSETS, NOT IN THE TRUST, IF ANY
Jointly owned Property. List all major property, whether included in the above Assets & Liabilities schedule or not, which are not in the Trust but are in joint names and can thus be transferred automatically to the other owner. *(Describe each form of joint-property ownership concerned — real estate, bank accounts, stocks and bonds, etc.)*

1. Type of Property
Address of property or by whom kept

2. Type of property
Address of property or by whom kept:

3. Type of property _____
　　Address of property or by whom kept _____

B. ADVISORS & TRUST TEAM

(Suggestion: Complete this section in pencil so that changes can frequently be made, as necessary)

1. Trustee(s) [Trusted person who manages your trust now; usually it will be you (and your spouse if applicable)].
Name(s) & Address(es): _____　Phone: _____

2. Successor or Back-up Trustee(s) [Trusted person, adult children, friend or even an institution) who steps in to manage your estate in the event of your disability or death]

#1 Choice:	Name _____	Address: _____ Phone: ___
#2 Choice: (Alternate) Name: _____	Address: _____ Phone: ___
#3 Choice: (2nd Alternate) Name _____	Address: _____ Phone: ___

3. Guardians For Minor Children [Trusted adult person who will raise your children if something happens to you & your spouse]

#1 Choice:	Name _____	Address: _____ Phone: ___
#2 Choice: (Alternate) Name: _____	Address: _____ Phone: ___
#3 Choice: (2nd Alternate) Name _____	Address: _____ Phone: ___

4. Trustees For Minor Children [Trusted adult who manages your children's inheritance. Can be the same person as your Successor Trustee or guardian, or could be another adult]

#1 Choice:	Name _____	Address: _____ Phone: ___
#2 Choice: (Alternate) Name: _____	Address: _____ Phone: ___
#3 Choice: (2nd Alternate) Name _____	Address: _____ Phone: ___

C. OTHER ADVISORS:

Name	**Address**	**Phone No.**
Immediate Family & Special Relatives		
Close Friends		
Business Associates		

Family Doctor: _____
Attorney: _____
Clergy: _____
Financial Advisor: _____
Stock Broker: _____
Insurance Agent: _____
Banker: _____
Accountant: _____
Conservator (if applicable): _____
Executor(s) & Alternate(s) of Will _____

D. BENEFICIARIES (Enter for you and for spouse, if applicable)

1. Primary Beneficiaries: Special Gifts to Charitable Organizations

List here gifts (cash or specific item) you wish to make to a charity, foundation, religious or fraternal organization, if any at all.

Name of organization	Description of gift or property

2. Primary Beneficiaries: Special Gifts Of Personal Effects to Individuals

Certain of my personal effects or other specific items have special meaning for me. I desire that upon my death the items listed below be given to these herein indicated (For example, "wedding ring to a daughter, gun collection to a son or nephew", etc.)

Name of Desired recipient & relation	Description of gift or personal property

3. Residuary Beneficiaries

List here the persons (spouse, children, grandchildren, relatives, friends, etc.) who you want to receive the rest of your estate after th gifts to organiza-tions and special gifts above, have been distributed. You can designate for each a dollar amount, or a percentage of the total gift available to this group. Designate each person by name.

Name/Address of each person/organization	Relationship	Amount/Percentage

(Have you made absolutely certain that you made EXACTLY the same provisions in your Trust/Will?)

4. Inheriting Instructions

List here your children, if any, who are minors who you would want to receive their inheritance in instalments, at certain ages, or all at once. Specify the age wanted for each child at which he/she will receive the inheritance

Child's Name	Recommended Age	Percentage of gift to receive & at what intervals

(Have you made absolutely certain that you made EXACTLY the same provisions in your Trust/Will?)

5. Dependents Who Require Special Care

List here, if any, any disabled child requiring special care for whom you want to provide basic care or luxuries to supplement his/her government benefits?

(Have you made absolutely certain that you made EXACTLY the same provisions in your Trust/Will?)

6. Alternate Beneficiaries

List here persons (spouse, children, grandchildren, relatives, friends, etc.) who you want to receive your estate if the beneficiaries you've named in paragraphs 2 & 3 above die before you (and your spouse). You may designate for each a dollar amount or a percentage of the total gift available to this group.

Name & Address of each Person/Organization	Amount/Percentage

(Have you made absolutely certain that you made EXACTLY the same provisions in your Trust/Will?)

Chapter 7

LET'S DRAW UP THE TRUST CREATION PAPERS:
THE STEP-BY-STEP PROCEDURES

A. Some Helpful Practical Procedures For Working Out A Good Living Trust Plan

1. First, you should review and understand some basic background facts, information and principles on estate planning, in general, and the Living Trust, in particular. [Read the following sections of the manual, at least: Chapter 1, "Let's Get The Background Information Straight First: The Trust Basics" (pp. 4-10); Chapter 2, "The Primary Estate Planning Reason(s) Why You Should Have A Revocable Living Trust: To Avoid Probate" (pp. 11-12); Chapter 3, "Other Probate Avoidance Methods of Transfer & When They May Just Be The Proper Tool For You" (pp. 15-25); and Chapter 4, "Major Factors To Consider & Decide On In Establishing A Living Trust" (pp. 26-37).

IN SHORT, (JUST FOR THE BASICS) YOU'VE GOT TO HAVE READ, STUDIED AND MASTERED AT LEAST CHAPTERS 1, 2, 3 & 4 (AMONG OTHERS), IN ADVANCE OF SETTLING DOWN TO BEGIN THE ACTUAL DRAFTING OF YOUR TRUST.

2. Before you start the actual writing up of the trust agreement itself, you should first sit down in a calm, quiet place, with you pen in hand and think. JUST THINK FOR A MOMENT. Run down, in general terms, the whole range of provisions you would want to make in your trust—for your wife or husband, children, relatives, friends, etc., as the case may be. Jot down the ideas as you go along.

3. Assemble, on an organized, detailed worksheet—as well as in your mind—the assets you own or have an interest in, and the debts owed to you; then the debts or obligations you owe to others. And if you have forgiven (or wish to forgive) any of the debts anyone owes you, make a note of them so that you can enter them in the Trust (and in your Will, as well). [Refer to Chapter 6 (pp. 55-62), and use Form LT-101, the ES-TATE INFORMATION ORGANIZER WORKSHEET therein, to aid you in properly and orderly assembling your assets, liabilities, and personal affairs and records]

In deed, among estate planners, this will usually be the starting point in the actual, practical writing of a trust (or will): the inventory and evaluation of the estate for a rough overall idea of what is owned, owed and so on.

4. Have you, by any chance, already made any significant gifts separately (e.g., say in a Will, or by annual $10,000 exclusion gift-making, etc.) to a beneficiary you also plan to name in the Trust? Make a note of it. That fact should be borne in mind as you draw up your Trust, and the provisions of the Trust should be *coordinated* and made compatible with the provisions in your Will. (In other words, don't give out or assign the same property TWICE, or to different persons).

5. Is there any extraordinary circumstance in your personal or family situation——e.g., a prior marriage that has not been completely terminated legally, children by a prior marriage, stepchildren or adopted children,

illegitimate children for which you are responsible, and the like? If there is, do not just merely lump everybody together in the trust documents under general terms like "my children" or "my wife." You must specify which children (or spouse) you refer to by his/her specific name in each instance.

6. Make sure you clearly describe and identify any property or asset, real or personal, that are assigned to beneficiaries in the trust in such a manner that there can be no misunderstanding whatsoever later about your exact intentions or which items in particular you have in mind. By this, we do not mean to say that you have to elaborately or specifically itemize in the trust each and every one or detail of the property—such as the policy numbers of stocks and bonds, the name and address of your broker or bank. We merely mean to say that any items bequeathed to beneficiaries should be sufficiently identified as to be reasonably clear which items are meant. (See sample Schedules A on p. 211 for an idea).

NOTE: Note that there are several ways by which one can "own" property, and that property owned in particular ways are treated in particular manners upon the owner's death. *The most common ownership forms are as follows:* i) individual or "sole" ownership, usually evidenced by being registered only in one name (this is the most basic ownership form); ii) "joint tenancy" of "tenancy by entirety" (shown mainly by being registered in names of BOTH husband and wife, and when the first party dies the surviving party owns the whole thing); iii) "tenancy-in-common" (ownership by two or more parties who are not marital partners; each party owns an equal proportional share only); iv) "partnership," involving two or more persons owning property together pursuant to a written (or oral) agreement and is usually more applicable in business deals (when one partner dies, the partnership is often dissolved and the deceased partner's share of the assets is considered part of his/her estate); and v) "community property," a form of marital partnership wherein all property obtained DURING the parties' marriage, except those acquired by gift or inheritance, are "community property"—i.e., belong equally to both spouses. With respect to community property, upon the death of one spouse, the surviving spouse is entitled only to his or her one half of the community property. (Property prior to marriage and property received solely by one spouse as a result of a gift or inheritance is the separate property of that spouse.) The 9 community property states are: AZ, CA, ID, LA, NV, NM, TX, WA, and WI.

7. In general, be simple and clear in the language you use in your Trust. (Avoid the usual legalese the lawyers love to use in writing Wills or Trusts, such as "I give, bequeath, and devise..." when you could simply say "I give..." and still mean exactly the same thing but with less confusion.)

8. In drawing up the Trust, allow for the unexpected and for different contingencies, if there should be an abnormal occurrence. For example, remember that while most wives often die after their husbands and most children after their parents, it doesn't always happen that way.

9. Allow for the possibility of there being a contest over the terms of your Trust—depending on your particular circumstances. (It's a relatively rare occurrence for a trust, but nevertheless always a possibility!)

B. Some Relevant General Information For Drafting The Papers

1. Generally, the rule is that you may create a living trust to be governed by the laws of any given state of your choice, as long as that state has some material connection with the trust—as in, say, the state wherein you reside at the time of the trust's creation, or where the trustee resides or has his place of business, or where the estate property is located.

2. Living Trusts may not last indefinitely or in perpetuity. Rather, they may only last for no more than a "life-in-being" (i.e., the duration of the life of a person who is living at the time the trust was created), plus 21 years.

3. One is not limited to only one trust. Quite to the contrary, you may establish as many trusts as you like, if you prefer or have good cause to do so. If you are married, for example, a more typical situation is for both spouses to consider most or all property they own as "shared property" owned by both, and hence to use one Living Trust for all property.[1]

To be sure,. it is not unusual to have more than one trust in one family—two separate ones, for example, for property acquired or inheritance had by each spouse BEFORE the marriage, and a trust for property acquired DURING the marriage. Certainly, if you'd prefer, you and your spouse could have separate trusts and separate estates while you are both alive. However, by far the overwhelming practice and preference among the vast majority of married couples is to view their property as common, shared property owned together by both, and a preference for one common living trust.

This is the practice recommended for the readership of this manual and followed in the illustrative samples presented. It is certainly a much more simple method since there will be only one set of documents to deal with because even with separately owned property you can just as well also handle them in one common trust document; and the assets will be kept in trust for a longer period, at least until one spouse dies.

C. Drawing Up The Trust-Creating Document: The Declaration Of Trust

1. Which One Of The Three Forms Of Living Trust Do You Need?

To begin to practically prepare the DECLARATION OF TRUST, which is the document by which the (revocable) Living Trust is legally created, here's the first thing you do. Ask yourself this basic question: which one of the three basic forms of the Living Trust do I best qualify and need to adopt—the Trust "A" type (i.e., the ordinary, regular Living Trust), or the Trust "A-B" type, or the Trust "A-B-C" type? (Turn to Section L of Chapter 5 at pp. 51-2, for the simple pointers on making this choice.)

2. By What State Rules To Be Governed

The next thing you need to do is to understand what your state's legal requirements for a valid Living Trust are. To do this, ask yourself: in what state do I maintain my residence as of the time of my making this trust? Then turn to Appendix A on pp. 187-210 of the manual for the specific statutory rules and requirements that relate to your particular state.

Of course, as pointed out above, generally speaking, the rule is that you may create a Living Trust to be governed by the laws of a particular state of your choice, as long as that state has some material connection with the trust as in, say, the state where you reside, or where the trustee resides or has his place of business or where the estate property is located. Nevertheless, a simple general yardstick used by the vast majority of people is simply to use the requirements of their state of residence at the time of the trust creation. And, anyway, the good news is that the basic concepts and rules governing the creation and operation of trusts are largely identical and interchangeable from state to state across the nation. So, just bear the requirements for your state in Appendix A strictly in mind as you go about the process of creating your trust.

3. Let's Actually Complete Your Living Trust Declaration Form

Now, in the pages ahead (from pp. 74-101) you'll find four (4) different Living Trust samples, each involving a particular situation or circumstance. The four sample forms are as follows:

---

[1]Occasionally, even in a shared-property situation between spouses, a couple may decide that each spouse should have the right to name the beneficiaries of his or her share of the property that is put in the trust. And in such a situation, all that happens is that when the first spouse dies, the shared marital property is divided into two trusts— called Trust 2, which will contain all property of the surviving spouse, and Trust 1, which will contain all property of the deceased spouse. The deceased spouse's property is transferred to the beneficiaries he/she designates in the trust—it may include the spouse, the children,children by a prior marriage, etc.This contrasts directly with the opposite situation where each spouse owns property separately and establish separate living trusts for each party's property. This situation is the far less typical case, however, even in states having "common law" "property ownership system under which one spouse may legally be the sole owner of much of the property. And the same thing is even more true in states which have the "community property" ownership system (see p. 64 and Appendix A for the list of states); there, shared ownership among the spouses is almost always the method followed. If the surviving spouse inherits property from the deceased spouse, the trust document would usually provide for the inheritance to be transferred to the surviving spouse's trust, so no paperwork is required. A common feature in such situations involving marital trust between spouses where shared property is employed, is that the both spouses who set up the trust are usually appointed co-trustees, and when one spouse dies, the other one continues as sole trustee.

Now, select the form that best suits your situation, and complete it by filling in the information in the blanks as necessary. An unmarried person can generally use the forms meant for married couples, but only with a slight modification to reflect the fact that only one person is making the trust, rather than two persons.

As a further aid to help you better complete the forms, you'll find at the end of each Living Trust sample form, a set of SQUARED NUMBERED INSTRUCTIONS that are keyed to the numbers listed on each sample form. These instructions will, where deemed necessary, indicate the type(s) of information or optional range of information that may be entered in a space to complete a form.

Form LT-I—Living Trust For A Single Person With No Children ("A" Type Trust) [See pp. 74-9 for this sample form]

Form LT-II—Living Trust For A Single Person With Children ("A" Type Trust) [See pp. 80-7 for this sample form]

Form LT-III—"A-B" Type of Living Trust For A Married (or Unmarried) Couple With Children [See pp. 90-8 for the sample form]

Form LT-IV—"A-B-C" Type of Living Trust For A Married Couple With Children [See pp. 101-9 for this sample form]

YOU MUST GO STEP-BY-STEP, STRICTLY IN ORDER

THIS IS VERY IMPORTANT: in preparing the forms, take the steps one (and only ONE) at a time, following the items EXACTLY in the same numerical order in which they are listed in the manual. In each clause or paragraph you come to, first read it (plus the instructions), to understand what is called for. Then, go one step (and only one step) at a time according to the order of the numbering. *Do not skip around from step to step or from page to page.*

Make Photocopies & Use Them As Your "Practice" Worksheets

A good practice in preparing the Trust forms, is to make some photocopies of the sample form and use a photocopy of the form as a "practice" worksheet. Fill in the appropriate information in all the photocopy Practice Sheets, from the first page to the last, and as you go along, if there are any paragraphs or provisions which do not apply to your particular situation, cross them out. You'll simply "pencil in" on the sample practice form the appropriate words and statements for a given entry. In each instance, be sure that the words or statements you fill in or enter do clearly state what you want to convey to the trustee, your beneficiaries, etc, or what you want them to do. CLUE: Ask yourself this question: "Would a stranger reading these words or statements readily know what I'm trying to say? Would they make simple sense to him or her? Are my intentions clear, straightforward and unambiguous? Then, after checking to make sure you have everything pretty much in order, type out the information on a final true sheet.

4. What To Do When You've Completed Making Up The Draft Copy Of Your Declaration Of Trust

Let's assume you've finished writing up the practice drafts. Now, run through the PRACTICE WORKSHEETS once again from its first page down, and carefully type (or print) out the full contents of each and every clause or paragraph you filled in or checked off. (Exclude all crossed out or inapplicable material.) Type (or print) out everything relevant onto a separate sheet of white paper to make out a final, true copy of your Trust document. (You should make two final copies of the Trust document, you may use carbon paper, but make sure that each copy is exactly the same in contents.)

Avoid any erasing, crossing out or other corrections in your final draft to avoid any suspicions that might arise later that such changes might have been slipped in by someone other than you. Run down the contents of your final draft once again and carefully proofread it; compare the items on the final draft with the items on the practice sheets. Did you get everything? Is there anything you might like to adjust or add in the final draft? Counter-check and make the necessary adjustments, accordingly. And if there has been any further corrections, then type (or write) out a final, perfect copy.

5. You've Got To Sign And Notarize Your Declaration Document Before A Notary Public

IT'S DONE NOW. The next order of business is the signing and notarizing of the Declaration of Trust document you've just finished drafting.

Here's what you do. *This is most, most important:* The law in just about every state requires that, for your trust to be legally valid, you've got to have your signature(s) to the trust document witnessed and <u>notarized</u> by a local Notary Public. Except for the state of Florida, which seemingly requires that the trust be witnessed by two adult persons, one of which must be the Notary Public, no other state requires live witnesses other than a duly licensed Notary Public to sign the trust document as a witness. So, it's simple as to what you've got to do. Just take your original Declaration of Trust document with you to a local Notary Public (you can find them in the banks, real estate broker's offices, courthouses, lawyers' officers, barber ships, everywhere). There, sign and date the trust document in the presence of the Notary Public. The Notary will then stamp and sign the "Acknowledgment" part on the last page of the trust document and give it back to you.

Note that if the trust is made by you and your spouse (or a mate) as common grantors or settlers, then BOTH you and your spouses must appear before the Notary Public and equally sign the trust document before him or her. Note, also, that it's not only a Notary Public that can sign a trust-maker's acknowledgment under oath. In most states in the country, an acknowledgment of your signature to the trust can be made as well by the following officials: a Justice of the Peace, a Court Judge, or a Clerk of a Court of Record.

Do You Need To File A Notice Of Living Trust?

IMPORTANT: One of the "changes" made by the drafters of something called "The Uniform Probate Code" in the 1970's, largely in a concerted attempt to strip away the much-desired secrecy that a Trust affords, is a provision which requires that a "Notice of Trust" be filed with the appropriate probate body of the given locality in the state.

But here's the good news: This requirement applies only to the handful of states (they are 12 in number) that adopted the so-called Uniform Probate Code: Alabama, Arizona, Colorado, Florida, Hawaii, Idaho, Minnesota, Montana, Nebraska, New Mexico, North Dakota and Utah.

So, here's the relevant information: IF YOUR STATE IS ONE OF THE 12 LISTED ABOVE, SIMPLY COMPLETE FORM LT-2 *"NOTICE OF LIVING TRUST"* (SAMPLE ON P. 110) AT THIS JUNCTURE BEFORE YOU PROCEED. AND SEND IT, BY CERTIFIED MAIL, TO THE CLERK OF COURT OF THE PROBATE COURT FOR YOUR COUNTY. RETAIN A COPY AND THE RECEIPT OF CERTIFIED MAIL ON FILE FOR YOUR PROOF.

D. The Next Order Of Business: Transfer The Trust Property Into The Trust

(a) THE EXTREME SIGNIFICANCE OF ACTUALLY TRANSFERRING THE TRUST PROPERTY INTO THE TRUST

To be able to have a valid trust, it is crucial that immediately following the drafting of the Trust document (the Declaration of Trust), the property designated for the trust be properly and actually transferred into the trust. How crucial is this move to the validity of the trust? Absolutely very crucial!

Picture, for instance, another term employed for transfer of property to a trust: the "funding" of the trust. This is a somewhat more apt definition of the concept because it conveys an idea or what it means to have a trust without property—it's somewhat like a bank without funds! *The important point of relevance to make here is that for the trust you just created to "own" property—for it to have funds—you must actually transfer property into it, you must actually "fund" it.* In deed, in the field of estate-planning and trust-creation, there *is probably no greater moral sin for a trust-maker to commit than to leave a trust unfunded!* SIMPLY PUT, WHEN YOU LEAVE A TRUST UNFUNDED, WHEN YOU, IN OTHER WORDS, DON'T ACTUALLY TRANSFER THE DESIGNATED TRUST PROPERTY INTO THE TRUST—THE PROPERTY IS, IN EFFECT, STILL CONSIDERED YOUR PERSONAL PROPERTY, AND NOT THE TRUST'S; THE ASSETS ARE LEGALLY NOT IN THE TRUST, AND HENCE THE TRUST IS LEGALLY NOTHING MORE THAN A TESTAMENTARY TRUST, MEANING THAT AT THE MAKER'S DEATH THE ASSETS MUST STILL GO THROUGH PROBATE!

In other words, in such a situation, it will just be as though no trust was ever created, and consequently you run a very real risk that the supposed property you thought was a "trust property" will be just as subject to probate as before when you die, or that it may not even go to the beneficiaries you designated in the trust. The trust would not be the legal "owner" of the property, and hence the successor trustees would have no legal authority to transfer that property to your beneficiaries upon your death. *To put it another way, the Trust Res (the Trust Property) is an essential, and integral element of the Trust without which the trust cannot—and does not—legally exist.*

Hence, next to the drafting of the Declaration of Trust document to create a trust (the subject matter of preceding passages), there is one other very important essential in making your newly created trust effective: THE ACTUAL TRANSFER OF THE PROPERTY'S OWNERSHIP TO THE TRUST.

What does the "transfer" of assets actually mean? Now, get this very clear: it does not just mean the mere listing of the assets on a "schedule" that is attached to the Trust document, as most people not experienced in this matter, including, reportedly, even many attorneys[2] typically think. *To properly transfer the property, the property in question has to be actually recorded in the name of the Trust, the legal title of the assets has to be transferred to the trust's name. Basically, you'll have to change the actual ownership papers of the property that is placed in the trust.* (But you should remember, however, that anything you put into or transfer to your trust can always be taken out at a later date if and when you should so desire, and that you actually do not lose control of your property.)

(b) HOW MUCH OF YOUR TOTAL WEALTH & PROPERTY DO YOU PUT IN THE TRUST?

So far as this writer's extensive experience and research on to matter has revealed, there is no set standard policy on this. Some experts would have you place ALL your property in the trust, while others would advocate the transfer of SOME, or even most of your property, by other estate planning methods—joint tenancy, checking accounts, life insurance, etc. Others, who subscribe to the orthodox school of living trust exclusivity, take to the extremist view that "you should leave nothing outside your trust," on the theory that, as they see it, only by doing so can one truly avoid probate on one's total estate.

Here is the more sensible and practical approach to this issue for you: in general, assuming that with you the decision is already settled that you'd use a living trust as one of your probate avoidance devices (see Chap. 3), you should mainly transfer your "big-ticket" items into the trust, unless you effectively have them already (or will have them) in other appropriate probate avoidance forms (see Chap. 3 esp. Section B thereof). Furthermore, you should bear in mind that only your ASSETS (e.g., a house, savings account, stocks, etc.) need to be transferred, and that liabilities (debts you owe on your assets or to others) and general insurance policies (e.g., house and automobile policies), are not transferred into the name of the Trust.

(c) GENERAL PRACTICAL PRINCIPLES OF TRANSFERRING PROPERTY

How do you actually "transfer" a property? Essentially, as one analyst aptly put it, the process itself "is really quite simple."[3]

FIRST, LET'S DIFFERENTIATE ALL TRUST ASSETS INTO TWO TYPES OF PROPERTY: **i)** those types of items for which NO ownership documents are usually had for them (the "loose items," for short), on the one hand, and **ii)** those for which documents of ownership are usually had for them, on the other hand.

---

[2] Abts, the veteran professional estate planner who has personally done or supervised the creation of well over 2,000 Living Trusts in his long professional career, laments that "all too often, attorneys create Trusts but then do not have the clients' assets transferred into the Trusts. Instead, the attorneys simply list the assets in 'schedules' attached to the Living Trusts...However, the client's assets are not actually recorded in the name of the Trust, and...this situation means that the Trust is legally nothing more than a Testamentary Trust. On the death of a spouse, the assets must still go through probate before they will pass into the Trust. Such situations happen all too frequently." Abts relates a particular 1979 case involving the mother of a client, a cancer patient, whom he had taken to an attorney to draw up a trust for. The attorney, claiming that he did not want to "bother" the mother with getting the signatures needed to transfer the assets into the Trust, and brushing aside Abts' repeated warnings that merely listing the assets in a schedule would not actually transfer them into the Trust with the typical lawyer-like attitude that "he was the attorney and that he knew the law," proceeded, instead, only to list the assets in a Schedule A. Then, 6 months later, the said mother died. "Then the trouble began, as the client discovered that, indeed, the assets were not legally in the Trust." (See Abts, The Living Trust, pp. 167 & 168).

[3] Abs, op. cit. p 169

1. Property Having No Documents Of Ownership

For property for which there is usually NO formal title documents or papers of ownership—household possessions and home furnishings, including audio, video and computer equipment, wearing apparel, furs, personal jewelry, antiques, art works, cash, precious metals and collectives, and the like—the procedure for transferring such property is simply this: you merely list them on a trust **SCHEDULE** or make a general descriptive statement about those items on the Schedule, and with a standard provision made in the Declaration of Trust document in reference to the property, you are said to automatically "sweep" all of such untitled property and personal possessions into your trust! The listing in a Schedule and a statement such as this, contained in the Trust, will suffice: "All personal property, household goods and furnishings owned by the grantor." Nothing more will need to be done to legally transfer such items to the Trust!

However, in some situations, there may be occasions or reasons why you may for personal reasons, wish—or even be well advised—to have some credible written evidence of the transfer, even though you need not necessarily have to have one from a technical standpoint. Perhaps, you just want to have a record of it, or some written proof for future reference, or its just your personal preference. In such an event, you could simply draw up an appropriately worded *Affidavit of Assignment of Transfer* which essentially describes the property involved and states that the property is transferred to and into the name of the Living Trust.

Illustrative samples of such an affidavit are reproduced on p. 111, Form LT-3, *"Grantor's Affidavit of Transfer of Chattel & Personal Property,"* which could be used to evidence the transfer of chattel property (moveable property such as trailer, equipment, personal property, motor vehicles, etc.); and Form LT-4, *"Grantor's Affidavit of the Transfer of Contents of a Rented House or Apartment,"* reproduced on p. 112.

2) Property That Generally Have Documents Of Ownership

With respect to those kinds of property for which ownership documents or title papers are usually had—vehicles, bank accounts, real estate, money market accounts, stocks, bonds, insurance policies and the like[4]—to transfer such items you'll have to formally re-register the property in the trust's name. For each of the assets listed on the trust SCHEDULE which has a document of title or ownership, you are to prepare a new document of title transferring ownership of that property from your own personal name to the trust's name.

There are two forms which the title change could take. You could transfer the title into the **name of the trustee**, or, alternatively, you could transfer title to the **trust's name.** For example, to transfer title to an insurance policy that is presently in the name of "John and Mary Doe, Husband and Wife," the policy will be redone either to read that the new owner is: "John and Mary Doe, Husband and Wife, Trustees under trust dated _____, 19___," **OR** "John and Mary Doe Trust." Either form of holding title or language of wording is just as legally valid and proper as the other. However, for our purposes in this manual, the recommended form of wording the title is the latter: PUTTING THE TITLE DIRECTLY IN THE <u>TRUST'S NAME</u>. In our view, this is a better method because it allows for flexibility for the entire life of the trust; you would not have to change the title all over again each time there may be a new change in the trustee. [There are exceptions where this rule may not be followed simply because of one practical problem that is unique to it, i.e., with respect to the transferring of real property].[5]

Then, additionally, to complete or effectuate the transfer process, often the newly retitled document will need to be signed and sworn to (notarized) by you, and be recorded in the public records with the office of the county recorder. And that's the extent of the whole transfer process. (In the case of an insurance policy and many other similar insurance policy instruments of ownership, an insurance broker or agent will usually complete for you on its own the necessary paperwork for transferring such asset, usually for a small, nominal fee.)

---

[4]The applicable assets will include the following: safe deposit boxes, trust deeds, time shares, bonds, corporations, sole partnership or partnerships, real estate, bank accounts, stocks and stock certificates, money market accounts, mutual funds, vehicles, etc.

[5]See p. 71 of this chapter on the transfer procedures for real property, for details concerning such exception.

(d) HERE'S HOW TO TRANSFER SPECIFIC TRUST ASSETS

We give below, some detailed specific procedures by which you may transfer specific assets and property of varying kinds to your Living Trust.

1. Safe Deposit Boxes

To transfer your safe-deposit box into your trust, simply ask your bank officer to rewrite your file card for the safe-deposit box in your trust's name.

2. Business Interests

The methods by which to transfer a business interest differs according to the type of business organization involved—i.e., in terms of whether it is a corporation, or a sole proprietorship, or a partnership.

I) Corporations

To transfer your privately-owned or solely-owned corporation, simply destroy or void your existing corporate stock certificates and have the "transfer agent" re-issue new stock certificates in the trust's name. Blank stock certificates usable for this purpose will typically be included in your corporate minutes book, and could also be purchased from a local legal stationer.

II) Sole Proprietorship

This type of business organization, the unincorporated, solely-owned business, is viewed as one of the easiest to transfer in that the business itself has no title document. To transfer this form of business organization, all you need to do is to list the business in the trust Schedule (see sample of a Schedule in Appendix B); then re-register in the trust's name any ancillary title documents of property owned by the business, such as the business licenses, bank account, trade name, copyright certificate, and the like. If, for example, the business is marketing a patented or copyrighted product, the patent and copyright should be assigned to the name of the trust. To undertake this, simply use Form LT-5, *"Grantor's Affidavit of Assignment of Business Interest to the Trust,"* (p. 113) to notify the persons, agencies or parties with an interest in the affairs of the business about the change in the ownership of the business. And, in most states where it is customary for a sole proprietorship or partnership to file a sworn Certificate of Doing Business in Trade Name with a state or county or local agency, it will also be necessary that the business be registered with such agency to amend the original certificate to reflect the change in ownership, or that the agency be notified as to the change in ownership of the trade name from your name to the trust's name.

III) Partnerships

When your owner's interest in a business is a general partnership interest, first you have to check the partnership agreement and the state laws to be sure they permit transfer of an owner's interest to a Living Trust, or whether or not a trust can legally be a partner under the laws of the state. Then follow exactly the same procedures as outlined above for a sole partnership situation and use the same Form LT-5, *"Grantor's Transfer/ Assignment of Business Interest To The Trust"* (p. 113), for purposes of formally notifying any parties in interest of the change in legal ownership of the business.

One solution, by the way, when and where it is determined under a given set of circumstances or by virtue of a state law or partnership agreement, that a general partner's interest in a partnership cannot be legally transferred to a Trust, without, say, terminating the partnership, would be simply to incorporate the partnership!

3. Transfer Of Real Estate

The process of transferring a piece of real property—a term broadly defined to include everything from a house or dwelling structure, to unimproved land, agricultural or farm land, mobile home, condominium or coop unit, and duplex boat or marina dock space, among other things—to a Living Trust essentially boils down to this: you'll need to complete, sign and notarize a "correction deed" (variously called by such names as a "quit claim," a "grant" or "trust-transfer" deed), listing the trust as the new owner of the property in place of you. And you'll then have that new deed recorded in the public record with the County Recorder of Deed's Office.

You're using a "correction" deed because you're simply *correcting* the title—as opposed to selling the property outright, or transferring the title. To put it another way, you should recall that you are only transfer-ring the BENEFICIAL INTEREST in these assets, not ownership, which means that it's not a change in ownership.

The process is quite simple:

- Locate the original DEED bearing your name(s) as the property's owner(s). (If unable to readily locate this, you can always acquire a certified copy from the County Recorder's Office.)

- Purchase a blank correction deed form (called also a "quitclaim" or "grant" or "trust transfer" deed form) from a local legal stationery store in the state where the property is located (see the sample form on p. 135).

- Complete the blank form, by essentially entering the *trustee's* name as the property's owner to whom the property is now "deeded to" or "granted to," in place of yours. Be sure to enter on the quitclaim form your own names, description of the property, etc., EXACTLY as they're shown on the original deed, and be sure to properly delete any language in the quitclaim deed which refers to "sale" or "purchase" of the real property, as transfer of property to a trust is not considered a sale. If, for example, the original deed says "See Exhibit A attached," then you must be sure to also provide the attached exhibit for the new deed, since it is considered to be part of the deed.) Take notice of the fact that here, with respect to transfer of title in real estate, we say that the title should be put in the TRUSTEE'S, rather than in trust's name. There's a special reason for this recommendation. It is unique to the real estate asset. By its policy Announcement 93-10 in early 1994, Fannie Mae (the Federal National Mortgage Association), and other financial institutions, decreed a new policy which now requires that when real estate is transferred to a trust, the trustee, and not the trust itself, should be listed as the owner on the new deed. Hence, from the practical standpoint, just so that your estate will avoid any potential problems with the mortgage companies and financial institutions, or with the title companies or private insurance enterprises, it is worth it simply to follow this rule in the transfer of real property!

- You, the grantor or grantors, as applicable, should also complete another form, Form LT-6, "*Grantor's Affidavit of Transfer of Real Property Deed to the Trust*," reproduced on p. 114.

- If married and the property in question is held only in one spouse's name, or this request for transfer has not been made by both spouses, then you generally have to prepare as well the *Spouse's Disclaimer Of Trust Asset* (sample Form LT-8 on p. 116), have your spouse sign and notarize it, and include it among the papers to be recorded in the county land and record's office.

- You (the grantor or grantors, as applicable) sign both forms, the deed and the assignment form, in the presence of a Notary Public and have them notarized.

- Attach thereto a covering letter of request, sample Form LT-10 on p. 118).

- Take both forms and the cover letter, to the County Recorder of Deed's office in the county where the real property is located, and have them officially "recorded"—registered. In many states, you may also be required to take with you and also record the *Declaration of Trust* document and, if applicable, the Disclaimer By Spouse form (Form LT-8), to be recorded at the same time with the deed. Check with your Recorder's office.

And, while we are at it, here's one piece of good news you should know in this connection: in most states, transferring your real estate to a revocable living trust should have no affect on the property's property taxes. In short, your property tax should not—and generally will not—increase when you place your home in a Living Trust!

NOTE: When the real property asset involved is an "interest" by the grantor in the real estate contract or agreement for sale, rather than a wholly-owned real property or one owned in "fee simple" by the grantor(s), then you should use Form LT-7, "Grantor's Affidavit of Assignment of Secured Real Property Interest," (sample on pp. 115), instead of Form LT-6. Simply notarize and have it recorded, and that alone should give effect to the transfer into the trust. You'll not need to record a quitclaim or other form of deed in such a situation.

What kind of "interest" in real property is covered by this? A simple way to know this is this: when ever the property involved is evidenced by any kind of DEED — i.e., if you were given any Deed on the property when you bought or negotiated for it—you probably don't fall under this category, for, in such a case, you apparently don't just have an "interest" in the real property but an ownership title to the property (the Deed). A mere "interest" in a secured realty will include such things as a beneficial interest in a Deed of trust; a seller's interest in an Agreement for Sale of Real Estate or in a Real Estate Contract; and an interest you may have as a mortgagee in a mortgage.

4. Transfer Of Bank, Brokerage Or Financial Accounts

Transfer procedures of a bank account to the trust is really pretty easy. Simply complete a transfer authori- zation form, such as sample Form LT-9 on p. 117, "Grantor's Affidavit to Transfer of Financial Account to the Trust," and have it notarized by a Notary Public. Attach thereto a covering letter of request, if necessary. (See sample Form LT-10 on p. 118). Then, ask your bank's officer for a copy of the appropriate bank form for transferring an account to the trust's name. Upon completion and submission of these two forms (plus the covering letter of request, if necessary) to you bank, the bank should go ahead and do all the necessary paper- work to effect the status change in the accounts.

Forms LT-9 **and** 10 (samples on p. 117 & 118) should also be sufficient in effecting the status change in your accounts kept with a brokerage firm in instances when the account consists of stocks or other securities held in the brokerage firm's name—in the so-called *"street name."*

Before you decide to put your bank account, particularly your checking account, into the trust's name, be sure you don't have all your maintenance or spending money in just that one account; be sure to have another account, other than the one you put in the trust's name, that you can freely draw on to make your normal everyday expenditures, without risking the possibility of having to face a hassle from some ill-informed bank or sales clerks who might occasionally give you a rough time about cashing a "trust" check.

5. Transfer Of Securities Or Stock Market Or Mutual Funds Accounts

To transfer your securities—stocks, bonds, U.S. Treasury notes, bonds, debentures, bills, mutual funds, etc[6]—into your trust's name, you essentially have to have them re-registered in the trust's name.

Basically, here's what you do. If your securities are kept with the brokerage firm in the firm's name (known as being held in the *"street name"*), then simply complete the transfer authorization form, such as sample Form LT-9 on p. 117, "Grantor's Affidavit of Transfer of Financial Account to the Trust," and have it notarized by a Notary Public. Submit it (along with the covering letter, Form LT-10 on p. 118) to the brokerage firm holding the securities, along with a copy of the Declaration of Trust. Thereafter, the brokerage firm should go ahead and do all the necessary internal paperwork to effect the status change in the accounts and on the certificates of ownership.

If, on the other hand, the stock or bond is in your personal name and you have personal possession of the certificates for the securities (this is generally the exception rather than the rule), then here's what you do. The easiest way to do this is to request your brokerage firm to transfer the securities for you. Or, if you do not have a stockbroker, you will need to arrange with the "transfer agent" of the corporation involved to issue new

[6]Other assets which will fall under this category may include "general assets" such as the following: money market accounts, certificates of deposit, Ginnie Maes, credit union accounts, limited partnerships, and promissory notes due. You should note that these general assets can generally be transferred into your Trust's name with similar Affidavit of Assignment as is used here which basically describes the asset and transfers it into the trust.

stock certificates or bonds in the trust's name as the new owner. Thereafter, you'll complete sample Form LT-11 on p. 119, "*Grantor's Affidavit of Transfer of Securities to the Trust,*" and have it notarized by a Notary Public and attach a covering letter of request (sample Form LT-10). Then submit this form and the covering letter to your broker or transfer agent, as the case may be, along with the stock certificates or bonds, and a copy of the *Declaration of Trust,* to request that new certificates be issued in the trust's name.

The same procedures as above should also be used in effectuating the re-registration of mutual funds and government bonds and securities in the trust's name.

6. Transfer Of Motor Vehicles

With respect to transferring your vehicles, particularly your automobile, into the name of your Living Trust, actually there is a primary issue that you should first consider: *should you do that, in the first place?* In deed, some analysts[7] in the field simply counsel against it as not worth the hassles that doing so often cause motorists. If you own an expensive or antique automobile, they say, or more than one moderately priced vehicle, or a motor home, that's another story, and in such instance it would be advisable from the standpoint of sound estate avoidance purposes to put those vehicles in the trust's name. But not so when all you have is just one vehicle, or a few averaged-priced ones. In such instance, the analysts say, you should leave the vehicle outside the trust and not transfer the titles because, they contend, the motor vehicle code in most states is exempt from the probate code.

Nevertheless, if for whatever reason you decide that you want to transfer your motor vehicle to your Living Trust's name, the easiest way to go about it is commonsensical. Simply contact your state's Department of Motor Vehicles and ask for its requirements for putting the vehicles into a trust's name.

7. Transfer Of Other Real Assets Having Documents Of Title

As stated in Parts b-2 of Section D above, the general principle is that to transfer any asset that usually has a document or title of ownership, essentially you'll generally have to re-register the asset or property in the trust's name. So, for virtually any asset you can conceive of which fall under this category which you list in the trust Schedule—certificates of deposits, ginni maes, credit union accounts, promissory notes due, patents and copyrights, etc.,— that's what you'll basically seek to do.

By and large, the basic procedure of effectuating the transfer is to send an appropriately worded Affidavit of Assignment to the financial institution or the government agency or other persons or entities having an interest in the change, detailing the specific asset and particulars (e.g., the account numbers, the ID number of the trust, etc.) and stipulating that the particular asset(s) are to be transferred into the designated trust's name. And assuming that the institution or agency is satisfied that proper authorization has been granted it, the transfer will be made and you should expect the ownership records or instruments to be changed accordingly, and/or to receive some written notification to that effect.

For example, let's say you wish to transfer an interest in a contract, say, specifically, in a contract with a publisher for the publication and distribution of your book. Then you'll prepare an appropriately worded *Affidavit of Assignment* of such contract, such as Form LT-12 reproduced on p. 120; have it signed and notarized by the grantor(s) as the assignors or transferror(s), and properly recorded and/or noticed.

E. A Final Word On The Transferring Of Property Into The Trust

As can be seen from the procedures outlined in the above passages, the actual formalities involved in transferring your assets into the Trust's name are not at all difficult or complex to do. BUT HERE'S PROBABLY THE "DIFFICULT" PART: YOU'VE JUST GOT TO TAKE THE TIME TO DO IT! *And, in any case, once again, you should always remind yourself that your trust is not really established or complete—until and unless you "fund" it, until you actually transfer the assets into it.* And any assets you leave out and do not transfer into the trust is not covered by the trust you have created, and will probably have to be probated.

---

[7]See Abts, op. cit., p. 169.

Copyright © 1994, Do-It-Yourself Legal Publishers, Newark, NJ 07102

Declaration Of Trust

(A Sample Form)

TYPE "A" TRUST—A SINGLE PERSON WITH NO CHILDREN

This revocable Living Trust Agreement (otherwise known as "DECLARATION OF TRUST"), is made on the date last signed and entered below, between the following person(s):

GRANTOR(S)/TRUSTOR(S): Mr/Mrs. ⬚1 of this address

of _____, city and state of _____ (hereinafter referred to as the

"Grantor(s)" or "Trustor(s)"; and

TRUSTEE(S): Mr/Mrs ⬚2 of this address

of _____ (hereinafter referred to as the _____, city and state

of _____ (hereinafter referred to as the "Trustee(s).")

WITNESSETH:

This Declaration is hereby made upon the following terms and conditions, and the parties intending to be legally bound by it, the Grantor(s) and the Trustee(s) do hereby covenant and agree as follows:

1. THE TRUST NAME

This trust shall be known as "The _____ ⬚3 _____ Trust."

2. NON-PERPETUITY CLAUSE

For the purpose of complying with the rule against perpetuities, any trust created herein that has not terminated sooner shall terminate twenty-one (21) years after the death of the rest of the last survivor of the class composed of _____ ⬚4 _____, and their children, grandchildren and any of their more remote descendents who are living when the trust is created.

3. TRUST INTENT & PROPERTY

A) The Grantors hereby declare that they have, without any consideration, transferred and delivered to the designated Trustee(s) herein, all their rights, title and interest in the property listed and described in Schedule A ⬚5 attached to this Declaration and hereby made a part of this Declaration, which property is to be held IN TRUST for the use, benefit and enjoyment of the beneficiaries named in this TRUST instrument and in accordance with the provisions set forth herein.

B) The said property listed and described in Schedule A is hereafter referred to as the "TRUST PROPERTY." The Trust Property shall be held, administered and distributed by the Trustee in accordance with the provisions of this trust instrument.

NOTE: See instructions for filling in the blank spaces on this form on pp. 88-9.

C) Each Grantor may, during his or her lifetime (or by testamentary Will), add or delete any asset at any time to the trust property. Such after-acquired property may be added to the trust simply by listing same on Schedule A.

4. POWERS & RIGHT OF GRANTORS TO AMEND OR REVOKE TRUST OR TO APPOINT/SUBSTITUTE TRUSTEES

A) The grantor(s) reserve(s) the authority and power to amend, modify or revoke this trust at any time during their lifetime, without prior notice or consent of any beneficiary or the trustee(s) or successor trustee(s), including the right to appoint, substitute or otherwise change the person(s) designated as trustee(s) or successor trustees.

B) All amendments, notices, or other notices affecting or furthering the purposes of this Declaration of Trust, brought pursuant to this Section, shall be in writing and upon proper form, duly notarized.

5. GRANTOR(S) RIGHTS TO TRUST INCOME & EXPENDITURES

The Trustees (the Successor Trustees) shall distribute the trust principal and income as follows:

A) During the live(s) of the grantor(s), the entire net income accrued from the trust property shall be paid to the Grantor(s) in monthly installment or at least once each quarter.

B) Providing, however, that the trustee considers that the net income is insufficient for the grantor's needs, the trustee may pay to the grantor(s), or apply to their benefits, as much of the principal as is necessary in the trustee's discretion for the grantors' adequate health care, maintenance or support. Pursuant to this provision, the trustee shall have liberal power to invade the principal, and the rights of the remainder persons in this trust shall be considered of secondary importance.

C) Incapacity of Grantor(s). If at any time, a grantor is certified in writing by two licensed physicians as being physically incapacitated, whether or not a court of competent jurisdiction has so declared, the trustee or successor trustee shall assume the active administration of the trust and shall apply for the benefit of the grantor(s) an amount of net income or trust principal necessary, in the Trustee(s)' discretion, for the proper health care, support and maintenance of the grantor(s), until the grantor(s), as certified by two licensed physicians, is (are) again competent to manage his or her own affairs or until his or her earlier death. Any income received by the Trust Property in excess of the amount applied for the benefit of the grantor(s) shall be accumulated and added to the Trust Property or Estate.

D) Upon the death of the grantor or surviving grantor(s), this trust becomes irrevocable and may not be amended, terminated or altered in any way except as specifically authorized by this instrument.

E) If a guardian or conservator is appointed for a grantor or the estate, the Trustee(s) shall take into account any such payments made by the guardian or conservator for the grantor's benefit.

F) The grantor(s) or surviving grantor may at any time direct the Trustee, in writing and proper form, to pay sums or make periodic payments to other persons or organizations.

6. TRUST BENEFICIARIES

A) Prime Beneficiaries

Upon the death of the grantor, the following beneficiaries (hereinafter called "Primary Beneficiaries") shall receive the following assets:

i) _____ 6a _____ shall be given _____ 7 _____ or, if

_____ 6a _____ does not survive the grantor, that property shall be given to _____ 6b _____ .

ii) _[name of beneficiary/beneficiaries]_ shall be given _____ _[items to be given]_ , or if _[name of alternate beneficiary/beneficiaries]_ does not survive the grantor, that property shall be given to _[name of beneficiary/beneficiaries]_ _____.

iii) _____ shall be given _____, or if _____, does not survive the grantor, that property shall be given to _____.

iv) _____ shall be given _____, or if _____, does not survive the grantor, that property shall be given to _____.

v) _____ shall be given _____, or if _____, does not survive the grantor, that property shall be given to _____.

vi) _____ shall be given _____, or if _____, does not survive the grantor, that property shall be given to _____.

B) Residuary Beneficiary Or Beneficiaries

i) Upon the death of the Grantor, or in any case the last grantor in this Trust to die, the Successor Trustee shall distribute all remaining trust assets and income not specifically or effectively disposed of by Paragraph 6 of this Declaration (which remaining trust property is hereinafter referred to as the "residuary property"), to the following beneficiaries:

_____
[Name(s) of the proposed residuary beneficiary or beneficiaries]

ii) The Successor Trustee shall distribute the said residuary property equally among the above-named Residuary Beneficiaries, if then living, and for any of them who is not then living, then to his or her descendants **per stirpes.**

7. DISTRIBUTION OF TRUST PROPERTY UPON DEATH OF GRANTOR & TIMETABLE

Upon the death of the Grantor, the Trustee (or Successor Trustee) shall distribute the trust property outright to the beneficiaries named above, subject to any provisions in this Declaration of Trust pertaining to children's subtrusts or custodianships, under the Uniform Transfer to Minors Act, if any is created in this Declaration.

8. TRUSTEES/SUCCESSOR TRUSTEES

A) The Trustee(s) of this Trust [and of all children's subtrusts created under this Declaration of Trust, if applicable], shall be: Mr/Mrs _____ of this address, _____.

B) _Incapacity of the Trustee._ Upon the death of the Trustee, or if he (she) is declared physically or mentally unable to handle his (her) financial affairs by any two licensed physicians, or shall for any reason be unable or fail to qualify or cease to act as Trustee, then the SUCCESSOR TRUSTEE shall be _____ , or if he/she is unable to serve or fails to qualify or cease to act as Successor Trustee, then the Successor Trustee shall be _____ .

C) Any trustee shall have the right to appoint additional successor trustees to serve in the order nominated, if and as deemed necessary in the trustee's sole discretion, except that such appointment shall be in writing and be notarized.

9. AUTHORITY OF THE SUCCESSOR TRUSTEE IN ADMINISTERING PROPERTY

A) The Successor Trustee(s) shall manage and administer the trust under the following conditions:

i) If both Trustee and Co-Trustee, in the event that this Declaration of Trust provides for more than one trustee, die at the same time;

ii) When the last surviving grantor dies; or

iii) If the last surviving grantor is not able to manage his or her financial affairs, as certified by the two licensed physicians; or

iv) If the grantor(s) for whatever reason(s) jointly express(es) their desire, in writing and duly notarized, to temporarily relinquish to his Successor Trustee his/her position as trustee(s) under this trust.

B) Successor Trustee(s) shall have all the rights and responsibilities of the original trustee(s) of this trust. They shall also have the right to appoint their successors, should they (the successor trustees) become unable to serve and no other successor has otherwise been appointed and available to serve.

10. TRUSTEE BOND, COMPENSATION & ACCOUNTING REQUIREMENTS

A) No bond or order of approval from a court shall be required of any Trustee, Co-Trustee or Successor Trustee named, or appointed or serving under this instrument. [OR, ALTERNATIVELY, IF PREFERRED: *'The trustee (and/or successor trustee) may receive reasonable compensation for his or her services on behalf of the Trust'*].

B) The trustees shall serve without compensation. [OR, ALTERNATIVELY, IF PREFERRED: *'The trustee (and/or successor trustee) may receive reasonable compensation for his or her services on behalf of the Trust'*].

C) No accounting shall be required of the Trustee, or Successor Trustee(s).

11. TRUSTEE'S POWERS, DUTIES & RESPONSIBILITIES

A) Statutory & Fiduciary Powers.

To manage this trust and any children's subtrusts created under this Declaration of Trust, if applicable, the Trustees and Successor Trustees shall have the full powers and authority allowed or conferred on a trustee under the state of *[Enter the applicable state's name]* law, subject to the trustee's fiduciary duty to the grantor(s) and the beneficiaries.

B) Record Keeping.

The Trustees' (or their successors') will keep accurate records of all transactions involving assets placed in this trust and make all such records readily available for inspection by any grantor(s) or beneficiary during normal business hours.

C) Payment of Valid Estate Debts & Expenses.

On the death of the grantor or surviving grantor, the Trustee shall pay the grantor's valid debts, and estate inheritance and death taxes, if any, and last illness and funeral expenses and other costs in administering the grantor's probate estate, out of the Trust Property and charge them against the said Trust Property, subject to Paragraph 19 below.

12. GENERAL POWERS OF TRUSTEES

A) The Trustee's powers and discretion shall include, but not be limited to:

a. The power to sell, encumber, mortgage, pledge, lease or improve the Trust Property, when such action is deemed to be in the best interest and in furtherance of the trust purposes, including the power to do same in order to make distribution provided for in this Declaration.

b. Power to manage securities, to include the power of all the rights, powers, and privileges of an owner.

c. Power to allocate to principal or increase all monies and properties received on behalf of the Trust.

d. Power to make distributions of the Trust property as required, pursuant to the provisions of this Trust.

e. Power to employ and pay reasonable fees to any custodian, investment advisor, attorney, accountant, or other consultant deemed necessary for information, assistance or advice related to the trust.

f. Power to hold and operate any business interest that may be or become a part of the Trust Property or Estate.

g. Power to pay with funds from Trust Property or Estate any tax, charge or assessment against the Trust which the Trustee shall be required to pay.

h. Power to deposit and hold trust funds in both interest bearing and non-interest bearing commercial, savings or saving & loan accounts, subject to the usual restrictions, upon withdrawal in effect at that time, and to enter into electronic fund transfer or safe deposit arrangements with such institutions.

i. Power to execute any documents necessary to effectuate or administer any trust created in this Declaration of Trust.

j. Power to retain and to continue to hold any property that becomes a part of the Trust Property or Estate.

k. Power to sell, dispose of, exchange, partition, convey, divide, repair, manage, control, and grant options and rights of refusal of property that becomes a part of the Trust Estate for cash, credit, deferred payments, or exchange.

l. Power to manage trust real estate belonging to the Trust, or to lease or rent same for any purpose, including exploration and removal of gas, oil and other minerals, to include community leases and pooling agreements.

m. Power to insure, at the expense of the Trust, insurance of any kind and in amounts as the Trustee deems advisable.

n. Power to invest all or any part of the Trust Property in every kind of property, whether real or personal, and in every kind of investment, such as bonds, debentures, notes, mortgages and stocks.

o. Power to litigate and compromise claims with respect to the Trust Estate as the Trustees deem advisable.

B) Any and all of the above specified or other authorized powers and duties may be exercised as may be necessary in the discretion of the Trustee, without being required to make application for more specific authority to any court of law or equity.

13. SPENDTHRIFT CLAUSE: INALIENABILITY OF BENEFICIARY'S INTEREST IN TRUST

No interest of a beneficiary in the principal or income of any trust created under this instrument shall be anticipated, assigned, encumbered, or subject to creditor's claim or legal process before being received by a beneficiary.

14. APPLICABLE STATE LAWS & SEVERABILITY OF PROVISIONS

The validity of this trust and the construction of its beneficial provisions shall be governed by the laws of the state of _____. If any clause(s) or provision(s) of this Declaration of Trust is (are) ruled invalid or unenforceable for any reason by a court of law, the remaining provisions shall nevertheless remain valid and in effect.

15. INTERCHANGABILITY OF TERMS

Any Trustee shall have the right to resign at any time by signing a notice of resignation and delivering same to the person or institution appointed or named in this Declaration of Trust to next serve as Trustee. The term "Trustee," as used in this instrument shall include also "Trustees," "Co-Trustees," "Sole Trustee," and "Successor Trustee or Trustees," and any singular terms also includes the plural.

16. NON-LIABILITY OF THE TRUSTEE

The trustee shall not be liable for any actions taken in good faith in the exercise or non-exercise of the powers and duties and responsibilities granted under this Declaration of Trust, and any provisions validly added by amendment. Such actions taken in good faith shall be binding on all parties concerned.

17. NON-LIABILITY OF THIRD PARTIES

A) Be it known that it is the express intent and understanding of the trust makers herein that any third person, including their Agents, Employees or Vendors, who upon the written request of the grantor(s), or under the color of authority granted to the Trustee(s) in this Declaration of Trust, performs any duties or renders any services pursuant to that authority, unless a showing of fraud can be made, shall be under no liability for the application or proper administration of any assets or properties that is the subject of the said third party's acts.

B) This limitation of liability is specifically intended to give protection to any third party who acts, performs or renders any services pursuant to any Notice, Instrument or Document reasonably believed and represented to be genuine, and to have been signed and presented by the proper party (parties).

C) It is further the express intent of this Trust that the non-liability of all Third Parties as herein above stipulated, be given broad and prospective application. In particular, financial, credit, or banking institutions or brokerage houses, or transfer agents, medical personnel or any other person or entity acting in a fiduciary capacity with regards to any assets or property comprising the Trust Property shall suffer no liability, nor incur any express or implied obligations when reasonably acting in the capacity of a Transferror or other such capacity, upon proper request, of any assets or property sought to be or comprising the Trust Property.

18. EXTENSION OF TRUST POWERS
This Declaration of Trust shall extend to and be binding upon the Heirs, Executors, Administrators and assigns of the undersigned Trustor(s) and upon the Successor(s) to the Trustee(s).

19. BENEFICIARY PROPORTIONATE LIABILITY FOR ESTATE TAXES
Each beneficiary under this Trust shall be liable for his (her) proportionate share of state or federal estate or inheritance taxes that may be levied, if any, upon the total taxable value of the Trust Property distributed to the said beneficiaries upon the death of either the donor or the surviving donor.

20. INTERPRETATION/DETERMINATION OF TRUST PROVISIONS
If any provision of this instrument shall be unclear or the subject of dispute among the parties to the trust, the Trustee (or the Successor Trustee, if the latter shall then be actively serving), is hereby fully authorized to interpret and determine such provision, and any such determination made by the Trustee shall be final and binding upon all such parties.

CERTIFICATION BY TRUST GRANTOR(S)

I (WE) CERTIFY that I (We) have read this *Declaration of Trust*, and that it correctly states the terms, conditions, covenants and agreements under which the trust estate is to be held, managed and administered and disposed of by the trustee (or the succesor thereof), and I (we) therefore approve the Declaration of Trust.

IN WITNESS WHEREOF, I (We) have signed these presents this _____ day of _____, 19___.

SIGNED X_____ 12
Trustor (Grantor)

SIGNED X_____ 12
Co-Trustor (Co-Grantor)

Acknowledgment

STATE OF _____
COUNTY OF _____) ss.

On this _____ day of _____, 19___, before me, the undersigned Notary Public duly authorized to administer oaths in and by the above captioned jurisdiction, personally appeared Mr/Mrs/Ms 1 _____, to me known or made known to me to be the individual(s) described in and who executed the foregoing Declaration Of Trust; thereupon the said person(s) acknowledged that he (she) (they) executed the same as his (her) (their) free act and deed.

My Commission expires _____ (Notary Public)

SWORN TO BEFORE
ME, THIS _____ 19___ .

Copyright © 1994, Do-It-Yourself Legal Publishers, Newark, NJ 07102

Declaration Of Trust

(A Sample Form)

TYPE "A" TRUST—A SINGLE PERSON WITH CHILDREN

This revocable Living Trust Agreement (otherwise known as "DECLARATION OF TRUST"), is made on the date last signed and entered below, between the following person(s):

GRANTOR(S)/TRUSTOR(S): Mr/Mrs ⬚1⬚ , of this address

"Grantor(s)" or "Trustor(s)"); and _____ , city and state of _____ (hereinafter referred to as the

TRUSTEE(S): Mr/Mrs ⬚2⬚ of this address

of _____ , city and state

_____ (hereinafter referred to as the "Trustee(s).")

WITNESSETH:

This Declaration is hereby made upon the following terms and conditions, and the parties intending to be legally bound by it, the Grantor(s) and the Trustee(s) do hereby covenant and agree as follows:

1. THE TRUST NAME

This trust shall be known as "The _____ ⬚3⬚ _____ Trust."

2. NON-PERPETUITY CLAUSE

For the purpose of complying with the rule against perpetuities, any trust created herein that has not terminated sooner shall terminate twenty-one (21) years after the death of the rest of the last survivor of the class composed of _____ ⬚4⬚ _____ , and their children, grandchildren and any of their more remote descendents who are living when the trust is created.

3. TRUST INTENT & PROPERTY

A) The Grantors hereby declare that they have, without any consideration, transferred and delivered to the designated Trustee(s) herein, all their rights, title and interest in the property listed and described in Schedule A _____ ⬚5⬚ _____ attached to this Declaration and hereby made a part of this Declaration, which property is to be held IN TRUST for the use, benefit and enjoyment of the beneficiaries named in this TRUST instrument and in accordance with the provisions set forth herein.

B) The said property listed and described in Schedule A is hereafter referred to as the "TRUST PROPERTY." The Trust Property shall be held, administered and distributed by the Trustee in accordance with the provisions of the trust instrument.

C) Each Grantor may, during his or her lifetime (or by testamentary Will), add or delete any asset at any time to the trust property. Such after acquired property may be added to the trust simply by listing same on Schedule A.

Note: See instructions for filling in the blank spaces on this form on pp. 88-89.

4. POWERS & RIGHTS OF GRANTORS TO AMEND OR REVOKE TRUST OR TO APPOINT/SUBSTITUTE TRUSTEES

A) The grantor(s) reserve(s) the authority and power to amend, modify or revoke this trust at any time during their lifetime, without prior notice or consent of any beneficiary or the trustee(s) or successor trustee(s), including the right to appoint, substitute or otherwise change the person(s) designated as trustee(s) or successor trustees.

B) All amendments, notices, or other notices affecting or furthering the purposes of this Declaration of Trust, brought pursuant to this Section, shall be in writing and upon proper form, duly notarized.

5. GRANTOR(S) RIGHTS TO TRUST INCOME & EXPENDITURES

The Trustees (the Successor Trustees) shall distribute the trust principal and income as follows:

A) During the live(s) of the grantor(s), the entire net income accrued from the trust property shall be paid to the Grantor(s) in monthly installment or at least once each quarter.

B) Providing, however, that the trustee considers that the net income is insufficient for the grantor's needs, the trustee may pay to the grantor(s), or apply to their benefits, as much of the principal as is necessary in the trustee's discretion for the grantors' adequate health care, maintenance or support. Pursuant to this provision, the trustee shall have liberal power to invade the principal, and the rights of the remainder persons in this trust shall be considered of secondary importance.

C) Incapacity of Grantor(s).

If at any time, a grantor is certified in writing by two licensed physicians as being physically incapacitated, whether or not a court of competent jurisdiction has so declared, the trustee or successor trustee shall assume the active administration of the trust and shall apply for the benefit of the grantor(s) an amount of net income or trust principal necessary in the trustee(s)' discretion, for the proper health care, support and maintenance of the grantor(s), until the grantor(s), as certfied by two licensed physicians, is (are) again competent to manage his or her own affairs or until his or her earlier death. Any income received by the Trust Property in excess of the amount applied for the benefit of the grantor(s) shall be accumulated and added to the Trust property or Estate.

D) Upon the death of the grantor(s) or surviving grantor, this trust becomes irrevocable and may not be amended, terminated or altered in any way except as specifically authorized by this instrument.

E) If a guardian or conservator is appointed for a grantor or the estate, the Trustee(s) shall take into account any such payments made by the guardian or conservator for the grantors' benefit.

F) The grantor(s) or surviving grantor may at any time direct the Trustee, in writing and proper form, to pay sums or make periodic payments to other persons or organizations.

6. TRUST BENEFICIARIES

A) Prime Beneficiaries

Upon the death of the grantor, the following beneficiaries (hereinafter called "Primary Beneficiaries") shall receive the following assets.

i)   6a   _____ shall be given   7   or, if

     6a _____ does not survive the grantor, that property shall be given to _____.

     6b _____ .

ii) *[name of beneficiary/beneficiaries]* _____ shall be given *[Items to be given]* _____ , or if *[name of beneficiary/beneficiaries]* _____ does not survive the grantor, that property shall be given to *[name of alternate beneficiary/beneficiaries]* _____ .

iii)
survive the grantor, that property shall be given to _____ , or if _____ does not

iv)
survive the grantor, that property shall be given to _____ , or if _____ does not

v)
survive the grantor, that property shall be given to _____ , or if _____ does not

vi)
survive the grantor, that property shall be given to _____ , or if _____ does not

B) Residuary Beneficiary Or Beneficiaries

i) Upon the death of the Grantor, or in any case the last grantor in this Trust to die, the successor trustee shall distribute all remaining trust assets and income not specifically or effectively disposed of by Paragraph 6 of this Declaration (which remaining trust property is hereinafter referred to as the "residuary property"), to the following beneficiaries:

8

(Name(s) of the proposed residuary beneficiary or beneficiaries)

ii) The Successor Trustee shall distribute the said residuary property equally among the above-named Residuary Beneficiaries, if then living, and for any of them who is not then living, then to his or her descendants **per stirpes.**

7. DISTRIBUTION OF TRUST PROPERTY UPON DEATH OF GRANTOR

Upon the death of the Grantor, the Trustee (or Successor Trustee) shall distribute the trust property outright to the beneficiaries named in above, subject to any provisions in this Declaration of Trust pertaining to children's subtrusts or custodianships, under the Uniform Transfer to Minors Act, if any is created in this Declaration.

8. TRUSTEES/SUCCESSOR TRUSTEES

A) The Trustee(s) of this Trust [and of all children's subtrusts created under this Declaration of Trust, if applicable], shall be: Mr/Mrs _____ 9 _____ of this address _____ .

B) Incapacity of the Trustee. Upon the death of the Trustee, or if he (she) is declared physically or mentally unable to handle his (her) financial affairs by any two licensed physicians, or shall for any reason be unable or fail to qualify or cease to act as Trustee, then the SUCCESSOR TRUSTEE shall be _____ 10 _____ ; or if he/she is unable to serve or fails to qualify or cease to act as Successor Trustee, then the Successor Trustee shall be _____ 11 _____ of this address _____ .

C)Any trustee shall have the right to appoint additional successor trustees to serve in the order nominated, if and as deemed necessary in the trustee's sole discretion, except that such appointment shall be in writing and be duly notarized.

9. AUTHORITY OF THE SUCCESSOR TRUSTEE IN ADMINISTERING PROPERTY
A) The Successor Trustee(s) shall manage and administer the trust under the following conditions:

i) If both Trustee and Co-Trustee, in the event that this Declaration of Trust provides for more than one trustee, die at the same time;

ii) When the last surviving trustee dies;

iii) If the last surviving grantor is not able to manage his or her financial affairs, as certified by two licensed physicians; or

iv) If the grantor(s) for whatever reason(s) jointly express(es) their desire, in writing and duly notarized, to temporarily relinquish to his Successor Trustee his/her position as trustee(s) under this trust.

B) Successor Trustee(s) shall have all the rights and responsibilities of the original trustee(s) of this trust. They shall also have the right to appoint their successors, should they (the successor trustees) become unable to serve and no other successor has otherwise been appointed and available to serve.

10. TRUSTEE BOND, COMPENSATION & ACCOUNTING REQUIREMENTS

A) No bond or order of approval from a court shall be required of any Trustee, Co-Trustee or Successor Trustee named, or appointed or serving under this instrument.

B) The trustees shall serve without compensation. *[OR, ALTERNATIVELY IF PREFERRED: 'The trustee (and/or successor trustee) may receive reasonable compensation for his or her services on behalf of the Trust].*

C) No accounting shall be required of the Trustee, or Successor Trustee(s).

11. TRUSTEE'S POWER, DUTIES & RESPONSIBILITIES

A) Statutory & Fiduciary Powers.

To manage this trust and any children's subtrusts created under this Declaration of Trust, if applicable, the Trustees and Successor Trustees shall have the full powers and authority allowed or conferred on a trustee under the state of *[Enter the applicable state's name]* law, subject to the trustee's fiduciary duty to the grantor(s) and the beneficiaries.

B) Record Keeping.

The Trustees (or their successors) will keep accurate records of all transactions involving assets placed in this trust and make all such records readily available for inspection by any beneficiary (or grantors) during normal business hours.

C) Payment of Valid Estate Debts & Expenses.

Upon the death of the grantor or surviving grantor, the Trustee shall pay the grantor's valid debts, and estate inheritance and death taxes, if any, and last illness and funeral expenses and other costs in administering the grantor's probate estate, out of the Trust Property and charge them against the said Trust Property, subject to Paragraph 19 below.

12. GENERAL POWERS OF TRUSTEES

A) The Trustee's powers and discretion shall include, but not be limited to:

a. The power to sell, encumber, mortgage, pledge, lease or improve the Trust Property, when such action is deemed to be in the best interest and in furtherance of the trust purposes, including the power to do same in order to make distribution provided for in this Declaration.

b. Power to manage securities, to include the power of all the rights, powers, and privileges of an owner.

c. Power to allocate to principal or increase all monies and properties received on behalf of the Trust.

d. Power to make distributions of the Trust property as required, pursuant to the provisions of this Trust.

e. Power to employ and pay reasonable fees to any custodian, investment advisor, attorney, accountant, or other consultant deemed necessary for information, assistance or advice related to the trust.

f. Power to hold and operate any business interest that may be or become a part of the Trust Property or Estate.

g. Power to pay with funds from Trust Property or Estate any tax, charge or assessment against the Trust which the Trustee shall be required to pay.

h. Power to deposit and hold trust funds in both interest bearing and non-interest bearing commercial, savings or saving & loan accounts, subject to the usual restrictions, upon withdrawal in effect at that time and to enter into electronic fund transfer or safe deposit arrangements with such institutions.

i. Power to execute any documents necessary to effectuate or administer any trust created in this Declaration of Trust.

j. Power to retain and to continue to hold any property that becomes a part of the Trust Property or Estate.

k. Power to sell, dispose of, exchange, partition, convey, divide, repair, manage, control, and grant options and rights of refusal of property that becomes a part of the Trust Estate for cash, credit, deferred payments, or exchange.

l. Power to manage trust real estate belonging to the Trust, or to lease or rent same for any purpose, including exploration and removal of gas, oil and other minerals, to include community leases and pooling agreements.

m. Power to insure, at the expense of the Trust, insurance of any kind and in amounts as the Trustee deems advisable.

n. Power to invest all or any part of the Trust Property in every kind of property, whether real or personal, and in every kind of investment, such as bonds, debentures, notes, mortgages and stocks.

o. Power to litigate and compromise claims with respect to the Trust Estate as the Trustees deem advisable.

B) Any and all of the above specified or other authorized powers and duties may be exercised as may be necessary in the discretion of the Trustee, without being required to make application for more specific authority to any court of law or equity.

13. SPENDTHRIFT CLAUSE; INALIENABILITY OF BENEFICIARY'S INTEREST IN TRUST
No interest of a beneficiary in the principal or income of any trust created under this instrument shall be anticipated, assigned, encumbered, or subject to creditor's claim or legal process before being received by a beneficiary.

14. APPLICABLE STATE LAWS & SEVERABILITY OF PROVISIONS
The validity of this trust and the construction of its beneficial provisions shall be governed by the laws of the state of _____. If any clause(s) or provision(s) of this Declaration of Trust is (are) ruled invalid or unenforceable for any reason by a court of law, the remaining provisions shall nevertheless remain valid and in effect.

15. INTERCHANGABILITY OF TERMS
Any Trustee shall have the right to resign at any time by signing a notice of resignation and delivering same to the person or institution appointed or named in this Declaration of Trust to next serve as Trustee. The term "Trustee," as used in this instrument shall include also "Trustees," "Co-Trustees," "Sole Trustee," and "Successor Trustee or Trustees," and any singular terms also includes the plural.

16. NON-LIABILITY OF THE TRUSTEE
The trustee shall not be liable for any actions taken in good faith in the exercise or nonexercise of the powers and duties and responsibilities granted under this Declaration of Trust, and any provisions validly added by amendment. Such actions taken in good faith shall be binding on all parties concerned.

17. NON-LIABILITY OF THIRD PARTIES
A) Be it known that it is the express intent and understanding of the trust makers herein, that any third person, including their Agents, Employees or Vendors, who upon the written request of the grantor(s), or under the color of authority granted to the Trustee(s) in this Declaration of Trust, performs any duties or renders any services pursuant to that authority, unless a showing of fraud can be made, shall be under no liability for the application or proper administration of any assets or properties that is the subject of the said third party's acts.

B) This limitation of liability is specifically intended to give protection to any third party who acts, performs or renders any services pursuant to any Notice, Instrument or Document reasonably believed and represented to be genuine, and to have been signed and presented by the proper party (parties).

C) It is further the express intent of this Trust that the non-liability of all Third Parties as herein above stipulated, be given broad and prospective application. In particular, financial, credit, or banking institutions or brokerage houses, or transfer agents, medical personnel or any other person or entity acting in a fiduciary capacity with regards to any assets or property comprising the Trust Property, shall suffer no liability, nor incur any express or implied obligations when reasonably acting in the capacity of a Transferror or other such capacity, upon proper request, of any assets or property sought to be or comprising the Trust Property.

18. EXTENSION OF TRUST POWERS

This Declaration of Trust shall extend to and be binding upon the Heirs, Executors, Administrators and assigns of the undersigned Trustor(s) and upon the Successor(s) to the Trustee(s).

19. BENEFICIARY PROPORTIONATE LIABILITY FOR ESTATE TAXES

Each beneficiary under this Trust shall be liable for his (her) proportionate share of state or federal estate or inheritance taxes that may be levied, if any, upon the total taxable value of the Trust Property distributed to the said beneficiaries upon the death of either the donor or the surviving donor.

20. INTERPRETATION/DETERMINATION OF TRUST PROVIISONS

If any provision of this instrument shall be unclear or the subject of dispute among the parties to the trust, the Trustee (or the Successor Trustee, if the latter shall then be actively serving), is hereby fully authorized to interpret and determine such provision, and any such determination made by the Trustee shall be final and binding upon all such parties.

21. CHILDREN'S SUBTRUST*

A) The Applicable Beneficiaries

If any of the following minors or young adult persons who are named as beneficiaries in paragraphs 6A & B above, namely, _____ [13] shall be under the age of ____ [14] at the time he or she becomes entitled to the distribution under this Declaration, then all trust property given to such beneficiaries under this Declaration shall not be paid, but shall be retained in trust for EACH such beneficiary in a separate subtrust of this "_____ [3] Trust," until each child or beneficiary attains the age of ____ [14] at which point each subtrust shall end with respect to that particular beneficiary, and any principal or income then remaining in the subtrust for the particular child or beneficiary, if any, shall promptly be distributed to the said child or beneficiary by the subtrust Trustee, subject, however, to the provisions of paragraph 21C below with reference to particular beneficiaries, if applicable.

B) Name Of Subtrust

Each and every separate subtrust herein shall be identified and referred to by adding the name of the subtrust's beneficiary to the name of this trust, and inserting it just before the name of this trust in this manner: "The ____ [3] ____ For ____ [13] ____, Minor."

C) Duration Of The Subtrust

With respect to these child(ren) or beneficiaries hereafter named, namely _____, if any is so named herein, upon the attainment of the age of ____ [14] years by each, the subtrust Trustee shall not make outright distribution of any balance of their inheritance then remaining in the subtrust, as stipulated in paragraph 21A above, but such balance, if any, shall be distributed to them as follows: one-third (¹/₃) promptly upon attainment of the said age; then another one-third (¹/₃) three years thereafter, and the final distribution of one-third (¹/₃) two years thereafter. And, thereupon, the children subtrust shall forthwith terminate with respect to such beneficiaries.

NOTE: Note that under the law, if you leave inheritance for your minor children under the children's subtrust in the Living Trust, you may not also use the Uniform Transfer to Minors Act to leave property for the same child or children. You may only use ONE; or the other, not both. See pp. 33-4 of the manual for more on this.

D) If any beneficiary survives the settlor(s) (grantor(s)) but dies before attaining the age of _____ [14] _____ years, at the death of such beneficiary the Trustee shall pass the beneficiary's entitlement under the subtrust to his/her heirs absolutely, per stirpes.

E) Powers Of Subtrust Trustee

i) In the meantime, until each child's term in the subtrust ends, the Trustee may distribute to or for the benefit of each designated beneficiary, as much of the net income or principal of the children's share of the subtrust as the Trustee in his/her discretion, deems necessary for the beneficiary's health, support, maintenance or education, only using his/her fiduciary discretion and best judgment and sense of fairplay and necessity, to provide for each beneficiary's individual needs as they may arise or be necessary. Education includes, but is not limited to, college, graduate, postgraduate and vocational studies, and reasonably related living expenses.

ii) In deciding how and in what manners and when to make a distribution to a beneficiary, the Trustee may take into account each beneficiary's other income, resources, and sources of support, his/her circumstances and real needs, character and demonstrated sense of responsibility.

iii) No intervention of any guardian or application to any court shall be necessary or permissible in the good faith exercise of these duties by the Trustee (or Successor Trustee).

iv) The Trustee may invest the subtrust assets in such income-yielding ventures as the Trustee may deem proper and prudent and the income as well as such amounts of the principal as are necessary, even to the extent of all, shall be applied to the support, general welfare and benefits of the beneficiaries, as directed in this Declaration.

F) No Assignment Of Interest Of Beneficiary

No interest of any beneficiary under this children's subtrust shall be anticipated, assigned or encumbered by voluntary or involuntary act or by operation of law before being received by the beneficiary. Nor shall these interests be subject to the claims of creditors or to attachments, execution, bankruptcy or other legal process to the fullest extent permitted by law.

G. Trustee's Rights of Compensation

Any Trustee of the children's subtrust created under this Declaration of Trust shall be entitled to reasonable compensation out of the subtrust assets, for his or her services on behalf of the Trust. *[Alternatively, if preferred:* '*Any 'Trustee of the children's subtrust shall serve without compensation.'*]

22. CUSTODIANSHIPS UNDER THE UNIFORM TRANSFERS TO MINORS ACT*

All trust property given to any of the minor or young adult beneficiaries listed below shall be given to each such beneficiary under the provisions of the _____ (*name of your state*) *Uniform Transfers To Minors Act.*

1. All Property to which _____ [15] _____ , hereinafter called a "Minor Beneficiary" under this Declaration, shall become entitled to receive, shall be given to _____ [16] _____ , as custodian for the said Minor Beneficiary under the Uniform Transfers To Minors Act, until the said Minor Beneficiary attains the age of _____ [17] _____ , or if no age is specified herein, until he/she attains the age provided under the Uniform Transfers to Minors Act at which the beneficiary becomes entitled to receive the property outright from the custodian.

2. All property to which _____ , hereinafter called a "Minor Beneficiary" under this Declaration, shall become entitled to receive, shall be given to _____ as custodian for the said Minor Beneficiary under the Uniform Transfers to Minors Act, until the said Minor Beneficiary attains the age of _____ , or if no age is specified herein, until he/she attains the age provided under the Uniform Transfers to Minors Act at which the beneficiary becomes entitled to receive the property outright from the custodian.

3. All property to which _____, hereinafter called a "Minor Beneficiary" under this Declaration, shall become entitled to receive, shall be given to _____ as custodian for the said Minor Beneficiary under the Uniform Transfers to Minors Act, until the said Minor Beneficiary attains the age of _____, or if no age is specified herein, until he/she attains the age provided under the Uniform Transfers to Minors Act at which the beneficiary becomes entitled to receive the property outright from the custodian.

CERTIFICATION BY TRUST GRANTOR(S)

I (WE) CERTIFY that I (We) have read this *Declaration of Trust* and that it correctly states the terms, conditions, covenants and agreements under which the trust estate is to be held, managed and administered and disposed of by the trustee (or the successor thereof), and I (we) therefore approve the Declaration of Trust.

IN WITNESS WHEREOF, I (We) have signed these presents this _____ day of _____ 19 ___.

SIGNED: ✗ _____
[12]　　Trustor (Grantor)

SIGNED: ✗ _____
[12]　　Co-Trustor (Co-Grantor)

Acknowledgment

STATE OF _____)
　　　　　　　　　)ss.
COUNTY OF _____)

On this _____ day of _____, 19 ___, before me, the undersigned Notary Public duly authorized to administer oaths in and by the above captioned jurisdiction, personally appeared Mr/Mrs/Ms _____ [1] to me known or made known to me to be the individual(s) described in and who executed the foregoing Declaration Of Trust; thereupon the said person(s) acknowledged that he (she) (they) executed the same as his (her) (their) free act and deed.

My Commission expires _____

_____
(Notary Public)

Spouse's Disclaimer Of Trust Asset Or Interest*

I, the undersigned legal spouse of the above-named Grantor, hereby waive all community property, dower or curtesy rights and interest which I may have in the property described in the foregoing Trust and give my assent to the provisions of the trust and to the inclusion of the said property in the said Trust.

✗ _____
(Spouse to sign here, when applicable)

SWORN TO BEFORE
ME, THIS _____ 19 ___.

_____
(Notary Public)

*NOTE: The signing of this clause is not applicable or necessary when the spouses have BOTH signed the Declaration of Trust. If married and you and your spouse have not jointly signed the Declaration of Trust, then you must have your spouse, as well, sign and notarize the statement in this box, if: (a) you've included in the Trust any property held only in one spouse's name and; (b) if your spouse is not the person that is designated in the trust as the primary beneficiary of the trust property.

Instructions For Completing The Blanks In The "A" Trust Declaration Of Trust Forms (pp. 74 & 80):

1️⃣ The names [and addresses] of the Trust-maker or makers go in here.

2️⃣ The name of the person (or institution) you appoint to act as the initial Trustee. Usually, in most family trust situations, you'll enter your own name here, and enter your spouse's name, if applicable, in the paragraph for designating the Successor Trustee.

3️⃣ Enter the name by which this Trust will be known and identified. Generally, trust-makers would simply use their own name(s). Example: *"The Mary Doe Trust;"* or, for a married couple: *"The Mary and John Doe Trust."* Also, if you create more than one trust, the trusts are usually differentiated by assigning a number to each trust. Example: *"The Mary and John Doe Trust, No. 1," "The Mary and John Doe Trust, No. 2," and so on.*)

4️⃣ The name of the Trust-maker or makers.

5️⃣ To create your trust, you'll have to identify which of your assets you are setting aside as the trust assets or property. And, the method generally recognized as the most convenient method of doing this, is to list all such assets you want to put into the trust on a separate sheet (or sheets) of paper called a **"SCHEDULE,"** and attach it to the back of the trust document. The assets listed on the schedule must be described in sufficient details and specifics on the Schedule, as is done in the sample copy set forth in the manual. (See Appendix B at p. 211, for sample of a Schedule.)

6️⃣ **a** Here, you enter in each of the next few paragraphs, the name or names of the beneficiary or beneficiaries you want to inherit the specific property you designate in 7️⃣ after you die. List each beneficiary (or group of beneficiaries) for specific trust property in each separate clause. In the blank space 6️⃣b, for each paragraph, you'll name the *alternate beneficiary* or beneficiaries who are to inherit that particular property in the event the primary beneficiary does not survive you. In marital situations, the better approach is for you to name beneficiaries for each spouse separately so that personal items can be distributed after each spouse dies. (See example below.) You should try to be consistent with the property listed in Schedule A, making sure to identify the items in the trust in exactly the same language as is used in the Schedule. *Example: "Bank Account No. 50-4967 with the Chase Savings Bank, New York," or, if there are more than one such account intended: "All bank accounts listed in Schedule A."*)

Example of the basic approach used in a marital situation involving shared marital property:

A. "Upon the death of the Grantor [the husband's name], the following beneficiaries shall receive the following assets: John Doe Jr., son of John and Mary Doe: A rare stamp collection located in a safe in the home of John and Mary Doe, 20 Trust Ave., Anytown, NY; hunting equipment located at the family vacation home at 20 Vacation Road, Anytown, Florida; all Mr. Doe's interest in the stock accounts listed on Schedule A.

B. Upon the death of the Grantor for Mrs [the wife's name], the following assets: Agnes Doe, daughter of John and Mary Doe: all books in the home library and all personal jewelry belonging to Mary Doe located in the master bedroom at 20 Trust Ave., Anytown, NY; and Agnes John and David Doe shall be given all my interest in the home listed in Schedule A in equal shares.

C. Upon the death of both spouses, Mr _____ and Mrs _____ shall be given $20,000 each for a total of $40,000 from the Money Market Account No. _____ at the Chase Savings Bank listed in

Schedule A; and thereafter the Successor Trustee shall distribute the remaining trust assets and income equally to Agnes, John and David Doe, the children of the Grantors, if then living, or if not then living, then to their descendents per stirpes."

⑧ Here you name all the *"residuary beneficiaries"*—those who are to inherit any assets (i.e., everything else) that have not otherwise been assigned to anyone in the trust.

⑨, ⑩, ⑪ Enter the full names of the persons (or institutions) you designate to serve as the Trustee in ⑨ [usually the spouse, when married], the **Successor Trustee** in ⑩, and the **Alternate Successor** in ⑪, respectively. [See Section C of Chapter 4 for an idea of the extreme significance of these positions].

⑫ You, the grantor or grantors, sign here—in the presence of a Notary Public.

⑬ Here you enter, if this clause is applicable to you—i.e., basically if you have minor or underage children and wish to set apart their inheritance for them in a separate subtrust until they are of age—the names and dates of birth of each child involved. This group may include persons who are underage or are incompetent whom you've named as alternate beneficiaries in Paragraphs ⑥ **A & B**. If, however, you list someone as a beneficiary under this paragaph, you may not also list that same person to receive gift under the Uniform Transfers To Minors Act (UTMA)—Paragraph 22 below. (Under the law, you can only leave property to a child by either **ONE** or the other method, and not both.)

⑭ Enter the age you prefer at which the minor(s) are to receive the distribution, or as the case may be, the first installment, of such inheritance. Example: at age 21, or 25, 30, or whatever you propose.

⑮ Here you enter , if this provision is applicable to you—i.e., basically, if you have minor or underage children and prefer to set apart their inheritance for them by means of your state's UTMA law until they are of certain age*—the names and dates of birth of each child involved. Enter in each paragraph the name of each child who is to be provided for under the UTMA provision.

⑯ Enter name of the custodian you designate to manage the child's inheritance.

⑰ Enter the maximum age specified under the state's Uniform Minors Transfer Act (see pp. 33-4).

> **NOTE:** Now that you shall have presumably completed the drafting phase of your Trust document (the first and final drafts and the signing and notarizing), now get back to the next phase that should follow in the trust creating process—the transfer of trust property into the trust (Chapter 7, from Section D thereof)—and systematically follow the rest of Chapter 7. Chapter 8 deals with the operation of the trust once you've created it.

---

*As elaborated in an earlier section of this manual, to be eligible to employ the UTMA law to leave property to your minor child, your state has to have enacted the UTMA law (See list of such states on p. 33.) and the method is generally more feasible when the leaving of a smaller estate is involved (generally, for gift of less than $25,000 to $50,000). Remember, however, that if the Living Trust's children's subtrust is used to leave an inheritance to a child, then the UTMA cannot also be used for the same child. (See pp. 33-4 for more on the children's subtrust and applicable UTMA states and the workings of the UTMA in leaving a gift for minors.)

Form LT—III

Declaration Of Trust

(A Sample Form)

TYPE "A-B" TRUST—A MARRIED COUPLE WITH CHILDREN

This revocable Living Trust Agreement (otherwise known as "DECLARATION OF TRUST"), is made on the date last signed and entered below, between the following person(s):

GRANTOR(S)/TRUSTOR(S): Mr/Mrs: ⟦1⟧ of this address

city and state of ⟦1⟧ of this address

(hereinafter referred to as the

"Grantor(s)" or "Trustor(s)"); and

TRUSTEE(S): Mr/Mrs ⟦2⟧ of this address

of (hereinafter referred to as the "Trustee(s).")

city and state

NOW THEREFORE, the Settlor(s) and the Trustee(s) intending to be legally bound by this agreement, do hereby covenant and agree upon the following terms and conditions:

WITNESSETH:

WHEREAS the Settlor(s) desire(s) at death to leave certain property in trust, and WHEREAS the Trustee(s) is (are) willing to accept and administer such funds as Trustee(s) under the terms of these presents,

1. THE TRUST NAME

This trust shall be known as "The ⟦3⟧ Trust."

2. NON-PERPETUITY CLAUSE

For the purpose of complying with the rule against perpetuities, any trust created herein that has not terminated sooner shall terminate twenty-one (21) years after the death of the last survivor of the class composed of ⟦4⟧ and their children, grandchildren and any of their more remote descendents who are living when the trust is created.

3. TRUST INTENT & PROPERTY

A) The Settlors hereby declare that they have, without any consideration, separately transferred and delivered to the designated trustee(s) herein, who is/are also named as Trust beneficiary to receive certain property, all his/her rights, title and interest in the property listed and described in Schedule A ⟦5⟧ attached to this Declaration and hereby made a part of this Declaration, which property is to be held IN TRUST for the use, benefit and enjoyment of the beneficiaries named in this TRUST instrument and in accordance with the provisions set forth herein.

NOTE: See instructions for filling in the blank spaces on this form on pp. 99-100.

B) The Trust Property

The said property listed and described in Schedule A, is hereafter referred to as the "TRUST PROPERTY." The Trust Property shall be held, administered and distributed by the Trustee in accordance with the provisions of the trust instrument, and the settlor reserves the right to add aditional assets to the Trust Property and/or to make them, including life insurance policies on the Settlor's life, payable to the designated beneficiaries.

C) Each Grantor may, during his or her lifetime (or by testamentary Will) add or delete any asset at any time to the trust property. Such after-acquired property may be added to the trust simply by listing same on Schedule A.

4. THE "MARITAL" & "NON-MARITAL" SHARES OF THE TRUST PROPERTY: THE "A" TRUST & "B" TRUST

Upon the settlor's death, the surviving spouse, as Trustee, shall divide the Trust Property or Fund into two parts. One part, herein termed the "Marital Share," (or **TRUST A part**), shall consist of property of value equal to the lesser of: **(a)** the maximum marital deduction allowable in determining the federal estate tax payable by the Settlor's estate, or **(b)** the minimum amount which, after taking into account all credits and deductions available to settlor's estate for federal estate tax purposes (other than the marital deduction), will result in no federal estate tax.* The other part, herein termed the "Non-Marital Share," (or **TRUST B**), shall consist of the remainder of the trust fund.

In apportioning to the marital and nonmarital trusts specific assets previously valued for estate tax purposes, the Trustee shall insure that the two trusts share proportionately in any subsequent appreciation or depreciation in the value of such assets. Assets which do not qualify for marital deduction status, or assets not includable in the Settlor's gross estate for federal tax purposes, shall not be included in the marital share of the trust.

5. INSTRUCTIONS WITH RESPECT TO THE 'MARITAL' SHARE OF THE TRUST PROPERTY (TRUST A)

A) With respect to the *'marital share,'* also called the Trust A part, the Trustee shall hold, manage, invest and reinvest the same as a trust and upon the following terms and conditions:

1) The Trustee shall pay to the Settlors surviving spouse _(John or Mary Doe)_ ⑥ _____ , in convenient monthly installments during his/her lifetime, the actual income accruing from the trust property or a sum equal to six (6%) percent per year of the value of the trust computed at the time of the Settlor's death and thereafter recomputed annually at the beginning of each calendar year, whichever is the greater, together with any sums from the principal that the Settlor's spouse may request to be paid from time to time.

2) Upon the death of the Settlor's surviving spouse, the Successor Trustee, who is hereinafter named in this Declaration, shall distribute the assets then contained in this part of the trust (i.e., in Trust A) to the surviving spouse's estate or the beneficiaries designated by the surviving spouse in his or her will or otherwise, in accordance with the directions of this Declaration of Trust. The Settlor hereby confers upon the said spouse the sole and unrestricted right to designate such beneficiaries by his or her Will, and to the extent that the said power is not effectively exercised, the surviving spouse's trust fund herein created shall be added to the remaining part of the Trust and shall be disposed of as hereinafter provided.

3) If the Settlor and the Settlor's spouse shall die in such circumstances that there is not, in the judgment of the Successor Trustee, whose decision shall be conclusive, sufficient evidence to determine readily which of them survived the other, then for the purposes of this trust, the Settlor's spouse shall be deemed to have survived the Settlor.

WITH RESPECT TO "NON-MARITAL"" SHARE OF TRUST PROPERTY (TRUST B)

B) With respect to the remainder of the trust fund, namely, the *"nonmarital"* part of the trust fund (hereinafter called Trust B) the Trustee shall, upon the death of the first spouse to die, hold, manage, invest and reinvest that non-marital part of the trust as a trust fund on the following terms and conditions:

*As elaborated in Chapter 5 of the manual, this statement describing the 'marital share' part (i.e, Trust A) basically means this: assuming that in this case the total value of the trust is LESS than $1.2 million, just one-half of the total value of the assets is all that is placed in this marital share part; and if, on the other hand, the total trust is MORE than $1.2 million, then everything else is placed in this part (Trust A)—except $600,000. In other words, only $600,000 of the decedent spouse's half of the total estate is placed in Trust B (since that is the maximum amount of his or her estate tax exemption), and the rest is placed in the other part (the surviving spouse's Trust A).

(1) If requested by the executor or administrator of the Settlor's Estate), the Trustee shall pay or reimburse the said executor or administrator for the amount of any pre-death claim, funeral expense or expense of administration which shall be allowed in connection with the settlement of such estate or, in the absence of any formal probate administration, the costs and expenses which the Trustee shall determine to be due and payable.

(2) The Trustee shall pay to the proper taxing authority or reimburse the executor or administrator of the Settlor's estate, for the amount of any state or federal succession, estate, transfer or similar tax, which shall lawfully be imposed upon the Settlor's taxable estate as a result of the Settlor's death. The proceeds of employee death benefits or employee life insurance policies on the Settlor's life shall not be used to pay death taxes or be otherwise paid to the executor of the Settlor's estate.

(3) From the balance of the trust fund remaining in the Trustee's hands, the Trustee shall pay to the Settlor's surviving spouse *(e.g., May Doe or John Doe)* □ ____ in equal monthly installments during such spouse's lifetime, a sum equal to six (6%) percent per year of the value of this nonmarital part of the trust fund as computed at the time of the Settlor's death and thereafter recomputed at the beginning of each calendar year.

(4) If the Trustee, pursuant to the provisions of paragraph 20 below, shall have resigned at any time after the Settlor's death, the Successor Trustee, hereinafter named below, is authorized thereafter at his or her sole discretion, to pay to the Settlor's spouse or expend on his/her behalf in addition to the income distribution specified above, such sums from the principal of the nonmarital part of the trust as the Successor Trustee shall deem necessary or desirable for the comfort or well-being of the Settlor's spouse.

(5) Upon the death of the Settlor's spouse, the Successor Trustee, if requested by the executor or administrator of the said spouse's estate, in his/her own discretion if there is no formal probate administration, shall pay or reimburse the said spouse's estate for the amounts of any funeral expenses or expense of the last illness and/or any taxes, debts or other post-death expense of the said spouse's estate.

(6) Thereafter, subject to the Children's Subtrust provisions in paragraphs 24 below, if applicable, the Successor Trustee shall dispose of the remaining Trust B trust fund specified in ____ ⑦ ____.

Cross off
TWO of the three
non-applicable ones
and initial them

| Box One below |
| Box Two below |
| Box three below |

Box One

The Trustee shall pay the entire balance of the trust fund to the Settlor's

(Daughter, nephew, friend etc.)

(Name)

and shall thereupon terminate the trust

Box Two

The Trustee shall divide the balance of the trust fund into as many equal parts as there shall be beneficiaries named below and shall pay one such part to each of the following, in equal shares, per stirpes;

(Name)

and shall thereupon terminate the trust.

Box Three

The Trustee shall pay the balance of the trust fund to the following, per stirpes, in the proportions shown:

Name   Proportion to be paid to such beneficiary

____ ____%
____ ____%

The share of any beneficiary who dies leaving no surviving issue shall be divided equally among the remaining named beneficiaries who are natural persons, per stirpes.

and shall thereupon terminate the trust.

6. COMMUNITY PROPERTY, IF APPLICABLE

With respect to community property*: (a) if the assets or any part of them, deposited in this trust shall constitute community property, they shall retain such character as community property after being transferred

*Community property designation (a form of jointly owned marital property between a married couple) will apply to you if you reside in these states, which are the "community property states": Arizona, California, Idaho, Louisiana, Nevada, New Mexico, Texas, Washington and Wisconsin.

to this trust; (b) in such event, all distributions of income from the trust while both parties are living shall be considered to be community property; (c) if and when community property applies, either party shall have the right to withdraw his or her portion of the community property either before or after the death of the Settlor, and (d) if the trust is revoked, any assets listed in Schedule A shall revert to the grantors as their community property and not as the separate property of either or both.

7. INCAPACITY OF GRANTOR(S).

If at any time, a grantor is certified in writing by two licensed physicians as being physically incapacitated, whether or not a court of competent jurisdiction has so declared, the trustee or successor trustee shall assume the active administration of the trust and shall apply, for the benefit of the grantor(s), an amount of net income or trust principal necessary in the trustee(s)' discretion for the proper health care, support and maintenance of the grantor(s), until the grantor(s), as certified by two licensed physicians, is (are) again competent to manage his or her own affairs or until his or her earlier death.

8. Upon the death of the grantor or surviving grantor, this trust becomes irrevocable and may not be amended, terminated or altered in any way except as specifically authorized by this instrument.

9. If a guardian or conservator is appointed for a grantor or the estate, the Trustee(s) shall take into account any such payments made by the guardian or conservator for the grantor's benefit.

10. TRUSTEE'S POWERS, DUTIES & RESPONSIBILITIES
A) Statutory & Fiduciary Powers.

To manage this trust and any children's subtrusts created under this Declaration of Trust, if applicable, the Trustees and Successor Trustees shall have the full powers and authority allowed or conferred on a trustee under the State of *[Enter the applicable state's name]* law, subject to the trustee's fiduciary duty to the grantor(s) and the beneficiaries.

B) Record Keeping.

The Trustees' (or their successors') will keep accurate records of all transactions involving assets placed in this trust and make all such records readily available for inspection by any grantor(s) or beneficiary during normal business hours.

C) Payment of Valid Estate Debts & Expenses.

On the death of the grantor or surviving grantor, the Trustee shall pay the grantor's valid debts, and estate, inheritance and death taxes, and last illness and funeral expenses and other costs in administering the grantor's probate estate, out of the Trust Property and charge them against the said Trust Property, subject to Paragraph 18 below.

11. GENERAL POWERS OF TRUSTEES.
A) The Trustee's powers and discretion shall include, but not be limited to:

a. The power to sell, encumber, mortgage, pledge, lease or improve the Trust Property, when such action is deemed to be in the best interest and in furtherance of the trust purposes, including the power to do same in order to make distribution provided for in this Declaration.

b. Power to manage securities, to include the power of all the rights, powers, and privileges of an owner.

c. Power to allocate to principal or increase all monies and properties received on behalf of the Trust.

d. Power to make distributions of the Trust property as required, pursuant to the provisions of this Trust.

e. Power to employ and pay reasonable fees to any custodian, investment advisor, attorney, accountant, or other consultant deemed necessary for information, assistance, or advice related to the trust.

f. Power to hold and operate any business interest that may be or become a part of the Trust Property or Estate.

g. Power to pay with funds from Trust Property or Estate any tax, charge or assessment against the Trust which the Trustee shall be required to pay.

h. Power to deposit and hold trust funds in both interest bearing and non-interest bearing commercial, savings or saving & loan accounts, subject to the usual restrictions, upon withdrawal in effect at that time, and to enter into electronic fund transfer or safe deposit arrangements with such institutions.

i. Power to execute any documents necessary to effectuate or administer any trust created in this Declaration of Trust.

j. Power to retain and to continue to hold any property that becomes a part of the Trust Property or Estate.

k. Power to sell, dispose of, exchange, partition, convey, divide, repair, manage, control, and grant options and rights of refusal of property that becomes a part of the Trust Estate for cash, credit, deferred payments, or exchange.

l. Power to manage trust real estate belonging to the Trust, or to lease or rent same for any purpose, including exploration and removal of gas, oil and other minerals, to include community leases and pooling agreements.

m. Power to insure, at the expense of the Trust, insurance of any kind and in amounts as the Trustee deems advisable.

n. Power to invest all or any part of the Trust Property in every kind of property, whether real or personal, and in every kind of investment, such as bonds, debentures, notes, mortgages and stocks.

o. Power to litigate and compromise claims with respect to the Trust Estate as the Trustees deem advisable.

B) Any and all of the above specified or other authorized powers and duties may be exercised as may be necessary in the discretion of the Trustee, without being required to make application for more specific authority to any court of law or equity.

13. APPLICABLE STATE LAWS & SEVERABILITY OF PROVISIONS

The validity of this trust and the construction of its beneficial provisions shall be governed by the laws of the state of _____. If any clause(s) or provision(s) of this Declaration of Trust is (are) ruled invalid or unenforceable for any reason by a court of law, the remaining provisions shall nevertheless remain valid and in effect.

12. INALIENABILITY OF BENEFICIARY'S INTEREST IN TRUST

No interest of a beneficiary in the principal or income of any trust created under this instrument shall be anticipated, assigned, encumbered, or subject to creditor's claim or legal process before being received by a beneficiary.

14. INTERCHANGABILITY OF TERMS

Any Trustee shall have the right to resign at any time by signing a notice of resignation and delivering same to the person or institution appointed or named in this Declaration of Trust to next serve as Trustee. The term "Trustee," as used in this instrument shall include also "Trustees," "Co-Trustees," "Sole Trustee," and "Successor Trustee or Trustees," and any singular terms also includes the plural.

15. NON-LIABILITY OF THE TRUSTEE

The trustee shall not be liable for any actions taken in good faith in the exercise or non-exercise of the powers and duties and responsibilities granted under this Declaration of Trust, and any provisions validly added by amendment. Such actions taken in good faith shall be binding on all parties concerned.

16. NON-LIABILITY OF THIRD PARTIES

A) Be it known that it is the express intent and understanding of the trust-makers herein, that any third person, including their Agents, Employees or Vendors, who upon the written request of the grantor(s), or under the color of authority granted to the Trustee(s) in this Declaration of Trust, performs any duties or renders any services pursuant to that authority, unless a showing of fraud can be made, shall be under no liability for the application or proper administration of any assets or properties that is the subject of the said third party's acts.

B) This limitation of liability is specifically intended to give protection to any third party who acts, performs or renders any services pursuant to any Notice, Instrument or Document reasonably believed and represented to be genuine, and to have been signed and presented by the proper party (parties).

C) It is further the express intent of this Trust that the non-liability of all Third Parties as herein above stipulated, be given broad and prospective application. In particular, financial, credit or banking institutions or brokerage houses, or transfer agents, medical personnel or any other person or entity acting in a fiduciary capacity with regards to any assets or property comprising the Trust Property, shall suffer no liability, nor incur any express or implied obligations when reasonably acting in the capacity of a Transferror or other such capacity, upon proper request, of any assets or property sought to be or comprising the Trust Property.

17. EXTENSION OF TRUST POWERS

This Declaration of Trust shall extend to and be binding upon the Heirs, Executors, Administrators and assigns of the undersigned Trustor(s) and upon the Successor(s) to the Trustee(s).

18. BENEFICIARY PROPORTIONATE LIABILITY FOR ESTATE TAXES

Each beneficiary under this Trust shall be liable for his (her) proportionate share of state or federal estate or inheritance taxes that may be levied, if any, upon the total taxable value of the Trust Property distributed to the said beneficiaries upon the death of either the donor or the surviving donor.

19. INTERPRETATION/DETERMINATION OF TRUST PROVISIONS

If any provision of this instrument shall be unclear or the subject of dispute among the parties to the trust, the Trustee (or the Successor Trustee, if the latter shall then be actively serving), is hereby fully authorized to interpret and determine such provision, and any such determination made by the Trustee shall be final and binding upon all such parties.

20. REVOCATION/AMENDMENT OF TRUST

This trust may be amended or revoked at any time during the lifetime of the Settlor(s) by written notice duly notarized from the Settlor(s) to the Trustee, without prior notice to or consent of any beneficiary or the Trustee(s) or Successor Trustee(s), including the right to appoint substitutes or otherwise change the person(s) designated as Trustee(s) or Successor Trustee(s). The Trustee may resign at any time during the lifetime of the Settlor(s) by written notice to the Settlor(s). The Trustee may resign after the death of the Settlor(s) upon written notice to the designated Successor Trustee and upon proper delivery of the assets of the trust to such Successor Trustee.

21. SUCCESSOR TRUSTEE(S)

In the event of the Trustee's physical or mental incapacity, death, resignation, or removal for cause, the Settlor(s) hereby appoints _____ 8 _____ as Successor Trustee. If the said first Successor Trustee, Mr/Mrs _____ 8 _____ , shall be unwilling or unable to carry out such duties, the Settlor(s) hereby appoints

Mr/Mrs _____ 9 _____ as Successor Trustee hereunder.

22. PRIVACY/CONFIDENTIALITY OF TRUST

The Trustee and any Successor Trustee are specifically instructed by the Settlor(s) to maintain the privacy and confidentiality of this instrument and the trust created hereunder, and are in no circumstances to divulge its terms to any probate or other court or other public agency with the exception of a tax authority.

23. Trustee Bond, Compensation & Accounting Requirements

A) No bond or order of approval from a court shall be required of any Trustee, Co-Trustee or Successor Trustee named, appointed or serving under this instrument.

B) The Trustee shall serve without compensation. [OR ALTERNATIVELY, IF PREFERRED: "The Trustee [and/or Successor Trustee] may receive reasonable compensation for his or her services on behalf of the Trust"]

C) No accounting shall be required of the Trustee.

24. CHILDREN'S SUBTRUST*

A) The Applicable Beneficiaries

If any of the following minors or young adult persons who are named as beneficiaries in paragraphs 5(B)(6) above, namely, _____ [10] _____ shall be under the age or _____ [11] _____ at the time he or she becomes entitled to the distribution under this Declaration, then all trust property given to such beneficiaries under this Declaration shall not be paid, but shall be deferred and be retained in common trust for all such beneficiaries in a separate subtrust of this "_____ [11] _____ Trust," until each child or beneficiary attains the age of _____ [1] _____, at which point the said subtrust shall end with respect to that particular beneficiary, and any principal or income then remaining in the subtrust for the particular beneficiary, if any, shall promptly be distributed to the said child or beneficiary by the subtrust trustee, subject to the provisions of paragraph 24C below with reference to particular beneficiaries, if applicable.

B) Name Of Subtrust

Each and every separate subtrust herein shall be identified and referred to by adding the name of the subtrust's beneficiary to the name of this trust, and inserting it just before the name of this trust in this manner: "The _____ [3] _____ For _____ [13] _____ Minor."

C) Duration Of The Subtrust

With respect to these child(ren) or beneficiaries named below, however, namely _____ if any is so named herein, upon the attainment of the age of _____ [14] _____ years by each, the subtrust Trustee shall not make outright distribution of any balance of their inheritance then remaining in the subtrust as stipulated in paragraph 24A above, but such balance, if any, shall be distributed to them as follows: one-third (1/3) promptly upon attainment of the said age; then another one-third (1/3) three years thereafter, and the final distribution of one-third (1/3) two years thereafter. And, thereupon, the children's subtrust shall forthwith terminate with respect to such beneficiaries.

D) If any beneficiary survives the (grantor(s)) but dies before attaining the age of _____ [14] _____ years, at the death of such beneficiary the Trustee shall pass the beneficiary's entitlement under the subtrust to his/her heirs absolutely, per stirpes.

E) Powers Of Subtrust Trustee

i) In the meantime, until each child's term in the subtrust ends, the Trustee may distribute to or for the benefit of each designated beneficiary, as much of the net income or principal of the child(ren') share of the subtrust as the Trustee in his/her discretion deems necessary for the beneficiary's health, support, maintenance or education, only using his/her fiduciary discretion and best judgment and sense of fairplay and necessity, to provide for each beneficiary's individual needs as they may arise or be necessary. Education includes, but is not limited to, college, graduate, postgraduate and vocational studies, and reasonably related living expenses.

ii) In deciding how and in what manners and when to make a distribution to a beneficiary, the Trustee may take into account each beneficiary's other income, resources, and sources of support, his/her circumstances and real needs, character and demonstrated sense of responsibility.

NOTE: Note that under the law, if you leave inheritance for your minor children under the children's subtrust in the Living Trust, you may not also use the Uniform Transfer to Minors Act to leave property for the same child or children. You may only use ONE or the other, not both. See pp. 33-4 of the manual for more on this.

iii) No intervention of any guardian or application to any court shall be necessary or permissible in the good faith exercise of these duties by the Trustee (or Successor Trustee).

iv) The Trustee may invest the subtrust assets in such income-yielding ventures as the Trustee may deem proper and prudent and the income as well as such amounts of the principal as are necessary, even to the extent of all, shall be applied to the support, general welfare and benefits of the beneficiaries, as directed in this Declaration.

F) No Assignment Of Interest Of Beneficiary

No interest of any beneficiary under this children's subtrust shall be anticipated, assigned or encumbered by voluntary or involuntary act or by operation of law before being received by the beneficiary. Nor shall these interests be subject to the claims of creditors or to attachments, execution, bankruptcy or other legal process to the fullest extent permitted by law.

G. Trustee's Rights of Compensation

Any Trustee of the children's subtrust created under this Declaration of Trust shall be entitled to reasonable compensation out of the subtrust assets, for his or her services on behalf of the Trust. *[Alternatively, if preferred: 'Any Trustee of the children's subtrust shall serve without compensation.']*

22. CUSTODIANSHIPS UNDER THE UNIFORM TRANSFERS TO MINORS ACT*

All trust property given to any of the minor or young adult beneficiaries listed below shall be given to each such beneficiary under the provisions of the *(name of your state)* Uniform Transfers To Minors Act.

1. All Property to which _____ [15] _____, hereinafter called a "Minor Beneficiary" under this Declaration, shall become entitled to receive, shall be given to _____ [16] _____ as custodian for the said Minor Beneficiary under the Uniform Transfers To Minors Act, until the said Minor Beneficiary attains the age of _____ [17] _____, or if no age is specified herein, until he/she attains the age provided under the Uniform Transfers to Minors Act at which the beneficiary becomes entitled to receive the property outright from the custodian.

2. All property to which _____, hereinafter called a "Minor Beneficiary" under this Declaration, shall become entitled to receive, shall be given to _____ as custodian for the said Minor Beneficiary under the Uniform Transfers to Minors Act, until the said Minor Beneficiary attains the age of _____, or if no age is specified herein, until he/she attains the age provided by the Uniform Transfers to Minors Act at which the beneficiary becomes entitled to receive the property outright from the custodian.

3. All property to which _____, hereinafter called a "Minor Beneficiary" under this Declaration, shall become entitled to receive, shall be given to _____ as custodian for the said Minor Beneficiary under the Uniform Transfers to Minors Act, until the said Minor Beneficiary attains the age of _____, or if no age is specified herein, until he/she attains the age provided by the Uniform Transfers to Minors Act at which the beneficiary becomes entitled to receive the property outright from the custodian.

---

*See footnote on the preceding page of this form, and on pp. 33-4 of the manual, including the footnote therein.

CERTIFICATION BY TRUST GRANTOR(S)

I (WE) CERTIFY that I (We) have read this *Declaration of Trust* and that it correctly states the terms, conditions, covenants and agreements under which the trust estate is to be held, managed and administered and disposed of by the trustee (or the succesor thereof), and I (we) therefore approve the Declaration of Trust.

IN WITNESS WHEREOF, I (We) have signed these presents this _____ day of _____, 19___.

SIGNED. ✗ _____ [12]
Trustor (Grantor)

SIGNED. ✗ _____ [12]
Co-Trustor (Co-Grantor)

Acknowledgment

STATE OF _____

COUNTY OF _____)ss.
)

On this _____ day of _____, 19___, before me, the undersigned Notary Public duly authorized to administer oaths in and by the above captioned jurisdiction, personally appeared Mr./Mrs./Ms. _____ to me known or made known to me to be the individual(s) described in and who executed the foregoing Declaration Of Trust, thereupon the said person(s) acknowledged that he (she) (they) executed the same as his (her) (their) free act and deed. [1]

My Commission expires _____

_____
(Notary Public)

Spouse's Disclaimer Of Trust Asset Or Interest*

I, the undersigned legal spouse of the above-named Grantor, hereby waive all community property, dower or curtesy rights and interest which I may have in the property described in the foregoing Trust and give my assent to the provisions of the trust and to the inclusion of the said property in the said Trust.

(Spouse to sign here, where applicable) ✗ _____

SWORN TO BEFORE ME, THIS _____ 19___

_____
(Notary Public)

*NOTE: The signing of this clause is not applicable or necessary when the spouses have both signed the Declaration of Trust. If married and you and your spouse have not jointly signed the Declaration of Trust, then you must have your spouse as well sign and notarize the statement in this box, if: (a) you've included in the Trust any property held only in one spouse's name and; (b) if your spouse is not the person that is designated in the trust as the primary beneficiary of the trust property.

98

Instructions For Completing The Blanks In The "A-B" And "A-B-C" Declaration Of Trust Forms (p. 90 & 101):

1. The names [and addresses] of the Trust-maker or makers go in here.

2. The name of the person (or institution) you appoint to act as the initial Trustee. Usually, in most family trust situations, you'll enter your own name here, and enter your spouse's name, if applicable, in the paragraph for designating the Successor Trustee.

3. Enter the name by which this Trust will be known and identified. Generally, trust-makers would simply use their own name(s). Example: *"The Mary Doe Trust;"* or, for a married couple: *"The Mary and John Doe Trust."* Also, if you create more than one trust, the trusts are usually differentiated by assigning a number to each trust. Example: *"The Mary and John Doe Trust, No. 1," "The Mary and John Doe Trust, No. 2," and so on.*

4. The name of the Trust-maker or makers.

5. To create your trust, you'll have to identify which of your assets you are setting aside as trust assets or property. And, the method generally recognized as the most convenient method of doing this, is to list all such assets you want to put into the trust on a separate sheet (or sheets) of paper called a **"SCHEDULE,"** and attach it to the back of the trust document. The assets listed on the schedule must be described in sufficient details and specifics on the Schedule, as is done in the sample copy set forth in the manual. (See Appendix B, at p. 211 for sample of a Schedule.)

6. Enter both spouses' names with an "<u>or</u>" in between, so that either one of them will be just as eligible. Example: "John Doe Or Mary Doe."

7. In this clause, you are to name and identify the beneficiary or beneficiaries who are to receive the balance of the estate (the Trust B and/or C part) remaining after the death of the surviving spouse. Pick just *one* option (one box) from the three options offered by the boxes; then properly cross out the other two boxes that are not picked, and enter in the box picked, the names and identities of the intended beneficiaries and specify the respective share each will get. The format used in this trust document does not specify particualr items of property for particular individuals and more specific designations may be made by will, if any, when desired. Notice that Box Two permits distribution of the property only in <u>equal</u> shares, while Box Three permits distribution in *non-equal* amounts, as you may wish. Number the beneficiaries you name, such as: *1. The couple's son, John Doe, Jr.; 2. The couple's daughter, Agnes Doe; and 3. The living children, natural or adopted, of the couple; son, David Doe and daughter, Mary Doe.*

8. Enter the full name of the person (or institution) you designate to serve as the **Successor Trustee**, if your spouse dies or is for any reason unable or unavailable to serve. [See Chapter 4, Section C of the manual for an idea of the extreme significance of this position.]

9. Enter the full name of the possible alternate successor for the designated first Successor Trustee.

10. Here you enter, if this clause is applicable to you—i.e., basically, if you have minor or underage children and wish to set apart their inheritance for them in a separate subtrust until they are of age—the names and

dates of birth of each child involved. This group may include persons who are underage or are incompetent whom you've named as alternate beneficiaries in Paragraph **5(B)(6)**. If, however, you list someone as a beneficiary under this paragaph, you may not also list that same person to receive gift under the Uniform Transfers To Minors Act (UTMA)—Paragraph 25 below. (Under the law, you can only leave property to a child by either **one** or the other method, and not both.)

11. Enter the age you prefer at which the minors are to receive the distribution, or, as the case may be, the first installment of such inheritance. Example: at age 21, or 25, 30, or whatever you propose.

12. Here you enter, if this provision is applicable to you—i.e., basically, if you have minor or underage children and prefer to set apart their inheritance by means of your state's UTMA law until they are of certain age*—the names and dates of birth of each child involved. Enter in each paragraph the name of each child who is to be provided for under the UTMA provision.

13. Enter the name of the custodian you designate to manage the child's inheritance.

14. Enter the maximum age specified under the state's Uniform Minors Transfer Act (pp. 33-4).

15. You, the Grantor or Grantors, sign here—in the presence of a Notary Public.

> **NOTE:** Now that you shall have presumably completed the drafting phase of your Trust document (the first and final drafts and the signing and notarizing), now get back to the next phase that should follow in the trust creating process—the transfer of trust property into the trust (Chapter 7, from Section D thereof)—and systematically follow the rest of Chapter 7. Chapter 8 deals with the operation of the trust once you've created it.

---

*As elaborated in an earlier section of this manual, to be eligible to employ the UTMA to leave property to your minor child, your state has to have enacted the UTMA law (see list of such states on p. 33), and the method is generally more feasible when the leaving off smaller estate is involved (generally, for gift of less than $25,000 to $50,000). Remember, however, that if the Living Trust's children's subtrust is used to leave an inheritance to a child, then the UTMA cannot also be used for the same child. (See pp. 33-4 for more on the children's subtrust and applicable UTMA states and the workings of the UTMA in leaving a gift for minors.)

Form LT—IV

Declaration Of Trust

(A Sample Form)

TYPE "A-B-C" TRUST—A MARRIED COUPLE WITH CHILDREN

This revocable Living Trust Agreement (otherwise known as "DECLARATION OF TRUST"), is made on the date last signed and entered below, between the following person(s):

GRANTOR(S)/TRUSTOR(S): Mr/Mrs: ___ ① ___, of this address

___, city and state of ___ (hereinafter referred to as the

"Grantor(s)" or "Trustor(s)"); and

TRUSTEE(S): Mr/Mrs ___ ② ___, of this address ___, city and state

of ___ (hereinafter referred to as the "Trustee(s)."

WITNESSETH:

WHEREAS the Settlor(s) desire(s) at death to leave certain property in trust, and WHEREAS the Trustee(s) is (are) willing to accept and administer such funds as Trustee(s) under the terms of these presents,

NOW THEREFORE, the Settlor(s) and the Trustee(s) intending to be legally bound by this agreement, do hereby covenant and agree upon the following terms and conditions:

1. THE TRUST NAME

This trust shall be known as "The ___ ③ ___ Trust."

2. NON-PERPETUITY CLAUSE

For the purpose of complying with the rule against perpetuities, any trust created herein that has not terminated sooner shall terminate twenty-one (21) years after the death of the rest of the last survivor of the class composed of ___ ④ ___ and their children, grandchildren and any of their more remote descendents who are living when the trust is created.

3. TRUST INTENT & PROPERTY

A) The Settlors hereby declare that they have, without any consideration, separately transferred and delivered to the designated Trustee(s) herein, who is/are also named as Trust beneficiary to receive certain property, all his/her rights, title and interest in the property listed and described in Schedule A ___ ⑤ ___ attached to this Declaration and hereby made a part of this Declaration, which property is to be held IN TRUST for the use, benefit and enjoyment of the beneficiaries named in this TRUST instrument and in accordance with the provisions set forth herein.

NOTE: See instructions for filling in the blank spaces in this form on pp. 99-100.

B) The Trust Property

The said property listed and described in Schedule A, is hereafter referred to as the "TRUST PROPERTY." The Trust Property shall be held, administered and distributed by the Trustee in accordance with the provisions of the trust instrument, and the settlor reserves the right to add additional assets to the Trust Property and/or to make them, including life insurance policies on the Settlor's life, payable to the designated beneficiaries.

C) Each Grantor may, during his or her lifetime (or by testamentary Will), add or delete any asset at any time, to the trust property. Such after-acquired property may be added to the trust simply by listing same on Schedule A.

4. THE "MARITAL" & "NON-MARITAL" SHARES OF THE TRUST PROPERTY: THE "A" TRUST & "B" TRUST

Upon the settlor's death, the surviving spouse, as Trustee, shall divide the Trust Property or Fund into two parts. One part, herein termed the "Marital Share," (or **TRUST A Part**), shall consist of property of equal value to one-half of the common total trust.* The other one-half part, hereinafter termed the "Non-marital Share" (or **Trust B and Trust C** parts) shall consist of the remainder of the total trust fund.

In apportioning to the marital and nonmarital trust specific assets previously valued for estate tax purposes, the Trustee shall insure that the two parts share proportionately in any subsequent appreciation or depreciation in the value of such assets. Assets which do not qualify for marital deduction status, or assets not includable in the Settlor's gross estate for federal tax purposes, shall not be included in the marital share of the trust.

5. INSTRUCTIONS WITH RESPECT TO THE 'MARITAL' SHARE OF THE TRUST PROPERTY (TRUST A)

A) With respect to the '*marital share*,' also called the Trust A part, the Trustee shall hold, manage, invest and reinvest the same as a trust and upon the following terms and conditions:

(1) The Trustee shall pay to the Settlor's surviving spouse *(John or Mary Doe)* _____ 6 _____, in convenient monthly installments during his/her lifetime, the actual income accruing from the trust property or a sum equal to six (6%) percent per year of the value of the trust computed at the time of the Settlor's death and thereafter recomputed annually at the beginning of each calendar year, whichever is the greater, together with any sums from the principal that the Settlor's spouse may request to be paid from time to time.

(2) Upon the death of the Settlor's surviving spouse, the Successor Trustee, who is hereinafter named in this Declaration, shall distribute the assets then contained in this part of the trust (i.e., in Trust A) to the surviving spouse's estate or the beneficiaries designated by the surviving spouse in his or her will or otherwise, in accordance with the directions of this Declaration of Trust. The Settlor hereby confers upon the said spouse the sole and unrestricted right to designate such beneficiaries by his or her Will, and to the extent that the said power is not effectively exercised, the surviving spouse's trust fund herein created shall be added to the remaining part of the Trust and shall be disposed of as hereinafter provided.

(3) If the Settlor and the Settlor's spouse shall die in such circumstances that there is not, in the judgment of the Successor Trustee, whose decision shall be conclusive, sufficient evidence to determine readily which of them survived the other, then for the purposes of this trust the Settlor's spouse shall be deemed to have survived the Settlor.

WITH RESPECT TO 'NON-MARITAL' SHARE OF THE TRUST PROPERTY (TRUST B & C)

B) With respect to the remaining one-half of the fund, namely the "nonmarital" part, the Trustee shall, upon the death of the first spouse to die, hold, manage, invest and reinvest that non-marital part of the trust as a trust fund on the following terms and conditions:

*As elaborated in Chapter 5 of the manual, this statement describing the 'marital share' part (i.e, Trust A) basically means this: assuming that in this case the total value of the trust is MORE than $1.2 million (say, specifically, it's $1.5 million), just one-half of the total value of the assets (i.e., $750,000 in this example) is all that is placed in the surviving spouse's marital share part; (his or her Trust A). The remaining one-half, the "non-marital" one-half belonging to the deceased spouse (i.e., $750,000 in our example), is, in turn divided into two parts—one part, his or her Trust B, will contain only $600,000 (since that is his/her maximum allowed federal estate tax exemption amount), while the other part, his or her Trust C, will contain the rest of his (that decedent spouse's) one-half share, which is $150,000 in our example (i.e., $750,000 - $600,000).

(1) This nonmarital half of the trust shall be divided into two sub parts so that only $600,000 of that is placed in one subpart to be called the decedent spouse's Trust B, and the rest of the nonmarital half of the trust shall be placed in the other subpart, to be called the decedent spouse's Trust C.

(2) If requested by the executor or administrator of the Settlor's estate (hereinafter also called the Decedent's Estate), the Trustee shall pay or reimburse the said executor or administrator for the amount of any pre-death claim, funeral expense or expenses of administration which shall be allowed in connection with the settlement of such estate or, in the absence of any formal probate administration, the costs and expenses which the Trustee shall determine to be due and payable.

(3) The Trustee shall pay to the proper taxing authority or reimburse the executor or administrator of the Settlor's estate, for the amount of any, state or federal succession, estate, transfer or similar tax, which shall lawfully be imposed upon the Settlor's taxable estate as a result of the Settlor's death. The proceeds of employee death benefits or employee life insurance policies on the Settlor's life shall not be used to pay death taxes or be otherwise paid to the executor of the Settlor's estate.

(4) From the balance of the trust fund remaining in the Trustee's hands, the Trustee shall pay to the Settlor's surviving spouse *(Mary or Lola Doe)* 6 , in equal monthly installments during such spouse's lifetime, a sum equal to six (6%) percent per year of the value of this nonmarital part of the trust fund as computed at the time of the Settlor's death and thereafter recomputed at the beginning of each calendar year.

(5) If the Trustee, pursuant to the provisions of paragraph 20 below, shall have resigned at any time after the Settlor's death, the Successor Trustee, hereinafter named below, is authorized thereafter at his or her sole discretion, to pay to the Settlor's spouse or expend on his/her behalf in addition to the income distribution specified above, such sums from the principal of the nonmarital part of the trust as the Successor Trustee shall deem necessary or desirable for the comfort or well-being of the Settlor's spouse.

(6) Upon the death of the Settlor's spouse, the Successor Trustee, if requested by the executor or administrator of the said spouse's estate, in his/her own discretion if there is no formal probate administration, shall pay or reimburse the said spouse's estate for the amounts of any funeral expenses or expense of the last illness and/or any taxes, debts or other post-death expense of the said spouse's estate.

(7) Thereafter, subject to the Children's Subtrust provisions in paragraphs 24 below, if applicable, the Successor Trustee shall dispose of the remaining nonmarital share of the trust specified in _____ 7 .

[Cross off TWO of the three non-applicable ones]	Box One below
	Box Two below
	Box Three below

Box One

The Trustee shall pay the entire balance of the trust fund to the Settlor's

_____
(Daughter, nephew, friend etc.)

_____
(Name)

and shall thereupon terminate the trust

Box Two

The Trustee shall divide the balance of the trust fund into as many equal parts as there shall be beneficiaries named below and shall pay one such part to each of the following, in equal shares, per stirpes

and shall thereupon terminate the trust.

Box Three

The Trustee shall pay the balance of the trust fund to the following, per stirpes, in the proportions shown: Proportion to be paid to such beneficiary
Name

_____ ___%

_____ ___%

The share of any beneficiary who dies leaving no surviving issue shall be divided equally among the remaining named beneficiaries who are natural persons, per stirpes.

and shall thereupon terminate the trust.

6. COMMUNITY PROPERTY, IF APPLICABLE

With respect to community property*: (a) if the assets or any part of them deposited in this trust shall constitute community property, they shall retain such character as community property after being transferred to this trust; (b) in such event, all distributions of income from the trust while both parties are living shall be considered to be community property; (c) if and when community property applies, either party shall have the right to withdraw his or her portion of the community property either before or after the death of the Settlor, and (d) if the trust is revoked, any assets listed in Schedule A shall revert to the grantor as their community property and not as the separate property of either or both.

7. INCAPACITY OF GRANTOR(S).

If at any time, a grantor is certified in writing by two licensed physicians as being physically incapacitated, whether or not a court of competent jurisdiction has so declared, the trustee or successor trustee shall assume the active administration of the trust and shall apply for the benefit of the grantor(s) an amount of net income or trust principal necessary, in the trustee(s) discretion, for the proper health care, support and maintenance of the grantor(s) until the grantor(s), as certified by two licensed physicians, is (are) again competent to manage his or her own affairs or until this or her earlier death.

8. Upon the death of the grantor or surviving grantor, this trust becomes irrevocable and may not be amended, terminated or altered in any way except as specifically authorized by this instrument.

9. If a guardian or conservator is appointed for a grantor or the estate, the Trustee(s) shall take into account any such payments made by the guardian or conservator for the grantor's benefit.

10. TRUSTEE'S POWERS, DUTIES & RESPONSIBILITIES

A) Statutory & Fiduciary Powers.

To manage this trust and any children's subtrusts created under this Declaration of Trust, if applicable, the Trustees and Successor Trustees shall have the full powers and authority allowed or conferred on a trustee under the state of _[Enter the applicable state's name]_ law, subject to the trustee's fiduciary duty to the grantor(s) and the beneficiaries.

B) Record Keeping.

The Trustees' (or their successors') will keep accurate records of all transactions involving assets placed in this trust and make all such records readily available for inspection by any grantor(s) or beneficiary during normal business hours.

C) Payment of Valid Estate Debts & Expenses.

On the death of the grantor or surviving grantor, the Trustee shall pay the grantor's valid debts, and estate inheritance and death taxes, and last illness and funeral expenses and other costs in administering the grantor's probate estate, out of the nonmarital Trust B and/or Trust C parts of the trust fund and charge them against the said Trust B and/or Trust C parts, subject to Paragraph 18 below.

11. GENERAL POWERS OF TRUSTEES

A) The Trustee's powers and discretion shall include, but not be limited to:

a. The power to sell, encumber, mortgage, pledge, lease or improve the Trust Property, when such action is deemed to be in the best interest and in furtherance of the trust purposes, including the power to do same in order to make distribution provided for in this Declaration.

b. Power to manage securities, to include the power of all the rights, powers, and privileges of an owner.

---

*Community property designation (a form of jointly owned marital property between a married couple) will apply to you if you reside in these states, which are the "community property states": Arizona, California, Idaho, Louisiana, Nevada, New Mexico, Texas, Washington and Wisconsin.

c. Power to allocate to principal or increase all monies and properties received on behalf of the Trust.

d. Power to make distributions of the Trust property as required, pursuant to the provisions of this Trust.

e. Power to employ and pay reasonable fees to any custodian, investment advisor, attorney, accountant, or other consultant deemed necessary for information, assistance or advice related to the trust.

f. Power to hold and operate any business interest that may be or become a part of the Trust Property or Estate.

g. Power to pay with funds from Trust Property or Estate any tax, charge or assessment against the Trust which the Trustee shall be required to pay.

h. Power to deposit and hold trust funds in both interest bearing and non-interest bearing commercial, savings or saving & loan accounts, subject to the usual restrictions, upon withdrawal in effect at that time, and to enter into electronic fund transfer or safe deposit arrangements with such institutions.

i. Power to execute any documents necessary to effectuate or administer any trust created in this Declaration of Trust.

j. Power to retain and to continue to hold any property that becomes a part of the Trust Property or Estate.

k. Power to sell, dispose of, exchange, partition, convey, divide, repair, manage, control, and grant options and rights or refusal of property that becomes a part of the Trust Estate for cash, credit, deferred payments, or exchange.

l. Power to manage trust real estate belonging to the Trust, or to lease or rent same for any purpose, including exploration and removal of gas, oil and other minerals, to include community leases and pooling agreements.

m. Power to insure, at the expense of the Trust, insurance of any kind and in amounts as the Trustee deems advisable.

n. Power to invest all or any part of the Trust Property in every kind of property, whether real or personal, and in every kind of investment, such as bonds, debentures, notes, mortgages and stocks.

o. Power to litigate and compromise claims with respect to the Trust Estate as the Trustees deem advisable.

B) Any and all of the above specified or other authorized powers and duties may be exercised as may be necessary in the discretion of the Trustee, without beng required to make application for more specific authority to any court of law or equity.

12. INALIENABILITY OF BENEFICIARY'S INTEREST IN TRUST
No interest of a beneficiary in the principal or income of any trust created under this instrument shall be anticipated, assigned, encumbered, or subject to creditor's claim or legal process before being received by a beneficiary.

13. APPLICABLE STATE LAWS & SEVERABILITY OF PROVISIONS
The validity of this trust and the construction of its beneficial provisions shall be governed by the laws of the state of _____. If any clause(s) or provision(s) of this Declaration of Trust is (are) ruled invalid or unenforceable for any reason by a court of law, the remaining provisions shall nevertheless remain valid and in effect.

14. INTERCHANGABILITY OF TERMS
Any Trustee shall have the right to resign at any time by signing a notice of resignation and delivering same to the person or institution appointed or named in this Declaration of Trust to next serve as Trustee. The term "Trustee," as used in this instrument shall include also "Trustees," "Co-Trustees," "Sole Trustee," and "Successor Trustee or Trustees," and any singular term also includes the plural.

15. NON-LIABILITY OF THE TRUSTEE

The trustee shall not be liable for any actions taken in good faith in the exercise or non-exercise of the powers and duties and responsibilities granted under this Declaration of Trust, and any provisions validly added by amendment. Such actions taken in good faith shall be binding on all parties concerned.

16. NON-LIABILITY OF THIRD PARTIES

A) Be it known that it is the express intent and understanding of the trust-makers herein, that any third person, including their Agents, Employees or Vendors, who upon the written request of the grantor(s), or under the color of authority granted to the Trustee(s) in this Declaration of Trust, performs any duties or renders any services pursuant to that authority, unless a showing of fraud can be made, shall be under no liability for the application or proper administration of any assets or properties that is the subject of the said third party's acts.

B) This limitation of liability is specifically intended to give protection to any third party who acts, performs or renders any services pursuant to any Notice, Instrument or Document reasonably believed and represented to be genuine, and to have been signed and presented by the proper party (parties).

C) It is further the express intent of this Trust that the non-liability of all Third Parties as herein above stipulated, be given broad and prospective application. In particular, financial, credit, or banking institutions or brokerage houses, or transfer agents, medical personnel or any other person or entity acting in a fiduciary capacity with regards to any assets or property comprising the Trust Property, shall suffer no liability, nor incur any express or implied obligations when reasonably acting in the capacity of a Transferror or other such capacity, upon proper request, of any assets or property sought to be or comprising the Trust Property.

17. EXTENSION OF TRUST POWERS

This Declaration of Trust shall extend to and be binding upon the Heirs, Executors, Administrators and assigns of the undersigned Trustor(s) and upon the Successor(s) to the Trustee(s).

18. BENEFICIARY PROPORTIONATE LIABILITY FOR ESTATE TAXES

Each beneficiary under this Trust shall be liable for his (her) proportionate share of state or federal estate or inheritance taxes that may be levied, if any, upon the total taxable value of the Trust Property distributed to the said beneficiaries upon the death of either the donor or the surviving donor.

19. INTERPRETATION/DETERMINATION OF TRUST PROVISIONS

If any provision of this instrument shall be unclear or the subject of dispute among the parties to the trust, the Trustee (or the Successor Trustee, if the latter shall then be actively serving) is hereby fully authorized to interpret and determine such provision, and any such determination made by the Trustee shall be final and binding upon all such parties.

20. REVOCATION/AMENDMENT OF TRUST

This trust may be amended or revoked at any time during the lifetime of the Settlor(s) by written notice duly notarized from the Settlor(s) to the Trustee, without prior notice to or consent of any beneficiary or the Trustee(s) or Successor Trustee(s), including the right to appoint substitutes or otherwise change the person(s) designated as Trustee(s) or Successor Trustee(s). The Trustee may resign at any time during the lifetime of the Settlor(s) by written notice to the Settlor(s). The Trustee may resign after the death of the Settlor(s) upon written notice to the designated Successor Trustee and upon proper delivery of the assets of the trust to such Successor Trustee.

21. SUCCESSOR TRUSTEE(S)

In the event of the Trustee's physical or mental incapacity, death, resignation, or removal for cause, the Settlor(s) hereby appoints _____ [8] _____ as Successor Trustee. If the said first Successor Trustee, Mr/Mrs

_____ ⑧ _____, shall be unwilling or unable to carry out such duties, the Settlor(s) hereby appoints

Mr/Mrs _____ ⑨ _____ as Successor Trustee hereunder.

22. PRIVACY/CONFIDENTIALITY OF TRUST

The Trustee and any Successor Trustee are specifically instructed by the Settlor(s) to maintain the privacy and confidentiality of this instrument and the trust created hereunder, and are in no circumstances to divulge its terms to any probate or other court or other public agency with the exception of a tax authority.

23. TRUSTEE BOND, COMPENSATION & ACCOUNTING REQUIREMENTS

A) No bond or order of approval from a court shall be required of any Trustee, Co-Trustee or Successor Trustee named, appointed or serving under this instrument.

B) The Trustee shall serve without compensation. _[OR, ALTERNATIVELY, IF PREFERRED: 'The Trustee [and/or Successor Trustee] may receive reasonable compensation for his or her services on behalf of the Trust']_

C) No accounting shall be required of the Trustee.

24. CHILDREN'S SUBTRUST*

A) The Applicable Beneficiaries

If any of the following minors or young adult persons who are named as beneficiaries in paragraphs 5(B)(7) above, namely, _____ shall be under the age of _____ ⑪ _____ at the time he or she becomes entitled to the distribution under this Declaration, then all trust property given to such beneficiaries under this Declaration shall not be paid, but shall be deferred and be retained in common trust for all such beneficiaries in a separate subtrust of this "_____ ③ _____ Trust," until each child or beneficiary attains the age of _____ ⑪ _____ at which point the said subtrust shall end with respect to that particular beneficiary, and any principal or income then remaining in the subtrust for the particular beneficiary, if any, shall promptly be distributed to the said child or beneficiary by the subtrust trustee, subject to the provisions of paragraph 24C below with reference to particular beneficiaries, if applicable.

B) Name Of Subtrust

Each and every separate subtrust herein shall be identified and referred to by adding the name of the subtrust's beneficiary to the name of this trust, and inserting it just before the name of this trust in this manner: "The

_____ ③ _____ For _____ ⑬ _____, Minor."

C) Duration Of The Subtrust

With respect to these child(ren) or beneficiaries named below, however, namely _____ if any is named herein, upon the attainment of the age of _____ ⑭ _____ years by each, the subtrust Trustee shall not make outright distribution of any balance of their inheritance remaining in the subtrust as stipulated in paragraph 24A above, but such balance, if any, shall be distributed to them as follows: one-third ($1/3$) promptly upon attainment of the said age; then another one-third ($1/3$) three years thereafter, and the final distribution of one-third ($1/3$) two years thereafter. And, thereupon, the children's subtrust shall forthwith terminate with respect to such beneficiaries.

D) If any beneficiary survives the (grantor(s)) but dies before attaining the age of _____ ⑭ _____ years, at the death of such beneficiary the Trustee shall pass the beneficiary's entitlement under the subtrust to his/her heirs absolutely, per stirpes.

---

*__NOTE:__ Note that under the law, if you leave inheritance for your minor children under the children's subtrust in the Living Trust, you may not also use the Uniform Transfer to Minors Act to leave property for the same child or children. You may only use ONE or the other, __not__ both. See pp. 33-4 of the manual for more on this.

E) Powers Of Subtrust Trustee

i) In the meantime, until each child's term in the subtrust ends, the Trustee may distribute to or for the benefit of each designated beneficiary, as much of the net income or principal of the child(ren') share of the subtrust as the Trustee in his/her discretion, deems necessary for the beneficiary's health, support, maintenance or education, only using his/her fiduciary discretion and best judgment and sense of fairplay and necessity, to provide for each beneficiary's individual needs as they may arise or be necessary. Education includes, but is not limited to, college, graduate, postgraduate and vocational studies, and reasonably related living expenses;

ii) In deciding how and in what manners and when to make a distribution to a beneficiary, the Trustee may take into account each beneficiary's other income, resources, and sources of support, his/her circumstances and real needs, character and demonstrated sense of responsibility.

iii) No intervention of any guardian or application to any court shall be necessary or permissible in the good faith exercise of these duties by the Trustee (or Successor Trustee).

iv) The Trustee may invest the subtrust assets in such income-yielding ventures as the Trustee may deem proper and prudent, and the income as well as such amounts of the principal as are necessary, even to the extent of all, shall be applied to the support, general welfare and benefits of the beneficiaries, as directed in this Declaration.

F) No Assignment Of Interest Of Beneficiary

No interest of any beneficiary under this children's subtrust created under this Declaration of Trust shall be entitled to reasonable compensation out of the subtrust assets, for his or her services on behalf of the Trust. *[Alternatively, if preferred: 'Any Trustee of the children's subtrust shall serve without compensation.']*

G) Trustee's Rights of Compensation

Any Trustee of the children's subtrust created under this Declaration of Trust shall be entitled to reasonable compensation out of the subtrust assets, for his or her services on behalf of the Trust. *[Alternatively, if preferred: 'Any Trustee of the children's subtrust shall serve without compensation.']*

22. CUSTODIANSHIPS UNDER THE UNIFORM TRANSFERS TO MINORS ACT*

All trust property given to any of the minor or young adult beneficiaries listed below, shall be given to each such beneficiary under the provisions of the *(name of your state)* Uniform Transfers To Minors Act.

1. All Property to which _____ 15 _____ , hereinafter called a "Minor Beneficiary" under this Declaration, shall become entitled to receive, shall be given to _____ 16 _____ as custodian for the said Minor Beneficiary under the Uniform Transfers To Minors Act, until the said Minor Beneficiary attains the age of _____ 17 _____ , or if no age is specified herein, until he/she attains the age provided under the Uniform Transfers to Minors Act at which the beneficiary becomes entitled to receive the property outright from the custodian.

2. All property to which _____ hereinafter called a "Minor Beneficiary" under this Declaration, shall become entitled to receive, shall be given to _____ as custodian for the said Minor Beneficiary under the Uniform Transfers to Minors Act, until the said Minor Beneficiary attains the age of _____ , or

if no age is specified herein, until he/she attains the age provided by the Uniform Transfers to Minors Act at which the beneficiary becomes entitled to receive the property outright from the custodian.

3. All property to which _____, hereinafter called a "Minor Beneficiary" under this Declaration, shall become entitled to receive, shall be given to _____ as custodian for the said Minor Beneficiary under the Uniform Transfers to Minors Act, until the said Minor Beneficiary attains the age of _____, or if no age is specified herein, until he/she attains the age provided by the Uniform Transfers to Minors Act at which the beneficiary becomes entitled to receive the property outright from the custodian.

CERTIFICATION BY TRUST GRANTOR(S)

I (WE) CERTIFY that I (We) have read this *Declaration of Trust* and that it correctly states the terms, conditions, covenants and agreements under which the trust estate is to be held, managed and administered and disposed of by the trustee (or the successor thereof), and I (we) therefore approve the Declaration of Trust.

IN WITNESS WHEREOF, I (We) have signed these presents this _____ day of _____ 19 ___.

SIGNED: **X** _____
[15]   Trustor (Grantor)

SIGNED: **X** _____
[15]   Co-Trustor (Co-Grantor)

Acknowledgment

STATE OF _____)
)ss.
COUNTY OF _____)

On this _____ day of _____ 19 ___, before me, the undersigned Notary Public duly authorized to administer oaths in and by the above captioned jurisdiction, personally appeared Mr/Mrs/Ms _____ [1] _____ to me known or made known to me to be the individual(s) described in and who executed the foregoing Declaration Of Trust; thereupon the said person(s) acknowledged that he (she) (they) executed the same as his (her) (their) free act and deed.

My Commission expires _____

_____
(Notary Public)

Spouse's Disclaimer Of Trust Asset Or Interest*

I, the undersigned legal spouse of the above-named Grantor, hereby waive all community property, dower or curtesy rights and interest which I may have in the property described in the foregoing Trust and give my assent to the provisions of the trust and to the inclusion of the said property in the said Trust.

_____ **X**
(Spouse to sign here, when applicable)

SWORN TO BEFORE
ME, THIS _____ 19 ___.

_____
(Notary Public)

---

*NOTE: The signing of this clause is not applicable or necessary when the spouses have BOTH signed the Declaration of Trust. If married and you and your spouse have not jointly signed the Declaration of Trust, then you must have your spouse, as well sign and notarize the statement in this box, if: (a) you've included in the Trust any property held only in one spouse's name and; (b) if your spouse is not the person that is designated in the trust as the primary beneficiary of the trust property.

Form LT-2

Notice of Living Trust
(Inter Vivos)

TO: _____

_____
Name of Court

_____
Address

_____
City/State/Zip Code

PLEASE TAKE NOTICE:

That pursuant to the applicable provisions of the The Uniform Probate Code, notice is hereby given that a Living Trust (an Inter Vivos Trust) was established in the jurisdiction of this court, this _____ day of _____ 19 _____, by the creator(s), as named below, upon the following facts:

Name of the Trust:
CREATOR(S):

(1) _____ (2) _____
(Name) *(Name)*

_____ _____
(Address) *(Address)*

_____ _____
(City/State/Zip Code) *(City/State/Zip Code)*

TRUSTEES:

(1) _____ (2) _____
(Name) *(Name)*

_____ _____
(Address) *(Address)*

_____ _____
(City/State/Zip Code) *(City/State/Zip Code)*

Hereby dated this _____ day of _____ 19 _____

Signed: _____ ✗
Trust Creator

_____ ✗
Co-Creator

Acknowledgment

STATE OF _____)
) ss.
COUNTY OF _____)

On this _____ day of _____, 19 _____ before me, the undersigned Notary Public duly authorized to administer oaths in and for the above-captioned jurisdiction, personally appeared _____ to me known or made known to me to be the individual(s) described in and who executed the foregoing instrument; whereupon the said person(s) acknwoeldaged that (he) (she) (they) executed the same as his (her) (their) free act and deed.

My Commission expires: _____

_____
Notary Public

NOTE: This NOTICE is only required if the State where you plan to establish the Living Trust requires the filing of a Notice with a Court of Jurisdiction, mostly in those states which have adopted the Uniform Probate Code (Alabama, Arizona, Colorado, Florida, Hawaii, Idaho, Minnesota, Montana, Nebraska, New Mexico, North Dakota, and Utah.) Even in those states, however, not all of them require it. Therefore do this: simply inquire with your local probate court clerk.

Form LT-3

Grantors' Affidavit Of Transfer Of Chattel & Personal Property To Trust

(Moveable Property, e.g., Motor Vehicles, trailer, boat, equipment, goods, household property, etc.)

KNOWN ALL MEN BY THESE PRESENTS:

That I (We) _[Enter name/names of the grantor(s)]_ _____ of this address: _____ County of _____ State of _____ the undersigned Transferor(s), who is (are) the Grantor(s) under a certain *Declaration Of Trust* named for the use and benefit of _____, and dated _____ 19 ____ a true copy of which is attached hereto and/or made a part hereof by this reference, do by these presents, hereby assign, transfer and deliver IN TRUST unto myself (ourselves) as Trustee(s) under the said Trust, all of my (our) rights, title and interest in the following Chattel and Personal Property, described as follows:

List the major items here

That the said Trustee(s) under the said Trust is/are TO HAVE AND TO HOLD all of the said Chattel and Personal Property unto and to the use of the said Trustee(s) and their successors in interest forever; and I (We) do hereby warrant and covenant to and with the said Trustees(s) and his/her successor(s) in interest, that I (We) am/are the legal owners of the said contents and have the absolute right to make this transfer and assignment without the consent of any third party, and will forever defend them against the lawful claims and demands of all persons whomsoever; and that neither I (We) for my (our) heirs or assigns shall have or make any claims or demands upon the said property.

IN WITNESS WHEREOF, I (We) have signed these presents this _____ day of _____ 19 ____ .

SIGNED **X** _____
(*Transferror-Grantor*)

X _____
(*Co-Transferror-Co-Grantor*)

Acknowledgment

STATE OF _____)
) ss.:
COUNTY OF _____)

On this _____ day of _____ 19 ____ before me, the undersigned Notary Public duly authorized to administer oaths in the above-captioned jurisdiction, personally appeared Mr/Mrs _____ to me known or made known to me to be the individual(s) described in and who executed the foregoing instrument; thereupon the said person(s) acknowledged that he (she) (they) executed the same as his (her) (their) free act and deed.

_____
Notary Public

My Commission Expires _____

Form LT-4

Copyright © 1994, Do-It-Yourself Legal Publishers Newark, NJ 07102

Grantor's Affidavit Of Transfer Of The Contents Of A Rented House Or Apartment

KNOW ALL MEN BY THESE PRESENTS:

That I (We) _____ _____ , of this address _____ , county
(Enter name/names of the grantor(s))

of _____ , state of _____ the undersigned Transferror(s) who is (are) the Grantors under the

DECLARATION OF TRUST named for the use and benefit of _____ and

dated _____ 19 _____ , a true copy of which is attached hereto and/or made a part hereof by this

reference, do by these presents, hereby assign, transfer and deliver IN TRUST unto myself (ourselves) as

Trustee(s) under the said TRUST, all of my (our) rights, title and interest in the contents of a rented house or

apartment located at _____ in the City/town of _____

State of _____ which shall include any and all items and property contained or possessed therein of

whatever nature or description, EXCEPT the following:

(List any exempt items, if any, otherwise, enter NONE and run two lines across the whole length of space)

That the said Trustee(s) under the said Trust is/are TO HAVE AND TO HOLD all of the said contents unto
and to the use of the said Trustee(s) and their successors in interest forever, and I (we) do hereby warrant and
covenant to and with the said Trustees(s) and his/her successor(s) in interest, that I (We) am/are the legal
owner(s) of the said contents and have the absolute right to make this transfer and assignment herein without
the consent of any third party, and will forever defend them against the lawful claims and demands of all
persons whomsoever; and that neither I (We) for my (our) heirs or assigns shall have or make any claims or
demands upon the said property.

IN WITNESS WHEREOF, I (We) have signed these presents this _____ day of _____ 19 _____ .

SIGNED X_____
(Transferror-Grantor)

X_____
(Co-Transferror-Co-Grantor)

Acknowledgment

STATE OF _____
COUNTY OF _____ }ss.:

On this _____ day of _____ 19 _____ before me, the undersigned Notary Public duly authorized to
administer oaths in the above-captioned jurisdiction, personally appeared Mr/Mrs _____
to me known or made known to me to be the individual(s) described in and who executed the foregoing
instrument; thereupon the said person(s) acknowledged that he (she) (they) executed the same as his (her)
(their) free act and deed.

My Commission Expires _____

_____
Notary Public

Form LT-5

Grantor's Affidavit Of Transfer Of Business Interest To The Trust

(Check which: ☐ Sole proprietorship ☐ Partnership)

KNOW ALL MEN BY THESE PRESENTS:

That I (We) ___ *[Enter name/names of the grantor(s)]* ___ of this address

County of ___, State of ___, the undersigned Transferror(s) who is (are) the Grantors under the

Declaration of Trust, named for the use and benefit of ___ and dated

___ 19 ___, a true copy of which is attached hereto and/or made a part hereof by this reference, do

by these presents, hereby assign, transfer and deliver IN TRUST unto myself (ourselves) as Trustee(s) under

the said TRUST, all of my (our) rights, title and interest in that certain Business organization, described as follows:

Name of business organization ___

Located at *(full address)* ___

which is a *(check one)* ☐ Sole Proprietorship ☐ Partnership, of which my (our interest) in said business entity

is ___ percent.

That the said Trustee(s) under the said Trust is/are TO HAVE AND TO HOLD all of the said Business

interest for the use of the said Trustee(s) and their successors in interest forever; and that neither I (We) or my

(our) heirs or assigns shall have or make any claims or demands upon the said Business Interest.

IN WITNESS WHEREOF, I (We) have signed these presents this ___ day of ___ 19 ___.

SIGNED ✗ ___

(Transferror-Grantor)

✗ ___

(Co-Transferror-Co-Grantor)

Acknowledgment

STATE OF ___

COUNTY OF ___ } ss.:

On this ___ day of ___ 19 ___, before me, the undersigned Notary Public duly authorized to

administer oaths in the above captioned jurisdiction, personally appeared Mr/Mrs ___

to me known or made known to me to be the individual(s) described in and who executed the foregoing

instrument; thereupon the said person(s) acknowledged that he (she) (they) executed the same as his (her)

(their) free act and deed.

___ Notary Public

My Commission Expires ___

Form LT-6

Grantor's Affidavit Of Transfer Of Real Property Deed To The Trust

114

KNOW ALL MEN BY THESE PRESENTS:

That I (We) _____ *(Enter name/names of the grantor(s))* of this address _____

county of _____, state of _____ the undersigned Transferror(s), who is (are) the Grantors under the

DECLARATION OF TRUST named for the use and benefit of _____ and

dated _____ 19 ___, a true copy of which is attached hereto and/or made a part hereof by this refer-

ence, do by these presents, hereby assign, transfer, convey and deliver IN TRUST, unto myself (ourselves) as

Trustee(s) under said TRUST, all of my (our) rights, title and interest in the Real Property situated in the city /

town of _____, county of _____, State of _____ and described as follows:

(Enter this street address, as well as the property description as contained in the deed)

The said Grantor(s) herewith warrant and covenant legal ownership of the said real property, and assert title
to the property pursuant to a Deed or other Instrument of Conveyance dated _____ 19 ___ and recorded
in the Official Land Records of _____ County, State of _____ in Book (Docket) (Volume) _____ at pages _____ thereof.

That the said Trustee(s) under the said Trust is/are TO HAVE AND TO HOLD all of the said real property
unto and to the use of the said Trustee(s) and his (her) (their) successors in interest forever; and that neither I
(We) for my (our) heirs or assigns shall have or make any claims or demands upon the said property.

IN WITNESS WHEREOF, I (We) have signed these presents this _____ day of _____, 19 ___.

SIGNED

X _____
(Transferror-Grantor)

X _____
(Co-Transferror-Co-Grantor)

Acknowledgment

STATE OF _____
COUNTY OF _____ ss.:

On this _____ day of _____, 19 ___, before me, the undersigned Notary Public duly authorized to
administer oaths in the above-captioned jurisdiction, personally appeared Mr/Mr/Ms
_____ to me known or made known to me to be the individual(s) described in
and who executed the foregoing instrument; thereupon the said person(s) acknowledged that he (she) (they)
executed the same as his (her) (their) free act and deed.

My Commission Expires _____

_____
Notary Public

Form LT-7 Copyright © 1994, Do-It-Yourself Legal Publishers Newark, NJ 07102

Grantor's Affidavit Of Assignment Of Secured Realty Interest To The Trust

(Check one) ☐ Deed of Trust   ☐ Real Estate Mortgage
              ☐ Realty Agreement   ☐ Realty Sales Contract

KNOW ALL MEN BY THESE PRESENTS:

That I (We) _____ *(Enter name/names of the grantor(s))* _____ of this address

_____ County of _____, State of _____ the undersigned Assignor(s), who is/are

also Grantor(s) under that certain DECLARATION OF TRUST named for the use and benefit of

_____ and dated _____ 19____, a true copy of which is attached hereto and/or made a part hereof

by this reference, do by these presents hereby assign, transfer and convey IN TRUST, unto myself (ourselves)

as Trustee(s) under the said TRUST, all of my (our) rights, title and interest in that certain secured realty

interest described as follows:

Check one:
☐ Agreement for sale of Real Estate   ☐ Real Estate Mortgage
☐ Beneficial Interest in Deed of Trust   ☐ Real Estate Sales Contract

and to the Note or other evidence of indebtedness secured by the said realty interest, dated _____ 19____ and

recorded in the Official Land Records of _____ County, State of _____, Book (Docket) (Vol-

ume) _____, at pages _____ thereof.

That the said Trustee(s) under the said Trust is/are TO HAVE AND TO HOLD all of the said Secured Realty

Interest, including all benefits payable thereunder, for the use of the said Trustee(s) and his (her) (their) succes-

sors in interest forever; and that neither I (We) for my (our) heirs or assigns shall have or make any claims or

demands upon the said Secured Realty Interest.

IN WITNESS WHEREOF, I (We) have signed these presents this _____ day of _____ 19____ .

SIGNED ✗ _____
                              (Assignor-Grantor)

✗ _____
                              (Co-Assignor-Co-Grantor)

I, the undersigned legal spouse of the above ASSIGNOR/GRANTOR, hereby waive all community property
rights which I may have in the hereinabove-described property and give my assent to the provisions of the trust
and to the inclusion in it of the said property interest.

Spouse sign here if applicable* ✗ _____

Acknowledgment

STATE OF _____
COUNTY OF _____ } ss.:

On this _____ day of _____, 19____, before me, the undersigned Notary Public duly authorized to administer oaths in the

above-captioned jurisdiction, personally appeared Mr/Mrs/Ms. _____ to me known or made known to

me to be the individual(s) described in and who executed the foregoing instrument; thereupon the said person(s) acknowledged that he

(she) (they) executed the same as his (her) (their) free act and deed.

_____
Notary Public

My Commission Expires _____

*NOTE: This (item enclosed in the box) is applicable only if and when you are married and the primary beneficiary named for the property is someone other than your
spouse. (For all real estate trust property matters, your spouse must also sign the quitclaim).

Form LT-8

Copyright © 1994, Do-It-Yourself Legal Publishers Newark, NJ 07102

Spouse's Disclaimer Of Trust Asset Or Interest

STATE OF _____
COUNTY OF _____

I, _____ *[full name of the spouse involved]* _____ the undersigned person hereinafter called the DEPONENT, first being duly sworn under oath, depose and say:

1. I am resident at this address _____ in the County of _____, State of _____, and I am the spouse, namely the *(Wife)(Husband)* of Mr/Mrs _____, the parties having been lawfully married on or about _____, 19___, in the City and State of _____, and the marriage has never been legally dissolved.

2. My said spouse is the maker of a certain DECLARATION OF TRUST, creating a Living Trust named _____ and dated _____, 19___.

3. My said spouse has previously acquired certain property with his/her own separate funds, which property is/are situated in the city/town of _____, County of _____, State of _____, and is/are described as follows:

_____
_____
_____

4. I have withdrawn all assets which I placed, or was placed in my name, in the trust, as Grantor or otherwise, and I herewith relinquish all my rights to the remaining Grantor, and assert no claims, interest, rights or title of any kind or description in and to the within designated property or trust, past, present or future.

5. I herewith waive all community property, dower or curtesy rights which I may have in the above-described property under any state laws, and give my assent to the provisions of the said Trust and to the inclusion of the said property in the said Trust.

NOW THEREFORE, in consideration of the foregoing, I, the undersigned Deponent, do hereby disclaim, release and quitclaim to the said spouse, his (her) heirs and assigns forever, all rights, title, interest, demand or claim, which I may in any way have in the aforesaid property.

IN WITNESS WHEREOF, I have signed this DISCLAIMER BY SPOUSE OF TRUST ASSET, this ___ day of ___ 19___.

SIGNED: ✗ _____

_____
(Deponent-Spouse)

Acknowledgment

STATE OF _____
COUNTY OF _____) ss.:

On this ___ day of _____, 19___, before me, the undersigned Notary Public duly authorized to administer oaths in the above-captioned jurisdiction, personally appeared Mr/Mrs _____ to me known or made known to me to be the individual(s) described in and who executed the foregoing instrument; thereupon the said person(s) acknowledged that he (she) (they) executed the same as his (her) (their) free act and deed.

_____
Notary Public

My Commission Expires _____

Grantor's Affidavit Of Transfer Of Financial Account To The Trust

KNOW ALL MEN BY THESE PRESENTS:

That I (We) _____ [Enter name/names of the grantor(s)] _____ of this address _____ State of _____, who is (are) the Grantors under the County of _____ State of _____, who is (are) the Grantors under the DECLARATION OF TRUST named for the use and benefit of _____ and dated _____ 19 ___, a true copy of which is attached hereto and/or made a part hereof by this reference, do by these presents hereby assign, transfer and convey IN TRUST, unto myself (ourselves) as Trustee(s) under the said TRUST, all of my (our) rights, title and interest in and to *(check which)*

☐ Bank/Financial Account No. _____
☐ Brokerage Account No. _____

kept or held in the Financial Institution or Brokerage Firm known as: _____ located at _____ in the city/town of _____ state of _____, including any and all cash and/or securities held in the said Account.

That the said Trustee(s) under the said Trust is/are TO HAVE AND TO HOLD all of the said Account, including any and all cash and/or Securities held therein, for the use of the said Trustee(s) and his (her) (their) successors in interest forever; and that neither I (We) nor my (our) heirs or assigns shall have or make any claims or demands upon said Financial Account.

IN WITNESS WHEREOF, I (We) have signed these presents this _____ day of _____ 19 ___.

SIGNED ✗ _____
(Transferror-Grantor)

✗ _____
(Co-Transferror-Co-Grantor)

Acknowledgment

STATE OF _____) ss.:
COUNTY OF _____)

On this _____ day of _____ 19 ___ before me, the undersigned Notary Public duly authorized to administer oaths in the above captioned jurisdiction, personally appeared Mr/Mrs _____ to me known or made known to me to be the individual(s) described in and who executed the foregoing instrument; thereupon the said person(s) acknowledged that he (she) (they) executed the same as his (her) (their) free act and deed.

_____ Notary Public

My Commission Expires _____

Sample Letter To An Institution Or Agency To Change Trust's Name & Designate The Trust As The Owner Of A Trust Property Or Asset

From: John & Mary Doe
24 Any Street
Anytown, NY 10003
Date: _____

RE: Change of ownership of below-designated asset/property from the undersigned Grantor(s), (John and Mary Doe), to John and Mary Doe Living Trust

ASSET/PROPERTY INVOLVED: _____

_____

Dear Sir/Madam:

Enclosed is an original of our (my) Affidavit of Transfer of the above-designated asset or property, formerly owned and in the name(s) of the undersigned, to authorize the change of name of the ownership. Enclosed also are the following other documents: _____.

Please change the name of the owner of the property (or asset) on the appropriate title documents to: "JOHN and MARY DOE LIVING TRUST" of _____, 19___.

Please record the change and send me an acknowledgment of the change, and a certified copy of the new instrument, if applicable. If you have any questions, please contact me.

Sincerely yours,

John Doe

John Doe

Form LT-11

Grantor's Affidavit Of Transfer Of Securities To The Trust

KNOW ALL MEN BY THESE PRESENTS:

That I (We) _____ *[Enter name/names of the grantor(s)]* _____ of this address _____ county of _____, state of _____, the undersigned Transferror(s), who is (are) the Grantors under the DECLARATION OF TRUST named for the use and benefit of _____ and dated _____ 19 ____, a true copy of which is attached hereto and/or made a part hereof by this reference, do by these presents hereby assign, transfer and convey, IN TRUST, unto myself (ourselves) as Trustee(s) under the said TRUST, all of my (our) rights, title and interest in and to the Securities, including common and preferred stocks, bonds, debentures, treasury bills, and mutual fund shares, etc., described as follows: *[e.g., 200 shares of IBM common stock; 100 shares of 6% New York Municipal Bonds; 100 shares of 7% 2nd preferred stock of AT&T]*

_____

_____

That the said Trustee(s) under the said Trust is/are TO HAVE AND TO HOLD the said securities for the use of the said Trustee(s) and his (her) (their) successors in interest forever; and that neither I (We) nor my (our) heirs or assigns shall have or make any claims or demands upon the said securities.

IN WITNESS WHEREOF, I (We) have signed these presents this _____ day of _____ 19 ____.

SIGNED **X** _____
(Transferror–Grantor)

X _____
(Co-Transferror–Co-Grantor)

Acknowledgment

STATE OF _____
COUNTY OF _____

On this _____ day of _____, 19 ____, before me, the undersigned Notary Public duly authorized to administer oaths in the above-captioned jurisdiction, personally appeared Mr/Mrs/Ms. _____ to me known or made known to me to be the individual(s) described in and who executed the foregoing instrument; thereupon the said person(s) acknowledged that he (she) (they) executed the same as his (her) (their) free act and deed.

My Commission Expires _____   _____ Notary Public

Form LT-12

Grantor's Assignment Of Contract For Literary Work Or Musical Composition To The Trust

KNOW ALL MEN BY THESE PRESENTS:

That I (We) _____ of this address _____
(Enter name/names of the grantor(s))

county of _____, state of _____, the undersigned Transferror(s) and Assignor(s), who is (are) the Grant-ors under the DECLARATION OF TRUST named for the use and benefit of _____

and dated _____ 19 ____, a true copy of which is attached hereto and/or made a part hereof by this reference, do by these presents hereby assign, transfer and convey IN TRUST, unto myself (ourselves) as Trustee(s) under the said TRUST, all of my (our) rights, title and interest in and to the certain contract (hereinafter called "the contract") dated _____ 19 ____ and signed by _____ on behalf of _____ in favor of _____ under the terms of which cetain royalties and/or other payments accrue to me (us) from the publication, distribution and/or performance of such woks by virtue of my work/services as *(check which)*;

☐ the author of literary works which was published, as more fully described below
☐ the composer of musical composition which was published, as more fully described below
☐ the registrant under design and/or utility patents numbered, as more fully described below
☐ others

Example of further description: "Design Patent No. 194405, pursuant to patent royalty contract signed by Alfa Industries Ltd in favor of John Doe., the grantor herein, dated ____ 19 ___."

That the said Trustee(s) under the said Trust is/are TO HAVE AND TO HOLD the said contract interest unto and for the use of the said Trustee(s) and his (her) (their) Successors in interest forever; and that neither I (We) nor my (our) heirs or assigns shall have or make any claims or demands upon the said contract interest.

IN WITNESS WHEREOF, I (We) have signed these presents this _____ day of _____ 19 ____.

SIGNED ✗ _____
(Transferror-Grantor)

✗ _____
(Co-Transferror-Co-Grantor)

Acknowledgment

STATE OF _____)
) ss.:
COUNTY OF _____)

On this _____ day of _____ 19 ____, before me, the undersigned Notary Public duly authorized to administer oaths in the above-captioned jurisdiction, personally appeared Mr/Mrs/Ms. _____ to me known or made known to me to be the individual(s) described in and who executed the foregoing instrument; thereupon the said person(s) acknowledged that he (she) (they) executed the same as his (her) (their) free act and deed.

_____
Notary Public

My Commission Expires _____

Chapter 8

THE OPERATION OF THE TRUST, REVOCATION OF THE TRUST, & SETTLING OF THE ESTATE

Alright. So, you have now established your Living Trust, and have had all trust property properly transferred into the trust (the subject matter of the preceding Chapter 7)? The next order of business, then, will be to manage and administer the trust—THE OPERATION OF THE TRUST. *In this chapter, we shall focus on the operation of the trust and the major practical issues which often arise in the operation of the trust, and the operational duties and functions the trustee may be called upon during his or her term of office to perform (or the successor trustee, upon the death of the trust-creator), in accordance with the intent, purposes and provisions of the Declaration of Trust.* Primarily, we shall do this by designating the forms which the grantor and/or the trustee could employ to perform different duties under various circumstances and situations.

A. To Change The Trust Property Or Beneficiaries

To add new property or more property to your trust, it is not necessary for you to formally amend of rewrite your trust document (the Declaration of Trust). All you do is simply list the additional trust property in question in the trust Schedule (See Appendix B) and be sure to formally transfer the title of the newly added property to the trust's name, if applicable. However, you must closely examine your Declaration of Trust to make sure that a beneficiary has been named for the newly added property, or that other proper disposition has been made of it, and if you determine that such provision has not been made, only then will it be necessary that you actually amend the trust to provide for that. Note that it is not required that notice of this change be served on the affected (or new) beneficiaries since it is a generally accepted principle of estate law that the heirs under a Living Trust or a Will instrument need not necessarily know that they are heirs until the document is read, that is, upon the death of the trust or will-maker.

Applicable forms: Form LT-13, *Amendment to Living Trust As to Trust Property or Beneficiaries.* (Form is to be signed and notarized by the grantor or grantors.)

To change a beneficiary (by deleting an existing one or adding a new one), or to delete property from the trust, simply use Form LT-13 and make the appropriate entries and modifications accordingly.

B. Substitution Of A Trustee Or Successor Trustee

To change a Trustee or Successor Trustee, simply use this form as necessary: Form LT-14, *"Amendment To The Trust To Substitute A Trustee Or Successor Trustee,"* (sample on p. 127). The grantor or grantors are to sign and notarize this.

C. Assumption Of Authority By Successor Trustee

When a person is duly appointed as the Successor Trustee of a trust, the person so appointed will have the opportunity to actually assume the duties under one of three basic circumstances: in the event that the grantor (or grantors) die; or in the event that the grantor(s) become incapacitated; or if the grantors were to voluntarily relinquish authority to the successor trustee to act as the trustee. The person assuming the successor trustee's position would need to have some documentary evidence he can show the appropriate persons or agencies he has to deal with in proof of his authority to act as successor trustee.

APPLICABLE FORMS:

i) Form LT-15, "*Affidavit Of Grantors Relinquishing Authority To Successor Trustee*" (sample on p. 128), usable when relinquishment of authority by the grantor applies. Form is to be signed and notarized by the grantor or grantors, as applicable.

ii) Form LT-16, "*Notice By Successor Trustee Of Authority To Administer Trust*" (sample on p. 129), to be signed and notarized by the party assuming the position of the successor trustee. And, of course, in the case of the grantor's incapacitation or death, a doctor's certification of incapacitation or a certified copy of the death certificate, respectively, will be necessary.

D. Revocation Of The Living Trust By The Grantor

There are essentially three broad circumstances under which the trust can be terminated: **1)** an accidental or inadvertent termination (e.g., termination necessitated by misplacement or theft of the trust property or by the mistaken sale of the trust assets); **2)** voluntary termination (e.g., termination necessitated by intentionally revoking the trust or otherwise disposing of the trust property); and **3)** an involuntary termination—termination, essentially, by the death of the trust creator(s).

Here in this section, we shall only treat the first and second forms of revocation of trust—basically revocation of the trust because you wish or prefer to pass your property, upon death, through other methods, such as a will, joint tenancy or the like, or because you wish to terminate the trust entirely (a rarely employed basis), or simply because the changes you wish to make in the present trust are so many and so extensive that it is less of a problem and more straightforward to simply make a new trust altogether.

(The third form of revocation, having to do with revocation compelled by the death of the trust maker, which will necessitate distribution of the estate, is addressed in Section E below.)

1. Revocation Of The Trust Simply To End It

Suppose the grantor (or grantors, as the case may be), is compelled by circumstances, or wishes to revoke the trust for good. To revoke the trust under that circumstance, simply use Form LT-17, "*Revocation Of Trust*" (sample on p. 130). Ideally, assuming that the trust is a family trust type jointly made and signed by both spouses, in using this form to revoke the trust, it should also be signed and notarized by BOTH spouses. You should note, however, that while it takes BOTH spouses to amend a trust, EITHER spouse (just one of them), on the other hand, can sign and legally revoke a jointly made trust. When this happens—i.e., when only one spouse revokes a joint trust—in such a situation it simply returns both spouses to the status quo, that is, to the status they were before they made the trust, back to each owning his or her separate property, or co-owning property under joint tenancy, community property, and so on, as the case may be.

Upon the actual revocation of a trust, the trust terminates and legally ceases to be, meaning that, as could be seen from the provision in Form LT-17, any property intended to have been transferred by the trust cannot now be so transferred and automatically goes back to the original owners as their personal property. And the implication? That you must then make sure that you provide another avenue from the standpoint of estate planning, by which to dispose of that property at death—whether it is be creating another trust, or drafting a will, a joint tenancy arrangement, or what have you.

If you must revoke an existing trust and create a new one, remember this one cardinal point: in creating the new trust, you must follow exactly the same formalities and procedures as are outlined in Chapter 7 for establishing a trust. Also, you should track down all copies of the old, now revoked, trust and destroy them, to diminish the possibility of the old trust being misused at the hands of an unscrupulous heir or other persons. To differentiate between your old, revoked trust(s) and your current one, the normal practice is to give the new, current trust a different name from the revoked one. Simply, add a number and the date of the signing of the new trust to the trust's old name: For example, the old joint revoked trust, "John and Mary Doe Trust of _____ 19 __," now becomes the new, current trust, "John and Mary Trust No. 2 of _____ 19 __."

NOTE: To make extensive changes or wholesale revisions in an existing trust, you should always desist from doing so by mere amendments, anyway. Rather, in such instances, the most prudent procedure is to revoke the trust instrument form altogether and completely prepare a new trust instrument from the scratch—strictly following all of the same formalities outlined in the manual (Chapter 7) for establishing a trust, from beginning to end.

2. Voluntary Termination Or Revocation Of Trust And Transfer Of Trust Property Back To Oneself

Suppose that, for whatever the reason, the grantor desires to simply revoke the trust and transfer the trust property back to himself/herself (or themselves), or to a third party. Then, in such a situation what you do essentially is to revoke the existing trust, and then re-assign or re-transfer the trust property from the trust back to yourself or to the intended third party.

Basically, you employ the following forms, according to the type of property involved, and/or adapt the forms to suit your particular situation or the types of property involved:

APPLICABLE FORMS:

1. Form LT-17, Revocation Of Trust—applicable in all cases (sample on p. 130);
2. Form LT-18. Trustee's Or Successor Trustee's Affidavit Of Chattel & Personal Property Transfer (sample on p. 131);
3. Form LT-19, Trustee's Or Successor Trustee's Affidavit Of Transfer Of The Contents Of A Rented House Or Apartment (sample on p. 132);
4. Form LT-20, Trustee's Or Successor Trustee's Affidavit Of Transfer Of Business Interest (sample on p. 133);
5. Form LT-21, Trustee's Or Successor Trustee's Affidavit Of Transfer Of Real Property Deed (applies in a fee simple, wholly-owned ownership situation in real property) [see sample of form on p. 134];
6. Form LT-22, Trustee's Or Successor Trustee's Quit Claim Deed (applies in a fee simple, wholly-owned ownership situation in real property) (See sample of form on p. 135);
7. Form LT-23, Trustee's or Successor Trustee's Affidavit Of Assignment Of Secured Realty Interest (sample on p. 136);
8. Form LT-24, Trustee's Or Successor Trustee's Affidavit Of Transfer Of Financial Account (sample on p. 137);
9. Form LT-25, Trustee's or Successor Trustee's Affidavit Of Transfer Of Securities (sample on p. 138);
10. Form LT-26, Trustee's or Successor Trustee's Affidavit Of Assignment Of Contract That Accrues Certain Payments (sample on p. 139).

SIGN THE REVOCATION AND TRANSFER DOCUMENTS & RECORD THEM, IF APPLICABLE

Then, upon your (i.e., the Trustee's or Successor Trustee's) completion of the applicable forms, they are to be **_signed_** and **_notarized_** by the Trustee or the Successor Trustee, whichever is applicable. Next, you will have to determine if there is any requirement for giving a notice, and/or making a public records recording of the transfer of title with the appropriate state agency or county records office, according to the procedures of your jurisdiction.

CLUE: If the title documents for the old, now revoked, trust was originally recorded, or if the property involved is a real property, then you can reasonably assume that this new property transfer documents would probably have to be recorded as well. (When recording is applicable, the revocation of trust form should also be recorded as well).. If, however, the original title documents were not recorded, or if the property involved is a non-realty property, then it's probably sufficient to merely give or send the proper parties appropriate notice of the trust revocation and transfer of property (basically, by providing them with a copy of the successor trustee's Affidavit Of Transfer & the Revocation Of Trust). As previously explained, the beneficiaries to the trust need not be given any notice of the revocation of trust or transfer of property, except in notification of distribution of the estate asset.

E. Involuntary Termination Or Revocation Of Trust & Transfer Of Trust Property To Beneficiaries Upon Surviving Grantor's Death

In this section, we should treat the third and final form of termination or revocation of trust first outlined in Section D above—INVOLUNTARY TERMINATION, basically termination occasioned by the death(s) of the trust maker(s), and the subsequent distribution of the estate to designated beneficiaries. In this connection, suppose the surviving spouse or grantor of the trust (the trust maker) dies, and that, upon his or her death, there is, for the purpose of simplification, no beneficiary under the adult age and hence no need for continuation of the trust, by way of, say, a Children's Sub-trust. Now, what does the Successor Trustee do under the circumstances?

Essentially, the successor trustee will seek to distribute the trust estate in accordance with the provisions of the trust, following which the trust will be terminated; it will be one of the successor trustee's main duties to terminate the trust in this instance, and hence it will fall on him or her to prepare and sign all the necessary papers for that. To this end, the trustee will, in effect, re-assign and re-transfer the trust property from the trust to the designated trust beneficiaries. Basically, you employ the following forms, according to the type of property involved, and/or adapt the forms to suit your particular situation or the type of property involved:

APPLICABLE FORMS:

1. Form LT-16, Notice By Successor Trustee Of Authority To Administer Trust (sample of form is on p. 129);

2. The Death Certificate(s) of the last surviving grantor (obtain a certified copy and attach same);

3. Form LT-18, Trustee's Or Successor Trustee's Affidavit Of Chattel & Personal Property Transfer (sample on p. 131);

4. Form LT-19, Trustee's Or Successor Trustee's Affidavit Of Transfer Of The Contents Of A Rented House Or Apartment (sample on p. 132);

5. Form LT-20, Trustee's Or Successor Trustee's Affidavit Of Transfer Of Business Interest (sample on p. 133);

6. Form LT-21, Trustee's Or Successor Trustee's Affidavit Of Transfer Of Real Property Deed (applies in a fee simple, wholly-owned ownership situation in real property) (see sample of form on p. 134);

7. Form LT-22, Trustee's Or Successor Trustee's Quit Claim Deed (applies in a fee simple, wholly-owned ownership situation in real property) (See sample of form on p. 135);

8. Form LT-23, Trustee's or Successor Trustee's Affidavit Of Assignment Of Secured Realty Interest (sample on p. 136);

9. Form LT-24, Trustee's Or Successor Trustee's Affidavit Of Transfer Of Financial Account (sample on p. 137);

10. Form LT-25, Trustee's or Successor Trustee's Affidavit Of Transfer Of Securities (sample on p. 138);

11. Form LT-26, Trustee's or Successor Trustee's Affidavit Of Assignment Of Contract That Accrues Certain Payments (sample on p. 139).

NOTE: In completing the property transfer documents, strict care should be taken to make sure that both the property description outlined in the papers and the designation of the beneficiaries, conform EXACTLY as they appear in the Declaration of Trust. Keep in mind, for example, that when the transfer of a property or inheritance is made to a trust beneficiary, that property is thereupon the "sole and separate" property of the married couple, "as husband and wife." The appropriate designation used should be according to the beneficiary's present status as of the time of the distribution. Thus, for a single beneficiary, John Smith, the designation on the new title of ownership should read: "John Smith, as his sole and separate property"; for a married couple beneficiary, John and Mary Doe, the designation should read: "John and Mary Doe, as husband and wife."[1]

---

[1] Other designations, in terms of the beneficiary's status or circumstances, include the following: For more than one beneficiary in equal share, "John Smith, John Doe, and Mary Doe, in equal shares, as their sole and separate property"; for a minor child through his/her legal guardian: "John Doe, the legal guardian of James Smith, a minor child"; for a person legally incapable of holding title, through his/her conservator: "John Doe, the conservator of David Jones, an incompetent person"; and for the estate of a deceased beneficiary: "The estate of Mary Smith, deceased."

SUCCESSOR TRUSTEE SIGNS THE TRANSFER DOCUMENTS, AND RECORDS THEM, IF APPLICABLE

Then, upon your (i.e., the trustee or successor trustee) completion of the applicable forms, they are to be *signed* and *notarized* by the Trustee or Successor Trustee, whichever is applicable.

Next, beyond having to give a notice to the designated beneficiaries, you will have to determine if there is any requirement for giving a notice, and for making a public records recording of the transfer of title with the appropriate state agency or county records office, according to the procedures of your jurisdiction.

CLUE: If the title document for the old, now revoked, trust was originally recorded, or if the property involved is a real property, then you can reasonably assume that this new property transfer documents would probably have to be recorded as well. (When recording is applicable, the revocation of trust form should always be recorded as well). If, however, the original documents were not recorded, or the property involved is a non-realty property, then it's probably sufficient to merely give or send the proper parties, more particularly, the designated beneficiaries, some appropriate notice of the trust revocation and transfer of property. (Basically, you'd send them a copy of the successor trustee's Affidavit of Transfer and the Revocation of Trust). *And in this instance, since distribution of the estate assets applies, the designated beneficiaries are to be given proper notification of that, among other parties.*

[See Chapter 10 for more on the procedures of settling a trust and distribution of estate-assets].

Copyright © 1994, Do-It-Yourself Legal Publishers Newark, NJ 07102

Amendment To Living Trust As To Trust Property And/Or Beneficiaries

KNOW ALL MEN BY THESE PRESENTS:

By the written DECLARATION OF TRUST dated _____ 19_____, (we) created a Revocable Trust named and Mr/Mrs _____ was named the Trustee of the said Trust.

WHEREAS, by the terms of the said Declaration of Trust, I (we) reserved the full power and right to amend (or revoke) the said Trust at any time without the consent or notice to any beneficiary of the said Trust,

NOW THEREFORE, pursuant to such power and right to amend (or to revoke) , I (we) do hereby amend the TRUST as follows:

1. The following provision(s) are deleted from and/ or added to the Trust, as follows:
The following assets (describe the trust assets) _____ accruing under the trust to: _____

_____

_____
(Insert Names of original beneficiary or beneficiaries)

Shall henceforth accrue to: *(check one)*
☐ the following individual
☐ the following individuals as primary and contingent beneficiary, respectively
☐ the following individuals, to share equally
☐ the following individuals primary beneficiary, with my children sharing equally as contingent beneficiaries
☐ No beneficiary or beneficiaries and the trust asset assigned to the above parties under the trust shall revert back to the trust as my (our) residuary estate, and/ or be distributed as set forth below.

(Insert name(s) of new beneficiary or beneficiaries:)

_____

2. The following is/are added to the Trust.
The trust creators hereby designate Mr/Mrs _____ as new beneficiary, subject ot the survivorship provisions of paragraph _____ of the Trust, namely: _(in equal shares)_ _(per stirpes)_ _(or the survivors of them)_ .

(Enter other changes, if any)

In all other respects, the trust, as previously executed by the grantors, is hereby affirmed.

IN WITNESS WHEREOF, I (We) have signed these presents this _____ day of _____ 19___.

SIGNED X _____

X _____

_____ (Grantor)

_____ (Co-Grantor)

Acknowledgment Before A Notary

STATE OF _____
COUNTY OF _____ } ss.:

On this _____ day of _____ 19___ before me, the undersigned Notary Public duly authorized to administer oaths in the above-captioned jurisdiction, personally appeared Mr/Mrs/Ms. _____ to me known or made known to me to be the individual(s) described in and who executed the foregoing instrument; thereupon the said person(s) acknowledged that he (she) (they) executed the same as his (her) (their) free act and deed.

My Commission Expires _____

_____
Notary Public

Form LT-14

Amendment To The Trust To Substitute A Trustee Or Successor Trustee

KNOW ALL MEN BY THESE PRESENTS:

By the written DECLARATION OF TRUST dated _____ 19___, I (we) created a Revocable Trust named _____ and Mr/Mrs _____ was named the Trustee of the said Trust.

WHEREAS, by the terms of the said Declaration of Trust, I (we) reserved the full power and right to amend (or revoke) the said Trust at any time without the consent of or notice to any beneficiary of the said Trust; NOW THEREFORE, pursuant to such power and right to amend (or to revoke), I (we) do hereby amend the TRUST as follows:

If substituting a Trustee:

☐ I (we) hereby appoint and substitute Mr/Mrs _____ as trustee, in place and stead of Mr/Mrs _____, the trustee thereinbefore named (or previously substituted).

If substituting a Successor Trustee:

☐ I (we) hereby appoint and substitute Mr/Mrs _____ as Successor Trustee, in place and stead of Mr/Mrs _____, the successor trustee thereinbefore named (or previously substituted).

IN WITNESS WHEREOF, I (We) have signed these presents this _____ day of _____ 19___.

SIGNED ✗ _____

(Grantor)

✗ _____

(Co-Grantor)

Acknowledgment

STATE OF _____)
COUNTY OF _____) ss.:

On this _____ day of _____ 19___, before me, the undersigned Notary Public duly authorized to administer oaths in the above-captioned jurisdiction, personally appeared Mr/Mrs/Ms. _____ to me known or made known to me to be the individual(s) described in and who executed the foregoing instrument; thereupon the said person(s) acknowledged that he (she) (they) executed the same as his (her) (their) free act and deed.

My Commission Expires _____

_____

Notary Public

Form LT-15

Copyright © 1994, Do-It-Yourself Legal Publishers Newark, NJ 07102

Affidavit Of Grantor(s) Relinquishing Authority
To Successor Trustee

STATE OF _____

COUNTY OF _____ ss.:

I (we) _____

Deponents," being duly sworn on oath, depose and say: _____ the undersigned person(s), hereinafter called "the

1. That I (we) am (are) the Grantors under the DECLARATION OF TRUST named as _____

and dated _____, 19____.

2. That as provided in paragraph _____ of the TRUST, the Grantor(s) may, at his/her (their) option and discretion, voluntarily relinquish authority as Trustee(s) to the Successor Trustee named therein (or previously substituted).

3. That, wherefore pursuant to the said provision, the undersigned Deponent(s), the Grantor(s) and Trustee(s) under the said TRUST, by this affidavit, hereby knowingly and voluntarily relinquish all authorities, powers and rights as Trustees under the said TRUST, to the Successor Trustee, *[name of such successor Trustee]* _____ who shall hereinafter have and exercise all of the powers vested in the Trustee as authorized in the Declaration of Trust.

Further the Deponent(s) sayeth not.

IN WITNESS WHEREOF, I (We) have signed these presents this _____ day of _____, 19____.

SIGNED **X** _____

_____ (Deponent-Grantor)

My (Our) Address(es) _____

_____ (Co-Deponent-Co-Grantor)

Acknowledgment

STATE OF _____

COUNTY OF _____ ss:

On this _____ day of _____, 19____, before me, the undersigned Notary Public duly authorized to administer oaths in the above-captioned jurisdiction, personally appeared Mr/Mrs/Ms. _____ to me known or made known to me to be the individual(s) described in and who executed the foregoing instrument; thereupon the said person(s) acknowledged that he (she) (they) executed the same as his (her) (their) free act and deed.

_____
Notary Public

My Commission Expires _____

Form LT-16   Copyright © 1994, Do-It-Yourself Legal Publishers Newark, NJ 07102

Notice By Successor Trustee Of Authority To Administer Trust

TO: Whom it may concern, and/or
Mr/Mrs/Ms _____
Address: _____ Zip _____

Please take notice that I, _____, the undersigned Successor Trustee under the DECLARATION OF TRUST named _____ and dated _____ 19____, a true copy of which is attached hereto and/or made a part hereof by this NOTICE, do by these presents, hereby give notice that pursuant to the provisions of the said Declaration of Trust, I have assumed the duties as Successor Trustee as provided in paragraph(s) _____ of the said Trust, for the reason(s) checked below:

(check one):

☐ The Grantor (or both Grantors, if applicable) are now incapacitated within the meaning of the applicable provisions of the said Declaration of Trust (see annexed Medical Certification)
☐ The Grantor (or both Grantors, if applicable) are now deceased (see annexed Death Certificate(s))
☐ The Grantors relinquished authority to me as successor (see annexed Grantor's Affidavit Relinquishing Authority)

WHEREFORE, I, the undersigned, hereby serve notice that I serve as the Successor Trustee, and that in my capacity as such Successor Trustee, all of the Trustee's rights, title and interest in and to the Real and Personal Property comprising the property and assets of the Trust have been assumed by me this date; and that the same will be administered in accordance with the discretionary provisions set forth in the said Declaration of Trust.

SIGNED ✗ _____
             (Successor Trustee)

            Name (print)

Acknowledgment

STATE OF _____
COUNTY OF _____) ss.:

On this _____ day of _____ 19____ before me, the undersigned Notary Public duly authorized to administer oaths in the above-captioned jurisdiction, personally appeared Mr/Mrs/Ms. _____ to me known or made known to me to be the individual(s) described in and who executed the foregoing instrument; thereupon the said person(s) acknowledged that he (she) (they) executed the same as his (her) (their) free act and deed.

_____
            Notary Public

My Commission Expires _____

Form LT-17

Copyright © 1994, Do-It-Yourself Legal Publishers Newark, NJ 07102

Revocation of Trust

(Inter Vivos)

KNOW ALL MEN BY THESE PRESENTS:

By the written DECLARATION OF TRUST dated _____ 19 ___, I (we) created a Revocable Trust named _____ and Mr/Mrs _____ was named the Trustee of the said Trust.

WHEREAS, by the terms of the said Declaration of Trust, I (we) reserved the full power and right to revoke (or amend) the said Trust at any time without the consent of or notice to any beneficiary of the said Trust;

NOW THEREFORE, pursuant to such power and right to revoke (or amend), I (we) do hereby take the following action with respect to the TRUST:

1. I (we) do hereby revoke in its entirety the said Trust, created and dated _____ 19 ___, and effective immediately, all property comprising the Trust property shall forthwith be free and discharged of all the terms and provisions of said TRUST contained in the said Declaration Trust, and shall be returned to the undersigned original grantor(s) of the said trust and be legally owned by them (he/her) unless as otherwise provided hereinafter in paragraph 2 below, if any.

2. _____

IN WITNESS WHEREOF, I (We) have signed these presents this _____ day of _____ 19 ___.

SIGNED ✗ _____

✗ _____
(Trust Grantor)

_____
(Trust Co-Grantor)

Acknowledgment

STATE OF _____)
COUNTY OF _____) ss.:

On this _____ day of _____ 19 ___ before me, the undersigned Notary Public duly authorized to administer oaths in the above-captioned jurisdiction, personally appeared Mr/Mrs/Ms. _____ to me known or made known to me to be the individual(s) described in and who executed the foregoing instrument; thereupon the said person(s) acknowledged that he (she) (they) executed the same as his (her) (their) free act and deed.

_____
Notary Public

My Commission Expires _____

Form LT-18   Copyright © 1994, Do-It-Yourself Legal Publishers Newark, NJ 07102

Trustee's or Successor Trustee's Affidavit of Chattel & Personal Property

(Moveable property, e.g., motor vehicles, trailer, boats, equipment, goods, household property, etc.)

KNOW ALL MEN BY THESE PRESENTS:

That I (We) _____ of this address
County of _____, State of _____, the undersigned Transferror(s) who is (check one) ☐ Trustee ☐ Successor Trustee under the DECLARATION OF TRUST named _____, and dated
_____ 19____, a true copy of which is attached hereto and/or made a part hereof by this reference, do
by these presents, hereby assign, transfer and deliver unto these parties: (enter the names of the trust-designated
beneficiaries for this item: EXAMPLE: *Edward E. Doe and John Johnson in equal shares*),
who are the TRANSFERREE(S) under the trust, all rights, title and interest which I as (check one) ☐ Trustee☐
Successor Trustee under the said Trust, have in and to the Chattel and Personal property described as
follows:

_____

_____
             [Use the major items here. Should be same items as in Form LT-13]
_____

The said Chattel Property had been previously assigned and transferred to this TRUST by the Grantor(s) on
_____ 19____, which assignment was:

(check applicable block)
☐ Not recorded in the Official Records of any county and state
☐ Recorded in the Official Records of _____ county and state of _____ in Book (Docket)
(Volume) _____.

That the said Transferree(s) is/are TO HAVE AND TO HOLD all of the said chattel and personal property unto
and to the use of the said Transferree(s) and his (her) (their) successors in interest forever free of trust; and that neither
I (We) nor my (our) heirs or assigns shall have or make any claims or demands upon the said Chattel property.

IN WITNESS WHEREOF, I (We) have signed these presents this _____ day of _____ 19____.

SIGNED X _____
                    (Transferror-Trustee or Successor Trustee)

Acknowledgment

STATE OF _____
COUNTY OF _____ ss.:
On this _____ day of _____ 19____, before me, the undersigned Notary Public duly authorized to
administer oaths in the above-captioned jurisdiction, personally appeared Mr/Mrs/Ms. _____
to me known or made known to me to be the individual(s) described in and who executed the foregoing
instrument; thereupon the said person(s) acknowledged that he (she) (they) executed the same as his (her)
(their) free act and deed.

My Commission Expires _____   _____ Notary Public

Trustee's Affidavit of Transfer
of the Contents of a Rented House or Apartment

KNOW ALL MEN BY THESE PRESENTS:

That I (We) _____

County of _____ State of _____, the undersigned Transferror(s) who is (check one) ☐ Trustee ☐ Successor Trustee under the DECLARATION OF TRUST named _____ of this address _____ and dated
_____ 19____, a true copy of which is attached hereto and/or made a part hereof by this reference, do
by these presents, hereby assign, transfer and deliver unto these parties: (enter the names of the trust-designated
beneficiaries for this property.)

who are the TRANSFEREE(S) under the trust, all rights, title and interest which I as (check one) ☐ Trustee ☐
Successor Trustee under the said Trust, have in and to the certain contents of a rented house or apartment
located at _____ in the city and state of _____, which shall
include any and all items and property contained or possessed therein of whatever nature or description
EXCEPT the following _____

_____ [List any exempt items, if any apply per the provision of the Trust; otherwise enter
'NONE' and run two lines across the whole length of space]

The said Property had been previously assigned and transferred to this TRUST by the Grantor(s) on
_____ 19____.

That the said Transferree(s) is/are TO HAVE AND TO HOLD the said property unto and to the use of the
said Transferree(s) and his (her) (their) successors in interest forever free of trust; and that neither I (We) nor
my (our) heirs or assigns shall have or make any claims or demands upon said property.

IN WITNESS WHEREOF, I (We) have signed these presents this _____ day of _____ 19____.

SIGNED X _____

(Transferror-Trustee or Successor Trustee)

Acknowledgment

STATE OF _____
COUNTY OF _____ ss.:

On this _____ day of _____ 19____ before me, the undersigned Notary Public duly authorized to
administer oaths in the above-captioned jurisdiction, personally appeared Mr/Mrs/Ms. _____
to me known or made known to me to be the individual(s) described in and who executed the foregoing
instrument; thereupon the said person(s) acknowledged that he (she) (they) executed the same as his (her)
(their) free act and deed.

My Commission Expires _____

_____
Notary Public

Trustee's or Successor Trustee's Affidavit of Transfer of Business Interest

(check one) ☐ Sole Proprietorship ☐ Partnership

KNOW ALL MEN BY THESE PRESENTS:

That I (We) _____, of this address _____, county of _____, state of _____, the undersigned Transferror(s) who is *(check one)* ☐ Trustee ☐ Successor Trustee under the DECLARATION OF TRUST named _____ and dated _____ 19___, do by these presents, hereby assign, transfer and convey unto these parties: *(enter the names of the trust-designated beneficiaries for this item. EXAMPLE: Edward E. doe, John Johnson and Mary Jones, per stirpes')* _____ who are the TRANSFERREE(S) under the trust, all rights, title and interest which I as *(check one)* ☐ Trustee ☐ Successor Trustee under the said Trust, have in and to the certain Business organization described as follows: _____

Name of business organization: _____, located at (full address) _____ which is *(check one)* ☐ Sole Proprietorship ☐ Partnership, of which my interest in said partnership is _____ percent.

The said Property had been previously assigned and transferred to this TRUST by the Grantor(s) on _____ 19___ .

That the said Transferree(s) named above, is/are TO HAVE AND TO HOLD the said Business Interst unto and to the use of the said Transferree(s) and his (her) (their) successors in interest forever free of trust; and that neither I (We) nor my (our) heirs or assigns shall have or make any claims or demands upon said Business Interest.

IN WITNESS WHEREOF, I (We) have signed these presents this _____ day of _____ 19___ .

SIGNED X _____
(Transferror-Trustee or Successor Trustee)

Acknowledgment

STATE OF _____)
) ss.:
COUNTY OF _____)

On this _____ day of _____, 19___, before me, the undersigned Notary Public duly authorized to administer oaths in the above-captioned jurisdiction, personally appeared Mr/Mrs/Ms. _____ to me known or made known to me to be the individual(s) described in and who executed the foregoing instrument; thereupon the said person(s) acknowledged that he (she) (they) executed the same as his (her) (their) free act and deed.

_____ Notary Public

My Commission Expires _____

Trustee's or Successor Trustee's Affidavit of Transfer of Real Property Deed

☐ Trustee ☐ Successor Trustee

KNOW ALL MEN BY THESE PRESENTS:

That I (We) _____, of this address _____
county of _____, state of _____, the undersigned Transferror(s) who is (check one) ☐ Trustee ☐ Successor Trustee under the DECLARATION OF TRUST named _____ and dated
_____ 19 ____, do by these presents, hereby convey unto these parties: (enter the names of the trust designated beneficiaries for this item,) _____
who are the TRANSFEREE(S) under the trust, all rights, title and interest which I as (check one) ☐ Trustee ☐
Successor Trustee under the said Trust, have in and to the certain contents of Real Property situated in the city
and state of _____ and described as follows: _____

The said Property had been previously conveyed and transferred to this TRUST by the Grantor(s) of the
Trust through a Deed or other instrument of Conveyance recorded in Book (Docket) (Volume) _____ at
pages _____, of the Official Land Records of _____ County, State of _____.

That the said Transferee(s) named above is/are TO HAVE AND TO HOLD all of the said real property unto and
to the use and benefit of the said Transferee(s) and his (her) (their) successors in interest forever free of trust; and
that neither I (We) nor my (our) heirs or assigns shall have or make any claims or demands upon said property.

IN WITNESS WHEREOF, I (We) have signed these presents this _____ day of _____ 19 ____.

SIGNED X _____
(Transferror-Trustee or Successor Trustee)

Acknowledgment

STATE OF _____
COUNTY OF _____ } ss.:

On this _____ day of _____ 19 ____, before me, the undersigned Notary Public duly authorized to
administer oaths in the above-captioned jurisdiction, personally appeared Mr/Mrs/Ms. _____
to me known or made known to me to be the individual(s) described in and who executed the foregoing
instrument; thereupon the said person(s) acknowledged that he (she) (they) executed the same as his (her)
(their) free act and deed.

_____
Notary Public

My Commission Expires _____

Form LT-22

Trustee's or Successor Trustee's Quit Claim Deed

To all people to whom these presents shall come, greetings:

Know YE, that I (we) _____ , of this address _____ County of _____ , State of _____ , the undersigned Successor Trustee(s) under the DECLARATION OF TRUST named _____ and dated _____ 19 _____ a true copy of which is attached hereto and/or made a part of this Deed by this reference, do by these presents, pursuant to the instructions contained in the said Declaration of Trust, hereby release and forever Quit-claim unto this/these person(s):

_____
[names of the beneficiary/beneficiaries, including you, if you are among them]

as beneficiaries under said Declaration, all right, title and interest and demand whatsoever which I as Successor Trustee under Declaration of Trust and as Releasor hereunder, have or ought to have in or to the property located in the city/town of _____ , County of _____ , State of _____ , and described as follows:

[Enter the description of the real property as it appears in the recorded Deed]

That the said beneficiaries named above is/are TO HAVE AND TO HOLD the said real property, with all the appurtenances, unto and to their use and his (her) (their) successors in interest forever free of trust; and that neither I (We) nor my (our) heirs or assigns shall have or make any claims or demands upon the said property.

IN WITNESS WHEREOF, I (We) have signed these presents this _____ day of _____ 19 _____ .

SIGNED ✗ _____
(Trust's Successor Trustee)

_____
Name (print)

Acknowledgment

Successor Trustee under Declaration of Trust executed by *[enter name(s) of the Trust Creators]* on this _____ day of _____ , in the city/town of _____ .

STATE OF _____ } ss.:
COUNTY OF _____ }

On this _____ day of _____ 19 _____ before me, the undersigned Notary Public duly authorized to administer oaths in the above-captioned jurisdiction, personally appeared Mr/Mrs/Ms. _____ to me known or made known to me to be the individual(s) described in and who executed the foregoing instrument; thereupon the said person(s) acknowledged that he (she) (they) executed the same as his (her) (their) free act and deed.

_____
Notary Public

My Commission Expires _____

136

Copyright © 1994, Do-It-Yourself Legal Publishers Newark, NJ 07102

Trustee's or Successor Trustee's Affidavit of Assignment of Secured Realty Interest

check one ☐ Deed of Trust   ☐ Real Estate Mortgage   ☐ Trustee ☐ Succes-
       ☐ Realty Agreement   ☑ Realty Sales Contract

KNOW ALL MEN BY THESE PRESENTS:

That I (We) _____ of this address

County of _____, State of _____, the undersigned Transferror(s) who is *(check one)* ☐ Trustee ☐ Successor Trustee under the DECLARATION OF TRUST named _____ and dated

_____ 19 ____ do by these presents, hereby assign, transfer and convey unto these parties:

(enter the name(s) of the true/designated beneficiaries for this item. EXAMPLE: ' Edward E. Doe, David A. Doe, in equal shares')

who are the assignee(s) under the trust, all rights, title and interest which I as *(check one)* ☐ Trustee ☐ Successor Trustee under the said Trust, have in and to the certain secured realty interest described as follows:

check one

☐ Agreement For Sale Of Real Estate   ☐ Real Estate Mortgage
☐ Beneficial Interest In Deed Of Trust   ☐ Real Estate Sales Contract

and to the Note or other evidence of indebtedness secured by the said realty interest, dated _____ 19 ____
and recorded in the Official Land records of _____ County and State of _____, in Book (Docket)
(Volume) _____ at pages _____ thereof.

The said Secured Realty Interest had been previously assigned to this trust by the Grantor(s) _____
19 ____, which assignment had been recorded in Book (Docket) (Volume) _____ on pages _____ in the official
land records of _____ County, State of _____.

That the said Assignee(s) and Transferree(s) is/are TO HAVE AND TO HOLD all of the said real property unto
and to their use and benefit and his (her) (their) successors in interest forever free of trust, and that neither I (We) nor
my (our) heirs or assigns shall have or make any claims or demands upon said Secured Realty Interest.

IN WITNESS WHEREOF, I (We) have signed these presents this _____ day of _____ 19 ____.

SIGNED **X** _____
(Transferror-Trustee or Successor Trustee)

Acknowledgment

STATE OF _____
COUNTY OF _____) ss.:

On this _____ day of _____, 19 ____ before me, the undersigned Notary Public duly authorized to
administer oaths in the above-captioned jurisdiction, personally appeared Mr/Mrs/Ms.
to me known or made known to me to be the individual(s) described in and who executed the foregoing
instrument; thereupon the said person(s) acknowledged that he (she) (they) executed the same as his (her)
(their) free act and deed.

My Commission Expires _____

_____
Notary Public

Form LT-24

Trustee's or Successor Trustee's Affidavit of Transfer of Financial Account

(☐ Financial Institution ☐ Brokerage Firm)

KNOW ALL MEN BY THESE PRESENTS:

That I (We) _____ of this address

_____, State of _____, the undersigned Transferror(s) who is *(check one)* ☐ Trustee ☐ Succes-

County of _____, State of _____, the undersigned Transferror(s) who is *(check one)* ☐ Trustee ☐ Successor Trustee under the DECLARATION OF TRUST named _____ and dated

19 ____ do by these presents, hereby assign, transfer and convey unto these parties:

_____ *[enter the names of the trust designated beneficiaries for this asset]*

who are the TRANSFEREE(S) under the trust, all rights, title and interest which I as *(check one)* ☐ Trustee ☐ Successor Trustee under the said Trust, have in and to *(check one)*

☐ Financial Account No. _____ kept or held at the Financial Institution or Brokerage Firm
☐ Brokerage Account No. _____

known as: _____ located at _____ in the City/town of _____

State of _____ including all cash and/or securities held in said Account.

That the said Transferree(s) named above is/are TO HAVE AND TO HOLD all of the said Account, including all the cash and securities held therein, unto and for their benefit and his (her) (their) successors in interest forever free of trust; and that neither I (We) nor my (our) heirs or assigns shall have or make any claims or demands upon said Account.

IN WITNESS WHEREOF, I (We) have signed these presents this _____ day of _____ 19 ____ .

SIGNED X _____
(Transferror Trustee or Successor Trustee)

Acknowledgment

STATE OF _____
COUNTY OF _____) ss:

On this _____ day of _____ 19 ____ before me, the undersigned Notary Public duly authorized to administer oaths in the above-captioned jurisdiction, personally appeared Mr/Mrs/Ms. _____ to me known or made known to me to be the individual(s) described in and who executed the foregoing instrument; thereupon the said person(s) acknowledged that he (she) (they) executed the same as his (her) (their) free act and deed.

My Commission Expires _____   _____ Notary Public

Form LT-25

Copyright © 1994, Do-It-Yourself Legal Publishers Newark, NJ 07102

Trustee's or Successor Trustee's Affidavit of Transfer of Securities

(☐ Stocks ☐ Bonds ☐ Other)

KNOW ALL MEN BY THESE PRESENTS:

That I (We) _____

County of _____, State of _____, the undersigned Transferror(s) who is (*check one*) ☐ Trustee ☐ Successor Trustee under the DECLARATION OF TRUST named _____ and dated _____ 19____, do by these presents, hereby, assign, transfer and deliver unto these parties:

_____ [*enter the names of the trust-designated beneficiaries for this asset designated in the trust*]

who are the TRANSFEREE(S), under the trust, all rights, title and interest which I as (*check one*) ☐ Trustee ☐ Successor Trustee under the said Trust, have in and to the securities described as follows: [*e.g., 200 shares of IBM common stock, 100 shares of 6% NY Municipal Bond, 100 shares of 7% 2nd preferred stock for AT&T*]

The said securities had been previously transferred to this Trust by the Grantor(s) of the Trust through an assignment document dated _____ 19____.

That the said Transferree(s) named above is/are TO HAVE AND TO HOLD all of the said securities unto and to the use and benefit of the said Transferree(s) and his (her) (their) successors in interest forever free of trust; and that neither I (We) nor my (our) heirs or assigns shall have or make any claims or demands upon the said Securities.

IN WITNESS WHEREOF, I (We) have signed these presents this _____ day of _____ 19____.

SIGNED X _____
(*Transferror-Trustee or Successor Trustee*)

Acknowledgment

STATE OF _____
COUNTY OF _____ } ss.:

On this _____ day of _____ 19____, before me, the undersigned Notary Public duly authorized to administer oaths in the above-captioned jurisdiction, personally appeared Mr/Mrs/Ms. _____ to me known, or made known to me to be the individual(s) described in and who executed the foregoing instrument; thereupon the said person(s) acknowledged that he (she) (they) executed the same as his (her) (their) free act and deed.

My Commission Expires _____

_____
Notary Public

Form LT-26   Copyright © 1994, Do-It-Yourself Legal Publishers Newark, NJ 07102

Trustee's or Successor Trustee's Assignment of Contract That Accrues Certain Payments

KNOW ALL MEN BY THESE PRESENTS:

That I (We) _____ of this address _____ County of _____, State of _____, the undersigned Transferror(s) who is (check one) ☐ Trustee ☐ Successor Trustee under the DECLARATION OF TRUST named _____, and dated _____ 19____, do by these presents hereby assign, transfer and convey unto these parties: *[enter the names of the trust-designated beneficiaries for this asset, EXAMPLE: 'Edward and David Doe, in equal shares']* who are the ASSIGNEE(S) under the Trust, all rights, title and interest which I as (check one) ☐ Trustee ☐ Successor Trustee under the said Trust, have in and to certain contract (hereinafter called "the contract"), dated _____ 19___ and executed by _____ on behalf of _____ in favor of _____, under the terms of which certain royalties and/or other payments accrue to the Grantor(s) from the publication, distribution and/or performance of certain works by virtue of the Grantors' work/services as (check which):

☐ the author of literary work which was published, as more fully described below
☐ the composer of musical composition which was published, as more fully described below
☐ the registrant under design and/or utility patents Numbered _____, as more fully described below
☐ others _____
☐ _____

The Trustee's interest in the above-stated contract was acquired by an ASSIGNMENT OF CONTRACT FOR LITERARY WORK OR MUSICAL COMPOSITION TO TRUST dated _____ 19____, which had been executed by the Grantor(s) hereinabove named, and was assigned to the trust.

That the said Trransferree(s) named above is/are TO HAVE AND TO HOLD the said contract interest unto and to their use and benefit and his (her) (their) successors in interest forever free of trust and that neither I (We) nor my (our) heirs or assigns shall have or make any claims or demands upon the said CONTRACT INTEREST.

IN WITNESS WHEREOF, I (We) have signed these presents this ____ day of _____ 19___.

_____
(Transferror-Trustee or Successor Trustee)

Acknowledgment

STATE OF _____)
) ss.:
COUNTY OF _____)
On this ____ day of _____ 19____, before me, the undersigned Notary Public duly authorized to administer oaths in the above-captioned jurisdiction, personally appeared Mr/Mrs/Ms. _____ to me known or made known to me to be the individual(s) described in and who executed the foregoing instrument; thereupon the said person(s) acknowledged that he (she) (they) executed the same as his (her) (their) free act and deed.

My Commission Expires _____   _____ Notary Public

Chapter 9

A Few Extra Estate Planning Instruments You Should Have For 'Total' Estate Plan Protection

In Chapter 3 (see, especially Sections E & F therein), we discussed the concept of adopting the 'total' estate planning approach in one's planning and plan-making, vigorously arguing against an absolutist, single-instrument approach to estate planning. The salient point is made that:

> "In point of fact, a lot of what are said to be "drawbacks" and "disadvantages" of particular traditional probate avoidance devices by critics and living trust absolutists, are not really faults in an intrinsic or structural sense, but actually one minor inadequacy or the other that a particular instrument may possess, but which frequently can be cured simply by using one other additional estate planning instrument or another in combination with the original instrument [such as a back-up will, a Living Will, Durable Power of Attorney, and the like]."

THE 'EXTRA' TOOLS WE SHALL CONSIDER IN THIS CHAPTER

In this chapter, we shall briefly discuss a few of these other estate planning tools which can often be employed to complement and supplement a good living trust, and should, in the view of many experts, generally be a part of any sound overall living trust estate "plan" for maximum legal protection effect. The objective is to, as much as is possible, provide further extra protection or "safety net," to attempt, through designing a living trust and appropriate accompanying and supporting instruments as well, to cover most (if not all) future possible contingencies. Thus, this category of tools focus on 'planning,' not for what happens just when we die or even when we are alive and physically and mentally able to control or decide on matters; but for when we may no more be in full control of our mental faculties, and may not quite be mentally or physically competent to make the important, day-to-day financial and/or medical decisions of our lives.

The following instruments in this category will be covered:

- ☐ The Back-up or Pour-Over will
- ☐ The Living Will
- ☐ The Durable Financial and Medical Power of Attorney

A. Drawing Up The Back-Up or Pour-Over Will

As is more fully elaborated in Chapter 3 [see, especially, item 4 of Section D therein, at pp. 20-4], certainly the Living Trust is quite a useful and versatile estate planning tool, but there's one important thing it can't do for you: it can't protect your assets that are somehow left outside of the trust, either inadvertently or intentionally—assets that have been simply forgotten or overlooked, or assets that could not have been anticipated, a last-minute inheritance, a settlement award from a lawsuit, a lottery winning, etc.

Hence, the prudent approach among many knowledgable people who have a living trust, is to also supplement the trust with a Will. The approach is to also include in your estate plan a "back-up" Will—a will to back up an existing trust, but which, among other things includes a "pour-over" provision that "pours" (transfers) into the trust any assets you might have left out of the trust. By providing that if any asset or property belonging to you should be left out of your trust, such assets or property should go ("pour-over") into the trust after probate, you shall have effectively guaranteed that ALL of your assets are eventually covered, and would almost surely end up in your trust and be governed by one set of distribution rules!

There are, in addition, other important estate planning purposes which are served by a back-up Will, and which make it all the more helpful, even necessary, to always complement your living trust with a Will. They include the following: it's the exclusive device by which you can provide for expressed disinheritance of an heir or relative, or for providing for a debt that is owed you to be forgiven, or for appointing a personal guardian to see to the custody, care and upbringing of your minor children, or for expressing specific funeral and burial instructions and preferences, among other purposes. [See Item 4, Section D of Chapter 3 for a fuller treatment of this].

Presented in Form LT-27 (p. 148), is a sample back-up Will containing the essential pour-over provisions. [For a far more elaborate and complete treatment of the subject matter of the Will and the Living Will in estate planning, you'll have to see a related title by the same author, *"How To Plan Your Total Estate With A Will & Living Will, Without A Lawyer's Fees"* published by Do-It-Yourself Legal Publishers.] Upon completion of the Will, you must be sure to properly "execute" (sign) it and have it witnessed and countersigned by some 2 or 3 adult persons (carefully follow the signing procedures set forth below).

IMPORTANT: Take note of the fact that under the laws of most states, for the pour-over provisions of a Will to be valid, the trust document must itself already have been in existence <u>BEFORE</u> your signing of the Will. Thus, this way, it will then be practicable for you to identify in the Will the specific trust your asset is to pour into.

The "Execution" (Signing) Of The Will

We'll assume that you have had your "Back-up" Will properly drawn up (sample on p. 148). *There's one other very important thing left to be done, now, before you can say you have a valid will*—THE PROPER "EXECUTION" (SIGNING) AND WITNESSING OF THE WILL.

For a will to be valid (other than a holographic type of Will), it must be properly signed and witnessed; and for it to be considered to be properly signed, and witnessed, certain required formalities must be observed. Primarily, the purpose of undertaking the required formalities is to ensure that the testator (the Will-maker), understands that he or she is executing a document that is of such serious and final implication, and to help prevent fraudulent documents being passed as wills.

Listed below are the general steps and requirements recommended for executing a will to ensure that the will is valid in just about every state in the nation under normal circumstances:

1. *Signature of the Testator:* The will must be signed by the testator, generally the signature must be at the foot or end of the will. (Note: if the testator is unable to sign, it may be signed for him by another person at the testator's request and in the presence of the testator and the witnesses).

2. Execute (sign) only one copy of the will, the original copy, do not sign the duplicate copy. Use a colored ink to sign so as to differentiate that copy with any photocopies of the original.

3. *Signature in Presence of Witnesses.* Immediately BEFORE the witnesses themselves sign the document, and at the same time and place, the Testator should sign the will in the presence of all witnesses to the will. (Note: The witnesses must observe the testator sign the will, but there is no requirement that they read or know the contents of the will.)

4. *'Publishing' the Will.* During the testator's own execution of the Will, the testator should 'publish' (i.e., announce openly, clearly and unambiguously) to the witnesses, something to this effect: "This is my Last Will and Testament."

5. *Number and signature of Witnesses.* The witnesses, in turn, should <u>each</u> and all sign the will at the spots just below the signature of the testator. They should sign in the presence of each other and of the testator, with each and all attentively observing. How many witnesses? Only 4 states (Maine, New Hampshire, South Carolina, and Vermont), require the use of three witnesses under the state law; the other states require the use of only two (2) witnesses.

6. *Nature of the Witnesses.* The witnesses you pick must be carefully picked; they should have sufficient mental capacity to understand and appreciate the nature of the act that they are witnessing.

Generally—and preferably—the witnesses used should be "disinterested" persons, that is, persons who are not beneficiaries under the Will. Since there may be a passage of time between when the Will is executed and the death of the testator, care should be taken to use relatively younger and healthy persons who will still be available, in case there are questions that may arise regarding the execution of the will.

7. *Finally, sign one other Document to make the Will 'Self-Proving'.* Finally, there is one more measure you should take, if at all possible: promptly take the signed Will and your witnesses before a Notary Public, and there have them (only them) sign a "Self-Proving Will" type of form in the presence of the Notary Public who will *notarize* their signatures on this form as witnesses to the Will. [See Form LT-28 on p. 151 for a sample of this form]. Upon completion of the notarization, you should recover the notarized form from the witnesses and attach same to the Will.

The advantage of a self-proving will is simple but of immense value and use: under the law, if a Will is a self-proved Will, it is "presumed" to be valid and thus (unless objected to) it is directly admitted to probate at the time of probate. Hence, it is highly advisable to hurry and meet the self-proving requirement—if at all possible for you.

[For more detailed and elaborate "ceremonies" and formalities of properly executing a Will, see another title by the same publisher, "*How To Properly Plan Your 'Total' Estate With A Will & Living Will, Without The Lawyer's Fees,*" authored by Benji O. Anosike (Do-It-Yourself Legal Publishers.)

B. Drawing Up The Living Will

The second important complementing instrument to the Living Trust which we shall consider in this guide-book, is the THE LIVING WILL.

What is a Living Will?[1] To be sure, this topic is beyond the scope of this present book, as it's more fully addressed in a separate sister volume also published by the same publisher.[2] However, for our more limited purpose here, suffice it to say simply that the term "Living Will" can more simply be defined in terms of what many people know as the "Right-to-Die" issue. To put it simply, this document says, in effect, to your doctors and loved ones: "Look, if I should become terminally ill, or otherwise sick or incapacitated or incompetent to the point where there's clearly no possibility of a return to a meaningful life, or my life is being sustained solely by artificial "life support" means, it is my desire that the plug be pulled, and I hereby so direct and authorize you to do so!"

Thus, by physically and actually making this election NOW—at a time when you are well and competent, and before the onset of any major medical problems—*you would have been able, legally, to tell your doctors and the hospitals later down the road that there's a certain 'quality of life' below which you cannot settle for, that you want to die with dignity—and not be subjected to being kept alive meaninglessly by a machine.* And, just as importantly, with the Living Will you would have been able to ensure that your wishes and instructions to doctors and loved ones will most likely be obeyed by them and be legally enforceable.

Furthermore, aside from your own specific directives in such a document, there's also one other important element you can provide for by use of the Living Will: you can also appoint a person in this document, called an "agent" or a "proxy," who will make the important life and death decision on your behalf in the event you were to become incompetent or mentally unable to make the decisions.

Many states (some18 of them as of this research) expressly require that a specific, state-designated "Statutory" Living Will form *must* be used, either precisely or susbtantially, while many others do not. Of this 17 states (plus the District of Columbia), 8 of them permit that the Living Will maker may include in the Living Will some other additional directives so long as they are consistent with the suggested form. The vast majority of states, however, including the larger ones, do not prescribe specific forms.

---

[1]"The Living Will goes by different names in different states—"Health Care Declaration," "Medical Directive," "Directive to Physician," "Durable Medical Power of Attorney," "Durable Power of Attorney for Health Care," and so on. By whatever specific name it goes in particular jurisdictions, however, they encompass essentially the same concept.

[2]For more detailed treatment of the topic, consult "*How To Plan Your 'Total' Estate With A Will & Living Will, Without The Lawyer's Fees*" by Benji O. Anosike (Do-It-Yourself Legal Publishers).

As of this writing and last research, the following 17 states and the District of Columbia expressly require that the "Statutory" living Will form (the specific form provided under the state's statutes) MUST be precisely or substantially used:

California	Mississippi
District Of Columbia*	North Carolina
Georgia	North Dakota*
Idaho	Oklahoma*
Indiana*	Oregon
Kansas*	South Carolina
Kentucky*	Utah
Maryland*	Washington*
Minnesota	Wisconsin

*In these states the law permits that the Living Will-maker may include additional directives but as long as it's consistent with the suggested form.

This means, in effect, that for the overwhelming balance of the states—that is, in the other 33 states besides the above-listed—**you** are permitted to draft and use your own individually tailored Living Will, one which presumably is legally adequate or perhaps, even better-drafted than a pre-provided stautory form. Hence, here is what you do. For those states listed above where the state-mandated Will is required, simply send for a pre-printed Living Will form for your state from the organization listed below and then fill out the sample form when you receive the pre-printed form from them. *Here is where you may send for the pre-printed form:*

National Council on Death & Dying
200 Varick Street
New York, N.Y. 10014

(It is supplied free of charge, but just enclose a self-addressed, stamped return envelope). Merely fill out the form for now, leave out the signing ("execution") part of the form for now till Paragraph D below. But for the other 33 states where it is not mandatory that either the statutory or a specific form be used, we have provided for the use and benefit of our readership, a Living Will Declaration form that is more comprehensive than the typical short form prevalent with the state-prescribed forms—*the Publisher's Comprehensive 'General Purpose' LIVING WILL DECLARATION* form set forth on pp. 152-4. And, accordingly, you may adapt this form to your particular needs and circumstances if your state falls under this category. [See the Living Will "execution" or signing procedures on p. 145].

As of this writing, 5 states (Massachusetts, Michigan, Nebraska, Ohio and Pennsylvania) do not yet have specific Living Will statutes, but Massachusetts, Michigan, Ohio and Pennsylvania have statutory provisions for durable power of attorney for health care.[3] And for any of these 5 states, you may employ the form on pp. 152-4. (If you happen to travel widely, or more frequently, or are likely to receive medical care in states other than the one in which you reside, it is advisable that you simply fill out and sign the statutory forms for each of those states as well. As far as is known, there is no law limiting the number of forms you may sign.

C. Drawing Up The Durable Financial And Medical Power of Attorney

Closely related to, and often used in conjunction with the Living Will, however, is another relatively new legal tool in the field of estate planning: THE DURABLE FINANCIAL & MEDICAL POWER OF ATTORNEY.

---

[3]It is possible that in the meantime your state may have revised the specific forms it uses, as has happened in some states in the last few years, usually to allow directives to discontinue therapy when the declarant is in a vegetative state, and to permit directives to withhold nutrition and hydration. Such revision, if made, do validate or decrease the coverage of the pre-existing Will form or the directives therein, but often increase such coverage. However, if you wish to be able to take advantage of any new developments that may have arisen, it will be advisable to check with your state's county probate court clerk to see if any newer statutory form has come to use lately. Or, check with The Choice in Dying organization in New York.

Basically, this document designates someone you name (called an "agent," a "proxy," or "attorney-in-fact") to make decisions for you in regards to both financial and health care matters, during the time you are incapacitated by reason of a physical or mental defect.

Here's the most fundamental piece of information to bear in mind about this document: this document, being a "durable" power of attorney, gives your appointed agent or proxy the power and right to act for you *only when you become or are incompetent or incapacitated*; it has no application whatsoever—it is not operational—while you are competent. (This contrasts with the regular "power of attorney" which gives the appointed agent the right to act on one's behalf while the indivdual is competent.) However, for you to validly create that document, you must do so while you are competent. Suppose, for example, you were to be involved in an accident and were rushed to the hospital. You were in a coma and in a state of unconsciousness and the doctors need an authorization to perform surgery? Well, such authorization can only be provided by a person who legally holds a Durable power of attorney from you, especially if you are unmarried or have no adult children around. In deed, even if you have adult children around, the shocking fact of the matter is that, as a matter of law, one's children do not have the authority to authorize the doctor or hospital to perform an important life-saving medical act on one's behalf—unless with a durable power of attorney!

The sample form for the *Durable Financial & Medical Power Of Attorney* is on p. 155. Note that you are only to fill out this form (and the Living Will) for now, and leave out the actual signing ("execution") of the form, till the next step below (p. 145).

Basically, to complete the POWER OF ATTORNEY (pp. 155-7), the most important task of all for many people is to find the person who is to serve as the agent (the "Attorney-in-Fact") to carry out the financial and health care duties spelled out in the document. As in the naming of an executor in a Will situation or trust case, many people name trusted family members for that function (though there is no law that says you necessarily must do so). It should be noted, though, that this is one instance when you may consider designating a trusted friend or family member other than a spouse, in that the spouse is the person most likely to be in the company of an injured person and thus runs a greater risk of being involved in a common accident with you than others. [CLUE: Look for a person who knows you well enough, a person of compatible mind with you about what you consider a good "quality life," a person of honor and reliability, and one who is younger than you and in relative good health.]

Before you proceed to designate a person, be sure to fully explain to him (or her) the full ramifications of his potential responsibilities and be sure that he (she) unequivocally volunteers and agrees that he'll discharge such responsibilities on your behalf if the need should arise.

For the Power of Attorney, you (the principal) are to complete the first part of the form, while the person(s) you designate as your agent (also called the "attorney-in fact" or the "proxy") is to complete the second part, the part captioned "*Affidavit of Agent as to Power of Attorney Being in Full Force*" (p. 158). The same person you enter as the designated agent or attorney-in-fact in your Power of Attorney form, is who **you** are also to enter as your agent in the Living Will (if the state form you employ makes provisions for designation of an agent in the form).

POINTER: Note that the most vital aspect to concern yourself with, in connection with the making of this Power of Attorney and the Living Will, is the making of a choice concerning the kinds of medical interventions will be acceptable or not acceptable under different kinds of conditions. Hence, first and foremost, discuss the issues, and respective medical options and situations, with your family, friends, religious mentors, but quite importantly, with your doctor.

IMPORTANT: Be absolutely sure to COORDINATE the provisions of the Living Will with the provisions of the Durable Power of Attorney. The terms and provisions of these two documents must be CONSISTENT with each other, and not be conflicting. The same person(s) must be named as the agents in the two documents. In the MEDICAL DIRECTIVE, you are to designate the name(s) of a person (or persons) who is to act as your agent or proxy decision-maker. This person would be the one who is to make decisions under circumstances in which your expressed wishes are not clear—when, for example, your specific situation is not covered in the Medical Directive you provide with the Living Will, or your preference is indeterminate or undecided. (Note that you can name more than one agent; if you do, just be sure to indicate whose opinion between them is to prevail in the event of a disagreement).

D. "Execution" (Signing) Of The Living Will & The Durable Power Of Attorney

Now, this is the time for you (and some witnesses as well) to formally sign— "execute" —the two above-described documents. To be sure that you'll have a valid set of instruments, *you MUST closely and strictly follow the following procedures in your signing act:*

1. You are to assemble the person(s) you have carefully picked who you will appoint to act as your agent or attorney-in-fact, and three (3) persons who will sign as witnesses to the signing event. *Any of these witnesses should <u>NOT</u>:*

   i) Be a minor under your state law (generally under 18)
   ii) Be related to you by blood or marriage or adoption
   iii) Be entitled to inherit from you under a Will or Codicil or under the law of intestate of your state
   iv) Have any claim against you or potentially have any claim against your estate
   v) Be your attending physician
   vi) Be a patient of the health care facility in which you are a patient or resident
   vii) Be an employee of your physician or of the health care facility in which you are being treated at the time of the signing of the Living Will
   viii) Be paid any compensation for acting as a witness
   ix) Have been the one who signed the Living Will itself for you, even if at your direction
   x) Have paid for you for your medical care
   xi) Be a person named in your Living Will or Power of Attorney as agent, proxy, or attorney-in-fact[2]

2. NOW, WE COME TO THE ACTUAL SIGNING EVENT. You are, first, only to sign one of the documents—THE LIVING WILL. Now, with all the witnesses looking on, you should briefly inform the witnesses (and your would-be attorney-in-fact) that the document you have in front of you, about to sign, is your *Living Will*. (You may say something like: *"Gentlemen (ladies), this document in front of me which I am about to sign, is my Living Will and Medical Directive to Mr/Mrs _____ who I'm appointing to act as my agent for the Living Will. I have read these documents, and with sound mind and without pressure from anyone, I ask you to witness my signature, and to sign your own names after me as witnesses."*)

And with this statement, as the witnesses watch you, you initial and date each and <u>every</u> page of the Living Will document at the top left-hand margin, and then sign your name in full on the last pages of the document. Sign in colored ink. (This way, the original document could be distinguishable.) Fill in the date of the signing of each page at the last page. (Sign only ONE original copy, but retain an unsigned copy.)

---

[2]NOTE: In South Carolina, the witness cannot be a physician. And if you are a patient in a hospital, or nursing or health care institution or facility in any of the states listed below, you should consider **using** as one of your witnesses, a patient embudsman, a patient advocate, or the director of the medical facility: California, Delaware, District of Columbia, Georgia, Massachusetts, Michigan, Nebraska, New Hampshire, New Jersey, Ohio, Pennsylvania, Rhode Island, and South Dakota.

3. It will now be the turn of the witnesses, next, to sign. Ask each of the witnesses to read out loud the statement on the last page of the Living Will—the one just below your signature but above where the witnesses are supposed to sign, which says something about the witnesses not having any particular relationship to you. (Note that it is not necessary that the contents of the Living Will or the other documents be read or made known to the witnesses; in fact, it is advised against!).

   Then, as you watch each of the witnesses, they will take their turns to sign and enter their individual addresses in the spaces provided for them. They'll do this—that is, sign as witnesses—only on one of the documents—on the Living Will (sample on pp. 152-4). *The second document, the DURABLE POWER OF ATTORNEY, need not be signed by the witnesses.*

4. Finally, to complete the "execution" (the signing) phase, there's one more thing that needs to be done before you're done: getting the papers *notarized* by you and by your witnesses and your appointed agents. Here's what you do. Just after the official signing ceremony, you should have your witnesses, as well as your agent or attorney-in-fact (all of them), stop by a Notary Public's office with the documents. This could be done on the same day of the Living Will signing affair; or later—but not too much later.

   First, concerning the witnesses. In the presence of a Notary Public (you can generally find one located in most banks, real estate and lawyers' offices, corner drug stores, and the like), you yourself will first sign your name this time, to only one document—the *LIVING WILL DECLARATION*. Then each of your 3 witnesses will sign their names after you on the Living Will paper. And the Notary Public will then "notarize" (i.e., stamp and sign) the document as confirmation that you and the witnesses did appear and sign the document in his presence. Thereafter, you should get the Declaration form back. It's now done.

   And finally, it will now be the turn of the person you have picked to serve as your Attorney-in-fact (also called 'agent' or 'proxy' or 'decision maker', etc.) to sign something. The agent is only to sign just one document—the second part of the Power of Attorney document that is titled *"AFFIDAVIT OF AGENT AS TO POWER OF ATTORNEY BEING IN FULL FORCE"* (sample on p. 158). First of all, you yourself have to sign the first part of this document, the Power of Attorney part (p. 157), and notarize that part before the Notary Public. And thereafter, the designated agent or agents will sign just the AFFIDAVIT OF AGENT part (p. 158), and have his or her own signature on this affidavit notarized by the Notary Public.

   NOTE: The value of the *Affidavit of Agent*, if and when it is signed by the appointed agent or attorney-in-fact, is that it serves as the agent's own word and legal assurance to outsiders that he was, in fact, granted the power of attorney and that the document still remains in force as of the time the agent is using or presenting it for any official use.

5. Have the needed number of copies of the documents made. Retain in your own records the original of the Living Will (Form LT-32) and copies of the Power of Attorney (Form LT-33). Give the originals of the Durable Power of Attorney, plus a copy of the Living Will, to your appointed attorney-in-fact (agent or proxy). Put the two documents in a thick envelope and seal it up with extra glue, and write these words on it: "The Living Will of ___(your name)___, and Related Documents." Then put away the envelope.

   Consider giving signed copies of the two documents, if appropriate for you, to the following parties: your family members, your attending or regular family physician (have him place a copy in your medical records file), your priest or paistor, and the executor of your Will. If you are a resident of a nursing home, give a copy to your nursing home director.

When distributing copies, the location of the original (the copy that is signed in colored ink) should also be noted, for the reason that it is only the presentation of the intact <u>original</u> that, to most people, will confirm that the documents continue to be valid at the particular time.

NOTE: For the Living Will to remain valid, California requires that you re-sign it (you have to go through the whole signing and witnessing formalities over again) every 5 years, while Georgia requires that you do so every 7 years.

E. How To Revoke Your Living Will And/Or Durable Power Of Attorney

Occasions may well arise when you'll want to change your Living Will and/or revoke them. There are any number of circumstances which could conceivably warrant that, as it is not unusual to find, with the passage of time, that there are many changes occurring in one's conditions, attitudes and position. It is not uncommon to find, for example, that persons who are designated attorneys-in-fact or proxies may at some point not be available any more to serve, by reason of death, relocation, change of mind, etc. Furthermore, persons appointed to act as attorneys-in-fact in a Living Will or a Medical Power of Attorney situation, may, at times, have second thoughts about it and may request to be removed, and so on.

In any event, if for whatever reason you should want or need to change or revoke your Living Will or Financial/Medical Power of Attorney, there are specific procedures you must follow for it to be legal and valid. In the first place, you should know that a Living Will (or Power of Attorney) may be revoked at any time by the declarant or maker, without regard to his (her) mental state or competence. This may be done by any one of the following methods: by destruction of the document (the original), by written (notarized) revocation, and by verbal expression of revocation.

FORM LT-27

Copyright © 1994, Do-It-Yourself Legal Publishers, Newark, NJ 07102

The Last Will and Testament

of _____
[Name of the Will-Maker (the "Testator")]

Article I: Your Identity

I, _____ *[Your (the Will-maker's) full name.]*, also known by the name(s) of _____, resident of this address _____, in the City/town of _____, in the State of _____, which state I hereby declare to be my place of domicile, being of sound and disposing mind and memory, DO HEREBY MAKE, PUBLISH AND DECLARE this to be my Last Will and Testament, and revoke all Wills and codicils to wills that I previously made.

Article II: Marital Status

A. I am NOT currently married. *If was never previously married/I was previously married but legally divorced in this Court _____ in or about _____ 19___ .]*

OR:

B. I am currently married, and the name of my spouse is _____ .

A. I am NOT currently married. *[I was never previously married/I was previously married but legally divorced in this Court _____ in or about _____ 19___ .]*

Article III: Children

A. I have _____ child(ren) living whose names and dates of birth (or ages) are: _____

B. I have _____ deceased child(ren) whose name(s) is/are: _____ and the said deceased child(ren) has/have a total of _____ living child(ren) whose names are: _____

Article IV: Guardian

A. If at my death any of my children are minors, and a guardian is needed, then I nominate _____ to serve as a guardian of the person(s) of the said minor children, to see to the proper care, maintenance and upbringing of the said children until they shall attain the majority age. If _____ is unwilling or cannot for any reason serve as personal guardian herein, then I nominate _____ to serve as said personal guardian.

B. I direct that no bond be required of any guardian appointed by this will.

Article V: Distribution

A. In addition to any other property I may give, by this will or otherwise, to the person(s) listed in Article II & III, I give each person listed there One Dollar ($1.00).

B. If any person, or devisee, legatee, or beneficary under this Will, and/or under the Revocable Living Trust named _____ Trust, and created by me on the _____ day of _____, 19___, as amended, or any legal heir of mine, or any person claiming to be a legal heir of mine, shall in any manner either directly or indirectly attack the distribution of my estate, or oppose, contest or attempt to set aside any part of this Will or of the said Revocable Living Trust, then and in such event, any gifts to that person or persons provided for in this Will or the said Revocable Living Trust, is revoked and that person or persons shall take only the sum of One Dollar ($1.00).

*NOTE: A general rule in respect to a Pour-Over Will is that the trust creator must clearly name and identify the trust at issue, in which the will is intended to [...] our over."

Article VI: Residuary Estate

I give all the residue and remainder of my estate, of whatever kind or character, and wherever situated, to the then serving Trustee of the Revocable Living Trust, named _____ Trust, which is created by me and dated the _____ day of _____, 19___, prior to the execution of this Will, as the said trust may be amended from time to time, the said residue to be added to the principal of that trust and held, administered, and distributed in accordance with the terms, limitations, and conditions of the DECLARATION OF TRUST creating the Revocable Living Trust. If this gift to that trust is ineffective for any reason, then and only then do I give the residue of my estate to the Executor of this Will, to hold in trust, subject to the same terms, conditions and limitations set forth in the said Declaration of Trust creating the Revocable Living Trust, the terms of which Declaration I herewith specifically incorporate into this Will by reference.

Article VII: Executor

A. I nominate _____ to serve as the Executor [Executrix] of this Will; or, if _____ is unable or unwilling to serve or continue serving as Executor, then I nominate _____ to serve as Executor.

B. No bond shall be required of any Executor of this Will.

Article VIII: Common Disaster

If my spouse and I or any other persons named in this Will should die simultaneously, or under such circumstances as to render it difficult or impossible to determine who predeceased the other, I shall be conclusively presumed to have survived my spouse or such other persons named in the Will for purposes of this Will.

Article IX: Out of State Estate

If it becomes necessary at any time to appoint a representative of my estate in any state other than the state in which I reside on the date of my death, I nominate and appoint such person or persons as may be selected by my Executor in this Will to serve as such representative.

Article X: Funeral Instructions

I direct that my body be buried or disposed of as follows: _____

Article XI: Debts

I direct that the Executor (Executrix) herein named in this Will pay (as soon after my death as practical) all of my just debts and obligations, including funeral expenses and the expenses incident to my last illness, but excepting those long-term debts secured by real or personal property which may be assumed by the recipient heir(s).

Article XII: Severability

In the event that any separate provision of this Last Will and Testament is held to be invalid by a Court of competent jurisdiction, then such finding shall not invalidate this entire Will but shall affect only the specific subject provisions so found to be invalid.

IN WITNESS WHEREOF, I have hereunto signed this my *Last Will and Testament* this _____ day of _____, 19___ in the City of _____ State of _____.　　SIGNED: ✗ _____

Testator/Testatrix

ATTESTATION CLAUSE (BY WITNESSES)

We, whose names are hereinafter signed below, **Do Certify**, under the penalty of perjury under the laws of this State, that on the above entered date, the Testator (Testatrix) above named, subscribed to and signed the annexed Will in our presence and in the presence of each of us at the same time; that in our presence and to the hearing of all of us, the said Testator declared that the said document was his/her last Will and Testament, and requested us, and each of us to sign our names thereto as witnesses to the execution thereof; we declare that at the time when the said person signed this document, he/she appeared to be of sound mind and memory and under no constraint or force whatsoever.

WHEREUPON, in the presence of the testator and of each other, we here subscribe our names as witnesses on the day of the date of the said Will, and write opposite our names our respective places of residence:

1. Mr/Mrs ✗ _____ of _____

Type or print same name of witness   _city/state_

2. Mr/Mrs ✗ _____ of _____

Type or print same name of witness   _city/state_

3. Mr/Mrs ✗ _____ of _____

Type or print same name of witness   _city/state_

4. Mr/Mrs ✗ _____ of _____

Type or print same name of witness   _city/state_

SAMPLE SHEET

PLEASE NOTE, Important: This LAST WILL AND TESTAMENT is a "Witnessed" Will, which means that it will not be valid unless it is properly signed by the required number of "disinterested" witnesses. For best results, you should use _no less than_ 3 adult witnesses; do not use relatives or persons who will receive property under the Will. See p. 41-2 for more on the proper signing & witnessing procedures for a Will.

Form LT-28
(Addendum to Last Will and Testament)

Copyright © 1994, Do-It-Yourself Legal Publishers, Newark, NJ 07102

Affidavit of Subscribing or Attesting Witnesses To Will

THE WILL OF MR/MRS/MS: _____, Testator.
(name of the Willmaker)

STATE OF _____)
) ss.:
COUNTY OF _____)

ON THIS DATE, the _____ day of _____, 19____, personally appeared before me, a Notary Public in and for the above captioned County and State, the undersigned persons.

WHEREUPON, the said persons, individually and severally signed and appended their respective names and addresses below, and while being severally sworn, stated under oath, that they witnessed the execution of the WILL of Mr/Mrs/Ms: _____ the within named Testator(trix), on _____ 19____; that the Testator(trix), in their presence, signed the Will at the end, and that at the time of his/her signing, he/she declared the instrument to be the Testator(trix)'s Last Will and Testament; that at the request of the Testator(trix) and in the Testator(trix)'s sight and presence, and in the sight and presence of each other, the said persons witnessed the execution of the Will by the Testator(trix) by signing their own names as witnesses to it; and that the Testator(trix) at the time of the execution of the Will, appeared to them to be of full age and sound mind and memory and was in all respects competent to make a will and was not under any restraint or duress.

The subscribing witnesses further state that this Affidavit was executed at the request of Mr/Mrs/Ms: _____ the Testator(trix) who made the Will and that at the time of the execution of this Affidavit, the original Will, above described, was exhibited to them and that they identified it as the said Will by appending their own signatures on it as subscribing witnesses.

Signatures, Names, & Addresses Of Witnesses:

1. Signature **X** _____
   Print Name _____
   Address _____

2. Signature **X** _____
   Print Name _____
   Address _____

3. Signature **X** _____
   Print Name _____
   Address _____

Severally subscribed and sworn
to before me on _____ 19____

_____
Notary Public

Form LT-32

Copyright © 1994, by Do-It-Yourself Legal Publishers, Newark, NJ 07102

The Living Will Declaration

OF

[The Publisher's General Purpose Form]

To my family, Doctors, Authorized Agents, and all those concerned with my health care:

I, _____, resident at _____, being of sound mind, willfully and voluntarily declare my desire that my life not be artificially prolonged under the circumstances set forth below, and, pursuant to all applicable laws, both statutory and common, in the state listed below or wherein I may become incapacitated, I declare that:

1. If at any time I shall have been diagnosed as being in a persistent vegetative state or should have an incurable injury, disease, or illness which causes me severe distress, and/or unconsciousness and has been certified to be a terminal condition by two (2) physicians who have both personally examined me, one of whom is my attending physician, and the physicians have determined that there can be no recovery from such condition and that death will occur therefrom without the administration of life-sustaining procedures, and if in the professional opinion of the said two physicians, the application of life-sustaining procedures would serve only to artificially prolong the dying process, then in that event I direct that such procedures or treatment be withheld or withdrawn and that I be permitted to die naturally with only the administration of medication, food or fluid or the performance of medical procedures deemed necessary to provide me with comfort or to alleviate pain.

In short, if I should, at any time be in an incurable or irreversible mental or physical condition and my physicians have, upon examination, duly certified that in their professional opinion there is no reasonable expectation of my recovery therefrom, or of regaining consciousness and meaningful state of health, I direct my attending physician(s) to withhold or withdraw treatment that merely prolongs my dying, and direct that treatment be limited only to measures to keep me comfortable and to relieve pain.

2. If I should become unable to give directions regarding my treatment or the use of life sustaining procedures in the above situations, it is my wish and expectation that my family, doctors, or my designated agent, if any, and any court of law, shall honor and be morally and legally bound by this Declaration, EXCEPT that all such persons and their actions shall always be guided in such an instance by the directives contained in the 3-page document executed by me and titled *"THE MEDICAL DIRECTIVE,"* which is annexed hereto [if any].

3. If I should become physically or mentally unable to communicate my instructions as stated in this Declaration, I designate and authorize the following person or persons, namely, Mr./Mrs. _____ to act in my behalf as my primary proxy. The said person or persons are also named in a separate written instrument titled DURABLE FINANCIAL & MEDICAL POWER OF ATTORNEY, and are to act in my behalf as my agent or attorney-in-fact thereof in accordance with the provisions therein, and of the Medical Directive.

4. No person or entity, whether designated in this Declaration or otherwise, or the attending physician, health care institution, or licensed health care profession, shall incur any legal or moral liabilities of any nature whatsoever for following or carrying out in good faith my directions in this Declaration.

5. If I am diagnosed, however, as pregnant, this Declaration shall have no force and effect or be inoperative during the course of my pregnancy.

6. This Declaration may be revoked by me, the Declarant, at any time, without regard to my physical or mental condition by: (a) being defaced, torn, obliterated, or otherwise destroyed by me or by someone else in my presence and at my direction; (b) either a written revocation signed and dated by me, or by verbal revocation by me duly communicated to the attending physician by me, expressing my intent to revoke the declaration.

In **Witness Whereof**, I, the undersigned Declarant, do hereby make and sign this Living Will Declaration consisting of _____ typewritten (or handwritten) pages, on the date hereinafter entered, and declare that I do so with a full and competent understanding as to its meaning, consequence, and impact, and that I am of sound mind and legal age and under no constraint or undue influence whatsoever.

DATED: _____

SIGNED: ✗ _____

(Declarant, or person signing for him/her, if applicable)

AT: _____

(Town/City) (State)

NAME (print): _____

Statement By The Witnesses (To The Living Will)

We, the witnesses whose names are signed below, do hereby declare that on _____ 19____ and in the presence of all of us, the above-named Declarant did sign the foregoing instrument designated as his/her LIVING WILL DECLARATION, and that thereupon, at the said Declarant's request, and in his (her) presence, and in each other's presence, we signed our names below as witnesses, and further declare, individually and severally under the penalty of perjury, that, to the best of our knowledge, the following are true:

1. The Declarant is personally known to us and we believe the Declarant to be at least 18 years of age and of sound mind.

2. Each of us is at least 18 years of age.

3. To the best of our knowledge, at the time of the execution of this of this Living Will Declaration, anyone of us:

   a) is not related to the Declarant by blood or marriage;

   b) would not be entitled to any portion of the Declarant's estate by any Will or by operation of law under the rules of descent and distribution of this state;

   c) is not the attending physician of the Declarant or an employer of the attending physician or an employee of the hospital or skilled nursing facility in which the Declarant is a patient;

   d) is not directly financially responsible for the Declarant's medical care; and

   e) has no present claim against any portion of the estate of the Declarant.

4. We all witnessed the execution of the within Living Will Declaration by the within named Declarant (or the signer for an oral declarant).

5. The said Declarant subscribed to and signed the said LIVING WILL DECLARATION and declared it to be his/her Living Will in our presence.

6. We thereafter subscribed to and signed the said document as witnesses, in the presence of the said Declarant, and in the presence of each other and at the request of the said Declarant.

7. We make this affidavit at the request of the said Declarant, _____ *(Declarant's name)*.

8. The Declarant fully appeared to us to have signed the said instrument freely and under no apparent constraint or undue influence, and was fully aware of the meaning and import of the action.

Witnesses sign here indicating their residency:

✗ _____ residing at _____ (Town or City/State)

✗ _____ residing at _____ (Town or City/State)

✗ _____ residing at _____ (Town or City/State)

[Witnesses (and party signing for oral declarant, if applicable) shall also sign as follows in the form of an affidavit before a Notary Public]

STATE OF _____)
) ss.
COUNTY OF _____)

Then and there personally appeared before me, a duly authorized notary public in and for the county and state above captioned, the within named persons, now listed as follows:

[name of first witness]   [second witness]   [third witness]

and *[the declarant or signer of Oral Declaration for Declarant, if any.]* _____ who being duly sworn, individually depose, attest and acknowledge:

That, in the presence of all the witnesses, the Declarant did sign the above Living Will Declaration; that at the Declarant's request, and in the presence of the Declarant and of each other, each of the witnesses signed as witnesses; that, to the best of their knowledge, the Declarant did sign the said Living Will Declaration freely, under no constraint or undue influence, and was of sound mind and memory and legal age, and fully aware of the meaning and import of this action; and that this affidavit is made by the witnesses at the direction of and in the presence of the Declarant.

SUBSCRIBED AND SWORN TO BEFORE ME
this _____ day of _____ 19 _____

Seal

_____
(Notary Public)

_____
(Notary Public)

(If this Declaration is signed in a nursing home or other extended care facility, the additional witness designated below should sign below as well.)

I hereby witness this Living Will and attest that I believe the Declarant to be of sound mind and to have made this Living Will Declaration willingly and voluntarily.

Witness ✗ _____
                                                    *

_____
*Medical director of skilled nursing facility or staff physician not participating in care of the patient, or chief of the health-care facility.

Form LT-33   Copyright © 1994, by Do-It-Yourself Legal Publishers, Newark, NJ 07102

Durable Financial & Medical Power of Attorney

Know all Men by these Presents,

That I, _____, as the principal, residing at _____, do hereby designate and appoint Mr/Mrs/Ms: _____, presently at this address _____ as my true and lawful Agent and Attorney-in-Fact, for the purpose of making financial decisions, and/or medical and health care decisions on my behalf if, DURING and owing to a condition resulting from illness or injury, I am deemed by my attending physician(s) to be incapable to make such decisions or to be incapable to competently or knowingly authorize or approve such decisions by reason of a physical or mental disability, incompetence or incapacitation.

Pursuant to this, I HEREBY authorize my above-named Attorney-in-Fact as follows, on the following two-part matters:

A. FinancialAffairs Decisions

(1) To enter upon and take possession of any lands, tenements and hereditaments that may belong to me, or to the possession of which I may be entitled;

(2) To ask for, collect and receive any rents, profits, issues or income of any and all of such lands, tenements and hereditaments, or of any part or parts thereof;

(3) To pay any and all taxes, charges and assessments that may be levied, assessed or imposed upon any of my lands, buildings, tenements or other structures;

(4) To make, execute and deliver any deed, mortgage or lease, whether with or without covenants and warranties, in respect of any such lands, tenements and hereditaments, or of any part or parts thereof, and to manage, repair, rebuild or reconstruct any buildings, houses or other structures or any part or parts thereof, that may now or hereafter be owned by me or be erected upon any such lands;

(5) To extend, renew, replace or increase any mortgage(s) now or hereafter affecting any of my lands, tenements and hereditaments and/or any personal property belonging to me, and, for any such purposes, to sign, seal, acknowledge and deliver any bond or bonds, or to make, sign and deliver any note or notes, or any extension, renewal, consolidation or apportionment agreement or agreements or any other instrument, whether sealed or unsealed, that may be useful or necessary to accomplish any of the foregoing purposes;

(6) To obtain insurance (and other similar instruments) of any kind, nature or description whatsoever, on any of my lands, tenements and hereditaments and/or in connection with the management, use or occupation thereof and/or on any personal property belonging to me and/or in respect to the rents, issues and profits arising therefrom, and to make, execute receipts, releases or other discharges therefor.

(7) To demand, sue for, collect, recover and receive all goods, claims, debts, monies, interests and demands whatsoever now due, or that may hereafter be due or belong to me (including the rights to institute any action, suit or legal proceedings for the recovery of any land, buildings, tenements or other structures, or any parts thereof, to the possession whereof I may be entitled) and to make and execute receipts, releases or other discharges therefor, for them.

(8) To make, execute, endorse, accept, collect and deliver any or all bills of exchange, checks, drafts, notes and trade acceptances;

*For any clause(s) or provision(s) not desired, completely delete same, but adequately initial them.

(9) To pay all sums of money that may hereafter be owing by me on any bill of exchange, check, draft, note or trade acceptance, made, or executed by me or for me, and in my name, by my said attorney;

(10) To make gifts, which shall in no event be more than $10,000, to each person per year ($20,000 to each marital couple, if applicable), to my lawful children (and spouse), if I have previously been in the pattern of making such gifts, and/or if at the good faith discretion of the attorney-in-fact such gifts are warranted for estate planning or other purposes and are affordable by my estate.

(11) To sell, mortgage or hypothecate any and all shares of stock, bonds or other securities now or hereafter belonging to me; and to make, execute and deliver assignments of any such shares of stock, bonds or other securities, either absolutely or as collateral security;

(12) To defend, settle, adjust, compound, submit to arbitration and compromise all actions, suits, accounts, reckonings, claims and demands whatsoever, that now are, or hereafter shall be pending between me and any person or entity in such a manner as my said attorney shall think fit;

(13) To file any proof of claim or of debt or take any other proceedings, under the Bankruptcy act, or under any law of demand, and to represent me in all respects in any such proceeding or proceedings, and to demand, receive and accept any dividend or dividends, or distribution or distributions that may be or become payable thereunder.

(14) To hire accountants, financial professionals, real estate agents, attorneys at law, clerks, workmen and others, and to remove them, and appoint others in their place, and to pay and allow to such persons who may be so employed such salaries, wages or other renumerations, as my said attorney shall think fit.

(15) To constitute and appoint, in his place and stead, and as his substitute, one or more attorney-in-fact, for me, with full power of revocation; and

(16) _____

(describe here any other or additional authority you wish not previously mentioned above)

B. Medical Care Decisions

(17) To consent, refuse to consent, withdraw consent, to any care, treatment, service, or procedure to maintain, diagnose, or treat my physical or mental condition.

(18) To inspect and disclose any information relating to my physical and mental health or condition.

(19) To sign documents, waivers, and releases, including documents, titled or purporting to be a "Refusal to Permit Treatment" and "Leaving the Hospital or Refusing Treatment Against Medical Advice," and to execute any waiver or release from liability required by a hospital, medical institution or physician.

(20) In general, to act in accordance with and in conformity to the directives in the 3-page document* titled "THE MEDICAL DIRECTIVE," which is executed by me and annexed hereto. The agent's decisions shall be overriden by my wishes in the DIRECTIVE wherever there is or appears to be a conflict in our positions.

(21) I DECLARE that this Power of Attorney in its entirety, and its validity or operation thereof, shall not be affected by my subsequent disability, incompetence or incapacity as recognized under the applicable state laws, and that the authority granted herein shall continue and remain in full force and effect in the event that I become, and during any period while I am disabled, incompetent or incapacitated, unless sooner revoked or terminated by me in writing.

(22) The foregoing power and authority granted herein are herewith granted without, in any way, limiting the said appointed Agent, generally to do, execute and perform any other act, deed, matter or thing whatsoever, that ought to be done, executed and performed, or that, in the opinion of my said agent or attorney-in-fact, ought to be done, executed or performed, in and about my premises, financial affairs,

*This provision assumes that the maker has also made a separate Medical Directive with far more specific details.

medical treatment, or health care, of every nature and kind whatsoever consistent with my directives, as fully effectual as I could do if personally present.

(23) And I do hereby ratify and confirm all things whatsoever that my said attorney-in-fact or his substitute or substitutes, shall do, or cause to be done, in or about the premises, and my affairs, by virtue of this power of attorney.

(24) This instrument may not be changed orally.

(25) If the first person I named above is unavailable to act as the agent or attorney-in-fact in my behalf, I hereby authorize the following person(s) _____

_____
(Name)

_____
(Address)

as the substitute agent(s) or attorney-in fact with the same powers, authority and responsibilities.

In Witness Whereof, I have hereunto set my hand and seal the _____ day of _____ 19____ .

SIGNED:: ✗ _____

Acknowledgment

STATE OF _____)
) ss.:
COUNTY OF _____)

On the _____ day of _____ 19____ before me, a duly authorized Notary Public by and for the above-designated state and county, personally came Mr/Mrs _____ to me known or made known to me to be the individual described in the foregoing POWER OF ATTORNEY, and who, upon first being duly sworn, executed the said POWER OF ATTORNEY, and thereupon acknowledged to me under oath that __he executed the same in all good faith

_____
(Notary Public)

Affidavit Of Agent As To Power Of Attorney Being In Full Force

(Attach to the Power of Attorney)

STATE OF _____)
COUNTY OF _____) ss.:

Mr/Mrs/Ms *(agent enters his/her name)*, being duly sworn, deposes and says under the penalty of perjury:

THAT *(your names is entered here)*, as principal, who resides at _____ *(your address)*, did, in writing, on the date of *(date when the Power of Attorney was signed)*, appoint me as his true and lawful Agent and Attorney-in-fact, and that annexed hereto, and hereby made a part thereof, is a true copy of the said Power Of Attorney;

THAT, as agent and attorney-in-fact of the said principal, and under and by virtue of the said power of attorney, I have this day executed the following described instrument(s):

(Enter any papers or documents you might be signing or presenting here in furtherance of your function as agent in this capacity)

THAT I hereby represent that the said principal is now alive; that at the time of the granting of this instrument ____ he is of sound mind; that ____ he has not, at any time, revoked or repudiated the said power or attorney; and that the said power of attorney is in current and full force and effect as of this time and date.

THAT I make this affidavit for the purpose of inducing any party, person, or entity in interest, to accept delivery of any such described instrument, as executed by me in my capacity as attorney-in-fact of the said principal, with the full knowledge that in accepting the execution and delivery of the aforesaid instrument, and/or in paying a good and valuable consideration therefor, the said party or entity herein being induced will rely upon this affidavit.

SIGNED: _____
(Attorney-in-Fact/Agent)

SWORN TO BEFORE ME
this ____ day of ____ 19 ____

_____
(Notary Public)

NOTE: This AFFIDAVIT part is to be filled in and notarized by the person appointed to act for you as your Attorney-in-Fact (agent), and not by you, the Principal.

Chapter 10

THE SETTLING OF YOUR TRUST ESTATE: HERE'S HOW YOU MUST ORGANIZE YOUR ESTATE NOW, OR YOUR TRUSTEE STILL WON'T BE SPARED THE AGONY OF PROBATE LATER

A. Having The Living Trust Is Not Enough; To Complete The Circle, You Must Now Organize Your Estate Also

Okay. So you've completed the essentials that assure that your estate will be settled with little or no probate: you've created your all-important revocable Living Trust, and properly transferred the trust property to the trust's name (the subject matter of the preceding Chapter 7)! And, probably, you have also drafted a few other estate planning tools that are necessary to assure extra legal protection, such as a Will, Living Will, and the like (the subject matter of the preceding Chapter 9). But, is that sufficient? Is that all you need to do—or should or can do—to assure that your estate will definitely avoid probate, or that your family or loved ones will surely be spared that "agony of probate" you seek to achieve in the settling of your estate upon death?

Emphatically NO, say many respected experts of estate planning who are vastly knowledgeable and experienced in the practical, day-to-day nitty gritty tasks of estate settlement. Not at all! According to experts, having a good living trust is certainly a very crucial piece of the essential structure for assuring the avoidance of the agony of probate for one's estate. But, nevertheless, it's only <u>one</u> element among <u>two</u> essential elements, each of which, experts emphasize, is just as crucial as the other in attaining the ultimate objective of probate agony avoidance in the settling of your estate. And that other essential element is this: GETTING YOUR ESTATE ORGANIZED; HAVING AN ORGANIZED ESTATE.

In deed, experts contend, so crucial is this second element that *without it—i.e., without a properly organized estate to go with the trust—all the efforts put into the establishment of the Living Trust shall have been disastrously negated and wasted, in that your heirs and loved ones shall still not have been completely spared the pains, agony and expense of probate in the settling of your estate, as had been intended.*

One expert, Henry W. Abts III, a hands-on professional estate planner who has created well over 2,000 Living Trusts in a lifetime of practical estate planning, sharply summed up the case this way:[1]

"There are two crucial, and equally important, elements in settling an estate: having a Living Trust and having an organized estate. The Living Trust avoids the agonizing probate process and unnecessary estate taxes; an organized estate facilitates a quick settlement and identifies what assets exist and where they are located.

For most people, the biggest problem involved in settling an estate of a loved one is just being able to find all of the pieces. Even spouses do not always keep track of what the other spouse is accumulating. For example, many widows do not really know all of the stocks and bonds their husbands have purchased or all the pension benefits their husbands have earned over many years...

Losing a loved one—especially a spouse—is a traumatic experience. People in mourning can think only of the loss and not of the many details that must be resolved to settle the estate...How large is the estate, and

[1] Abts, pp. 149 & 151.

In sum, the point, simply, is that a well organized estate, with all the necessary documents and information properly assembled in one (or a few) place(s) and orderly organized, is an essential and integral element of the living trust and a good and complete estate plan, without which the trust cannot really yield you the full benefits. Aside from having a good living trust, the next best thing you can do for your heirs—and, even more especially, the best thing you can do for your trustee or estate executor in terms of making the task easy for him—is to have a well organized estate.

To put it still another way, if you want to truly reap the full benefits of all the efforts you put into establishing the Living Trust, you had better taken one further additional step: YOU MUST PROPERLY ORGANIZE YOUR ESTATE!

Hence, in this chapter, the focus will be on the issue of how to get your estate organized, and how your trustee can use your organized estate plan to orderly and smoothly settle your estate—without the pain or agony of probate.

B. Use Of The Estate Information Organizer Worksheet & The Final Operational Instructions For Settling The Estate

Basically, for our purposes in this guidebook, there are two tools you need to use for the organizing of your estate:

    i) Form LT-101, The *Estate Information Organizer Worksheet* (which is on pp. 55-62); and
    ii) Form LT-102, *The Final Operational Instructions To The Trustee For Settling The Estate* (which is on pp. 163-9).

Both of these forms, exclusively developed by the author, are especially designed so that you can more easily use the information on the forms for systematically gathering, coordinating, and orderly organizing your estate at one and the same time that you do your estate planning and make your estate plans. The central objective is to provide one place where to put and to assemble all the essential information, documentations, and records you'd need both for your estate planning and trust-making work, and for your successor trustee to use in the settling of the estate.

Thus, if fully completed by you, the *Estate Information Organizer Worksheet*, which you shall have already come across (and assembled) when you prepared your trust document (see Chapter 6), shall have enabled you to make an orderly and complete gathering of your vital affairs—assets, liabilities, records, personal data, beneficiaries, advisors, etc—in one data sheet. And, if made available for the benefit of the successor trustee, as it is most likely to be, the Worksheet will also give him (her) the advantage of having the information all assembled in one spot for his ready use.[2]

On the other hand, the second form, *The Final Operational Instructions To The Successor Trustee,*" if and when fully completed by you (by the trust grantor), can be systematically followed by your successor trustee (or by the trustee, as the case may be), and easily take him or her step-by-step through the estate settling process.

where are the assets? Where is the deed to the house? Where are the checking and savings accounts and certificates of deposit? (The banks love to retain unclaimed accounts.) Who was your last stockbroker, and where are all those U.S. Government savings bonds? [And so on and on].

People "know" where their important papers are—until they go to retrieve them. I have watched both spouses, even in the most organized families, search high and low for missing documents. Imagine [then what would be] the dilemma if one spouse were removed. Similarly, trying to step in and assemble the estate of a single person is a nightmare...

Without organization, you have a nightmare; however, with organization, you create an orderly process for your surviving spouse, children, or other heirs. The orderly process allows the survivors to quickly identify your assets, legal documents, and distribution desires and then to settle your affairs—and then get back to living their own lives...[You do] not have to leave a jumble of jigsaw pieces as your legacy to your family..."

[2]It is, of course, entirely possible that with some this Worksheet may be completed only later in the estate planning and trust-making process and mainly for the purpose of helping the successor trustee in his estate settling tasks. However, as has been advised in several sections elsewhere in this manual (see, for example, Chapters 6 & 7), it is even far more advantageous—and highly advisable—that you do it right at the start of your estate planning or living trust drafting work. This way, you get to reap the benefits in two, and not just one way: as an aid in and in helping you think up and work through the serious decisions involved in your trust-making, as well as serving as an aid in helping your designated successor trustee to more easily settle your estate upon your death.

Hence, it cannot be emphasized enough: HERE'S WHAT YOU DO: *Take the time and the trouble to actually complete these two forms*—*The Information Organizer Worksheet* (p. 52), most preferably even BEFORE you shall have first prepared your trust papers; and *The Final Operational Instructions For Settling The Estate* (pp. 163-9). Fill in every bit of the two forms. [And, as you go about the process of doing so, it is advisable that you make it a point always to re-read sections of the manual that may apply to each issue or consideration in question, especially where you are not immediately certain on the law or the procedures.]

C. General Instructions On Completing The Two Forms

Here are a few helpful general instructions you should observe in completing the ESTATE INFORMATION ORGANIZER WORKSHEET & THE FINAL OPERATIONAL INSTRUCTIONS.

1. Print or type in the information legibly—so that it can be clearly read. However, considering that you'll probably have to be changing the entries from time to time to allow for changes in your life or circumstances, it's probably better to simply use a pencil to "pencil in" the entries.

2. Use back of the page, or add additional sheets of paper for continuation whenever you need more space to complete the information required.

3. Clearly make clear your marital status on the forms, and complete the appropriate sections that are appropriate for your status.

4. Make absolutely certain (check and compare the contents of the three documents), that the entries you make in the Worksheet and the Final Instructions (e.g., about the persons you name as beneficiaries, special gifts for individuals) conform <u>exactly</u> to your provisions in your trust instrument.

5. Bear this in mind: these two forms (Forms LT-101 and LT-102) are a "workbook"—i.e., they are something you should be working with on a continuous basis, adding to and deleting from, and changing and revising, constantly. Hence, you should keep them readily accessible and handy at all times; keep them in your bookshelf or a drawer, for example, and not put them away at a distinct safe-deposit box that is remote or inaccessible. AND REMEMBER (this is very important) TO KEEP YOUR TRUSTEE(S), INCLUDING ANY NEW ONES YOU MAY APPOINT, ALWAYS INFORMED ABOUT THE EXACT LOCATION OF THESE CRUCIAL PIECES OF YOUR ESTATE PLAN RECORDS!!

6. FINALLY: Take all the time you'd need to actually complete these two forms, and don't rush it. Don't skip around. But do it, though!

D. "The Estate Records Book" Binder

NEXT, IS THE ORGANIZING AND STORING OF THE PHYSICAL RECORDS AND DOCUMENTS. Here's what you do. Get a moderate sized, loose-leaf binder (or a file cabinet or drawer) with dividers. Designate this binder by a name, say *"The Estate Records Book."* Now, carefully label the dividers to designate under each label or folder a separate subject matter and subheading listed in (keyed or tied into) the *Estate Information Organizer Worksheet*—e.g., "Family Information," "Special Medical Care Needs," "Business Interests & Agreements," "Records," "Estate Plan Documents—Trusts, Wills, Durable Power of Attorney, Living Will, Etc.," "Cash or Equivalent Funds," "Investments," "Loans," "Trustees & Successor Trustee," "Advisors & Trust Team," "Beneficiaries," "The Estate Information Organizer Worksheet," "The Final Operational Instruction For Settling The Estate," etc.

Make photocopies of each of the documents and records relating to your affairs. Then, selectively assemble and segregate and place the photocopies of your documents and records (just the photocopies) under the proper subheadings or labels. (With respect to the originals of the documents and records, put these away separately, preferably in a more secure but separate location away from the home, such as in a safe deposit box).[3]

---

[3]Laws vary from state to state on this, but many states allow the surviving spouse (or executor or a will) access to the box promptly upon a spouse's death. However, a good practice would be to verify your state's policy in advance. It's simple to do: simply ask your bank (a responsible officer) whether the box will have to be "sealed" upon one's ₁th.

THE ESTATE RECORDS BOOK

BOOK

For: John & Mary Doe

Form LT-102   Copyright © 1994, by Do-It-Yourself Legal Publishers, Newark, NJ 07102

The Final Operational Instructions To The Trustee Or Successor Trustee For Settling The Estate

To The Trustee/Successor Trustee: These are the more immediate information you would need, and the more immediate steps that may need to be taken, following my death or the death of my spouse, for purposes of orderly settlement of the estate and to facilitate the process.

IMPORTANT: The thick folder or binder [or file cabinet or drawer] containing all my important back-up personal and family records and documents for use in settling the estate, is located at: _____

"THE ESTATE RECORDS BOOK." This binder (folder, file cabinet, drawer) labelled: _____. Look for a binder (folder, file cabinet, drawer) contains only the photocopies (no originals) of the records and documents. The complete duplicate originals of these records and documents are kept with and located at _____.

(✔) Telephone	Name & Addresses	Phone
Check, if accomplished		

_____ Notify Family Doctor

_____ Notify Clergy

_____ Notify Hospital for Anatomical Gifts (if applicable)

_____ Notify Funeral Home

_____ Place & Manner of Interment

_____ Get data for completing Death Certificate from Section A of Estate Information Organizer Worksheet

_____ Make Funeral Arrangements

_____ If a veteran, take Military Papers to funeral home*

_____ Order 12 Death Certificates through funeral home

_____ Special Funeral/Burial instruction (type of service, cremation, special people to contact)

_____ I (we) have a cemetery lot, located at: _____

Cemetery name   City   State

_____ Prepare and deliver notice to newspaper (include date, time and place of funeral)

_____ Promptly notify these relatives & friends (see names listed herein, or on the attached list).

_____ Notify Successor Trustee

_____ Notify Executor of Will & Estate Representative

_____ Notify Insurance Agent and Trustee (if you have Insurance Trust)

*NOTE: The Veterans Administration will provide $150 towards funeral expense and headstone marker and an American Flag, if desired

The Final Operational Instructions To The Trustee (cont'd)

Name & Addresses   Phone

_____ Advise Social Security (if receiving or eligible for benefits)

_____ Notify Employer's Personnel Department

_____ For immediate cash for settling the funeral and
other immediate expenses, confirm with the banks
amount of available funds in checking accounts).*

_____ Check in each safe deposit box for original
documents and special instructions or messages
grantor(s) may have left

      _____ Location of key(s)

      _____ Individuals authorized to open box

_____ Notify these personal advisors

_____ Meet with my family advisor promptly to:
review funeral arrangements, trust instrument and instructions

NOTE: Another executed copy of my Trust (and Wills) is located at (with) _____

IMPORTANT: Keep an accurate record of last medical and funeral costs, collect any bills and start a ledger of
all bills paid and income received.

_____ Review the entire ESTATE RECORDS BOOK,
as well as the ESTATE INFORMATION ORGANIZER WORKSHEET,
a copy of which should be in this Records Book folder, for
information on every piece of personal data you may need.

SPECIAL INSTRUCTIONS

If the decedent was living alone:

      _____ Remove important documents and valuables to a safe location

      _____ Notify utility companies and landlord

      _____ Advise post office where to send mail

Other(s): I Designate these other special personal instructions to be carried out upon my (my spouse's) death:

TO THE TRUSTEE/
SUCCESSOR TRUSTEE: I systematically follow the "TRUSTEE'S" CHECKLIST OF DUTIES" on the
following pages (pp. xxx) below, to complete the rest of your estate settling
responsibilities under your appointment as a trustee or successor trustee of
my (our) Living Trust.

*NOTE that, for simplicity, it's a good practice for you to keep your checking account (or at least one such account) outside the living trust but in joint tenancy with your
spouse or one of your designated successor trustees. This gives the person (your spouse or successor trustee) easy, rapid access to funds that may be immediately needed
upon your death for urgent expense and funeral arrangements.

The Final Operational Instructions To The Trustee (cont'd)

Trustee's Checklist Of Duties

FROM: The Grantor

TO: The Trustee/Successor Trustee: For simplicity, to complete the balance of your responsibilities and duties under your appointment as Trustee or Successor Trustee of my (our) Living Trust, simply follow the following CHECKLIST step-by-step and systematically:

A. ASSEMBLING THE ASSETS

1. _____ Determine, from your review of the Trust provisions: Are any of the deceased spouse's or party's assets to be immediately distributed, rather than remaining in trust for the benefit of the surviving spouse? (If so, see "Distribution" below).

2. _____ Review the following to determine the size and extent of the Estate: **i)** the Declaration of Trust document and the Trust Schedule of Assets; more specifically, the sections on such matters as "Trust Property or Assets," and "Allocations and Distributions to Beneficiaries," and **ii)** the "Assets" part of the Financial Information" Section of the *Estate Information Organizer Worksheet*. (Is the estate's net worth reasonably current, and is the estate of the size to make it subject to Federal Estate or Inheritance taxes? If so, see part B below, for filing of estate tax returns and payment of the taxes.)

3. _____ Check the assets and determine that all assets are within the Trust, and, if not, which assets are outside the Trust and must therefore be probated. (If the value of all assets OUTSIDE the trust exceeds the value set by the state for probate, the assets outside the trust must go through probate.)

NOTE: If any assets are held in other "probate avoidance" forms (e.g., under jointly held property or assets, U.S. bonds, life insurance, pension funds & death benefits, pay-on-death bank accounts, etc., they need not be probated.

4. _____ Notify each of the Life Insurance Companies (if any is applicable)—File claims for life insurance benefits for which the trust is the beneficiary (basically, obtain Form 712 from each insurance company). Include certified copy of Death Certificate and a photocopy of the face page of the policies from Trust files.

5. _____ File claim for any pension or profit sharing benefits from the employer (if applicable), and for any other work-related benefits payable to the trust.

6. _____ File Notice of Fiduciary Relationship (IRS Form 56), with the IRS. (If the trust does not have a tax identification number, file IRS Form SS-4 to get one).

7. _____ Write to the appropriate banks (with copies of the trust document and Death Certificate attached) for information as to the balances of any bank accounts as of the date of death, and to allow withdrawals for immediate cash needs.

The Final Operational Instructions To The Trustee (cont'd)

8. _____ Obtain, as of the date of death of a grantor, written valuation and appraisal of each real and personal asset owned by the trust. [Note: this is one of the most important functions that must be completed upon a trust grantor's death, as this is necessary in order to establish, in writing, a new cost basis (evaluation) of all trust assets as of the date of a grantor's death as a basis for substantiating a new "stepped-up" cost basis of the assets to the IRS when you eventually sell the property).*

To obtain the current market value of a real estate, simply call up three different real estate brokers (or agents) from separate firms in the area and tell them you'd wish to sell your property; then request from each, written estimates of the value for which you could sell your property. Select the two evaluations from them that are closer to each other and take an average of the two estimates.

To obtain the current market value of any stocks and bonds in the trust, simply look up price quotations in the newspapers on or near the date of the death. Then, put the newspaper pages(the whole page with the date thereof intact) bearing the stock quotation in your estate settlement file. Alternatively, any broker can readily give you the actual stock or bond prices as of the date of the death, and in writing, if requested.

9. _____ Review the business agreement (if applicable) for action, disposition and benefits. (See "Business Interests and Agreements" section of the Information Organizer Worksheet.) Determine: are there any partnerships, buy-sell agreements, stock-redemption agreements, and the like? Is there a business or an interest in a business that is of substantial value? If there is, then be aware of this: such businesses must be valued very skillfully and wisely. Otherwise, the IRS will come up with an outrageously high valuation for the business (The IRS is said to have a many as 14 different methods by which it could compute a corporate evaluation). So, to cut what would otherwise be a long story short, the suggestion is that you simply do this: hire a certified public accounting firm and have it value the business and ask them to look at the various available options to freeze or establish the value of the business.

10. _____ Review credit cards issued to the deceased individual (if applicable)—determine if they should be changed or cancelled and destroyed (See Liabilities in the "Financial Information" section of the Estate Information Organizer Worksheet for a list of the cards, if applicable). Definitely destroy these any issued only in the deceased's name or for business use only.

11. _____ Analyze and review trust assets and investments (real estate securities, etc) with emphasis on preserving trust assets, if consistent with trust provisions, and to see if they meet the objectives of income. Determine if some assets should be reinvested to provide adequate income as well as appropriate growth for hedge against inflation. Review assets at least annually to determine if assets should be reinvested for best balance between growth and income and if assets should be shifted among A, B and/or C trusts, if applicable, to preserve anticipated appreciation. Or if, on the other hand, in the context of the deceased person's death the types of investment in the estate have ceased to make sense or to correspond to the needs of the survivors or the beneficiaries.

12. _____ Identify which assets are to be placed in the A Trust, and which ones in the B trust (if applicable). [See "Distributions" section below.]

13. _____ Obtain last three years of fiduciary income-tax returns and last three years of canceled checks of the trust (if any).

14. _____ Review all accountings and distributions that have taken place for the last five years (or since the trust was established, if these records apply or are available).

---

*A "stepped-up" cost basis for an asset enables you to keep the value of the asset at the same amount, thus minimizing the taxable gain attributed to the assets months or possibly years later, when they are eventually sold. The written valuation provides a valid documentation for the asset's current market value for determining stepped-up valuation.

The Final Operational Instructions To The Trustee (cont'd)

B. FILING OF TAX RETURNS, PAYMENTS OF TAXES & EXPENSES

15. _____ File "U.S. Individual Income Tax Return," IRS Form 1040. Explain to the surviving spouse (if applicable) that he/she has a right still to file a joint income tax return (Form 1040) for that year in which the spouse died, if the couple was of the practice of filing joint returns prior to the deceased spouse's death. He/she should also be told to be sure to keep strict record of the decedent spouse's last medical and funeral expenses, as these expenses can be deducted from the surviving spouse's own taxable income, and the funeral expenses deducted for estate tax purposes.

The surviving spouse should use his or her own personal social security number to identify and report all asset and income in the whole Trust (those in Trust A as well as in Trust B and Trust C, if applicable), because this way it permits you (i.e., the trustee) to transfer the trust assets back and forth between Trust A and Trust B (and Trust C, as well, where applicable) as necessary. [If this were to involve the death of a single grantor, however, of the second spouse, then IRS Trust Identification Number will have to be used, in stead, in that situation]. For a marital trust, the surviving spouse, as the trustee, will typically pay out the income from the trust to himself or herself, and merely continue to report the said trust income on his/her own personal IRS Form 1040 income tax return.

16. _____ File Form 1041s (Trust Income Tax Return), if the Trust involved is an A-B type or A-B-C- type trust and if the death involved is the death of the first spouse to die, but only for that part of the trust that becomes irrevocable upon the decedent's death—i.e, for the decedent B Trust, and/or C Trust. [Note that this form, which is a simplified shorter version of the regular Form 1041, is not well known even by the professionals, the CPAs and the lawyers. Hence, you must be persistent on the specific form you want when you order the blank Form 1041S from the IRS.]

Here is how this works in a nutshell. Assuming the Trust involved is an A-B trust or A-B-C Trust, upon the death of a spouse, one-half of the Trust, (the Decedent's B Trust, if an A-B Trust, or his B and C Trusts, if an A-B-C Trust) becomes frozen and *irrevocable*. A form, Form 1041S (S for simple), should then be filed—but only for the *irrevocable* part of the trust, the Decedent's B Trust, or his/her B Trust and C Trust, in an A-B-C Trust. Form 1041S must continue to be filed annually until no assets remain in any irrevocable part of the trust. [Trust Employer Tax Identification Number is the number to use on Form 1041S for the purposes of identifying the decedent's estate; to have this number assigned you, obtain Form SS-4 from an IRS office, and fill it out and submit to the IRS and they'll assign you the number.]

17. _____ If Form 1041S is filed, then you must also file SCHEDULE K-1 to accompany it, and use the same trust "Employer Identification Number" on the said Schedule K-1. Typically, since all of the income in Trust B (and Trust C, if applicable) will be paid to the surviving spouse, who is also still a grantor of the Trust, the net effect is paying income to oneself; hence the taxable income (and the tax) you'll find on Form 1041S is zero! On Form 1041S, the surviving spouse would subtract from the income of Trust B, or of Trust B and Trust C (the decedent's share) an income distribution deduction (income received) in the same amount—giving a taxable income of zero on the form. Hence, Form 1041S is merely an "information" return. The surviving spouse would, as usual, continue to report the income received from the trust on his or her regular Form 1040 personal tax return. And Schedule K-1 "Beneficiary's Share of Income, Deductions, Credits, etc," which is attached to the filed Form 1041s, clearly shows, however, who receives the income distribution from the Trust.

The Final Operational Instructions To The Trustee (cont'd)

18. _____ File Form 1041S (Trust Income Tax Return) upon the death of both spouses in a marital situation, or of the individual, in a non-marital situation, since the entire Living Trust becomes irrevocable in such a situation, and the social security numbers belonging to the trust grantor(s) ceases to be usable upon their death.

19. _____ Review the size of the estate (see the "Financial Information" section of the Estate Information Organizer Worksheet, and the net worth therein). Determine its current net worth of the estate of the size to make it subject to Federal estate or state inheritance taxes? (**CLUE:** See the Net Worth in the "Financial Information" section of the Organizer Worksheet; review the grantor's last year's federal and state income tax returns to determine whether any gifts were reported on IRS Form 709 or 709A, and if there was, and if this is the death of the surviving spouse (the last party to die), then you can assume the estate is subject to federal estate taxes and state inheritance taxes and the trustee should, in such a case, ascertain which forms need to be filed and how much tax needs to be paid).

20. _____ If and when you should determine that the estate is large enough (up to a gross estate of more than $600,000 for a single person, or of more than $1.2 million for a married couple), then an IRS Form 706 (Federal Estate Tax Return) must be filed within 6 months of death, and any taxes due must be paid within 9 months. However, the good news is: you don't even have to file this complicated, forbidding tax return, if there is no federal estate tax payable; no Form 706 is necessary, if no estate tax is owed! (If you find that the filing of this form is required, it may be generally advisable to hire the services of a tax accountant for a modest charge and let him handle it.)

C. DISTRIBUTION

21. _____ Review the Declaration of Trust document and the Trust Schedule of Assets attached to the Trust (and the Estate Information Organizer Worksheet, if need be); more specifically, the clauses on such matters as "Trustees," "Successor Trustees," and "Allocation and Distributions To Beneficiaries." Check these sections to be sure on the specific authority you have in administering the Trust and on the specific directions on distribution of trust assets.

22. _____ Determine, from your review of the Trust provisions: Are any of the deceased spouse's (or party's) assets to be immediately distributed, rather than remaining in trust for the benefit of minor children or the surviving spouse?

23. _____ Identify which assets are to be placed in the A Trust, and in the B and/or C Trust. (CLUE: Generally, place growth and appreciating assets in Trust B (the Decedent's Trust), being that whatever is in that portion of the trust is "frozen"—insulated from further estate taxes as from that time on.) If only an A Trust is involved, skip this issue for it's not relevant in such a case; it's only relevant if an A-B or an A-B-C Trust is involved.

The Final Operational Instructions To The Trustee (cont'd)

Basic Procedures Of Asset Allocation Among The A, B and C Trusts:

i) First, identify the decedent spouse's share of the community property (i.e., basically one-half of the common property), and add that to his/her separate property; then place the VALUE of that—not merely the physical property—in the decedent's B Trust, with any excess over $600,000 placed in the C Trust, if applicable;

ii) Next, identify the surviving spouse's share of the community property (i.e., basically one-half of the common property), add his/her separate property to that, and place that in the surviving spouse's A Trust;*

iii) In other words, think of the *dollar value* of the property involved—instead of the physical property itself—as what is being placed in the Decedent's Trust B and/or Trust C; hence, even a decedent spouse who owns just one-half of, say, the family home, may still have the entire house put into either A or B, as long as an equal value of assets (i.e., a value equal to his one-half of the house) is put into the other Trust;

iv) To place an asset in an A, B or C Trust, the trustee merely needs to describe the particular asset, give the valuation amount, the date and the source of the valuation, and indicate from which Trust the asset is being taken and to which Trust it is being transferred. (Use sample Form LT-29 on p. 170 for such allocation of assets among the trusts);

v) Upon the asset allocation being made among the A, B, C Trusts, the trustee may totally ignore the allocation, except that he must make sure he files the annual report of income on the IRS Form 1041S Trust tax return, and must comply with the provisions of the Trust regarding the use of the assets in B and C Trusts.

24. _____ Distribute the personal effects, as per the provisions of the trust (or the Will, if applicable), with particular attention paid to the special instructions given, under the section titled "Special Gifts of Personal Effects to Individuals" in the Estate Information Organizer Worksheet. Make special estate distributions, if called for, per relevant provisions of the Trust Agreement.

25. _____ If assets are to be distributed or retained in Trust for the spouse, or for the minor children or young adult (or other) heirs: Determine which assets, and real estate, should be distributed, sold or converted to income. (Determine debts outstanding to be paid prior to distribution of estate.)

26. _____ Prepare an accounting of receipts and disbursements; make distributions, give accounting to beneficiaries and obtain receipts and release from them; make a written record of all assets and of all bills paid.

27. _____ Notify state attorney general, if charitable gifts are involved.

28. _____ Transfer assets in accordance with distribution instructions set forth in the trust.

---

*In short, the VALUE of the decedent's separate property (whatever it is), plus one-half of the asset VALUE which represents the Decedent's share of the community or common property, must be put into Trust B (and Trust C, if applicable).

Form LT-29

ASSET TRANSFER & DISTRIBUTION FORM—TRUST TO TRUST

Asset Description	Valuation Amount	Valuation Date	Source of Valuation	Transfer From To	Trustee Signature	Date of Signature

Chapter 11

A FEW OTHER ESTATE TAX-SAVING TOOLS YOU MAY CONSIDER TO SUPPLEMENT YOUR LIVING TRUST

A. Other Tax Saving and Tax Reducing Devices Beyond the A-B or A-B-C Trust

In a previous section of the book (see Chapter 5), we discussed tax savings and tax planning as a major aspect of overall estate planning, and placed it on level that is, in some respects, as high as the goal of probate avoidance in the field of estate planning. In that chapter, the primary tool relied in for the tax savings and tax planning task is the use of the A-B and the A-B-C forms of Revocable Living Trust, and the focus there is on the use of this device in minimizing estate and inheritance taxes that are paid on the estate at death, the so-called death taxes.

The A-B and A-B-C revocable living trust may not be enough, however, in providing you all the tax savings you'd need or should have, depending on the size or nature of your estate, or your particular estate planning needs and objectives. In this chapter, we shall consider a few other major planning device that are used by estate planners for tax planning. *It is important to emphasize however, that in general, these devices should be used not as substitutes for the revocable living trust, but primarily to supplement — i.e, in addition to — the living trust.* Hence, in using these devices, you should endeavor to consider each one in conjunction with a (revocable) living trust.

There are many other instruments that fall under the subject matter of this chapter, but only the following instruments shall be considered here:

- The Irrevocable Life Insurance Trust
- Gift-Making

We shall discuss the irrevocable life insurance trust first. But, first, as background for our discussion, we shall discuss the overall concept of life insurance as an investment tool.

B. Life Insurance: An Overview

Some basic questions, as a good background for our purposes here, are: What is life insurance? Should you have it, and if so, when and for what purposes? How much of it and at what cost?

An observation by one analyst, a lawyer, certified public accountant and financial planner with over 30 years experience in the field, goes to the very heart of these questions, especially as they relate to life insurance within the context of estate planning:

"As a general proposition, it is safe to say that almost no one has 'enough' life insurance coverage. There are many individuals who have virtually no coverage … On the other hand, almost probably everyone has met the self-important person who does not wish to disclose his income, but who 'subtly' lets you know his or her great worth by casually mentioning how much life insurance he or she carries. This individual may, without realizing it, be revealing that he or she does not understand very much about life insurance relative to his or her total financial picture. This person may, in fact, be outrageously overcommitted to insurance and may therefore be wasting money…

[The point is that there are no] hard and fast rules about coverage. There is no fool-proof formula for knowing how much coverage is 'enough.' We are dealing here with the *concepts* of insurance in order to show you how to relate these concepts to you and your family's needs. *If you buy life insurance you do so mainly in order to replace wages, provide for the liquidity of your estate, and pay debts ... [to make decisions regarding life insurance] you should decide first what what your needs are, and then, how much you can afford.* This is the only reliable method for selecting the right amount of insurance and kind of coverage for your life situation."[1] [Emphasis added by the writer]

TRANSLATION: The central key by which to determine whether you should get a life insurance coverage or not, and if so what type or how much of it to get, is WHAT YOUR NEEDS ARE! (And then, next in order of priority, you've got to go according to what you can afford!!)[2]

The point is that, from the standpoint of prudent estate planning, there may be times and situations when you actually don't need to have a life insurance policy in your particular estate planning portfolio, and should not have one. To put it another way, it is neither automatic nor a foregone conclusion that you must necessarily have a life insurance policy in your estate plan, and sometimes you can be just as prudent and as well served not to have one — depending on your particular estate planning needs, circumstances, and objectives and means.

C. The Purposes For Having Life Insurance

A key question, then, is: for what "estate planning" purposes do people buy life insurance? For our purposes, basically, the main estate planning-related purposes for which people typically have life insurance can be summed up as follows:

i) to supplement their other assets and provide for their families in the event they die unexpectedly or prematurely; and

ii) to pay their accumulated debt and immediate expense needs, such as personal loans, funeral expenses, mortgages or rents, and income or death taxes, and not burden their families with them in the event of their premature death.

Quick, immediate cash at the insured's death, is easily the prime attraction of this instrument. Thus, because of this instrument's ability to provide "ready cash" directly to the insurance policy's designated beneficiaries upon the death of the insured person, often without redtape or probate, you will be able to guarantee, for example, that your family is not evicted from their homes for lack of funds, or to assure that you'll have a decent burial outright without having to compel your family to pay off your funeral expenses by installments, or having to be compelled to hastily "unload" (sell-off) some non-liquid assets (your small business, real estate, car, etc...) probably at a substantial loss, just to pay such bills.

D. Who Really Needs To Have Life Insurance?

The above-described purposes are, certainly, worthwhile and legitimate purposes. They are worthy of pursuit in their own right. But does everyone have the need to pursue this objective? Is everyone, for example, in such a financial condition as to warrant that the or she should purchase insurance to provide financial help for family members in the event of his or her premature death?

Not so, say experts. If you are not the main family provider, or you have no one really dependent on you, then you probably don't need to have life insurance to serve that purpose in the event of your death. Nor

---

[1] Jerome R. Rosenberg, in *Managing Your Own Money* (Newsweek Books, N.Y., 1979) p. 205-6.

[2] "Other analysts make pretty much the same point. Witness this reaction by one insurance professional who, after making the case that "for a variety of reasons" many people would not buy life insurance, states: "Thus, life insurance isn't a product everyone believes in, can afford, or needs. A life insurance agent will disagree with this, but [that is the fact.]" [Jeff O'Donnell, in Insurance Smart, John Wiley & Sons, (N.Y., 1991) p. 121.]. And witness this statement by another report, by a lawyer and author on estate planning: "Having indicated some reasons life insurance can be desirable, let me again emphasize that simply buying some [of it] is not an adequate way to plan an estate. Indeed, many people simply don't need life insurance. Those who decide to purchase insurance should know exactly why they are buying it, the best type of policy for their needs, and of course, should buy no more than they need." Denis Clifford, in *Plan Your Estate With A Living Trust* (Nolo Press, Berkley CA: 1992) p. 12/1.

would you need to have one if, say, there are other likely sources of income and support available in your own particular situation, or if you have (or there otherwise are) other assets available in your own case to meet the financial needs of the family, and so on and so forth.

For this reason, by and large *financial planners counsel the purchase of life insurance mainly when one's family is young, particularly when one has children, as it is maintained that that is when the loss of the family provider can be devastating.*

E. What Is The "Right" Amount Of Life Insurance?

And how much life insurance do you need — what is the "right" amount to have? That question is a highly complicated one. Insurance brokers and financial planners employ what they call a "capital needs analysis," or "financial needs analysis" — a straightforward process that estimates the coverage necessary to provide sufficient income for a family's needs.[3] Another approach the brokers and financial planners take, adds up the large, lump-sum expenses, and seeks to provide what would be sufficient to pay off the larger expenditures for the family in the event of death: the house, major bills, and enough money for a decent funeral.

A far less complicated but yet comprehensible approach, to the writer's knowledge, is one by Henry W. Abts III.[4] Abts' truly "very simple but effective way" —his formulas—for determining the right amount of insurance is simply this: you determine your gross family income amount per year (the husband's and the wife's, if married); deduct from that the amount of saving you make on that per year, and that amount — the amount of savings per year — is presumed to be the amount of money which, if lost, will be needed for the family to continue maintaining it's normal standard of living, and hence is the amount of money that the insurance should provide for the family. You then multiply that amount (the annual savings amount) by a factor of 10 (assuming a 10% return on investment, if invested[5]) to account for the expected interest it will earn annually if invested (where both spouses are working, then both will have to be insured for the loss of the income amount involved).

The Abts formula, in short, is as follows:

Gross annual income (call it "A"), minus the assumed amount saved ("B") per year, multiplied by 10 (or any other rate of return you assume on its investment).

Simply: (A-B) x 10. A truly "very simple" formula!

---

[3] Here's essentially how the method works. You start by estimating your "income objective", expressed in today's dollars. Based on current spending patterns and financial obligations — i.e., that which your income covers at present, plus your debts — how much gross income will your family need? $35,000 a year? $60,000 a year? Next, list other financial resources your survivors could tap:

1) Current liquid assets (mainly the cash and securities used to pay expenses or generate income after death). The more you have, the less insurance you need.

2) Other insurance proceeds (insurance provided by your employer, such as group term insurance; the rights your estate may have to a lump sum payment from your pension plan, including Social Security benefits payable to a spouse and children [by completing Form SSA 7004, Request for Statement of Earnings, you can learn from the Social Security Administration what benefits you and your survivors have coming]); and

3) Survivors' earning power — the more your spouse can earn in the years ahead, the less insurance you need. Make a conservative estimate in today's dollars, allowing for only small raises beyond inflation unless you know that a lucrative new job or promotion is in the cards. The shortfall between your other financial resources and your income objective equals your life insurance needs.

EXAMPLE: Say your income objective is $60,000 a year and your spouse earns $20,000 a year; Social Security is good for $13,000; and other investments will generate $2,000, for a total of $35,000. Thus, insurance has to contribute about $25,000 to make up the difference. (Analysis, as provided by insurance expert Jeff O'Donnell, in *Insurance Smart*, pp. 146-7).

[4] Abts, op. cit. pp. 134-6.

[5] Actually, the more elaborate explanation for multiplying by 10 goes as follows. First, it's assumed that the annual saved amount will earn a 10% return on investment. Therefore, the amount of life insurance needed to maintain the same standard of living on the death of the provider (or providers, if applicable), is taken to be the amount which, earning 10% annually, would provide $50,000 per year (the amount representing the gross income, minus the annual savings).

ILLUSTRATIVE EXAMPLE #1[6]: Assume a single or a married but sole provider, with an annual gross income (income before taxes), "A," of $60,000, and savings "B," of $10,000 per year on that — which leaves $50,000 ($60,000 - $10,000) per year, as the amount necessary to maintain the same standard of living if the provider were to die. The calculation will be as follows:

FIGURE 11-A

GROSS INCOME PORTION NEEDED AS REPLACEMENT

Gross income	("A")	$60,000
Less: savings	("B")	-($10,000)
Amount of gross income to replace		$50,000

INSURANCE NEEDED

Amount of income needed	$50,000
Annual return (based on 10% rate of return)	X 10
Insurance (Investment)	$500,000

Thus, in this case, the amount of life insurance policy the provider should have for his heirs is $500,000.

ILLUSTRATIVE EXAMPLE #2: Assume a working married couple, with the husband earning a gross annual income (income before taxes), "A," of $40,000, and the wife earning $20,000 gross, "A". The couple make a savings "B", of $10,000 per year on their earnings — which leaves $50,000 ($60,000 - $10,000) per year, as the amount necessary to maintain the same standard of living if the providers were to die.

FIGURE 11-B

THE COUPLE'S COMBINED GROSS INCOME & LIVING EXPENSES

Husband's gross income		$40,000
Wife's gross income		+ $20,000
Combined gross income	("A")	$60,000
Less: savings	("B")	-$10,000
Living expense		$50,000

The calculation will be as follows. First, realize that since both spouses are contributors to the family income, then the amount of insurance to be had will have to be assessed on BOTH spouses — the total potential loss of income amount involved.

[6]These two hypothetical cases are taken from samples cited in Abts, op.cit. pp.135-6.

For the husband (if he were to die): since the family needs $50,000 and the wife provides $20,000 of that, the difference is $30,000. The amount that would need to be invested at 10 percent annually to yield the $30,000 difference per year would be $300,000. Therefore, the husband should have $300,000 of insurance on his own life, calculated as follows:

FIGURE 11-C

IF THE HUSBAND WERE TO DIE
GROSS INCOME PORTION NEEDED AS REPLACEMENT

Living expense	$50,000
Less Wife's gross income	-$20,000
Amount of gross income to replace	$30,000

INSURANCE NEEDED

Amount of income needed	$30,000
Annual return (based on 10% rate of return)	x 10
Insurance (investment)	$300,000

For the wife (if she were to die): since the family needs $50,000 and the husband provides $40,000 of that, the difference is $10,000. [Or, another way of putting it, is to say that since the wife provides $20,000 of income and the couple were saving $10,000, then the death of the wife would result in a loss of $10,000 (her $20,000 income minus the $10,000 family savings)]. So, what is the amount that would need to be invested at 10 percent annually to yield $10,000 potential difference or "loss" per year? That amount is $100,000. Therefore, the wife should have $100,000 of insurance on her life, calculated as follows:

FIGURE 11-D

IF THE WIFE WERE TO DIE
GROSS INCOME PORTION NEEDED AS REPLACEMENT

Living expense	$ 50,000
Less Husband's gross income	-$40,000
Amount of gross income to replace	$10,000

INSURANCE NEEDED

Amount of income needed	$10,000
Annual return (based on 10% rate of return)	x 10
Insurance (investment)	$100,000

F. But Here's The Even Bigger Problem: Can You Afford It?

Alright. So, you've finally figured out how to estimate the proper amount of life insurance you'd need, and finally figured out the "right" amount of it you should purchase. But now comes the far harder and more relevant question: CAN YOU AFFORD IT? Analysts who have made detailed analyses of the issue character-ize that aspect as "the hard part" in the whole issue of deciding on whether or not to secure the life insurance policy, adding that "it takes a mountain of cash to create that much [to be able to pay for a reasonable level of insurance] for decades to come."[7] Jeff O'Donnell, a family insurance professional and specialist who studied the insurance company methods of estimating how much life insurance consumers need, calculates that "[In order] to earn $25,000 a year from 9 percent Treasury bonds, you need $277,778 worth. And that' just for income [you should have]; you would have to provide separately for any lump sums you want to set aside to pay off the mortgage or send your kids to college."[8]

Once again, we come full circle as to the reason why experts have overwhelmingly counseled that there are essentially two prime considerations upon which to base the decision on whether to purchase a life insurance policy and when and how much of it to: YOUR SPECIFIC NEEDS, AND YOUR OWN FINANCIAL RESOURCES.

O'Donnell, an insurance sales professional and a keen insurance analyst, clearly sums up the relevant points this way:[9]

"Now comes the hard part. [After you've made the calculations], you know what you need, but the amount seems beyond reach. One possibility is to wait. Plenty of people do just that. If you are single or your death wouldn't visit financial hardship upon anyone, life insurance is a luxury. Benefits from your group policy at work would more than suffice.

To me, it really starts with how much money you can comfortably spend per month on life insurance. Don't let the agent get carried away with your money. If we all bought enough life insurance to pay our debts, educate our children, and provide an income for our spouse until age 65, we'd be broke.

There's no doubt that large amounts of life insurance are required to satisfy what [insurance agents and financial planners say] most financial-needs analyses show that a young family would require. The FNA [for "Financial Needs Analysis" methods of figuring out a family's amount of insurance needed used by insurance brokers and financial planners] works great in figuring what you need, but how many people can afford this much? Some people can and some can't...

I always feel more comfortable when people tell me honestly how much money they can budget monthly for life insurance. This helps me plan a program that does a couple of things: (1) accomplishes at least the most important of their goals, whether it's paying off their house, providing an education for their children, or replacing the deceased spouse's income; and (2) keeps them happy by staying within their budget.

Instead of ignoring the issue and not buying insurance [at all]... *Figure the amount of money you can spend comfortably on life insurance every month. No more, no less. You can grow into a program as your income increases and your financial situation improves."* (Italics added by the writer).

G. Using The Irrevocable Life Insurance Trust As A Device For Estate Tax-Saving

As we have attempted to establish in the preceding section of this chapter, ordinarily you need not necessar-ily or automatically have to have a life insurance policy in your estate plan portfolio. Rather, you may pur-chase a policy under certain circumstances and if you are in a certain situation — depending on your particu-lar needs, and the amount of insurance you can financially afford. In essence, the point made is that, as a general principle of financial or estate planning, a person who otherwise has an estate that is sufficient to provide for his and his family needs — or who strictly can't afford to pay for a policy — need not necessarily have to have a life insurance. The implication is that for such a person, the A-B or the A-B-C living trust instruments, or some other instruments, would have provided him all the estate tax-savings he (or she) can afford to have under the circumstances to be able to pass on his estate to his heirs.

[7] Ibid. p. 147-8. And witness this assertion by Jerome R. Rosenberg, who cautions about the crucial necessity for every individual to "understand very much [the connection] about life insurance relative to his or her total financial picture," and adds: "You should make decisions regarding life insurance only after you have examined your financial resources ...first, what your needs are, and then, how much you can afford ... for your life situation." (Rosenberg, *Managing Your Own Money*, op. cit, pp. 205-6).

[8] Ibid. p. 147.

[9] Jeff O'Donnell, *Insurance Smart*, op. cit. 148.

(a) SITUATION WHEN USE OF THIS SPECIAL KIND OF LIFE INSURANCE MAY BE ADVISABLE

There is one distinct situation, however, when a certain kind of life insurance could be usable in securing crucial estate tax savings even to such a person who has "sufficient" assets. And, in the field of estate planning, that situation is when, specifically, you reach that crucial "crossing point" — when your assets EXCEED the federal estate tax equivalent exemption ($600,000 for a single person, and $1.2 million for a married couple). At that point, say estate planning experts, that would be one situation where and when you should have a life insurance policy, a certain kind — THE IRREVOCABLE LIFE INSURANCE TRUST. The reason? Because the use of the life insurance trust would be the cheapest way for such a person with a "large" estate to pay estate taxes on the assets that exceed the federal estate tax equivalent exemption. (Which is also to say, that unless you have an estate with a gross value over $600,000, if single, or over $1.2 million, if married, this device is not of much relevance to you!)

How does the *irrevocable* life insurance Trust device work? First, we should clear up one common source of confusion among the public. Get this clear: true, upon death, life insurance proceeds are not included in the probate estate, and are not subject to probate, but are rather paid directly to the designated beneficiary without going through probate. *Those proceeds are, however, includable in your estate — they are counted as part of your estate — when determining the estate taxes assessable on your estate, that is, the estate taxes.* Estate planners consistently report that this fact frequently comes as a great surprise, even shock, to clients, and that most people interested in estate planning are totally unaware that life insurance proceeds are subject to federal taxation. But the fact is that they really are! What is exempt from taxation, in other words, is INCOME TAXATION ("income" tax type of taxation) on the life insurance proceeds, but not the "estate" type of taxation. And that may well be the main source for the confusion. Here's how to clear up the confusion: the life insurance proceeds are not subject to PROBATE and are not subject to INCOME taxes; but they are subject to federal ESTATE TAXATION (assuming, of course, that the estate is large enough to qualify for estate taxation).

So, to see how the irrevocable life insurance trust works, and how you can employ it to save your estate some estate taxes, let's say your estate falls within the "large estate" category — defined as an estate with assets worth in excess of $600,000, if single, or in excess of $1.2 million, if married. Specifically, let's say you are a married couple with a net estate (i.e., the estate after subtracting out the loans, debts, and liabilities) of $1,200,000, plus life insurance which will pay $300,000 at the spouse's death. So, you have a total net estate of $1,500,000 — which means that using the A-B-C type of trust, still you are over the $1,200,000 federal estate tax equivalent exemption by $300,000. If you were to let that $300,000 stand as it is, it will be subject to the federal estate tax of a whopping $115,000, assuming you use an A-B-C form of trust. (The rate starts at 37% of anything over $1.2 million, remember). So, from an estate planning standpoint, what you want to do is simply this: you'd want to remove altogether the insurance proceeds (the $300,000) from your estate, so you don't have to pay the estate taxes on it that you would otherwise have to pay. So, what you do is to create an IRREVOCABLE LIFE INSURANCE TRUST and have this trust "own" the insurance; with that, the $300,000 value now ceases to be counted as an asset of your own estate — since it is now "owned" by the trust, and not by you — meaning that no estate taxes would have to be paid on it! You have, in this example, saved your estate and beneficiaries the $115,000 in federal estate taxes that would have been payable on the $300,000!!!

Here's how the tax-savings works out comparatively between an estate with a life insurance trust and an estate without a life insurance trust.

EXAMPLE I: SINGLE PERSON

Here, we are assuming the following facts: a single person with a net estate of $400,000, plus life insurance which will pay $300,000 at the person's death. In one case, the Living Trust is the beneficiary of the insurance policy but is not placed in an Insurance Trust; while in the other case, the party has an Insurance Trust into which he places the $300,000 insurance policy.

The contrasting tax consequences will be as in Figure 11-E below.

FIGURE 11-E

TAXATION OF SINGLE PERSON'S ESTATE ($700,000)

	WITHOUT INSURANCE TRUST	WITH INSURANCE TRUST
Other assets, less debts	$400,000	$400,000
Insurance	300,000	300,000
Total estate (net worth)	$700,000	$700,000
Insurance Trust	— 0 —	- 300,000
Taxable estate	$700,000	$400,000
Less: Federal estate tax equivalent exemption	- 600,000	- 600,000
Taxable excess	$100,000	— 0 —
Estate tax @ 37%	$ 37,000	— 0 —

INTERPRETATION: use of the insurance trust device alone saves his/her estate a federal estate tax of $37,000!

EXAMPLE II: MARRIED COUPLE

Here, take a case that involves an estate with a net worth, including insurance, that is in excess of $1.2 million. Let's say it's a married couple with a net estate (net worth) of $1.5 million, $500,00 of which is a life insurance policy.

If the estate has no Insurance Trust (the $500,000 insurance policy is not placed in an Insurance Trust), here's what happens. Using an A-B-C Trust, upon the death of one spouse, the surviving spouse, through the device of using the "C" part of the Trust, will be able to defer paying any taxes immediately on the entire $1.5 million estate. However, eventually, upon the death of the second spouse, there will be a federal estate tax, which amounts to $115,000 due on the estate. On the other hand, if this estate has an Insurance Trust, and places the $500,000 in an Insurance Trust, the estate even does better—it avoids paying any federal estate tax at all. Here's how. Here, the A-B Trust will be used because, with the value of the Insurance Trust removed from the estate, the remainder of the estate is less than $1.2 million. Being that the Insurance Trust is considered "owned" by the Insurance Trust, that amount is not counted as an asset of the estate. That means, therefore, that the value of the asset in the Trust is just $1 million (i.e., $1.5 million minus the $500,000 that is in the insurance Trust).

Hence, as an estate with no more than $1.2 million, with an A-B Trust, upon the death of the surviving spouse, no taxes would be due on the estate in that, as explained in Chapter 5, with an A-B Trust no federal estate taxes are assessed or payable on an estate worth less than $1.2 million. So, by this device of creating an Insurance Trust, the couple in this second example would have saved $115,000 in estate taxes in comparison to a couple with the same $1.5 million net worth, and an A-B-C Trust, but which has no Insurance Trust.

(b) HOW DO YOU SET UP THE LIFE INSURANCE TRUST?

As explained in the section immediately preceding, the key to having the proceeds which accrues from your life insurance policy exempted from estate taxation under the irrevocable life insurance trust device, is to have the insurance policy "owned" by the trust (rather than by you). The question for us here, is how do you set up the life insurance trust? And how does it operate, in practice?

Essentially, what you need to do is create a life insurance trust to which you then "transfer" or give the ownership of your life insurance policy. In other words, you make the trust the owner of the policy, not you. This way, with the insurance policy now legally "owned" by the trust, rather than by you, you shall have effectively removed the proceeds of the insurance policy from your taxable estate, thereby simultaneously reducing the death taxes, particularly the federal estate taxes, on your estate.

But why don't you rather assign the life insurance policy directly to someone else, you may ask? Say to your spouse or other person you wish to designate as beneficiaries, anyway? Well, there just may be no one you'd rather give your policy directly to, because you simply feel that that way you'll breathe easier or you prefer to retain control yourself over the policy. Since, under the applicable rules, this insurance policy must be <u>irrevocable</u> in order to qualify, you'll have no more or control over the policy if you were to give its ownership away to someone else; once given to him or her, who knows what the new owner can do; he can go ahead and change the beneficiaries, cash in the cash value of the policy, or even cancel the policy and leave you without insurance!

So, a better way that will give you greater peace of mind but yet allow you to ensure that the proceeds of the insurance policy are distributed the way you want, is by setting up a life insurance trust. You'll designate a trustee to manage the trust (under the rules, you can't yourself be the trustee of the trust), but since the TRUSTEE will be subject to your instructions in the trust, you're more or less guaranteed that the funds will be distributed to your beneficiaries as you directed — and without probate, or income taxes or estate taxes.

(c) AN IMPORTANT CONSIDERATION, THOUGH: CAN YOU LIVE WITH THE RESTRICTIONS AND OTHER TERMS?

Setting up the irrevocable life insurance trust and giving it ownership (making it the owner) of the insurance policy is a fairly simple matter. But, first of all, there's one major consideration you had better be sure you're willing to live with, before you can finally decide to do this: YOU HAD BETTER MADE SURE THAT YOU CAN ABIDE BY THE STRICT REQUIREMENTS AND RESTRICTIONS THAT GOVERN THE LIFE INSURANCE TRUST.

Basically, here are the restrictions you've got to decide for yourself whether they are worth abiding by, in exchange for you merely to gain the estate tax savings:[10]

---

[10]The IRS rules governing this basically boils down to determining whether you have, in fact, relinquished ownership of the insurance policy and irrevocably assigned it the ownership to the life insurance trust, and the IRS bases this essentially on this question: do you appear to have, in fact, given up any "incidents of ownership" in the policy, as defined by the IRS. Basically, the IRS would consider that you still retain incidents of ownership of a life insurance policy (i.e., that you are still effectively the owner) if: you still pay the premiums or control or exercise significant power over the policy (such as the power to change beneficiaries, to borrow against the policy, power to select a payment option, such as to decide if the payments to the beneficiaries can be made in a lump sum or in installments, or the power to have a reversionary interest of more than 5% of the value of the policy immediately prior to your death, since that would be an indication that you, and not your designated beneficiary, still retain control over who will relieve the proceeds if your beneficiary dies before you).

• Unlike the living trust, which is revocable, the Life Insurance Trust must be an <u>irrevocable trust</u> — once done, you can't change the beneficiaries or other terms of the insurance trust you designate therein. (You can, however, always change around the beneficiaries or other terms of the living trust, and since your trust (which you control) owns the insurance policy, and since you can always change around the provisions of the living trust, you effectively retain continuous control of the insurance proceeds as well).

• Unlike the living trust, you can't be the trustee of the life insurance trust. Rather, you've got to name someone else (an adult person or corporate institution) to serve as the trustee.

• You cannot, as a previous owner, still retain any "incidents of ownership" (indication of effectively being the owner) over the life insurance.

• To qualify, the life insurance trust must have been established at least 3 years before your death, otherwise the trust will not qualify for estate tax purposes and the life insurance proceeds will still be included in your (the trust maker's) estate.

(d) TO SET UP A LIFE INSURANCE TRUST, SIMPLY FOLLOW THE FOLLOWING PROCEDURES, STEP-BY-STEP:

1. You set up the IRREVOCABLE LIFE INSURANCE TRUST, and in it you name someone else (it cannot be you) to serve as it's trustee to manage the trust for you. (Note that you may not be the trustee of a life insurance trust for which you are the grantor).

2. Following your instructions in your trust, the trustee will purchase a new life insurance policy with you (or both spouses, if applicable) as the insured person(s), and name the trust as the owner of the policy. (Or, if you've already bought an existing life insurance policy, then you can easily transfer it into the new trust by simply completing the *Transfer or Assignment of Life Insurance* form (see sample Form LT-30 on p.184) and submitting it to the life insurance company to make the assignment from you to the trust. Insurance companies generally have their own blank transfer forms, which you may often use for this purpose. *The transfer of the policy into the trust must be done, however, at least 3 years prior to your death).*

3. You should also name the trust as the beneficiary of the insurance policy. [11] As with your living trust, you can name anyone you wish as beneficiaries of the insurance trust and designate any purposes for which the proceeds should be used — e.g., provision for use of the funds to provide for your surviving spouse or for the education of your children or grandchildren, use of the proceeds specifically to pay estate taxes, use of a minor or incompetent beneficiary's designated share to provide for his or her care and distribution of the remaining proceeds, if any, when he's of certain age; giving authorization for the trustee to purchase assets from the living trust, if and when necessary, and to be able to replace non-liquid assets with cash to pay, say, income or estate taxes to prevent a distress disposal of the estate assets, and so on and so forth. [12]

4. Upon your (the insured's) death, assuming you have named the trust as the beneficiary what happens is that the insurance company will pay the proceeds to the trust, and hence the funds shall have been effectively removed from being includable in your estate for tax purposes. Then, your trustee will, in turn, use the proceeds according to your instructions in the trust.

---

[11] According to one report, however, said to have been based on a recent court decision, in order to avoid an IRS challenge, individuals with "large estates" — defined therein as those exceeding $2 million—are to name their heirs, rather than their living trust, as the beneficiaries of their insurance trust. (Abts, op. cit. p. 138).

[12] For example, the specific characteristics carried by life insurance trusts created by Henry W. Abts III, a professional estate planner and living trust specialist who has physically created living trusts counting in the thousands, are designed to include the following: Primarily the insurance is to provide the income to the spouse for life, and the way this is achieved is that upon the spouse's death, the insurance company is to pay the face value of the insurance policy to the trustee of the insurance trust, the trustee then invests those funds and pays the income from the investments to the surviving spouse during his or her lifetime. The surviving spouse is further granted the right to borrow against the insurance if his or her own estate were to substantially diminish. Thereupon, since the insurance shall not have been "owned" by the trust grantors and was therefore never an asset of their estate, 60 days after the death of the second spouse, the proceeds from the insurance in the insurance trust "pour over" (directly pass) to the designated heirs without being subject to federal estate taxation. (Account as given by Henry W. Abts III, *The Living Trust*, op. cit. p. 144.)

(e) HOW YOU FUND THE INSURANCE TRUST

In order to protect the insurance trust from challenge by the IRS, the trustee must get the funds with which to fund the insurance trust from you — *but in a special way*. There are two things you want to avoid. You want to avoid doing anything that will smack of your still having any "incidents of ownership" in the insurance policy; and you don't want to give the money directly to the trustee, since such will provoke gift taxes being assessed on that. (It should be noted, however, that it has been well established by analysts, that, in general, even if one were to pay a gift tax, the amount of the gift tax assessed will still be considerably less than the tax cost of having the policy in your estate, given that the life insurance policy is effectively valueless while the insured lives, and that, hence, the proceeds collectible from an insurance policy at the insured's death will almost always be considerably more than the worth of the policy during the insured's lifetime.) So, what you want to do is to find a way to fund the insurance policy while at the same time avoiding or at the very least minimizing these two pitfalls. How do you do this?

Setting Up A Separate Bank Account For Premium Payments

Henry W. Abts III, the living trust creation specialist, suggests this method: to set up a separate bank account, a checking account, to be used exclusively to pay the premiums for the insurance policy used in the insurance trust, and advises that you (the trust creator) "make contributions to this checking account in different amounts and at different frequencies than are required to make the premium payments — in order to protect the insurance trust from challenge by the Internal Revenue Service."[13]

Under this method, true, you may not retain legal right to pay the premiums as they become due — that is, it cannot be your legal obligation to do so. The new owner of the insurance policy (i.e., the Insurance Trust, or it's trustee, in this case) is to make all premium payments, alright. However, "if the new owner doesn't have sufficient funds to make the payments, the previous owner, (i.e., you, as the trust creator) could give her money to be used for those payments. In other words, it's okay for the previous owners to make payments indirectly by giving money to the new owner, but it's a no-no for the previous owner to make payments directly to the insurance company."[14]

The 'Demand Right' Method Of Gift-Making

A slightly more elaborate method to achieve the same objective of funding your insurance trust, is described as the DEMAND RIGHT method. Under this method,[15] you are to take advantage of the lifetime gift-making provision of the Economic Recovery Tax Act of 1981 to fund the life insurance trust. And here's how the funding works, according to the experts: the law allows you (an individual) to give away, during your lifetime, up to $10,000 per year to each individual or organization ($20,000 where both spouses consent) to as many people as you wish, with no gift tax, which means that you can give up to $10,000 each year (or $20,000 if giving to a married couple) to each beneficiary of your insurance trust. However, instead of making a gift directly to the beneficiaries, you turn around and give it to the trustee of your INSURANCE TRUST. The trustee, in turn, then sends a written notice (called a *"Crummey letter,"* because the procedure was based on a court case brought by a Mr. Crummey) to each of the trust beneficiaries informing him or her that a gift has been received on his/her behalf, and that unless he/she elects to receive the gift now, he (the trustee) will

---

[13]Abts, op. cit. p.144.

[14]Denis Clifford, *Plan Your Estate With A Living Trust*, p.12/8.

[15]Method as described by Schumacher, *Understanding Living Trusts*, p. 141-2.

invest the funds by using it to pay the premium on the insurance trust's insurance policy. (See Form LT-31 on p. 184, for sample copy of such a letter.) For this to work perfectly well, you shall have, of course, first discussed the matter with the beneficiaries concerned and arrived at a common understanding with them that they would wait for the insurance proceeds down the road.

Then, finally, there's one other thing you are to do. If you want to gift the full $10,000 per year (or $20,000 by married couples) per beneficiary, you'll have to include an additional provision in the insurance trust, dividing it into separate shares, one for each of your beneficiaries with the insurance policy allocated among the shares. That's because under the rules, if a beneficiary of your insurance trust were to refuse your gift that exceeds $5,000 or 5% of his/her individual share of the trust, the excess is considered to be a "gift" by that beneficiary to the other beneficiaries; it will not qualify for the $10,000 gift tax exclusion and will therefore be subject to gift tax liability. Hence, by dividing the insurance trust into separate shares for the respective beneficiaries, when a beneficiary refuses a gift from the trust grantor that exceeds the $5,000 or 5% limitation, that beneficiary is deemed to be making a "gift" (the excess over the $5,000 or 5% limitation) to himself or herself, and not to the other beneficiaries, and hence no gift tax liability will result.

NOTE: You should note, however, that this method is not without some problems, though. As already stated above, gifts of items or property which the recipient cannot use or enjoy immediately, or over which you still retain some rights or power, such as the right to revoke it, do not qualify. *To be a true gift which qualifies under the tax code for this purpose, the gift must be absolute and irrevocable once made. It's gone, once made, and you can't claim it or try to recover it.*

So, ultimately, whatever the supposed "tax advantages" of gift-making for estate purposes, there's really one underlying consideration you must first think about: can you afford to give away something in the first place? Would you have enough to cope with, for example, if after you've transferred large chunks of your estate to others you are struck by a sudden, unanticipated change in your economic status? (See section H of this chapter for more on the use of the gift-making as a device for estate tax savings)

FIGURE 11-F

SCHEMATIC ILLUSTRATION OF HOW IRREVOCABLE LIFE INSURANCE TRUST BY 'DEMAND RIGHT' FUNDING WORKS

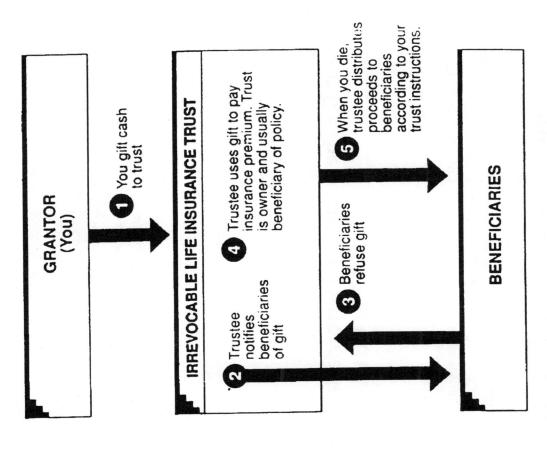

GRANTOR (You)

1 You gift cash to trust

IRREVOCABLE LIFE INSURANCE TRUST

2 Trustee notifies beneficiaries of gift

3 Beneficiaries refuse gift

4 Trustee uses gift to pay insurance premium. Trust is owner and usually beneficiary of policy.

5 When you die, trustee distributes proceeds to beneficiaries according to your trust instructions.

BENEFICIARIES

Illustration, reproduced by courtesy of Vickie and Jim Schumacher, *Understanding Living Trusts* (Schumacher and Co., Los Angeles, CA; 1990), to whose authors and publisher the present author is deeply grateful.

Form LT-30

Transfer Or Assignment Of Life Insurance

Mr/Mrs _____ of this address _____ hereinafter called the "Original Owners," and _____ of this address _____ hereinafter called the "New Owner," hereby covenant and agree as follows:

1. That the life insurance policy issued to the said Original Owner on his/her life, described as Policy No. _____ issued by the company named _____ is hereby assigned to the New Owner as his/her sole property.

2. That the Original Owner releases and waives to the New Owner any and all rights he/she may have to any incidents of ownership in the said insurance policy, including:

(a) the right to change or name beneficiaries of the policy; (b) the right to borrow against the policy, or pledge any cash reserve it has or cash it in; (c) the right to surrender, convert or cancel the policy; (d) the right to select payment option; and (e) the right to make payments on the policy.

Dated, this _____ day of _____ 19___

SIGNED: X _____

Signature of Original Owner

X _____

Signature of New Owner

Form LT-31

Letter Of Notification On The Receipt Of Gift Made To You By Mr/Mrs/Ms _____, The Gift Maker

Date: _____

Dear Mr/Mrs/Ms _____

PLEASE TAKE NOTICE, and this is to so inform you that I am in receipt of a certain gift in the amount of $_____ made by the above-named person(s), Mr/Mrs _____ of this address _____ to and for you through me, the undersigned trustee of THE JOHN AND MARY DOE LIFE INSURANCE TRUST.

Please take note that I currently retain the said gift for you, and if you prefer you may promptly collect it from me in its original form. Unless you elect to receive the said gift now (at the latest within _____ days from the date of this letter), I shall invest the funds on your behalf, by using same to pay the premium on the insurance policy taken out on the life of the said gift-maker(s), with you as the ultimate contingent beneficiary. If I do not hear from you by the date last stated above, I shall presume that you have no objection to my investing same accordingly.

Thank you.
Yours truly,

SIGNED X _____

Trustee, The John and Mary Doe Life Insurance Trust

H. Another Estate Tax-Saving Device: Use Of Life-Time Gift Making Provision

This is probably the most primary traditional method used by the estate-planning professionals for the purpose of making estate tax savings. Under a provision of the Economic Recovery Tax Act of 1981, known as "the $10,000 annual gift exclusion," during your lifetime you may give away anything of value (cash, jewelry, fine art, stocks and bonds, real estate, a trust, bank accounts, etc) in amounts of NO MORE THAN $10,000 per person or non-charitable institution, per year, to as many individuals as you choose, without the gifts being subject to estate taxation. To put it another way, under this law, you can give away anything or property you have, to anybody (Christmas present, anniversary or birthday gifts, etc) and that's your personal business. But the moment that gift is worth *more than* $10,000 to any one person or institution in a year, except for gifts between spouses, you've got an issue with the federal tax authorities—how you'll pay gift tax on the gift, on the excess over the $10,000 limitation! And if you are a married couple, you can give double that $10,000 amount ($20,000) per year tax-free to one person, and $40,000 if you choose to incude the spouse of the recipient in your gift-giving program. Most people confine this gift to their children or grandchildren.

(a) ADVANTAGES OF THIS METHOD

Gifting part of your estate using the $10,000 annual gift exclusion, is considered by many as an excellent way of passing an estate by some people to one's beneficiaries at a substantial estate tax savings. It's easy to see by simple multiplication, that by using this $10,000 exclusion as fully possible, you can quickly parcel out a good deal of your estate to intended heirs—estate-tax free. For example, let's say you have 5 children. Each year, you (the father) could gift $10,000 to each of the children (for a total of $50,000) and your spouse (the mother) could also gift additional $10,000 to each child per yer (an additional $50,000). Thus, in this example, the gift exclusion alone would have allowed the parents to give their children a grand total of $100,000 each year. If you make the same level of gifts to the same number of people for, say, ten years, you've distributed $1,000,000—tax-free. (The recipients of the gift would not be liable for either gift tax or income tax on it). Then, to add even more to that, if your children are married and you and your spouse wish to include their spouses in the gift-giving, the amounts would be double that—$2,000,000 in the same 10 year period!

(b) MAJOR DISADVANTAGES OF THIS MEHOD: CAN YOU REALLY AFFORD TO PART WITH THE GIFTS?

Certainly this method of distributing one's assets to one's would-be heirs is particularly suited to, and advantageous for, persons who have several children, grandchildren or other beloved ones *and who can afford the gifts.*

Experts strictly caution, though, that such tax-exempt gift-giving works well only for people who can afford it, especially since the gifts are irrevocable and the deal is done and final once made. Consequently, experts[16] recommend that *use of gifts to reduce eventual estate taxes is most advisable and ideal only under certain circumstances* such as these:

- When you estimate that your estate will be far in excess of $600,000
- The property you want to give has not greatly appreciated in value since you acquired it. (In other words, give those property you think will appreciate in the future, rather than the ones that have already appreciated)
- Most importantly, when you're absolutely sure you don't or won't need all of your resources and income to live on now and in the future.

Denis Clifford's measured analysis very aptly sums up the somewhat ambivalent but relevant considerations that should be carefully weighed by an individual before he can make a prudent determination as to when or whether to make a gift or not, this way:[17]

---

[16]Denis Clifford, *Plan You Estate With a Living Trust,* op. cit, pp. 15/7.

[17]Ibid. p. 15/8

"Before plunging into this subject (game might be a better word) [of using gifts to save on estate taxes], take stock of what you feel about gifts. Does it detract from the spirit of making a gift to save it for reducing taxes?

Making a gift, under common understanding and the law, means you've given away ownership of some property; you no longer control it. This loss of ownership is precisely why many people don't make substantial gifts. Sometimes this makes good sense; they need, or may need, the money. Often, however, with larger estates, the refusal to make gifts makes little economic sense. Some people, it seems, want to hang on to every nickel they've got while they're alive, whether they will ever need it or not. The pleasure of keeping all their property outweighs any possible tax benefits.

Certainly, I wouldn't encourage a person to give away money if it meant risking sacrifices in lifestyle or the possibility of money fears or anxieties. However, those with more than adequate wealth for their forseeable needs should seriously consider the giving of tax-exempt gifts while alive. Aside from any tax savings, the giver can feel pleasure and satisfaction in making a gift while living and seeing the help it brings." (Italics added by the present author)

(C) WHAT ARE THE CONSEQUENCES IF YOU GIVE A GIFT WORTH IN EXCESS OF $10,000?

Finally, while we are on this subject, you should be aware that upon your making an annual exclusion gift, you must file a Gift Exemption Form 709A on or by April 15th of the following year (when a regular income tax return is filed), and declare the gifts to each of the recipients. This is required although no tax is assessed for this gift (none is assessed, unless, of course, you've made a non-exempt gift in excess of $10,000 to a single person or organization in a year.)

Let's say you were to give a gift worth $20,000 in a single year to a recipient. The first $10,000 of that is exempt from gift taxes; the remaining $10,000 (the amount in excess of the allowed $10,000) is subject to gift taxes, and the gift taxes are steep, the same rate as the estate tax rate levied on property transferred at death (see p. xxdx for the applicable tax rates). Secondly, all such gift amounts OVER the $10,000 exclusion limit (the totality of all of them added up for all the applicable years), would be counted towards the $600,000 estate tax exemption. For example, if the amount of "taxable gifts" (i.e., the amount of gifts that are over the $10,000 per year, per person exclusion limit) totals, say, $300,000 during your lifetime, that amount will be deducted from your $600,000 estate tax exemption allowance, meaning that only $300,000 worth of your property ($600,000, less the $300,000 "taxable gifts" made) can be transferred free of federal estate tax upon your death.

Note that, on the other hand, all property given by one spouse to another, is totally exempt from any gift taxes, no matter the worth of the gift. However, if the spouse involved (the recipient spouse) is not a citizen of the United States, the rules are drastically different, in that case there's no "unlimited marital deduction" for the couple. All that the U.S. citizen spouse can give his or her non-citizen spouse free of federal estate or gift taxes, is $100,000 worth of property per year and no more![18] (The $600,000 exemption would remain available, and a spouse, even if a non-citizen, can still be left that much property tax-free under this exemption).

---

[18]There's one exception to this rule. Property left by a U.S. citizen spouse to a non-citizen spouse in what the IRS calls a "Qualified Domestic Trust" qualifies for the unlimited marital deduction.

Appendix A

SUMMARY OF BASIC TRUST RULES & REQUIREMENTS IN ALL 50 STATES AND OTHER JURISDICTIONS

The broad principles underlying the trust creation, in particular, and estate planning instruments, in general, are basically identical from state to state among the vast majority of states. The following notes explains the heading terms and entries in this appendix. Terms not otherwise explained are either explained in the glossary or are self-explanatory.

UNIFORM ACTS ADOPTED: Indicates that the state has adopted the specific act(s).

THE UNIFORM PROBATE CODE: Essentially is concerned with supposedly "streamlining" the probate procedures, but has something to say on matters such as what trustees may charge, whether they have to post bond, whether they should file a report of the trust creation with a public agency, and so on.

THE UNIFORM TESTAMENTARY ADDITIONS TO TRUST ACT: Allows the property of a person with a "pour-over" provision in his will, to be transferred from his or her will to the living trust after he or she dies.

THE UNIFORM TRUSTS POWERS ACT: sets forth the different types of rights and responsibilities and powers a trustee may have; it typically becomes relevant mostly when the trustee's powers are not adequately or unambiguously spelled out in the trust document and there's some dispute over the exact interpretation of the powers.

THE UNIFORM STATUTORY RULE AGAINST PERPETUITIES: The rule against perpetuities governs how long a trust (a private trust) may last, and the Uniform Statutory Rule Against Perpetuities simplifies the process of determining whether a trust violates the rule against perpetuities.

There are two versions of the rule in use among states. One version practiced by less than half the states, is called the rule against perpetuities *"in full,"* or more popularly known as the *"common-law rule,"* and states that a trust may not last longer than the life of a person already alive at the time the trust is created, plus an additional 21 years, and if it is considered that it will last longer then the trust is deemed illegal and void. And the other version of the rule, practiced by a second group compromising more than half of the states, is called the modified *"wait-and-see"* version of the common-law rule, in that it allows a wait to see what happens. That is, the trust is deemed valid anyway, so long as the beneficiary obtains a full interest in the trust property within the regular 21-years plus time limits of the rule — even if it's theoretically possible that the beneficiary might not have obtained a full interest in time.

INTESTATE-SHARE LAWS: State laws which stipulate who gets what, and how much from a deceased person's estate when a person dies without leaving a will.

ELECTIVE (SPOUSAL) RIGHTS: Under state law, if a surviving spouse is unhappy with what a deceased spouse leaves her under a will, he (or she) can refuse to take what is left him under the will, and "elect" to take the share of the estate provided for one in such a situation by statute. This is called the "elective right" of a spouse. Thus, by filing the appropriate NOTICE OF ELECTION with the court within the time designated under the state law for doing so, a spouse can assert the right to take, say, one third of the decedent spouse's estate, in lieu of the bequests made under the will, depending on the specific provisions of the state law involved.

AUTOMATIC-SHARE LAWS: Under the laws of most states, the decedent's spouse (the surviving spouse) is granted the right to take a portion of the estate free of the claims of others. The share of the estate allowed the spouse under this circumstance is called the "automatic share", and is in addition to intestate and elective rights shares.

Alabama

Uniform acts adopted: Uniform Testamentary Additions to Trusts Act.

Court with probate jurisdiction: Probate Court.

Must trustee be a state resident? No provision.

Must trustee post bond? No provision.

Age of majority to be grantor or trustee: 19.

Rule Against Perpetuities: The common-law rule applies.

Forms of property ownership: Common law state. There is no tenancy by the entirety. Tenancy in common presumed in real estate if held jointly, unless title (deed) shows joint tenancy with the "right of survivorship" or similar words.

Note: Trusts are considered irrevocable unless powers to revoke are stated.

Any intestate-share law? Yes. Spouse gets everything if deceased has no surviving children or parents. If there are surviving parents and/or surviving children, the spouse usually gets a certain fixed dollar amount and always gets half of the estate.

Any elective rights? Yes. Spouse may elect to take up to one-third of the deceased's estate.

Any automatic-share law? Yes. Homestead: $6,000. Personal property: $3,500. Allowance for family living expenses.

State gift, inheritance, or estate taxes: No gift tax; no inheritance tax; imposes state estate tax equal to federal credit for state death taxes.

Alaska

Uniform acts adopted: Uniform Probate Code; Uniform Testamentary Additions to Trusts Act.

Court with probate jurisdiction: Superior Court.

Must trustee be a state resident? No, but if out of state trustee is appointed, trust must be registered.

Must trustee post bond? No, unless required by trust, requested by beneficiary or ordered by court.

Age of majority to be grantor or trustee: 18.

Rule Against Perpetuities: Wait and see approach; common-law rule is modified by actual rather than possible events.

Forms of property ownership: Common law state. No joint tenancy in personal property. Persons with undivided interests in real estate are tenants-in-common. Spouses who acquire real estate are presumed to hold it as tenants by entirety unless stated otherwise.

Any intestate-share law? Yes. Spouse gets everything if deceased has no surviving children or parents. If there are surviving parents and/or surviving children, the spouse usually gets a certain fixed dollar amount and always gets one-half of the estate.

Any elective rights? Yes. Spouse may elect to take one-third of the estate.

Any automatic-share law? Yes. Homestead: $27,000. Personal property: $10,000. Allowance for family living expenses if estate is insolvent.

State gift, inheritance, or estate taxes: No gift tax; no inheritance tax; imposes state estate tax equal to federal credit for state death taxes.

Arizona

Uniform acts adopted: Uniform Probate Code; Uniform Trustees' Powers Act; Uniform Testamentary Additions to Trusts Act.

Court with probate jurisdiction: Superior Court.

Must trustee be a state resident? No, but if out of state trustee is appointed, must qualify to do business in Arizona.

Must trustee post bond? No, unless required by trust.

Age of majority to be grantor or trustee: 18.

Rule Against Perpetuities: The common-law rule applies.

Forms of property ownership: Community property state. Property acquired during marriage outside the state before moving into state, is quasi-community property controlled by Arizona law. To create joint tenancy between spouses, deed or other document must clearly state that it is intended to be joint property with the "right of survivorship" provision. No tenancy by the entirety.

Any intestate-share law? Yes. If the deceased had any children which were his or hers alone, such as from a previous marriage, the surviving spouse gets half of the deceased's "separate property" and half of the deceased's "community property". Otherwise, the surviving spouse takes all.

Any elective rights? No.

Any automatic-share law? Yes. Homestead: $12,000. Personal property: $7,000. Allowance for family living expenses. Half of all "community property".

State gift, inheritance, or estate taxes: No gift tax; no inheritance tax; imposes state estate tax equal to federal credit for state death taxes.

Arkansas

Uniform acts adopted: Uniform Testamentary Additions to Trusts Act.

Court with probate jurisdiction: Probate Court.

Must trustee be a state resident? No, but if out of state trustee is appointed, must qualify to do business in Arkansas.

Must trustee post bond? Yes, unless not required by trust.

Age of majority to be grantor or trustee: 18.

Rule Against Perpetuities: The common-law rule applies.

Forms of property ownership: Common law state. Property acquired in another state is community property if considered so in other state. Tenancy in common, and joint tenancy recognized. Spouses are presumed to hold real estate by tenancy by entirety unless the deed expressly states otherwise.

Any intestate-share law? Yes. Spouse gets everything if there are no surviving children and if he/she was married to the deceased for more than three years. If there are no surviving children but he/she was married to the deceased for less than three years, spouse gets half of the estate. If there are any surviving children the spouse gets no intestate share.

Any elective rights? Yes. Arkansas has an intricate right-of-election statute tied into a spouse's "dower" or "courtesy" rights. If considering exercising a right of election, you should probably consult a local professional estate appraiser knowledgeable in this area, and you should do so quickly: spouses have only one month after the claims filing deadline expires to use their right of election.

Any automatic-share law? Yes. Homestead: $2,500. Personal property: $1,000. Half of all community property. Allowance for family living expenses of up to $500 for 2 months. Family furnishings.

State gift, inheritance, or estate taxes: No gift tax; no inheritance tax; imposes state estate tax equal to federal credit for state death taxes.

California

Uniform acts adopted: Uniform Testamentary Additions to Trusts Act; Uniform Statutory Rule Against Perpetuities.

Court with probate jurisdiction: Superior Court.

Must trustee be a state resident? No, but if out of state trustee is appointed, trustee's actions are severely limited.

Must trustee post bond? No, unless required by trust.

Age of majority to be grantor or trustee: 18.

Rule Against Perpetuities: The common-law rule is modified by wait-and-see approach.

Forms of property ownership: Community property state. Property held in both names of spouses as joint tenants is not community property unless so stated. No tenancy by entirety.

Any intestate-share law? Yes. Half of any property acquired during the marriage when and if the couple was not living in California. Depending upon the number and relationship of surviving family members, spouse also gets from one-third to all of the deceased's separate property.

Any elective rights? No.

Any automatic-share law? No.

State gift, inheritance, or estate taxes: No gift tax; no inheritance tax; imposes state estate tax equal to federal credit for state death taxes.

Colorado

Uniform acts adopted: Uniform Probate Code; Uniform Testamentary Additions to Trusts Act; Uniform Statutory Rule Against Perpetuities.

Court with probate jurisdiction: District Court (Probate Court in Denver).

Must trustee be a state resident? No, but if out of state trustee is appointed, trust must be registered.

Must trustee post bond? No, unless required by trust or requested by beneficiary.

Age of majority to be grantor or trustee: 18.

Rule Against Perpetuities: The common-law rule is modified by wait-and-see approach.

Forms of property ownership: Common law state. There is no tenancy-by-the-entirety. Tenancy-in-common is presumed unless otherwise stated. Joint tenancy recognized if explicitly titled as joint tenancy with right of survivorship.

Any intestate-share law? Yes. Spouse gets everything if there are no surviving children. If any children are those of the deceased's only, such as from a prior marriage, the spouse gets $25,000 and half of the estate.

Any elective rights? Yes. Spouse may take half of the estate.

Any automatic-share law? Yes. Half of all community property. Personal property: $7,500. Allowance for family living expenses if estate is insolvent.

State gift, inheritance, or estate taxes: No gift tax; no inheritance tax; imposes state estate tax equal to federal credit for state death taxes.

Connecticut

Uniform acts adopted: Uniform Testamentary Additions to Trusts Act; Uniform Statutory Rule Against Perpetuities.

Court with probate jurisdiction: Probate Court.

Must trustee be a state resident? No, but if out of state trustee is appointed, a resident agent must also be appointed.

Must trustee post bond? Yes, unless not required by trust.

Age of majority to be grantor or trustee: 21.

Rule Against Perpetuities: The common-law rule is modified by wait-and-see approach.

Forms of property ownership: Common-law state. There is no tenancy-by-the-entirety. In joint ownership, tenancy-in-common is presumed unless words "joint tenants" follows names. Joint tenancy automatically includes right of survivorship.

Any intestate-share law? Yes. Spouse gets everything if the deceased leaves no surviving children or parents. Otherwise, depending on whether there are surviving children and/or surviving parents of the deceased, the spouse can get up to three-fourths of the estate plus the first $100,000.

Any elective rights? Yes. Spouse gets a "lifetime use" of one-third of the estate.

Any automatic-share law? Yes, but very limited. The court may allow for family living expenses and use of any car during the administration of the estate.

State gift, inheritance, or estate taxes: No gift tax; no inheritance tax; imposes state estate tax equal to federal credit for state death taxes.

Delaware

Uniform acts adopted: None.

Court with probate jurisdiction: Chancery Court.

Must trustee be a state resident? No.

Must trustee post bond? No provision.

Age of majority to be grantor or trustee: 18.

Rule Against Perpetuities: The common-law rule is modified by wait-and-see approach.

Forms of property ownership: Common-law state. Tenancy in common presumed. If joint owners are married, tenancy by entirety created. Joint tenancy created only if expressly so stated.

Any intestate-share law? Yes. Spouse gets everything if the deceased leaves no surviving children or parents. Otherwise, depending on whether there are surviving children and/or surviving parents of the deceased, the spouse may or may not get the first $50,000 of the estate, but will always get (1) half of the decedent's real estate until the spouse dies.

Any elective rights? Yes. Spouse may take one-third of the estate. The definition of "estate" is, however, tied to the definition of "adjusted gross estate" under federal estate tax law.

Any automatic-share law? Yes, but very limited. There is a $2,000 allowance for living expenses.

State gift, inheritance, or estate taxes: imposes a state gift tax; an inheritance tax of up to 16%; and a state estate tax equal to federal credit for state death taxes less any amounts paid on state inheritance tax.

District of Columbia

Uniform acts adopted: Uniform Testamentary Additions to Trusts Act

Court with probate jurisdiction: Superior Court.

Must trustee be a state resident? No provision.

Must trustee post bond? Yes, if appointed by the court.

Age of majority to be grantor or trustee: 18.

Rule Against Perpetuities: The common-law rule applies.

Forms of property ownership: Common-law state. Tenancy-in-common presumed unless joint tenancy is stated. Joint tenancy, tenancy by entirety, can be created if at least one of the granting owners is also a recipient owner. Joint ownership by husband and wife presumes tenancy by entirety.

Any intestate-share law? Yes. Spouse gets everything if there are no surviving children of the spouse and/or the deceased and no surviving relatives or parents of the deceased. Otherwise, the spouse's intestate share will be from one-third to one-half of the deceased's estate.

Any elective rights? Yes. Spouse can elect to take either: (1) half of the deceased's estate, after debts, or (2) use of one-third of the deceased's real property until the spouse dies and half of the deceased's other property, after debts.

Any automatic-share law? Yes. Allowance for $10,000 in family living expenses, minus $750 in funeral costs.

State gift, inheritance, or estate taxes: No gift tax; no inheritance tax; imposes state estate tax equal to federal credit for state death taxes.

Florida

Uniform acts adopted: Uniform Trustees' Powers Act; Uniform Testamentary Additions to Trusts Act; Uniform Statutory Rule Against Perpetuities.

Court with probate jurisdiction: Circuit Court.

Must trustee be a state resident? No, but if out-of-state trustee is appointed, may be required to register trust if requested by beneficiary or directed by trust.

Must trustee post bond? No, unless required by trust, or by court order, or requested by beneficiary.

Age of majority to be grantor or trustee: 18.

Rule Against Perpetuities: The common-law rule is modified by wait and see approach. Personal property or real estate owned by husband and wife is presumed to be tenancy by the entirety and survivorship. Joint tenancy includes survivorship only if expressly stated.

Forms of property ownership: Common-law state.

Any intestate-share law? Yes. Spouse gets everything if there are no surviving children. If there are any children, the spouse gets the first $20,000 and half the estate. If any children are not those of the surviving spouse, such as from a prior marriage of the deceased, then the surviving spouse gets half the estate.

Any elective rights? Yes. Spouse may take 30 percent of the fair market value of all estate property in Florida (excepting joint bank accounts and after mortgages or other liens.)

Any automatic-share law? Yes. Household property: $10,000. Lifetime use of the spouse's real estate: $6,000. Allowance for family living expenses during the administration of the estate, and $1,000 of the deceased's personal effects.

State gift, inheritance, or estate taxes: No gift tax; no inheritance tax; imposes state estate tax equal to federal credit for state death taxes.

Georgia

Uniform acts adopted: Uniform Testamentary Additions to Trusts Act; Uniform Statutory Rule Against Perpetuities.

Court with probate jurisdiction: Probate Court.

Must trustee be a state resident? No.

Must trustee post bond? Court may require a successor trustee to post bond; otherwise only if required by trust or requested by beneficiary.

Age of majority to be grantor or trustee: 18.

Rule Against Perpetuities: The common-law rule is modified by wait-and-see approach.

Forms of property ownership: Common-law state. No tenancy by entirety. Tenancy in common presumed unless ownership papers refer to "joint tenants with right of survivorship" or similar language.

Any intestate-share law? Yes. Spouse gets everything if there are no surviving children. If there are surviving children, the spouse and the children get equal shares of the estate, but the spouse always gets at least one-fourth of the estate. Thus, if there are four or more children, they will divide the remaining three-fourths of the estate between themselves.

Any elective rights? No.

Any automatic-share law? Yes, but very limited. The court makes an allowance for family living expenses which starts at $1,600.

State gift, inheritance, or estate taxes: No gift tax; no inheritance tax; imposes state estate tax equal to federal credit for state death taxes.

Hawaii

Uniform acts adopted: Uniform Trustees' Powers Act; Uniform Testamentary Additions to Trusts Act.

Court with probate jurisdiction: Circuit Court.

Must trustee be a state resident? No, but if out-of-state trustee is appointed to a living trust, trust must be registered.

Must trustee post bond? No, unless required by trust or requested by beneficiary or ordered by court.

Age of majority to be grantor or trustee: 18.

Rule Against Perpetuities: The common-law rule applies.

Forms of property ownership: Common-law state. Tenancy-in-common is presumed unless expressly stated as joint tenancy or tenancy-by-entirety with "right of survivorship".

Any intestate-share law? Yes. Spouse gets everything if there are no surviving children or parents of the deceased. If there are surviving parents and/or surviving children, the spouse gets half of the estate.

Any elective rights? Yes. Spouse may take one third of the estate in the deceased's will and one third of any real estate not in the will if owned by the deceased prior to July of 1977.

Any automatic-share law? Yes. Homestead: $5,000. Personal property: $5,000. Allowance for family living expenses.

State gift, inheritance, or estate taxes: No gift tax; no inheritance tax; imposes state estate tax equal to federal credit for state death taxes.

Idaho

Uniform acts adopted: Uniform Probate Code; Uniform Trustees' Powers Act; Uniform Testamentary Additions to Trusts Act.

Court with probate jurisdiction: District Court.

Must trustee be a state resident? No, but if out of state trustee is appointed, must qualify to do business in Idaho. A trustee, whether a resident or not, must register the trust.

Must trustee post bond? No, unless required by trust, requested by beneficiary or ordered by court.

Age of majority to be grantor or trustee: 18.

Rule Against Perpetuities: Wait-and-see approach; common-law rule is modified by actual rather than possible events.

Forms of property ownership: Community property state. Tenancy-in-common is presumed unless joint tenancy is stated or property is acquired as partnership or community property, but ownership document must expressly state "joint tenancy with right of survivorship". Tenancy by entirety is not recognized.

Any intestate-share law? Yes. Spouse gets everything if there are no surviving children or parents of the deceased. If there are any surviving children who are not the spouse's, such as from a prior marriage of the deceased, the spouse gets half of the esate. In all other situations, the spouse gets half the estate plus the first $50,000.

Any elective rights? Yes. Half of any property acquired during the marriage when and if the couple was not living in Idaho.

Any automatic-share law? Yes. Half of all community property. Homestead: $4,000, unless there were dependent children living with the spouse, then $10,000. Personal property: $3,500. Allowance for family living expenses during the administration.

State gift, inheritance, or estate taxes: No gift tax; an inheritance tax of up to 30%; imposes state estate tax equal to federal credit for state death taxes less any amounts paid on state inheritance tax.

Illinois

Uniform acts adopted: Uniform Testamentary Additions to Trusts Act.

Court with probate jurisdiction: Probate Court.

Must trustee be a state resident? No.

Must trustee post bond? No, unless required by trust.

Age of majority to be grantor or trustee: 18.

Rule Against Perpetuities: Wait-and-see approach; common-law rule is modified by actual rather than possible events.

Forms of property ownership: Common law state. Tenancy-in-common presumed. Joint tenancy with right of survivorship is created only by a declaration being made on the ownership papers that estate including personal property, is held in joint tenancy with right of survivorship, and not as tenants-in-common. Tenancy by entirety is recognized.

Any intestate-share law? Yes. Spouse gets everything if there are no surviving children, the spouse gets half of the estate.

Any elective rights? Yes. Spouse may take half of the estate.

Any automatic-share law? Yes. Homestead: $7,500. Allowance for nine months of living expenses up to $10,000. Additional $2,000 for each dependent.

State gift, inheritance, or estate taxes: No gift tax; no inheritance tax; imposes state estate tax equal to federal credit for state death taxes.

Indiana

Uniform acts adopted: Uniform Testamentary Additions to Trusts Act; Uniform Statutory Rule Against Perpetuities.

Court with probate jurisdiction: Circuit or Superior Court. (Probate Court in St. Joseph and Vigo Counties).

Must trustee be a state resident? No.

Must trustee post bond? No, unless required by trust.

Age of majority to be grantor or trustee: 18.

Rule Against Perpetuities: The common-law rule is modified by wait-and-see approach.

Forms of property ownership: Common-law state. Joint tenancy, tenancy-in-common and tenancy by entirety, are recognized; but tenancy by entirety is not recognized for personal property only.

Any intestate-share law? Yes. Spouse gets everything if there are no surviving children, the spouse gets three-fourths of the estate. If there are no surviving children or parents. If there are surviving children, the spouse gets half of the estate. Special rules apply if the surviving spouse is not the deceased's first spouse.

Any elective rights? Yes. Spouse may take half of the estate, but special rules apply if the surviving spouse is not the deceased's first spouse.

Any automatic-share law? Yes, but very limited. Automatic share is limited to $8,500 in personal property.

State gift, inheritance, or estate taxes: No gift tax; an inheritance tax up to 20%; imposes state estate tax equal to federal credit for state death taxes less any amounts paid on state inheritance tax.

Iowa

Uniform acts adopted: Uniform Testamentary Additions to Trusts Act.

Court with probate jurisdiction: District Court.

Must trustee be a state resident? No.

Must trustee post bond? No, unless required by trust or ordered by court.

Age of majority to be grantor or trustee: 18.

Rule Against Perpetuities: Wait-and-see approach; common-law rule is modified by actual rather than possible events.

Forms of property ownership: Common-law state. Tenancy-in-common presumed unless joint tenancy is stated. Tenancy by entirety is not recognized.

Any intestate-share law? Yes. Spouse gets everything if there are no surviving children who are children of the deceased only, such as from a prior marriage of the deceased. Otherwise, the spouse can get either the first $50,000 of the estate or half the estate over $50,000.

Any elective rights? Yes. Spouse may take one-third of the real estate owned by the deceased during the marriage and one-third of the deceased's personal property. In thre alternative, the spouse can elect to live in the family home for life.

Any automatic-share law? Yes, but very limited. Spouse gets living expenses for one year and some personal property.

State gift, inheritance, or estate taxes: No gift tax; an inheritance tax up to 15%; imposes state estate tax equal to federal credit for state death taxes less any amounts paid on state inheritance tax.

Kansas

Uniform acts adopted: Uniform Trustees' Powers Act; Uniform Testamentary Additions to Trusts Act.

Court with probate jurisdiction: District Court.

Must trustee be a state resident? No, but if out-of-state trustee is appointed, a resident agent must also be appointed.

Must trustee post bond? Yes, unless not required by trust.

Age of majority to be grantor or trustee: 18.

Rule Against Perpetuities: The common-law rule applies, although a trust holding a stock bonus plan, disability or death benefit plan, is exempt from the rule against perpetuities.

Forms of property ownership: Common-law state. Tenancy-in-common is presumed unless joint tenancy is stated on ownership papers and transfer is from the sole owner to himself or herself and one other. Tenancy by entirety is not recognized.

Any intestate-share law? Yes. Spouse gets everything if there are no surviving children. If there are surviving children, the spouse gets half the estate.

Any elective rights? Yes. Spouse can elect to take intestate share.

Any automatic-share law? Yes. Personal property: $7,500. Spouse is also entitled to lifetime use of a certain amount of the deceased's real estate, which varies from 1 acre to 60 acres depending upon whether it is urban land or farm land.

State gift, inheritance, or estate taxes: No gift tax; an inheritance tax up to 15%; imposes state estate tax equal to federal credit for state death taxes less any amounts paid on state inheritance tax.

Kentucky

Uniform acts adopted: Uniform Trustees' Powers Act; Uniform Testamentary Additions to Trusts Act.

Court with probate jurisdiction: District Court.

Must trustee be a state resident? No provision.

Must trustee post bond? No, unless required by trust, requested by beneficiary or ordered by court.

Age of majority to be grantor or trustee: 18.

Rule Against Perpetuities: Wait-and-see approach; common-law rule is modified by actual rather than possible events.

Forms of property ownership: Common-law state. Tenancy-in-common is presumed in a husband-and-wife situation unless tenancy by entirety is stated, but deed or other document must expressly state that spouses own property as tenants by entirety with "rights of survivorship." Joint tenancy is worthless as there are no rights of survivorship permitted for joint tenants.

Any intestate-share law? Yes. Spouse gets everything if there are no surviving children, parents or relatives of the deceased. Otherwise the spouse's intestate share share is simply what the spouse gets as his or her automatic share.

Any elective rights? Yes, but for practical purposes they are irelevant as they are virtually identical to the automatic share.

Any automatic-share law? Yes. Spouse gets half of all community property and half of the real estate owned by the deceased at death, plus lifetime use of one-third of other real estate. Further, the spouse gets half of the deceased's separate personal propery and living expenses up to $7,500.

State gift, inheritance, or estate taxes: No gift tax; an inheritance tax up to 16%; imposes state estate tax equal to federal credit for state death taxes less any amounts paid on state inheritance tax.

Louisiana

Uniform acts adopted: None.

Court with probate jurisdiction: District Court.

Must trustee be a state resident? No.

Must trustee post bond? Yes, unless not required by trust.

Age of majority to be grantor or trustee: 18.

Rule Against Perpetuities: The common-law rule applies.

Forms of property ownership: Community property state. Joint ownership (called "indivision") if two or more persons are listed as owners. Louisiana law, which is based on French civil law, does not recognize either tenancy by entirety or tenancy-in-common.

Any intestate-share law? Yes. Spouse gets everything if there are no surviving children or parents of the deceased. If there are surviving parents but no surviving children, spouse gets half of the estate. If there are any surviving children, spouse gets lifetime use of deceased's separate property which terminates if the spouse remarries.

Any elective rights? No.

Any automatic-share law? No.

State gift, inheritance, or estate taxes: No gift tax; an inheritance tax up to 10%; imposes state estate tax equal to federal credit for state death taxes less any amounts paid on state inheritance tax.

Maine

Uniform acts adopted: Uniform Probate Code; Uniform Testamentary Additions to Trusts Act.

Court with probate jurisdiction: Probate Court.

Must trustee be a state resident? No, but if out-of-state trustee is appointed, he must qualify to do business in Maine.

Must trustee post bond? No, unless required by trust or requested by beneficiary or ordered by court.

Age of majority to be grantor or trustee: 18.

Rule Against Perpetuities: The common-law rule applies.

Forms of property ownership: Common law state. Ownership by two or more persons presumes tenancy-in-common unless joint tenancy is expressly stated. There is no tenancy by entirety.

Any intestate-share law? Yes. Spouse gets everything if there are no surviving children or parents of the deceased. If there are surviving parents and/or surviving children, the spouse usually gets a certain fixed dollar amount and in no event may he/she get less than half of the estate.

Any elective rights? Yes. Spouse may take one third of the estate.

Any automatic-share law? Yes. Homestead: $5,000. Personal property: $3,500. Allowance for living expenses during term of estate administration and if estate is insolvent.

State gift, inheritance, or estate taxes: No gift tax; no inheritance tax; imposes state estate tax equal to federal credit for state death taxes.

Maryland

Uniform acts adopted: Uniform Testamentary Additions to Trusts Act.

Court with probate jurisdiction: Orphans Court (Circuit Court in Hartford and Montgomery Counties).

Must trustee be a state resident? No Provision.

Must trustee post bond? No.

Age of majority to be grantor or trustee: 18.

Rule Against Perpetuities: The common-law rule applies.

Forms of property ownership: Common-law state. Tenancy-in-common is recognized. Joint tenancy must be expressly stated. Joint ownership by spouses presumes tenancy by entirety unless it is otherwise stated.

Any intestate-share law? Yes. Spouse gets everything if there are no surviving children or parents of the deceased. If there are surviving parents and/or surviving children, the spouse usually gets a certain fixed dollar amount and in no event does he/she get less than half of the estate.

Any elective rights? Yes. Spouse may take half of the estate if there are no living children, one-third of the estate if there are living children. Spouse must file notice of election within 30 days after creditor claims due.

Any automatic-share law? Yes, but very limited. There is a $2,000 allowance for living expenses plus an additional $1,000 for every child under 18.

State gift, inheritance, or estate taxes: No gift tax; an inheritance tax of up to 10%; imposes state estate tax equal to federal credit for state death taxes less any amounts paid on state inheritance taxes.

Massachusetts

Uniform acts adopted: Uniform Testamentary Additions to Trusts Act; Uniform Statutory Rule Against Perpetuities.

Court with probate jurisdiction: Probate and Family Court.

Must trustee be a state resident? No, but if out-of-state trustee is appointed and trust holds Massachusetts land, trust must be registered.

Must trustee post bond? No, unless required by trust.

Age of majority to be grantor or trustee: 18.

Rule Against Perpetuities: The common-law rule is modified by wait-and-see approach.

Forms of property ownership: Common-law state. Tenancy in common, joint tenancy and tenancy by entirety are recognized. Joint ownership by husband and wife creates tenancy in common, unless it is otherwise stated in the document of ownership, and should contain the phrase "with rights of survivorship".

Any intestate-share law? Yes. Spouse gets everything if there are no surviving children, parents or other relatives of the deceased. If there are no surviving children but there are other surviving relatives, the spouse usually gets the first $200,000 and half of everything over that amount. If there are surviving children, the spouse gets half of the estate.

Any elective rights? Yes. Spouse may take anywhere from one-third of the estate, if there are surviving children, to $25,000 and half of the estate, if there are no surviving children or relatives.

Any automatic-share law? Yes. Homestead: use of home for anywhere from six months up to death or remarriage; living expenses for six months.

State gift, inheritance, or estate taxes: No gift tax; no inheritance tax; there is a state inheritance tax of up to 16% not tied to federal estate tax credit.

Michigan

Uniform acts adopted: Uniform Probate Code; Uniform Testamentary Additions to Trusts Act; Uniform Statutory Rule Against Perpetuities .

Court with probate jurisdiction: Probate Court.

Must trustee be a state resident? No, but if out-of-state trustee is appointed, he/she must qualify to do business in Michigan.

Must trustee post bond? No, unless required by trust.

Age of majority to be grantor or trustee: 18.

Rule Against Perpetuities: The common-law rule is modified by wait-and-see approach.

Forms of property ownership: Common-law state. Tenancy-in-common, joint tenancy and tenancy by entirety are recognized. Joint tenancy is created only if expressly so stated. Joint tenancy by spouses and joint ownership of real estate by spouses is presumed to be tenancy-by-entirety unless otherwise stated. Joint tenancy and tenancy by entirety document must contain the statement "with right of survivorship".

Any intestate-share law? Yes. Spouse gets everything, if there are no surviving children or parents of the deceased. If there are surviving parents and/or surviving children, the spouse usually gets a certain fixed dollar amount and in no event does he/she get less than half of the estate.

Any elective rights? Yes. Spouse has choice of taking half of the estate or lifetime use of one third of the real estate owned during the marriage.

Any automatic-share law? Yes. Homestead: $10,000. Personal property: $3,500. Allowance for living expenses.

State gift, inheritance, or estate taxes: No gift tax; an inheritance tax of up to 17%; imposes state estate tax equal to federal credit for state death taxes less any amounts paid on state inheritance tax.

Minnesota

Uniform acts adopted: Uniform Probate Code; Uniform Trustees' Powers Act; Uniform Testamentary Additions to Trusts Act; Uniform Statutory Rule Against Perpetuities.

Court with probate jurisdiction: Probate Court.

Must trustee be a state resident? No provision.

Must trustee post bond? No provision.

Age of majority to be grantor or trustee: 18.

Rule Against Perpetuities: The common-law rule is modified by the wait-and-see approach.

Forms of property ownership: Common-law state. Tenancy-in-common is presumed unless the deed or other document of ownership expressly states it is in joint tenancy. Tenancy by entirety is not recognized.

Any intestate-share law? Yes. Spouse gets everything if there are no surviving children. If there are surviving children, the spouse usually gets a certain fixed dollar amount and always gets half of the estate.

Any elective rights? Yes. Spouse may take one-third of the estate.

Any automatic-share law? Yes. Personal property: $9,000 and one car. Use of homestead and allowance for living expenses..

State gift, inheritance, or estate taxes: No gift tax; no inheritance tax; imposes state estate tax equal to federal credit for state death taxes.

Mississippi

Uniform acts adopted: Uniform Trustees' Powers Act; Uniform Testamentary Additions to Trusts Act.

Court with probate jurisdiction: Chancery Court.

Must trustee be a state resident? No, but if out of state trustee is appointed, must qualify to do business in Mississippi.

Must trustee post bond? No, unless required by trust.

Age of majority to be grantor or trustee: 18.

Rule Against Perpetuities: The common-law rule applies.

Forms of property ownership: Common-law state. Tenancy-in-common, joint tenancy and tenancy by entirety are recognized. Ownership by two or more persons presumes the title to be tenancy-in-common, unless joint tenancy or tenancy by the entirety is expressly stated, and should contain a phrase such as "with right of survivorship".

Any intestate-share law? Yes. Spouse gets everything if there are no surviving children. If there are surviving children, the spouse and children take equal shares of the estate.

Any elective rights? Yes. Spouse may take one-third of the estate if there are surviving children, but no more than intestate share.

Any automatic-share law? Yes. Homestead: lifetime use up to $30,000 and 150 acres. Allowance for living expenses.

State gift, inheritance, or estate taxes: No gift tax; no inheritance tax; there is a state estate tax of up to 16% not tied to federal credit for state death taxes.

Missouri

Uniform acts adopted: None.

Court with probate jurisdiction: Circuit Court.

Must trustee be a state resident? No, but if out of state trustee is appointed, must qualify to do business in Missouri.

Must trustee post bond? Yes, unless not required by trust.

Age of majority to be grantor or trustee: 18.

Rule Against Perpetuities: The common-law rule applies, but court may change a trust to make it valid.

Forms of property ownership: Common-law state. Tenancy-in-common, joint tenancy and tenancy by entirety are recognized. Ownership by two or more persons presumes tenancy in common, unless joint tenancy is stated and should contain a phrase "with rights of survivorship."

Any intestate-share law? Yes. Spouse gets everything if there are no surviving children or parents of the deceased. If there are surviving parents and/or surviving children, the spouse usually gets a certain fixed dollar amount and in no event does he/she get less than half of the estate.

Any elective rights? Yes. Spouse may take half of the estate if there are no surviving children. If there are surviving children, spouse may take one third of the estate.

Any automatic-share law? Yes. Homestead: $7,500 or up to half of the estate, whichever is less. Some personal property and an allowance for living expenses.

State gift, inheritance, or estate taxes: No gift tax; no inheritance tax; imposes state estate tax equal to federal credit for state death taxes.

Montana

Uniform acts adopted: Uniform Probate Code; Uniform Trustees' Powers Act; Uniform Testamentary Additions to Trusts Act; Uniform Statutory Rule Against Perpetuities.

Court with probate jurisdiction: District Court.

Must trustee be a state resident? No, but if out-of-state trustee is appointed, he/she must qualify to do business in Montana.

Must trustee post bond? No provision.

Age of majority to be grantor or trustee: 18.

Rule Against Perpetuities: The common-law rule is modified by wait-and-see approach.

Forms of property ownership: Common-law state. Partnership interests, tenancy-in-common and joint tenancy (called "interests in common" and "joint interests") are recognized. There is no tenancy by entirety in personal property. Tenancy in common is presumed unless joint tenancy ("joint interests") is expressly stated in the deed or other ownership document.

Any intestate-share law? Yes. Spouse gets everything if there are no surviving children who are the deceased's only, such as from a prior marriage. If there are surviving children of the deceased's only, the spouse gets one-third of the estate.

Any elective rights? Yes. Spouse may take one-third of the estate.

Any automatic-share law? Yes. Homestead: $20,000. Personal property: up to $3,500. Allowance for living expenses.

State gift, inheritance, or estate taxes: No gift tax; an inheritance tax of up to 32%; imposes state estate tax equal to federal credit for state death taxes less any amounts paid on state inheritance tax.

Nebraska

Uniform acts adopted: Uniform Probate Code; Uniform Testamentary Additions to Trusts Act; Uniform Statutory Rule Against Perpetuities.

Court with probate jurisdiction: County Court.

Must trustee be a state resident? No, but if out-of-state trustee is appointed, he/she must qualify to do business in Nebraska.

Must trustee post bond? No, unless required by trust.

Age of majority to be grantor or trustee: 18.

Rule Against Perpetuities: The common-law rule is modified by wait-and-see approach.

Forms of property ownership: Common-law state. Tenancy-in-common and joint tenancy recognized, but must be expressly stated and certain such statements as "joint tenants with the right of survivorship." There is no tenancy by entirety.

Any intestate-share law? Yes. Spouse gets everything if there are no surviving children or parents of the deceased. If there are surviving parents and/or surviving children, the spouse usually gets a certain fixed dollar amount and in no event does he/she get less than half of the estate.

Any elective rights? Yes. Spouse may take half of the estate.

Any automatic-share law? Yes. Homestead: $7,500. Personal property: $5,000. Allowance for living expenses.

State gift, inheritance, or estate taxes: No gift tax; no inheritance tax; no state estate tax.

Nevada

Uniform acts adopted: Uniform Testamentary Additions to Trusts Act; Uniform Statutory Rule Against Perpetuities.

Court with probate jurisdiction: District Court.

Must trustee be a state resident? No provision.

Must trustee post bond? No, unless required by trust or ordered by court.

Age of majority to be grantor or trustee: 18.

Rule Against Perpetuities: The common-law rule is modified by wait-and-see approach.

Forms of property ownership: Community property state. Tenancy-in-common, joint tenancy and community property recognized. No tenancy by entirety.

Any intestate-share law? Yes. Spouse gets all of the deceased's separate property if there are any surviving children, parents, brother or sisters, the spouse gets from one-third to half of the deceased's separate property.

Any elective rights? No.

Any automatic-share law? Yes. In addition to half of the community property, the spouse gets a homestead exemption, some personal property, and possibly an allowance for living expenses.

State gift, inheritance, or estate taxes: No gift tax; no inheritance tax; no state estate tax.

New Hampshire

Uniform acts adopted: Uniform Trustees' Powers Act; Uniform Testamentary Additions to Trusts Act.

Court with probate jurisdiction: Probate Court.

Must trustee be a state resident? No, but if out-of-state trustee is appointed, a resident agent must also be appointed.

Must trustee post bond? No, unless required by trust or ordered by court.

Age of majority to be grantor or trustee: 18.

Rule Against Perpetuities: Wait-and-see approach; common-law rule is modified by actual rather than possible events.

Forms of property ownership: Common-law state. Tenancy-in-common is presumed unless joint tenancy is expressly stated on the document of ownership, which should also contain statement such as "joint tenancy with rights of survivorship". There is no tenancy by entirety.

Any intestate-share law? Yes. Spouse gets everything if there are no surviving children or parents of the deceased. If there are surviving parents and/or surviving children, the spouse usually gets a certain fixed dollar amount and always gets half of the estate.

Any elective rights? Yes. Spouse may take one-third of the estate if there are surviving children. If there are no surviving children, but there are surviving parents, brothers or sisters, the spouse gets $20,000 and half of the rest of the estate. If there are no surviving children, parents, brothers or sisters, the spouse gets $10,000, $2,000 for every year of marriage, and half of the rest of the estate.

Any automatic-share law? Yes, but very limited. Spouse may use home for 40 days after death and gets an allowance for living expenses which will be deducted from his or her inheritance.

State gift, inheritance, or estate taxes: No gift tax; an inheritance tax of up to 15%; imposes state estate tax equal to federal credit for state death taxes less any amount paid on state inheritance tax.

New Jersey

Uniform acts adopted: Uniform Probate Code; Uniform Testamentary Additions to Trusts Act; Uniform Statutory Rule Against Perpetuities.

Court with probate jurisdiction: Surrogate's Court.

Must trustee be a state resident? No.

Must trustee post bond? No, unless party is not the appointed trustee, or the trust requires it or the court orders it.

Age of majority to be grantor or trustee: 18.

Rule Against Perpetuities: The common-law rule is modified by wait and see approach.

Forms of property ownership: Common-law state. Tenancy by the entirety is recognized for both real and personal property, but deed or other document must be explicit in naming both spouses as "husband and wife". Ownership by spouses presumes tenancy-by-entirety unless stated otherwise. Joint tenancy is recognized for both real and personal property, but deed or other document must expressly state the intent to create joint tenancy. Tenancy-in-common is also recognized.

Any intestate-share law? Yes. Spouse gets everything if there are no surviving children or parents of the deceased. If there are surviving parents and/or surviving children, the spouse usually gets a certain fixed dollar amount and always gets half of the estate.

Any elective rights? Yes. Spouse may take one-third of the estate.

Any automatic-share law? Yes. The spouse gets only an allowance for living expenses.

State gift, inheritance, or estate taxes: No gift tax; an inheritance tax of up to 16%; imposes state estate tax equal to federal credit for state death taxes less any amounts paid on state inheritance tax.

New Mexico

Uniform acts adopted: Uniform Probate Code; Uniform Trustees' Powers Act; Uniform Testamentary Additions to Trusts Act.

Court with probate jurisdiction: Probate or District Court.

Must trustee be a state resident? No.

Must trustee post bond? No, unless required by trust.

Age of majority to be grantor or trustee: 18.

Rule Against Perpetuities: Wait-and-see approach; common-law rule is modified by actual rather than possible events.

Forms of property ownership: Community property state. Tenancy-in-common, joint tenancy and community property are recognized. Spouses may hold real estate as joint tenants. There is no tenancy by entirety.

Any intestate-share law? Yes. Spouse gets everything if there are no surviving children. If there are surviving children, the spouse gets the deceased's half of all community property and one-fourth of the deceased's separate property.

Any elective rights? No.

Any automatic-share law? Yes. Half of all community property. Homestead: up to $10,000. Personal property: $3,500. $10,000 allowance for living expenses.

State gift, inheritance, or estate taxes: No gift tax; no inheritance tax; imposes state estate tax equal to federal credit for state death taxes.

New York

Uniform acts adopted: Uniform Testamentary Additions to Trusts Act.

Court with probate jurisdiction: Probate Court.

Must trustee be a state resident? No.

Must trustee post bond? No, unless required by trust.

Age of majority to be grantor or trustee: 18.

Rule Against Perpetuities: The common-law rule applies, with certain modifications designed to eliminate invalidity in specified cases.

Forms of property ownership: Common-law state. Tenancy-in-common, joint tenancy and tenancy by entirety are recognized. Joint ownership by spouses presumes tenancy by entirety, unless otherwise expressly specified in the document of ownership. Joint ownership by couples not legally married but who are described as husband and wife, presumes joint tenancy unless tenancy-in-common is expressly stated. Tenancy-in-common is presumed unless joint tenancy is expressly stated. Tenancy-by-the entirety is allowed for real property only, and is not recognized in personal property.

Any intestate-share law? Yes. Spouse gets everything if there are no surviving children or parents of the deceased. If there are surviving parents and/or surviving children, the spouse gets the firts $4,000 to $25,000 of the estate and from one-third to the rest.

Any elective rights? Yes. Spouse may take from one-third of the estate.

Any automatic-share law? Yes, but very limited. Personal property: up to $6,000.

State gift, inheritance, or estate taxes: has a gift tax; no inheritance tax; imposes state estate tax of up to 21% or not less than any federal credit for state death taxes.

North Carolina

Uniform acts adopted: Uniform Testamentary Additions to Trusts Act.

Court with probate jurisdiction: Superior Court.

Must trustee be a state resident? No, but if out-of-state trustee is appointed, a resident agent must also be appointed.

Must trustee post bond? No, unless party is not the appointed trustee, or unless required by trust or ordered by court.

Age of majority to be grantor or trustee: 18.

Rule Against Perpetuities: The common-law rule applies.

Forms of property ownership: Common-law state. Tenancy-in-common, joint tenancy and tenancy-by-entirety are recognized. Tenancy by entirety is allowed for real property only and is not recognized for personal property. The deed or other document must, in the case of joint tenancy, expressly contain the statement "joint tenants with rights of survivorship".

Any intestate-share law? Yes. Spouse gets everything if there are no surviving children or parents of the deceased. If there are surviving parents and/or surviving children, the spouse gets $15,000 to $25,000 in personal property and one-third of the balance of the estate.

Any elective rights? Yes. If the provision for the spouse in the will is less than what the spouse would have received as his or her intestate share if the deceased had died intestate, the spouse may take one-third of the real estate owned during the marriage, or to have the use of the decedent's home for the spouse's lifetime.

Any automatic-share law? Yes. Allowance for living expenses from $5,000 to half of the deceased's annual income prior to date of death.

State gift, inheritance, or estate taxes: No gift tax; an inheritance tax of up to 17%; imposes state estate tax equal to federal credit for state death taxes less any amounts paid on state inheritance tax.

North Dakota

Uniform acts adopted: Uniform Probate Code; Uniform Testamentary Additions to Trusts Act Uniform Statutory Rule Against Perpetuities.

Court with probate jurisdiction: County Court.

Must trustee be a state resident? No provision.

Must trustee post bond? No provision.

Age of majority to be grantor or trustee: 18.

Rule Against Perpetuities: The common-law rule is modified by wait-and-see approach.

Forms of property ownership: Common-law state. Tenancy-in-common and joint tenancy are recognized. Tenancy by the entirety is not recognized.

NOTE: Trust is considered irrevocable unless power to revoke is stated in the instrument.

Any intestate-share law? Yes. Spouse gets everything if there are surviving children or parents of the deceased. If there are no surviving parents and/or surviving children, the spouse usually gets a certain fixed dollar amount and always gets half of the estate.

Any elective rights? Yes. Spouse may take one-third of the estate.

Any automatic-share law? Yes. Spouse gets homestead for life. Personal property: $5,000. Allowance for living expenses.

State gift, inheritance, or estate taxes: No gift tax; no inheritance tax; imposes state estate tax equal to federal credit for state death taxes.

Ohio

Uniform acts adopted: Uniform Testamentary Additions to Trusts Act.

Court with probate jurisdiction: Court of Common Pleas.

Must trustee be a state resident? No provision.

Must trustee post bond? Yes, unless not required by trust.

Age of majority to be grantor or trustee: 18.

Rule Against Perpetuities: The common-law rule is modified by wait-and-see approach.

Forms of property ownership: Common-law state. Tenancy-in-common, joint tenancy and tenancy by entirety are recognized. If joint tenancy, term must be stated in the document of ownership and reference made to ownership as a "survivorship tenancy."

NOTE: Trust is considered irrevocable unless power to revoke is stated in the trust instrument.

Any intestate-share law? Yes. Spouse gets everything if there are no surviving children. If there are surviving children, the spouse gets from the first $20,000 to the first $60,000 of the estate and from one-third to half of the balance of the estate.

Any elective rights? Yes. Spouse may take from one-third to half of the estate.

Any automatic-share law? Yes, but very limited. Spouse gets use of the homestead for one year and $5,000 allowance for living expenses. Living expenses are deducted from spouse's inheritance.

State gift, inheritance, or estate taxes: No gift tax; no inheritance tax; imposes state estate tax of up to 7% or not less than any federal credit for state death taxes.

Oklahoma

Uniform acts adopted: Uniform Testamentary Additions to Trusts Act.

Court with probate jurisdiction: District Court.

Must trustee be a state resident? No, but if out of state trustee is appointed, a resident agent must also be appointed.

Must trustee post bond? Yes, unless not required by trust.

Age of majority to be grantor or trustee: 18.

Rule Against Perpetuities: The common-law rule applies, but court can modify trust to make it valid.

Forms of property ownership: Common-law state. Tenancy-in-common, joint tenancy and tenancy by entirety are recognized. For joint tenancy, the statement "joint tenancy with rights of survivorship" must be stated in the deed or other ownership document.

Any intestate-share law? Yes. Spouse gets everything if there are no surviving children, parents, borthers or sisters of the deceased. If there are surviving parents, children, brothers or sisters, the spouse gets from half to all the property acquired by "joint industry" during the marriage and from up to half of the estate.

Any elective rights? Yes. Spouse may take half of all the property acquired by "joint industry" during the marriage.

Any automatic-share law? Yes. Use of homestead, personal property and an allowance for living expenses.

State gift, inheritance, or estate taxes: No gift tax; no inheritance tax; imposes estate tax of up to 15% but not less than the federal credit for state death taxes.

Oregon

Uniform acts adopted: Uniform Trustees' Powers Act; Uniform Testamentary Additions to Trusts Act; Uniform Statutory Rule Against Perpetuities.

Court with probate jurisdiction: Circuit or County Court.

Must trustee be a state resident? No provision.

Must trustee post bond? No provision.

Age of majority to be grantor or trustee: 18.

Rule Against Perpetuities: The common-law rule is modified by wait-and-see approach.

Forms of property ownership: Tenancy by the entirety is recognized for real property but not for personal property. Equivalent of joint tenancy is recognized for real property and personal property, if the deed or other document expressly states that the property is to be held "not as tenants-in-common but with the right of survivorship".

Any intestate-share law? Yes. Spouse gets everything if there are no surviving children who are children of the deceased's only. If there are surviving children of the deceased's only, such as from a prior marriage, the spouse usually gets half of the estate.

Any elective rights? Yes. Spouse may take one-fourth of the estate.

Any automatic-share law? Yes. Use of homestead for one year and allowance for living expenses of up to two years.

State gift, inheritance, or estate taxes: No gift tax; no inheritance tax; imposes state estate tax equal to federal credit for state death taxes.

Pennsylvania

Uniform acts adopted: Uniform Probate Code; Uniform Testamentary Additions to Trusts Act.

Court with probate jurisdiction: Court of Common Pleas.

Must trustee be a state resident? No.

Must trustee post bond? No, unless required by trust or ordered by court.

Age of majority to be grantor or trustee: 18.

Rule Against Perpetuities: Wait-and-see approach; common-law rule is modified by actual rather than possible events.

Forms of property ownership: Common-law state. Tenancy-in-common and tenancy by entirety are recognized. Joint tenancy with right of survivorship recognized only if stated on the document of ownership with a statement such a "joint tenants with right of survivorship". Real estate jointly owned by spouses are presumed held in tenancy by the entirety unless stated otherwise. Tenancy by the entirety in personal property is recognized.

Any intestate-share law? Yes. Spouse gets everything if there are no surviving children or parents of the deceased. If there are surviving parents and/or surviving children, the spouse usually gets a certain fixed dollar amount and always gets half of the estate.

Any elective rights? Yes. Spouse may take one-third of the estate.

Any automatic-share law? Yes, but very limited. There is an allowance of up to $2,000 for living expenses.

State gift, inheritance, or estate taxes: No gift tax; an inheritance tax of up to 15%; imposes state estate tax equal to federal credit for state death taxes less any amounts paid on inheritance tax.

Puerto Rico

Uniform acts adopted: None.

Must trustee be a state resident? No.

Must trustee post bond? No, unless ordered by court.

Age of majority to be grantor or trustee: 21.

Rule Against Perpetuities: A trust is void if there is an established order of succession extending beyond the lives of two persons in being.

Forms of property ownership: Community property state. Co-ownership, community and cojugal property recognized. Property acquired during marriage belongs to both spouses in equal parts; property is presumed to belong to the marriage. Each spouse may dispose of half of community property by will. *NOTE:* Trust is considered irrevocable unless power to revoke is expressly stated in the trust instrument.

Rhode Island

Uniform acts adopted: None.

Court with probate jurisdiction: Probate Court.

Must trustee be a state resident? No provision.

Must trustee post bond? No provision..

Age of majority to be grantor or trustee: 18.

Rule Against Perpetuities: Wait-and-see approach; common-law rule is modified by actual rather than possible events.

Forms of property ownership: Common-law state. Tenancy-in-common is presumed unless stated otherwise. Tenancy-in-common, joint tenancy and tenancy by entirety are recognized.

Any intestate-share law? Yes. Spouse gets $50,000 in personal property, up to $75,000 in real estate and lifetime use of the rest of the real estate, and half of the balance of the estate if there are no surviving children. If there are surviving children, the spouse gets only half of the deceased's personal property.

Any elective rights? Yes. Spouse may elect to use all of the estate's real estate for his or her lifetime.

Any automatic-share law? Yes. Some personal property and a six-month allowance for family living expenses.

State gift, inheritance, or estate taxes: No gift tax; no inheritance tax; imposes state estate tax equal to federal credit for state death taxes.

South Carolina

Uniform acts adopted: Uniform Probate Code; Uniform Trustees' Powers Act; Uniform Testamentary Additions to Trusts Act; Uniform Statutory Rule Against Perpetuities.

Court with probate jurisdiction: Probate Court.

Must trustee be a state resident? No, but if out-of-state corporate trustee is appointed, must have capital of at least $250,000. All out of state trustees must qualify to do business in South Carolina.

Must trustee post bond? No, unless required by trust.

Age of majority to be grantor or trustee: 18.

Rule Against Perpetuities: The common-law rule is modified by wait-and-see approach..

Forms of property ownership: Common-law state. There is no tenancy by entirety. Tenancy-in-common and joint tenancy are recognized, but for joint tenancy the document of ownership must state that ownership is to be held in joint tenancy "with the right of survivorship".

Any intestate-share law? Yes. Spouse gets everything if there are no surviving children. If there are surviving children, the spouse gets half of the estate.

Any elective rights? Yes. Spouse may take one-third of the estate.

Any automatic-share law? Yes. Some personal property and $5,000.

State gift, inheritance, or estate taxes: No gift tax; no inheritance tax; imposes state estate tax of up to 8% but not less than the federal credit for state death taxes.

South Dakota

Uniform acts adopted: Uniform Testamentary Additions to Trusts Act.

Court with probate jurisdiction: Circuit Court.

Must trustee be a state resident? No provision.

Must trustee post bond? No provision.

Age of majority to be grantor or trustee: 18.

Rule Against Perpetuities: Wait-and-see approach followed.

Forms of property ownership: Common-law state. Tenancy-in-common and joint tenancy are recognized. There is no tenancy by entirety. Creditors' rights are reserved against surviving joint owner(s).

Any intestate-share law? Yes. Spouse gets everything if there are no surviving children, parents, brother, sisters, nephews or nieces of the deceased. Otherwise, spouse usually gets one-third of the estate to $100,000 and half of the balance of the estate.

Any elective rights? Yes. Spouse may take one third of the estate.

Any automatic-share law? Yes. Lifetime use of homestead. Personal property: up to $1,500. Allowance for family.

State gift, inheritance, or estate taxes: No gift tax; an inheritance tax of up to 30%; imposes state estate tax equal to federal credit for state death taxes less any amounts paid on state inheritance tax.

Tennessee

Uniform acts adopted: Uniform Probate Code; Uniform Testamentary Additions to Trusts Act.

Court with probate jurisdiction: Chancery Court (Probate Court in Davidson and Shelby Counties).

Must trustee be a state resident? No, but if out-of-state trustee is appointed, must qualify to do business in Tennessee.

Must trustee post bond? No, unless required by trust.

Age of majority to be grantor or trustee: 18.

Rule Against Perpetuities: The common-law rule applies.

Forms of property ownership: Common-law state. Tenancy-in-common and joint tenancy are recognized. If joint tenancy is intended, deed or other document must contain expressed statement such as "joint tenancy with rights of survivorship".

Any intestate-share law? Yes. Spouse gets everything if there are no surviving children. If there are surviving children, the spouse can divide the estate equally with the children or take one-third of the estate, whichever is larger.

Any elective rights? Yes. Spouse may take one-third of the estate.

Any automatic-share law? Yes. Homestead: $5,000. Allowance for living expenses.

State gift, inheritance, or estate taxes: No gift tax; an inheritance tax of up to 16%; imposes state estate tax equal to federal credit for state death taxes less any amounts paid on state inheritance tax.

Texas

Uniform acts adopted: Uniform Testamentary Additions to Trusts Act.

Court with probate jurisdiction: County or Probate Court.

Must trustee be a state resident? No provision.

Must trustee post bond? Yes, if corporate trustee. Otherwise not required unless required by the trust.

Age of majority to be grantor or trustee: 18.

Rule Against Perpetuities: The common-law rule applies.

Forms of property ownership: Community property state. All property acquired by either spouse during marriage is community property. Tenancy-in-common is recognized. There is no tenancy by entirety. Joint tenancy is allowed for real property if the deed or other document expressly creates a joint tenancy and refers to a "right of survivorship".

Any intestate-share law? Yes. Spouse gets everything if there are no surviving children, parents, brothers, sisters, nephews or nieces of the deceased. Otherwise, the spouse gets a half of the community property and certain portions of the deceased's separate property.

Any elective rights? No.

Any automatic-share law? Yes. Half of all community property. Lifetime use of homestead as well as some personal property, additional real estate acreage, and an allowance for living expenses.

State gift, inheritance, or estate taxes: No gift tax; no inheritance tax; imposes state estate tax equal to federal credit for state death taxes.

Utah

Uniform acts adopted: Uniform Probate Code; Uniform Trustees' Powers Act; Uniform Testamentary Additions to Trusts Act.

Court with probate jurisdiction: District Court.

Must trustee be a state resident? No, but if out-of-state trustee is appointed, party must qualify to do business in Utah.

Must trustee post bond? No, unless required by the trust or requested by beneficiaries or ordered by court.

Age of majority to be grantor or trustee: 18.

Rule Against Perpetuities: The common-law rule applies.

Forms of property ownership: Common-law state. Tenancy-in-common, joint tenancy and tenancy by entirety are recognized. Tenancy by the entirety is recognized for real property only. Real estate presumed to be in tenancy in common, and in joint tenancy only if expressly so stated.

Any intestate-share law? Yes. Spouse gets everything if there are no surviving children who are children of the deceased only, such as from a prior marriage. If there are any children who are children of the deceased's only, the spouse gets half of the estate.

Any elective rights? Yes. Spouse may take one-third of the estate.

Any automatic-share law? Yes. Homestead: $10,000. Personal property: $5,000. Up to $25,000 in automobiles but no more than four automobiles. Allowance for family living expenses.

State gift, inheritance, or estate taxes: No gift tax; no inheritance tax; imposes state estate tax equal to federal credit for state death taxes.

Vermont

Uniform acts adopted: Uniform Testamentary Additions to Trusts Act.

Court with probate jurisdiction: Probate Court.

Must trustee be a state resident? No, but if out of state trustee is appointed, a resident agent must also be appointed.

Must trustee post bond? Yes, unless not required by the trust.

Age of majority to be grantor or trustee: 18.

Rule Against Perpetuities: Wait-and-see approach; common-law rule is modified by actual rather than possible events.

Forms of property ownership: Common-law state. Tenancy-in-common, tenancy by the entirety and joint tenancy are recognized. The presumption is that a real estate is held by tenancy-in-common rather than in joint tenancy, unless otherwise expressly stated that there is a "right of survivorship."

Any intestate-share law? Yes. Spouse gets everything if there are no surviving children or other relatives of the deceased. If there are no surviving children, but there are surviving relatives, the spouse gets $25,000 and half of the rest of the estate. If there are surviving children, the spouse gets one-third of the estate's personal property and one-third to half of the estate's real estate.

Any elective rights? Yes. Spouse's right of election is from one-third to half of the estate, depending on the number of surviving children.

Any automatic-share law? Yes. Homestead: $30,000. Allowance for family living expenses.

State gift, inheritance, or estate taxes: No gift tax; no inheritance tax; imposes state estate tax equal to federal credit for state death taxes.

Virgin Islands

Uniform acts adopted: None...
Must trustee be a state resident? No.
Must trustee post bond? No, unless required by trust.
Age of majority to be grantor or trustee: 18.
Rule Against Perpetuities: No information available.
Forms of property ownership: Common-law state. Tenancy-in-common, joint tenancy and tenancy-by-entirety are recognized. Tenancy-by-entirety recognized for real property only, and spouses are presumed to hold real estate by tenancy-by-the entirety unless the deed expressly says otherwise. Joint tenancy recognized for both real property and personal property, but only if the deed or other document expressly creates a joint tenancy.
Any intestate-share law? Yes. Spouse gets everything if there are no surviving children, parents, brothers, sisters, nephews or nieces of the deceased. Otherwise, the spouse usually gets from $5,000 to $10,000 and always gets from one-third to half of the estate.
Any elective rights? Yes. Spouse may take up to half of the estate.
Any automatic-share law? Yes, but very limited. Court determines a homestead and living allowance for the spouse.

Virginia

Uniform acts adopted: None.
Court with probate jurisdiction: Circuit Court.
Must trustee be a state resident? No, but if out of state trustee is appointed, a resident agent must also be appointed unless trustee is a corporation authorized to do business in Virginia, or is a parent, sister or brother of the decedent and has qualified to do business in Virginia.
Must trustee post bond? No provision.
Age of majority to be grantor or trustee: 18.
Rule Against Perpetuities: The common-law rule is modified by wait-and-see approach.
Forms of property ownership: Common-law state. Joint tenancy is recognized, but only where "right of survivorship" is stated in the ownership document. Tenancy-in-common and tenancy by the entirety recognized.
Any intestate-share law? Yes. Spouse gets everything if there are no surviving children who are children of the deceased's only, such as from a prior marriage. If there are children of the deceased's only, the spouse gets one-third of the estate.
Any elective rights? Yes. Spouse may take half of the estate if there are no surviving children. If there are surviving children, the spouse gets one-third of the estate.
Any automatic-share law? Yes, but very limited. Homestead: $5,000. Personal property: $3,500. Allowance for family living expenses.
State gift, inheritance, or estate taxes: No gift tax; no inheritance tax; imposes state estate tax equal to federal credit for state death taxes.

Washington

Uniform acts adopted: Uniform Testamentary Additions to Trusts Act.
Court with probate jurisdiction: Superior Court.
Must trustee be a state resident? No provision.
Must trustee post bond? No provision.
Age of majority to be grantor or trustee: 18.

Rule Against Perpetuities: Wait and see approach; common-law rule is modified by actual rather than possible events.

Forms of property ownership: Community property state. Tenancy-in-common and joint tenancy are recognized. Technically, tenancy by the entirety is recognized for both real property and personal property, but it is worthless as no rights of survivorship is included. Joint tenancy, however, is recognized for both real property and personal property if the deed or other document expressly creates a joint tenancy and refers to a "right of survivorship". Property acquired during marriage is community property.

Any intestate-share law? Yes, and very generous. Surviving spouse always gets all of the community property, which usually is the bulk of the estate. If there are any surviving parent and/or children, they may be entitled to from one-fourth to half of the deceased's separate property, if any. Surviving spouse is entitled to all community property, if deceased did not otherwise dispose of his/her own share of the community property by will.

Any elective rights? No.

Any automatic-share law? Yes. Half of all community property and an allowance for living expenses. Spouse may also be entitled to take an additional $30,000 in homestead allowance and personal property.

State gift, inheritance, or estate taxes: No gift tax; no inheritance tax; imposes state estate tax equal to federal credit for state death taxes.

West Virginia

Uniform acts adopted: Uniform Testamentary Additions to Trusts Act.

Court with probate jurisdiction: County Commissioner.

Must trustee be a state resident? No.

Must trustee post bond? No provision.

Age of majority to be grantor or trustee: 18.

Rule Against Perpetuities: The common-law rule applies.

Forms of property ownership: Common law state. Tenancy-in-common, joint tenancy and tenancy-by-the-entirety are recognized. Tenancy-by-the-entirety and joint tenancy are recognized but the deed or other document of ownership must expressly create such a tenancy and must refer to a "right of survivorship". If there are

Any intestate-share law? Yes. Spouse gets everything if there are no surviving children. If there are surviving children, the spouse gets one-third of the estate.

Any elective rights? Yes. Spouse may take one-third of the estate.

Any automatic-share law? Yes. Use of homestead. Personal property: $1,000.

State gift, inheritance, or estate taxes: No gift tax; no inheritance tax; imposes state estate tax equal to federal credit for state death taxes.

Wisconsin

Uniform acts adopted: None.

Court with probate jurisdiction: Circuit Court.

Must trustee be a state resident? No, but if out of state trustee is appointed, party must qualify to do business in Wisconsin.

Must trustee post bond? Yes, unless not required by trust or ordered by court.

Age of majority to be grantor or trustee: 18.

Rule Against Perpetuities: The common-law rule cannot invalidate a trust if the trustee can buy and sell trust property.

Forms of property ownership: Community property state. Tenancy-in-common and joint tenancy are recognized. Ownership by spouse presumes property is held in joint tenancy unless the document of ownership expressly states otherwise. There is no tenancy by entirety.

Any intestate-share law? Yes. Spouse gets everything if there are no surviving children who are children of the deceased's only, such as from a prior marriage. If there are surviving children who are children of the deceased's only, the spouse gets half of the estate.

Any elective rights? No.

Any automatic-share law? Yes. Half of all community property from January 1, 1986 to date of death. Homestead: $10,000. Personal property: $1,000. Allowance for family living expenses.

State gift, inheritance, or estate taxes: a gift tax; an inheritance tax of up to 20%; imposes state estate tax equal to federal credit for state death taxes less any amounts paid on state inheritance tax.

Wyoming

Uniform acts adopted: Uniform Trustees' Powers Act; Uniform Testamentary Additions to Trusts Act.

Court with probate jurisdiction: District Court.

Must trustee be a state resident? No.

Must trustee post bond? No provision.

Age of majority to be grantor or trustee: 18.

Rule Against Perpetuities: The common-law rule applies.

Forms of property ownership: Common-law state. Tenancy-in-common, joint tenancy and tenancy by the entirety are recognized. Tenancy by the entirety and joint tenancy are recognized for both real and personal property. For joint tenancy to be recognized, though, the deed or other document must expressly create such a tenancy and must refer to a "right of survivorship".

Any intestate-share law? Yes. Spouse gets everything if there are no surviving children. If there are surviving children, the spouse gets half of the estate.

Any elective rights? Yes. Spouse may take from one-fourth to half of the estate, depending on whether or not there are any surviving children.

Any automatic-share law? Yes. Homestead: up to $30,000. Some personal property. Allowance for family living expenses.

State gift, inheritance, or estate taxes: No gift tax; no inheritance tax; imposes state estate tax equal to federal credit for state death taxes.

Appendix B

SCHEDULE OF TRUST ASSETS

Shown below is a sample Schedule that is customarily attached to the Living Trust. If you are married, you can fill out separate forms for you (Schedule A) and your spouse (Schedule B); or you can use only one form, Schedule A, to list your shared-ownership property together, the format adopted in the sample used in this manual. A third schedule, Schedule C, can also be used by someone to list property.

It should be made absolutely clear that listing the trust property on this schedule does not in any way mean or signify the making of the property as a gift to beneficiaries. Rather, ITS PRIMARY PURPOSE IS THIS: to help you remember and be clear what property you've placed in the trust. Nor does the listing of assets on the schedule mean or signify the actual transfer of the assets to the trust. Quite to the contrary, to accomplish the actual transfer of property to the trust, you would also have to re-register or re-title the ownership papers of the property into the name of the trust (see Sections of Chapter 7 for the procedures for that). To put it bluntly, simply listing assets, especially titled ones which have papers of ownership, without re-titling them, means absolutely nothing in terms of actually "transferring" the assets to the trust.

There is no particular form or set of rules by which to list property in a schedule. There's one principle you'd need to follow, though, for the listing of trust property on a Schedule: simply identify each item of property in a clear and concise way; be sure to describe or identify the items in such a way that all interested parties—your trustee, successor trustee, beneficiaries, etc.—will unambiguously know exactly what property is meant or being referred to.

Schedule A—A Sample

	Husband	Wife	Joint	Market Value
(Real Estate)			House and real estate located at 20 Trust way, Tarrytown,NY	$200,000
				$150,000
	Summer house and real estate located at 20 Vacation Rd., Miami Beach, FL			
	The unimproved lot owned by grantor on Probate Road, Bronx, NY			$ 20,000
(Furnishings & Household goods)			All personal property and household furnishings located at 20 vacation Rd., Miami Beach, FL	$45,000
			All personal property and household furnishings located at 20 Trust Rd., Tarrytown, NY	$50,000
(Automobiles)	1990 Chevy Impala	1992 Honda Accord		
(Valuable Personal possessions, antiques, collectibles, etc.,)			The collection of 18th century European paintings and American coins owned by the grantors	$7,500 & $12,000 respectively
(Cash)			Funds accrued in savings acct no. 44-145 held at Chase National City Bank, Brooklyn, NY	$40,000
(Securities, stock accounts, money market accounts)		400 shares of AT&T stock Certificate No. 2434567, located in wife's pesonal file drawer		$56,000
				$20,000

SCHEDULE A—A SAMPLE (*CONTINUED*)

Husband	Wife	Joint	Market Value
	200 shares of 6% IBM preferred stock		$10,000
	IRA acct no. 48344 held at XYZ Credit Union, Newark, NJ		$7,000
		All stock accounts or other assets in brokerage acct no. 3A-1234 at Merrill Lynch & Co. NYC	$10,000

(Business Interests)

XYZ Stationery Store, Hoboken NJ
all interest of husband in the XYZ partnership

$30,000

DATE last updated* _____ 19___

*NOTE: A good estate planning practice is to make it a duty to always UPDATE the Schedule at a regular interval (say every two or three years or so), and particularly after a major purchase or sale of assets, or occurrence of significant events, such as a divorce, birth of a child or marriage, and definitely whenver you've made any changes to (added to or sold, reassigned or otherwise taken out of) a trust property.

Appendix C

Look, Chances Are You May Just Not Have An Estate Tax Problem In The First Place!

A. The (New) Realities About Estate Tax Savings Through Some Planning Gimmickry: You May Not Have A Big Enough Estate

To begin with, let's get one fundamental point clear outright: CHANCES ARE THAT YOU MAY NOT HAVE AN ESTATE TAX 'PROBLEM', IN THE FIRST PLACE; ONLY IF YOU FALL WITHIN THAT TINY PROPORTION OF ALL ESTATES WHICH COMES WITHIN THE SOCIETY'S UPPERMOST WEALTH BRACKET, SHOULD YOU ACTIVELY AND ACTUALLY BEGIN TO WORRY!

Traditionally, lawyers would give you a big argument contending that one "major pitfall" why non-lawyers should never even attempt to draft their own wills or trusts (but should, of course, pay a lawyer to do it!), is that a non-lawyer would need to be skilled in the ins and outs of working the maximum possible estate "tax savings" into his self-made Will!! This has been the lawyer's claim historically.[1] It so happens, though, that like all such claims by tradesmen who have some underlying vested interest to protect, it has all along been a myth— an exaggeration of the truth.

It has always been more of a myth than reality for one basic reason: *in the overwhelming majority of estates in the United States, no "tax consequence" of any type do generally rise, in the first place.* For example, under the tax law that preceded the Tax Reform Act of 1976 (which had allowed only $60,000 in federal estate tax exemption, plus the marital deduction allowance), the proportion of estates which was subject to federal estate tax was only 7 per cent of all estates. Just 7 per cent! The remaining 93 per cent were not large enough to be taxable; hence no big, extraordinary tax expertise would have really been called for concerning those. Then came the Tax Reform Act of 1976 which, principally by providing a much larger exemption and marital deduction allowance, curtailed the number of estates that were subject to federal estate taxation still further—down to a mere 3 per cent of all estates per year (from the previous 7 per cent)!

But, even then, many lawyers had remained unmoved, and would still pretend that "tax planning" in estate planning in general, and in Will-making or Trust-making, in particular, was of such a crucial importance in the average estate. Then, on August 31, 1981, Congress dropped the other shoe: it passed the *Economic Recovery Tax Act of 1981*. By this law, the proportion of all estates that could be subject to Federal transfer taxes was still reduced further-to a tiny ¹/₃ of 1 per cent of all estates, according to figures provided by Congressional staff members! (Congress did this primarily by dramatically raising the Federal "exemption" ceiling [the size of estate assets that can be transferred to one's heirs tax-free], and by making all property that passes from one spouse to a surviving spouse totally exempt from federal estate taxes—the so-called *"unlimited marital deduction."*)

[1]In a recent article on the subject, for example, a lawyer who would have ordinarily been expected to take a less than conventional lawyers' view, an author of a "do-it-yourself" Will guide and an ardent supporter of the self-help law approach, was cited as holding to the same rather misleading notion that one necessarily needs to use a lawyer if, as the writer put it, "the estate is worth more than $600,000 and therefore likely to be subject to the federal estate tax." (See statement attributed to Denis Clifford in "The Do-It Yourself Will: Good Idea, Sometimes," N.Y. Times, Sept. 23, 1993 p. 36.)

Translated, what it all boils down to is that, from 1987 (when all the changes of the 1981 law become fully effective) *fewer than 5 estates out of every 1,000 would possibly have been subject to any federal estate taxes, compared to about 28 out of every 1,000 previously. To put it in more relevant, personal terms, what this means for you, the average estate planner or Trust or Will-maker, is that for all practical purposes you probably don't have to worry about needing any fancy special expertise in estate tax planning; only if you happen to be so blessed as to belong to that tiny minority of Americans who fall within the society's uppermost wealth brackets, may you begin to worry!*

The central point is that the claim often voiced by tax lawyers and some estate planning professionals, to the effect that the average Trust or Will-drafter needs some great expertise in estate tax code methods and planning, is a little too overstated. Some knowledge of some basic procedures, maybe. But nothing really extraordinary or critical by any means!

Indeed, in all fairness, many experts, lawyers as well as non-lawyers, have changed their tune, somewhat, and lately would now admit to the new reality. Said one such expert, John W. Hamm of the New York accounting firm of Arthur Young & Company, "It used to take a lot of maneuvering to try to divvy up an estate appropriately. We would try to utilize both spouses' maximum tax credits and try to take advantage of the progressive estate tax rates by splitting the estate. But both of these areas have changed drastically as a result of the new (1981) law."

"It [the new 1981 law] would, of course, create an enormous change in our perspective towards planning," said another estate plan professional, Sondra Miller, a New York lawyer and member of the Westchester County Estate Planning Council. "[For example] now, if an estate is not going to be taxed until it is in excess of $600,000, much of the old techniques of planning are going to be out the window."[2]

B. Look, Is Your Estate Big Enough To Be Taxable, In The First Place?

The point is that, as a factual matter, the 1981 tax law has just about made it absolutely certain that for the overwhelming majority of estates in the United States, any exercise in elaborate "tax planning" gimmickry in trust or will-making will now more than ever be neither too fruitful nor necessary. Or, to put it another way, it is for only a very tiny portion of all estates in America —some $1/3$ of one percent of the total which fall within the society's uppermost wealth bracket—that an estate taxation "problem" actually exists! Hence, in light of this reality, we elect in this chapter to focus on an aspect of the tax issue which, in the author's view, is even the more primary and relevant tax question for the vast majority of estate plan makers vis-a-vis tax planning, namely: DO YOU HAVE A BIG ENOUGH ESTATE THAT IS TAXABLE, IN THE FIRST PLACE?

Think about it for a moment. If your estate is not big enough and would not be subject to a tax, in the first place, then isn't the issue clearly a mute one for you as to how much of a "tax saving" you could supposedly make by drafting a Will (or a trust) in one way, rather than another, or by having it drawn up by a lawyer, as opposed to yourself!?

THE TWO TYPES OF TAXES THAT ARE RELEVANT HERE: ESTATE TAXES, AND 'INHERITANCE' OR 'DEATH' TAXES

There are primarily two kinds of taxes to which an estate which qualifies to be taxed may be subject: **1)** Federal estate tax —which is one imposed by the federal government on a decedent's entire "taxable estate"; and **2)** State inheritance tax (also known as state "estate", "inheritance" or "succession" tax)—which is a kind of the right-to-transfer-property tax imposed by most state governments upon that part (and only that part) of the decedent's estate transferred as inheritance to particular beneficiaries. Of the two kinds of taxes, the Federal estate tax is by far the major one to concern yourself with, not only because it is often the much larger one, but also because most states which impose state death or inheritance taxes use the federal tax figures as the "base" from which the state tax is calculated.

[2]Along the same line, Michael Richards of HALT, the Washington DC. legal reform organization, states bluntly that: "The long term effect of the new estate tax law will be to reduce taxpayers' dependence on estate lawyers…As fewer estates become subject to federal tax, the need for retaining an estate lawyer for tax planning will be eliminated."

Now, back to the main question at hand. The primary question, of course, is: what makes an estate subject to an estate tax liability?

The answer is simple. *Whether an estate will be taxable will be dependent entirely on one major consideration:* THE SIZE AND NATURE OF THE ESTATE ASSETS. Under the Internal Revenue Code of 1981, the federal estate tax return (from which a tax liability, if any, is determined) is not even required to be filed, unless the value of a decedent's "gross estate" approximately exceeds the following amounts as of the date of death:

For death in or gifts made in:	No filing unless gross estate Is More than:
1981	$175,000
1982	225,000
1983	275,000
1984	325,000
1985	400,000
1986	500,000
1987 and after	600,000

NOTE: Note that these limits cease to apply if the beneficiary is the giver's spouse. That is, when the gift is between spouses, the tax-free amount that may be transferred is "unlimited," meaning that it would then be any amount whatsoever (see footnote on p. 218 below). Furthermore, if you made any gifts of "taxable" nature to others (i.e., gifts made to others during your lifetime that are over the permitted annual $10,000 limit per person), such gifts—to the extent that they exceed the $10,000 per person allowed, will be used to reduce the amount of your gross estate that can pass tax-free at your death.

To put it simply, therefore, here's the "acid test": if the value of your "gross estate" is not likely to exceed the above amount in the given years, your estate would probably not be a "taxable estate" for federal estate tax purposes! (Another way of saying this, is that these amounts represent for the appropriate years, what you can transfer to anyone(s) you prefer, free of federal estate tax.) To put it another way, what this means for you, as an estate planner (or Will-maker), is this: if you can't see the size of your "gross estate" being worth in excess of the above-given "maximum exemption" limits (basically, $600,000 as from 1987 onwards), then for all practical purposes you shouldn't worry about having any federal estate tax problems or liability. And, *if you determine that you are in that situation, you should just as well skip the rest of this chapter and forget all the big, fancy talks about estate tax planning for your estate!*[3]

C. First, Estimate The Size Of Your "Gross Estate"

As explained above, the size of your "gross estate" is a central figure in determining whether or not you may have to file a federal estate tax return, or possibly have a federal estate tax liability. Hence, the all-important question is: how do you determine this figure—THE SIZE OF YOUR GROSS ESTATE?

THE GROSS ESTATE

With respect to determining a person's (or decedent's) "gross estate" for tax purposes, technically speaking there is really one (and only one) important thing to bear in mind: namely, that as defined by the IRS the "gross estate" comprises MORE THAN just the property owned outright by the decedent or only intended by him to pass through his Will, and does, also, include different other kinds of property, including even those property

---

[3]One knowledgeable tax practitioner, Julian S. Bush of the New York law firm of Shea & Gould, put it quite accurately this way: "A [married] couple whose assets are not expected to go above a combined $600,000 need not get involved with fancy [tax planning techniques in] Wills. Above that number, it gets more complicated."

which he may not have owned completely or outrightly.[4] Briefly summarized, a decedent's "gross estate" can be defined as *roughly the total of everything the decedent owned or shared an interest in, or that is due to his estate.*

For our limited purposes in this manual, however, it will suffice for you to simply define your estimated "gross estate" as follows: ESTIMATED "NET WORTH"—that is, your assets minus liabilities. (See Chapter 6, especially the Financial Information section of the Estate Information Worksheet on p. 55). This should suffice for the purposes here, since, after all, you really don't need to know the precise value of your gross estate to be able to do the planning work intelligently; you merely need to have, for our purposes here, a rough but educated estimate so that you can assess the likelihood of your being liable for (federal) estate taxes, if at all.

How do you make this determination of an estate? It's simple: from your "gross estate" (i.e., your net worth) figure, you then subtract the total of all the "allowable deductions" (p. 218). And whatever balance you have left thereafter (if any), is the "taxable estate." If no balance is left, then the estate at issue is a non-taxable estate—one that would owe no federal estate tax whatsoever.

D. Next, Determine If Your Estate Is A "Taxable Estate" By Subtracting From It The "Allowable Deductions"

Alright. Let's say you have now calculated the value of your gross estate, meaning, actually, the value of your net worth. The next relevant question for you is this: is the estate big enough to be classified as a "taxable estate"?

What constitutes the "allowable deductions" of an estate?

---

[4]More specifically, as more fully defined by the IRS (See IRS Publications 559 and 448, for example), one's gross estate would include such items as the following:

i) All property of any kind owned by the decedent (or testator) at the time of his death, regardless of where it is located, and that was transferred at death by Trust or Will or by local intestacy laws: real property, stocks, bonds, furniture, personal effects, jewelry, works of art, interest in a business, cash surrender value (or installment proceeds) of life insurance on another's life, notes, and other evidences of indebtedness to the decedent, etc.

ii) Gifts made or property transferred for less than full and adequate consideration within 3 years of decedent's death. (Bona fide sales made for adequate consideration, or gifts (other than a life insurance policy) for which the decedent was not required to file a gift tax return, are not includable as part of the decedent gross estate. However, gift taxes paid on any gifts made during this 3-year period is includable.]

iii) Under most circumstances, the proceeds of a life insurance policy, including accidental death policies, even if they are paid directly to the named beneficiary by the insurance company.

iv) The value of any annuities (or other payments) payable to any other person surviving the decedent (to the extent of the contributions made to it by both the decedent and the employer, if payment to the beneficiary is under a "non qualified plan," and by the decedent only, if payment to the beneficiary is made under a "qualified plan.") [The value of any long term (over 36 months of annuity payment to a beneficiary—other than an executor—under the Individual Retirement Arrangement (IRA), is generally excluded, however, part of a decedent's gross estate.]

v) With respect to all pre-1977 joint interests, the total value of property owned (or held) by the decedent and others as joint tenants (or as tenants by the entirety) with the right of survivorship—except the part, if any, proven as paid for by the other surviving joint tenant or tenants.

vi) With respect to all "qualified joint interests" (as well as pre-1977 joint interests for which an election is made to treat them as qualified joint interests), only one-half of the fair market value of the joint interests is includable in the gross estate of the spouse who died first, even if the surviving spouse furnished the total purchase money for the property. (The term "qualified joint interest" for an estate of a person dying after 1981 is defined as any interests in property held by the decedent and the decedent's spouse as: 1) tenants by the entirety, or 2) as joint tenants with the right of survivorship, but only if the spouses are the only joint tenants.)

vii) Life insurance proceeds on decedent's life, if it is payable to his estate or to another person for the benefit of his estate; the proceeds of a policy payable to other beneficiaries but over which the decedent had some "incidents of ownership" (meaning things like the tight to change the beneficiary, or to cancel, assign or borrow against the policy);

viii) Insurance proceeds on another's life (to the extent of the cash surrender value of the policy);

ix) Any income earned but still uncollected by the decedent at the time of his death;

x) Property over which the decedent had 'a general power of appointment' (meaning the right to na*me who the property should go to);

xi) Distributions from pension and profit-sharing plans made in lump-sum to decedent's beneficiaries;

xii) Dower or curtesy (or statutory estate in lieu thereof) of the surviving spouse.

THE ALLOWABLE DEDUCTIONS (FROM THE GROSS ESTATE)

In a word, "allowable deductions" are simply the kinds and amounts of deductions the law says are allowable under the tax code as legitimate to be made from the "gross estate" to arrive at one's "taxable estate." (This would seem logical since the taxable estate is defined as the "gross estate," minus the total "allowable deductions," remember?)

Briefly defined, the following are what constitute the 'allowable deductions' of an estate.

i) the total funeral expenses of the decedent;

ii) the total amount of expenses made (or losses suffered) in administering the estate;

iii) the total debts owed by, or claims made against, the estate;

iv) losses in the estate arising from theft or casualties (storms, fires, and the like), incurred during the settlement of the estate—to the extent that is not compensated for by insurance or otherwise;

v) marital deduction allowance[5]—the value of any and all property passing to the surviving spouse through joint ownership, by Will, by being a beneficiary under life insurance upon decedent's death, by gift or in trust for which the principal of the trust passes to the survivor's own estate at her death, or for which the survivor has a "general" (i.e., sole) power to appoint whom the trust principal would go to, or any other property passing by other means, and which "qualifies" for the marital deduction; and

vi) charitable deduction allowance—the value of property or gifts in the decedent's gross estate donated by the decedent either during his lifetime or by Will to charity.

E. Computing The "Net" Federal Tax Liability Of An Estate

It has been explained above that the "taxable estate" (what is left after you deduct the total "allowable deductions" from the "gross estate"), is the amount upon which the estate tax liability is assessed. Using the tax table, called the *Unified Federal Estate And Gift Tax Rate Schedule* (see p. 222), you can easily determine what is known as the "tentative tax" on the taxable estate you have arrived at—the tax which an estate of a given size would likely be liable for.

In using this schedule to compute the tentative tax, however, there's one more factor of great importance to take into account. The law provides for a system of "**credits**" that can be applied, on a straight dollar-for-dollar basis, as offsets against the tentative tax amount—that is, credits that may be used to reduce the tax (the "tentative tax") assessed on one's estate, dollar-for-dollar. A "credit" is a direct reduction of the tax itself, as distinguished from a "deduction." In other words, what this means is that an estate may show a "tentative tax" liability but still not necessarily owe or have to pay any tax, nevertheless. So long as the amount of previously unused "credits" available to the estate (if any), is in excess of the "tentative tax" amount assessed to it, then that estate would have no "net" estate tax payable, and would in effect be a non-taxable estate.

There are five types of "**credits**" allowable against an estate's tentative tax (on the combined total of the taxable estate and the adjusted taxable gifts) to determine the "net estate tax payable": Unified credit (representing credit for lifetime gifts); credit for state death taxes paid; credit for gift taxes paid; credit for tax on prior transfers; and credit for foreign death taxes.

To illustrate the computation method, let's look at some examples just to see how the tax Schedule (see p. 222 below) is read.

---

[5]NOTE THIS: Marital deduction is a deduction allowable to only a surviving spouse from the decedent partner's gross estate, providing the property on which such allowance is made "qualifies." For estates of spouses who die after 1981, this allowance is unlimited—i.e., it could be any amount or proportion of the estate property, even to the extent of the whole estate, and which "qualifies."

Basically, in making the estate tax computation, the way the marital deduction allowance works out is that the total of any property that have gone or will go to the surviving spouse, say the wife, is deducted from the estate of the deceased spouse, and any property inherited by the surviving spouse as a marital deduction allowance goes untaxed, but is later taxable in her (the surviving spouse's) own estate when she dies. (See pp. 219-221 for more on actual estate tax computation procedures.)

To be eligible for this deduction, the property involved must "qualify"; that is: i) the property must actually be going to or have gone to the surviving spouse; ii) the spouse must survive the decedent and must be legally married at the time of death; iii) the property must have been denoted or bequeathed to her/him under conditions which make the property includable in his/her own taxable estate when he/she dies.

F. Schematic Illustration Of Federal Estate Tax Computation Method For 4 Different Estates

EXAMPLE 1: Assume the following facts: Mr. A died in 1994. His gross estate was valued at $800,000. He made no lifetime taxable gifts. His surviving spouse was to receive all the assets of the estate.

The estate tax is computed as follows:

Gross Estate (use, essentially, the net worth).. $800,000

Minus: (allowable deductions')

i)	Funeral expenses...........................	$ 20,000
ii)	Administration expenses.................	40,000
iii)	Estate debts & losses.....................	100,000
iv)	Charitable deductions.....................	40,000

    -200,000

Adjusted Gross Estate.. 600,000

Minus: Marital deduction (Mr. A left everything to spouse).. -600,000

Taxable Estate... -0-

Add: Adjusted taxable gifts* (assuming none).. -0-

Taxable Amount.. -0-

NET ESTATE TAX PAYABLE BY MR. A's ESTATE... -0-

EXAMPLE 2: Assume the following facts: Mr. B estimates that the value of his gross estate (his net worth) today is about $4.9 million. He anticipates the exemptions and allowable deductions and expenses (funeral and administrative expenses, charitable gifts, etc.) will amount to approximately $400,000, as listed in the illustration below, leaving him a Net Estate of about $4,500,000. He plans to leave $3,250,000 to his wife, and $1,250,000 to his children.

Explanation: First, the property ($3,250,000) Mr. B leaves his wife is totally exempt from any federal estate tax because of the "unlimited marital deductions." Mr. B is thus left with a remaining net estate of $1,250,000 which is subject to federal estate tax. Looking at Column C of the Tax Rates Chart (p. 222), you find that the tax assessable on a $1,250,000 estate is $448,300. From this $448,300 Mr. B deducts the amount for "tax credit" allowed every individual, $192,800.* That leaves the balance of $255,500, which represents the estimated federal estate tax that Mr. B's estate will pay.

Gross Estate (use, basically, the net worth).. $4,900,000

Minus ('allowable deductions')

i)	Funeral expenses...........................	$60,000
ii)	Administration expenses.................	90,000
iii)	Estate debts & losses.....................	150,000
iv)	Charitable deductions.....................	100,000

    -400,000

Adjusted Gross Estate.. 4,500,000

Minus: Marital deduction... -3,250,000

Taxable Estate... 1,250,000

Add: Adjusted taxable gifts* (assuming none).. -0-

Taxable Amount.. -0-

Tax assessable on $1,250,000................... $448,300

Less "credits": Unified Credits*.................. 192,800

NET ESTATE TAX PAYABLE BY MR. B's ESTATE.. $255,500

---
*See Footnote on p. 221 for definition of this concept.

EXAMPLE 3: Let's just say that Mr. C has a net taxable estate (that is, what would be left of the estate after all the 'allowable deductions', such as the funeral and administrative expenses, charitable gift exemptions, marital deductions, etc. shall have been deducted), amounting to $1,300,000. But, the individual exemption of $600,000 has not been deducted at this point.

His estate is computed as follows:

Gross Estate		$1,800,000
Minus:	i) Funeral expenses	$50,000
	ii) Administration expenses	40,000
	iii)Estate debts & losses	100,000
	iv)Charitable deductions	10,000
		-200,000
Adjusted Gross Estate		1,600,000
Minus: Marital deduction		-300,000
Taxable Estate		1,300,000
Add: Adjusted taxable gifts* (assuming none)		-0-
Taxable Amount		1,300,000
Tax assessable on $1,300,000		$469,800
Less "credits": Unified Credits*		-192,800
NET ESTATE TAX PAYABLE BY MR. B's ESTATE		**$277,000**

EXPLANATION OF METHOD OF CALCULATION:

1. Enter the numbers in Column A and B between which the value of your Net Taxable Estate falls

Column A =	$1,250,000
Column B =	$1,500,000

2. Subtract from the value of your net estate the amount in Column A

$1,300,000
-1,250,000
50,000

3. Multiply this remainder by the applicable percentage in Column D

50,000
X .43
$21,500

4. Add together the resultant amount and the tax for $1,250,000 listed in Column C

21,500
+448,300
469,800

5. Subtract the federal estate tax credit ($192,800) from the last amount

469,800
-192,800
277,000

This is your ESTATE TAX PAYABLE ⟶ 277,000

EXAMPLE 4: (Illustrating how the "credits" are made use of): Assume the following: In 1979, while still alive, Mr. D gave his daughter a gift of property valued at $253,000, for which he had filed a gift tax return and paid a net gift tax of $32,800 (tentative tax, $70,800, minus unified credit of $38,000). He made no other prior gifts. Mr. D died in 1982 with a gross estate valued at $607,000. State death taxes of $25,000 were paid by the estate. The estate is valued as of the date of death. The value of the gift as of that date was $300,000.

The net estate tax on Mr. D's estate is computed as follows: [The value of the gift to the daughter at date of Mr. D's death - $300,000—is not included in the gross estate; but the value of the gift taxes paid ($25,000) would be. However, the taxable gift ($250,000)** is added to the taxable estate for purposes of determining the gross estate tax. No marital deduction is applicable.]

---

*See footnote on p. 221 for definition of this concept.

The permissible limit for non-taxable gifts under the law operating when the gift was made (1979) was $3,000 per recipient (it's now $10,000 as of this writing since 1981). Hence, any gift in excess of the $3,000 limit is a "taxable gift" meaning $253,000-$3,000 or $250,000 **in our present example.

Appendix C: Look, Do You Have A Big Enough Estate For A Tax 'Problem'?

Gross Estate..$607,000

Minus:

    i) Funeral expenses.................... $15,000

    ii) Administration expenses............ 45,000

    iii) Estate debts & losses................ 37,000

    iv) Charitable deductions............... 10,000

                                                    −107,000

Taxable Estate..500,000

Add: Adjusted taxable gifts[6] ($253,000-$3,000)..250,000

Taxable Amount...750,000

Tentative Tax (computed on Taxable Amount from the Unified Rate Schedule)...........248,300

Minus "Credits"[7]:

    Gift taxes payable...... $32,800

    Unified credit............ 62,800 (limit for the 1982 year)

    State death tax credit

    (based on adj, taxable

    estate of $440,000)...... 10,000

                                       105,600

NET ESTATE TAX PAYABLE BY MR. D's ESTATE..142,700

---

[6] **"Adjusted taxable gifts"** include only the value of the taxable gifts that were made by the testator (or decedent) after 1976 and that are not includable in the testator's gross estate. (The permissible amount for non-taxable gifts under the law operating since 1981 is $10,000 per recipient. Hence, any gift in excess of that amount is a "taxable gift.")

[7] NOTE THIS: This is where the 'tax credit' comes from. For every individual, the federal tax law exempts from federal estate tax property worth up to $600,000, no matter who he or she leaves the property to—i.e., you are allowable to transfer that much property free of federal estate tax. But, with the one important qualification: this exemption is reduced by 'taxable gifts' if any, that one may make during one's lifetime, to the extent that such gifts are larger than $10,000 per person per year. Thus, let's say you give $40,000 to your son in a single year, then $30,000 ($40,000 - $10,000) will be subject to gift tax. However, the gift tax assessed is not paid in the year you make this gift; rather, the total amount of the excess taxable gift is deducted from your $600,000 estate/gift exemption.

The $600,000 exemption works, however, by means of "tax credits" which in effect, exempts the first $192,800 of tax due in an estate—the equivalent of the payable tax on $600,000.

There are five types of "credits" allowable against an estate's tentative tax before the "net' estate tax payable is finally arrived at. These are: 1) unified credit (representing credit for lifetime gifts); 2) credit for state death taxes paid; 3) credit for gift taxes paid; 4) credit for tax on prior transfers; and 5) credit for foreign death taxes. A "credit' is a direct reduction of the tax itself, as distinguished from a "deduction."

In particular, the **"unified credit"**—which is so-called because it may be used to cover tax-free gifts made before death—is a credit of $192,800 that can be used to reduce the transfer tax (which is different from the income tax) on both taxable gifts and estates. And, if a decedent did not make any taxable gifts at all during his/her lifetime, the totality (100%) of the credit can be used to reduce the tax on his estate at his death. (A "taxable gift" is one that does not fall into any of these categories: gifts made by one spouse to another, annual gifts of $10,000 or less per recipient, or charitable contributions).

Take, for example, the case of a person who dies any time after 1987, meaning that his "unified credit" is $192,800. What this means, in effect, is that lifetime gifts or the estate of this decedent can escape tax entirely if they, together, total no more than $600,000—since $192,800 is exactly the "tentative" tax chargeable on an estate of that ($600,000) size. Thus, this decedent could have made a taxable gift of, say, $100,000 and left a $500,000 estate—without becoming subject to any federal transfer tax. That is, a combined gifts and estate worth up to $600,000 will not be subject to any federal estate tax.

G. United Federal Estate And Gift Tax Rates (Schedule)

The following table, the *Unified Federal Estate and Gift Tax Rates*, gives the federal estate and gift tax rates for estates of people who have died after 1987. As discussed elsewhere in this manual (see, for example, p. 216), these taxes will only begin to apply if and when your taxable estate is worth $600,000 or more. Basically, to calculate the tax owed, here's the process: first, determine your taxable estate—your net worth, minus the exempt amounts (funeral expenses, charitable gifts, any amount left to a surviving spouse). Then, check on the Tax Rates chart below for the tax owed on the taxable estate. Finally, subtract from that amount the "tax credit" that is allowed for the amount that would be owed on the first $600,000 (appx. $192,000). (Of course, you'll recall from our previous discussion that if you have given gifts of more than $10,000 per year per person during your life, then this "credit" will have to be reduced by the total excess amount of excess gifts over the limit).

Unified Federal Estate and Gift Tax Rates (Schedule)

Column A		Column B	Column C	Column D
If taxable estate is more than		But not more than	Tax owed on amounts in A	Rate of tax on excess over amounts in A
$ 0		$10,000	$ 0	18%
10,000		20,000	1,800	20
20,000		40,000	3,800	22
40,000		60,000	8,200	24
60,000		80,000	13,000	26
80,000		100,000	18,200	28
100,000		150,000	23,800	30
150,000		250,000	38,800	32
250,000		500,000	70,800	34
500,000		750,000	155,800	37
750,000		1,000,000	248,300	39
1,000,000		1,250,000	345,800	41
1,250,000		1,500,000	448,300	43
1,500,000		2,000,000	555,800	45
2,000,000		2,500,000	780,800	49
2,500,000			1,025,800	50

Federal Estate Tax:
How Much Will Your Estate Pay?

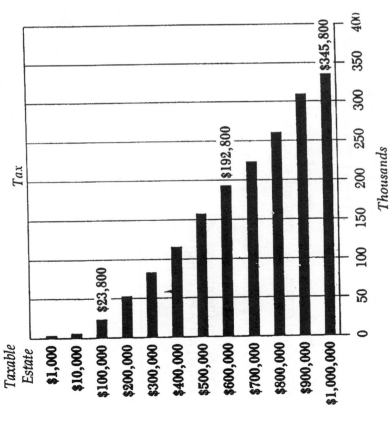

Taxable Estate	Tax
$1,000	
$10,000	
$100,000	$23,800
$200,000	
$300,000	
$400,000	
$500,000	
$600,000	$192,800
$700,000	
$800,000	
$900,000	
$1,000,000	$345,800

Thousands

Taxing Estates

The Federal marginal tax rate on each portion of a person's estate. No more than 55 percent goes to taxes, but a 5 percent surcharge is imposed on estates of $10 million to $21.04 million, effectively taxing the entire 55 percent.

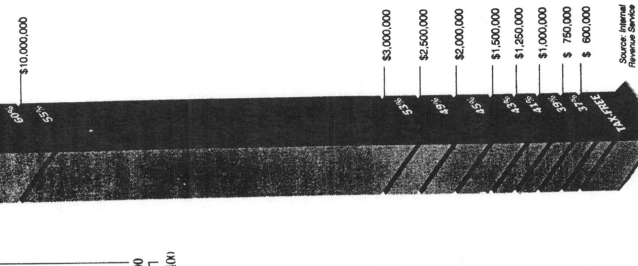

60%
55%
$10,000,000

53% — $3,000,000
49% — $2,500,000
45% — $2,000,000
43% — $1,500,000
41% — $1,250,000
39% — $1,000,000
37% — $ 750,000
— $ 600,000
TAX-FREE

Source: Internal Revenue Service

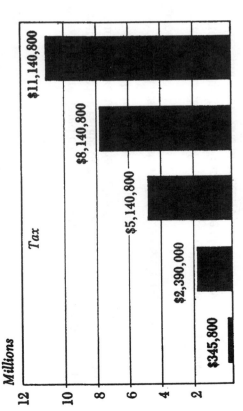

Millions

	Tax
	$11,140,800
	$8,140,800
	$5,140,800
	$2,390,000
	$345,800

TAXABLE ESTATE: $1,000,000 $5,000,000 $10,000,000 $15,000,000 $20,000,000

Appendix D

GLOSSARY OF
ESTATE & LEGAL TERMS

Abatement Clause A clause in a Will by which the Will-maker ensures that in the event he had overestimated the value of his estate, or that it had substantially decreased in value at the time of his death or became smaller than he had anticipated when he made his will and the bequests therein, certain bequests would have preference or priority over others.

Acknowledgment A declaration in front of a person who is qualified to administer oaths (such as a Notary Public) that a document bearing your signature was actually signed by you.

Act Of God An accident which could not have been foreseen or prevented, e.g., those caused by earthquakes, storms, forest fires, and the like.

Ademption The cancellation of a bequest by reason of some act of the will-maker, such as the subsequent sale of a bequeathed item by the will-maker.

Administration The conservation, management and distribution of the property (estate) of a dead person.

Administrator A male person (or a corporation) appointed by a court to manage and settle the estate of a person who died "intestate"—i.e., without leaving a will. The female counterpart is called Administratrix.

Administrator Cum Testamento Annexo (With the will annexed, abbreviated c.t.a.) A person or corporation appointed by a court to manage and settle the estate of a deceased (dead) person who left a will but failed to name an executor in the will; or a person so appointed when the person named in the will fails to qualify or is unable to act.

Affinity Relationship by marriage. (This contrasts with "consanguinity," which is relationship by blood.)

Ancestor One who precedes another in the line of inheritance (father, mother, grand-parents, children, etc., are said to be in "direct" line of ancestry, and uncles, aunts, and cousins, in "collateral" line of ancestry)

Ante-nuptial (Contract) A contract made by a man and a woman prior to their marriage, in which they detail their property-rights.

Appraisal A valuation of property; the opinion of an expert as to the true value of real or personal property based on facts and experience.

Appreciation Increase in value; opposite of depreciation.

Attest
To witness a document in writing, such as the witnessing of the signing of a will.

Attestation Clause
That clause in a will which contains the statement of the persons witnessing the signing of the will; the clause that immediately follows the signature of the will-maker.

Beneficiary
One who is the recipient of benefits, such as: 1) the profits or rents of an estate or transaction; or 2) the proceeds of an insurance policy; or 3) the income or profits from a trust fund.

Bequest
A gift of personal property by will (same as Legacy, but contrasts with devise, which is a gift of real property).

Bond
A written pledge or obligation, usually issued by a bonding company for a fee, by which the bonding company is to pay a sum of money in case of failure to fulfill an obligation, or of conflicting damages or mishandling of funds

Charitable Bequest
A gift of personal property by will to a charity.

Codicil
An addition or amendment of a will.

Collateral
Incidental; something that is additional to, or an off-shot to a matter. E.g., the term "collateral heir," means a person who falls outside the "direct line" of inheritance, such as a nephew, uncle or aunt.

Community Property
The property owned in common or together by husband and wife during their marriage, based on the legal doctrine in certain states that property acquired by either or both parties during marriage belongs to the "marital community."

Competent
(Testator or witness). A person who, at the time of his making and signing of his will, had a reasonably sound mental capacity to do so. When used in connection with a witness, the term is generally used to refer to the fitness of the witness to a will to testify credibly in court concerning his role as a witness to the signatory.

Conservator
A guardian, protector or preserver.

Corpus
Latin word meaning the "body" or principal of an estate, as contrasted with its income or interest.

Curtesy
The right of a surviving widower, under an old common law practice, to have an interest in the real property the wife leaves, irrespective of the provisions of her will to the contrary, and irrespective of any debts she might owe, etc.

Death Taxes
Same as estate and inheritance taxes.

Decedent
The dead person.

Demise
1) Death, decease; 2) To pass by Will or inheritance.

Depreciate
To decrease in value; the opposite of appreciate.

Descendant
One who descends (proceeds) from the body of another, e.g., a child, grandchild, etc.

Descent
The passing on of an estate to another person by inheritance.

Devise
A gift of real property by will. The giver is called the devisor, and the person to whom it is given, the devisee.

Direct Heir
A person in "direct" line of descent, such as a child or parent.

Distribution
Generally, the distribution or apportionment of property or money by an Executor or the court to the heirs or beneficiaries of an estate. More commonly, the term is used to describe a situation where the court distributes the property of a person who dies without leaving a will to those entitled to receive them under the applicable state law. (A "distributee" is one who gets or is entitled to a share in the distribution).

Domicile
One's permanent or legal home, as opposed simply to his temporary place of abode. This differs from a person's "residence" which is used to describe where the person may be living for the time being.

Dower
The right of a surviving widow under an old common law practice, to have an interest in the real property the husband leaves, irrespective of the provisions of his will to the contrary, or any debts he might owe, etc.

Election
The choice of an alternative, such as the right of a widow (or widower) to take the share of her deceased husband's estate to which she is entitled under the law, if she dissents from the provision made in her husband's will.

Encumbrance
A right in real property which, while it diminishes the net value of the property, does not prevent its transfer from one person to another, e.g., liens, outstanding debts or taxes on a house.

Entirety
The phrase "ownership or tenancy by the entirety," is used to describe a situation where two or more persons (but more commonly a husband and wife) jointly own a real property, so that the property cannot be divided up between them. Hence, if one of the parties should die, the whole property goes to the remaining survivor(s).

Escheat
The reversion of property to the state if no heirs or beneficiaries can be found.

Estate
The sum total of the property, both real and personal, owned by a decedent at the time of his death.

Execution
The completion of the making of a document (such as a deed, contract or Will) by officially signing it.

Executor
A male person (or a corporation) named in a Will to see that the terms of the Will are carried out. If a female, she is called an Executrix.

Fiduciary
A general term used to describe a relationship that requires a high trust and confidence. Persons like guardians, trustees, executors and administrators of estates, fall under such a category.

Gift Causa Mortis
A gift of personal property made by a person in contemplation or expectation of death, which is actually delivered by the gift-maker but effective only if the gift-maker dies.

Gift inter Vivos
A gift of personal property made by a living person to another, which becomes effective only if actually delivered by the gift-maker.

Gift tax
A tax imposed upon the value of a gift.

Guardian
A person who is legally assigned the responsibility of taking care of and managing the property of another person who is incapable of managing his own affairs (e.g., a minor or an incompetent)

Guardian ad Litem
A person assigned by a court to represent a minor or an incompetent while a court action or probate proceedings are pending.

Heir
A person who inherits by virtue of descent or relationship from a deceased person.

Holographic Will
A will written, dated and signed entirely by the will-maker in his own handwriting.

Income
The returns from a property or asset, as opposed to the principal or capital itself (the "corpus"). Rents, interest and dividends are examples of income.

Incompetent
A person who lacks the ability or fitness to understand and manage his own affairs or to discharge the required function.

Infant	A person who is not of the required legal age. (Same as minor)
In Extremis	Something done in extreme circumstance, e.g., the one's last illness.
Inheiritance Taxes	A tax assessed on the person who receives a proprty by inheritance. This tax is based on the recipient's right to receive such a gift, and differs from an "estate" tax, which is assessed on the decedent's estate itself.
Inter Vivos	A trust or gift between living persons; something done during one's lifetime.
Intestacy	The state or condition of dying without having made a valid will. One who dies without having left a valid will is said to have died "intestate."
Issues	One's offspring, children or descendents.
Joint Tenancy	The phrase "joint tenancy or joint ownership" is used to describe a situation where two or more persons (usually non-marital partners) own or hold property in joint names, so that if any of them should die, the entire property goes to the remaining survivors. (Nearly the same as "tenancy by the entirety," especially when non-marital partners are involved)
Kin (or Kindred)	Persons related by blood, or with a common ancestry. (Next-of-kin is a person who is next closest relation to a decedent by blood)
Legacy	A gift of personal property by will. (Same as bequest). One who receives or is entitled to receive a personal property under a will is known as a legatee.
Letters Testamentary	A document issued by a court to an executor, by which the said executor is authorized to settle a particular estate.
Lien	A claim on the property of another resulting from some charge or debt.
Mutual Wills	Two separate wills in which each testator (usually a husband and wife) make similar or reciprocal provisions concerning the beneficiaries and executor or executrix.
Natural Guardian	The mother, father or grandparent of a minor.
Non Compos Mentis	Latin for "not of sound mind. Term is used to indicate a state of insanity or intoxication when one has no knowledge of the full meaning or consequences of his act.
Noncupative Will	An oral statement by a person on his death bed or under similar circumstance, as to what should be done with his property, which then becomes the basis of his last will if he should die.
Pecuniary Legacy	A gift of money by will.
Per Capita	Latin, meaning "by the head." When used in wills, it is taken to mean that the property or gift involved should be distributed in equal or share-by-share parts to each of the beneficiaries named.
Per Stirpes	This is the opposite of "Per Capita." When a will-maker makes a gift to a group of beneficiaries 'per stirpes,' it means that if any of the named beneficiaries should die before he could receive the gift, then his children would get, as a class or family, that portion to which their parent would have been entitled if alive.
Perjury	False testimony made under oath.
Personal Property	Any other property other than real property. (Same as personalty)
Posthumus Child	A child born after the father's death.

Principal The capital of an estate or trust; or the original fund of money or deposit on which interest is paid.

Probate of Will The formal presentation of the will to a proper court for the purpose of establishing that the will presented is actually the maker's last will.

Pro Se A person, usually a non-lawyer, who is acting for himself or representing himself in a court case.

Public Administrator A government official who acts as the administrator of a deceased person's estate when there is no one else named or available or qualified to assume the duty.

Real Property Land and everything growing or erected on it.

Residuary Estate The property that is left over in a testator's estate after all the liabilities, bequests and devises are paid out.

Reversion The return of real property to the original owner or his heirs, after the expiration of a stated period. E.g., when a testator gives a house to his wife for her lifetime only, the house 'reverts' (goes back) to the testator's estate upon the death of the wife.

Revocation of Will The cancelling or renouncing of an existing will by a subsequent act of the testator, such as making a new will or destroying the old one.

Settlement The final distribution of an estate by an executor or administrator.

Statutory Share That portion of a person's property or estate which is allowed to his spouse by the law of the state.

Signature A signed name or mark on a document to identify the person who made the document.

Subscribe To write your name yourself, by putting your signature to a written statement or document, such as a will.

Subscribing Witness One who signed his name on a will as a witness to its execution by the will-maker.

Succession The state of someone becoming entitled to the property of a deceased person, whether by law or by the provision of a will.

Tenancy by the Entirety See "Entirety."

Tenancy in Common The holding of property by two or more persons in such terms that each has an undivided interest in the property, and on the death of one of them, his undivided interest automatically passes to his heirs or devisee(s) and not to the other survivors.

Testamentary Capacity (Testamentary power). The competency or mental capacity sufficient to make a will.

Testamentary Guardian A guardian named in the will of a decedent.

Testamentary Trust A trust established by the provisions of a will.

Testate The opposite of intestate; the state of having made or left a valid will at one's death.

Testator A person (male) who dies leaving a valid will. (Called a testatrix, if a female)

Trust An obligation upon a person (the "trustee") which arises out of the terms of a special grant, to hold or apply property according to those terms, for the benefit of others (the "beneficiaries").

Verification Written confirmation of the truth of a document made out and sworn to by a person.

Void

An act or statement which has no legal force, effect or legitimacy from the beginning. (When something is "voidable," it means it has a legal force or legitimacy until and unless someone takes an action that makes it void, or a court declares it so.)

Ward

A person who is under the protection of a guardian.

Widow's allowance

The allowance given to a widow for her immediate needs after the death of her husband.

Appendix E

SOME RELEVANT BIBLIOGRAPHY

Henry W. Abts III, *The Living Trust: The Foolproof Way To Pass Along Your Estate To Your Heirs Without Lawyers, Courts, Or Other Probate System*, (Contemporary Books, Chicago; 1989)

George T. Bogart, *Trusts* (West Publishing Co., St. Paul, MN; 1987)

Denis Clifford, *Plan Your Estate With A Living Trust*, (Nolo Press, Berkely, CA; 1992)

Norman F. Dacey, *How To Avoid Probate—Updated!* (Crown Publishers, New York; 1979)

Robert A. Esperti and Renno L. Peterson, *Loving Trust: The Smart, Flexible Alternative To Wills and Probate* (Penguin Books, New York; 1991)

Michael J. Klug, A Report On Probate: *Consumer Perspective and Concerns* (American Assoc. of Retired Persons, Wash. DC; 1990)

Jeff O'Donnell, *Insurance Smart* (John Wiley & Sons, New York; 1991)

Charles K. Plotnick and Stephen Leimberg, *How To Settle An Estate* (Consumer Reports Books, Yonkers, NY; 1991)

Chris J. Prestopino, *Introduction To Estate Planning* (Kendall-Hunt, Dubuque, IA; 1992)

Cliff Roberson, *Avoiding Probate: Tamper-Proof Estate Planning* (Tab books, Summit PA; 1989)

Jerome R. Rosenberg, *Managing Your Own Money* (Newsweek Books, New York; 1979)

Theresa Meehan Rudy, Kay Ostberg & Jean Dimeo, *How To Use Trusts To Avoid Probate & Taxes* (Random House, NY; 1992)

Vickie and Jim Schumacher, *Understanding Living Trust* (Schumacher and Company, Los Angeles, CA; 1990)

Austin W. Scott and William F. Fratcher, *Scott on Trusts*, 12 Volumes (Little Brown & Co, Boston, Mass.; 1991)

Edward Siegel, *How To Avoid Lawyers* (Ballantine Books, New York; 1989)

Appendix F

ORDERING YOUR BLANK FORMS FOR CREATING YOUR OWN LIVING TRUST ESTATE PLAN

For our readers' added convenience, the *Do-It-Yourelf Legal Publishers*, the nation's original and leading self-help law publisher, makes available to its readership a package of forms usable for the standard needs. Taken together, the package comprises the essential forms a planner will need in a "complete" or "total" estate plan scheme (Chapter 3, Section E of the manual). Whether married or single, with children or not, if your situation is uncomplicated and straightforward (as most peoples' situations often are, actually!), you can just as well use these forms for a faster, quicker, less involved effect. (Or, at least, adapt them to your use accordingly.)

The following forms are included in our STANDARD LIVING TRUST KIT FORMS PACKAGE:

1) The Living Trust
2) The Pour-over/Back-up Will, with Affidavit of Attesting Witnesses
3) The Living Will (General Purpose form), with a "Medical Directive" component
4) Durable Financial & Medical Power of Attorney
5) Affidavit of Agent As To Power of Attorney Being In Full Force

---

(Customers: For your convenience, just make a zerox copy of this page and send it along with your order. All prices quoted here are subject to change without notice.)

TO: **Do-It-Yourself Legal Publishers,** Legal Forms Division
         60 Park Place # Suite 1013,
         Newark, NJ 07102

Please send me the publisher's "all-in-one" STANDARD LIVING TRUST KIT OF FORMS: [Prices: $35.90 per set]

Form	Quantity (Sets)	Price
For unmarried person WITH minor child(ren)...........	_____	$ _____
For unmarried person WITHOUT minor child(ren)......	_____	$ _____
For married couple WITH minor child(ren)...............	_____	$ _____
For married couple WITHOUT minor child(ren).........	_____	$ _____
(Prices: $35.90 per set)	Subtotal...........................	$ _____
	Postage @ $4 per set..........	$ _____
	Sales Tax*.........................	$ _____
	GRAND TOTAL..................	$ _____

Answer the following:
My permanent domicile is the city and county of _____, State of _____.
Which type of Trust do you want—the "A," or "A-B," or "A-B-C" type? _____ *(Turn to pp. 51-2 for some pointers on how to pick)*
My marital status is _____. I have children _____ Yes _____ No. The child(ren) are: Adults _____ Minors _____
I bought your book, or read, learned about it from this source (bookstore, library, medium): _____

Enclosed is the sum of $ _____ to cover the order, which includes $4 per set for shipping and local sales tax,* as applicable.
Send this order to me:
     Mr/Mrs/Ms/Dr. _____
     Address: _____
     City & State: _____ Zip _____ Tel # (____) _____

*New Jersey residents enclose 6% sales

IMPORTANT: Please do NOT rip out the page. Consider others! Just make a photocopy and send. And have you please completed our 'Readers Opinion Sheet' on p. 233?

Please DO NOT tear out this page. Consider others!

Appendix G

PUBLICATIONS FROM DO-IT-YOURSELF LEGAL

PUBLISHERS/SELFHELPER LAW PRESS

The following is a list of books obtainable from the Do-it-Yourself Legal Publishers/Selfhelper Law Press of America.

✓(Customers: For your convenience, just make a photocopy of this page and send it along with your order. All prices quoted here are subject to change without notice.

1. How To Draw Up Your Own Separation/Settlement Agreement Without, Before, Or During Marriage.
2. How To Win Your Tenant' Legal Rights Without A Lawyer (New York Edition)
3. How To Probate, Administer & Settle An Estate Without The High-Cost Lawyer ($35)
4. How To Adopt A Child Without A Lawyer
5. How To Form Your Own Profit/Non-Profit Corporation Without A Lawyer
6. How To Plan Your 'Total' Estate With A Will & Living Will, Without The Lawyer's Fees
7. How To Declare Your Personal Bankruptcy Without A Lawyer ($29)
8. How To Buy Or Sell Your Own Home Without A Lawyer Or Broker ($29)
9. How To File For Chapter 11 Business Bankruptcy Without A Lawyer ($29)
10. How To Legally Beat The Traffic Ticket Without A Lawyer (forthcoming)
11. How To Settle Your Own Auto Accident Claims Without A Lawyer ($29)
12. How To Obtain Your U.S. Immigration Visa Without A Lawyer ($29)
13. How To Do Your Own Divorce Without A Lawyer [State-By-State Edition] ($35)
14. How To Legally Change Your Name Without A Lawyer
15. How To Properly Plan Your Total Estate With A Living Trust Without The Lawyers' Fee ($35)
16. Before Your Say 'I Do' To Him Or Her, Here's How To First Protect Yourself Legally

Prices: Each book, except for those specifically priced otherwise, costs $25, plus $3.00 per book for postage and handling. New Jersey residents please add 6% sales tax. ALL PRICES ARE SUBJECT TO CHANGE WITHOUT NOTICE.

(CUSTOMERS: Please make and send a xerox copy of this page with your orders)

Order Form

TO: *Do-It-Yourself Legal Publishers* (Books Division)
       60 Park Place #1013,
       Newark, NJ 07102

Please send me the following:

1. _____ copies of _____
1. _____ copies of _____
1. _____ copies of _____
1. _____ copies of _____

Enclosed is the sum of $ _____ to cover the order. *Mail my order to:*

Mr/Mrs/Ms/Dr. _____
Address (include Zip Code please):_____

Phone No. and area code: (_____) _____ Job: (_____) _____

_____ Zip _____

*New Jersey residents enclose 6% sales tax.

IMPORTANT: Please do NOT rip out the page. Consider others! Just make a photocopy and send. And have you please completed our 'Readers Opinion Sheet' on p. 233?

READERS OPINION SHEET

The author (the Publisher as well) is interested in serving YOU, the reader, as he's deeply of the view that YOU, the consumer, are the KING or QUEEN! He'd love to know: Did this book meet your needs? Did it answer the more general, basic questions that you had; was it to the point? Most importantly, did it get the job done for you—of getting you a good Living Trust and/or a "Total" estate plan? If you would like to express your views directly to the author, *please complete and return this sheet to: the author, in care of the Publisher.* And we'll make sure your opinion promptly gets directly to him. *Please use the reverse side, if you need extra space. [Please do NOT tear out the sheet; just make a photocopy and send that]*

1. The areas (subject matters, chapters, issues, etc.) this book covers that were of interest to me were:

   They were _____ were not _____ covered in sufficient depth.

2. Areas not covered by this book that I would like to see are: _____

_____

3. The most helpful chapter(s) was (were): 1 2 3 4 5 6 7 8 9 10 11 Other: _____

4. The least helpful chapter(s) was (were): 1 2 3 4 5 6 7 8 9 10 11 Other: _____

5. The organization of the contents and writing style make the manual easy to read and use? Yes___No___
   (Explain/Elaborate:) _____

6. What did you like the best about the book? _____

7. The concept of do-it-yourself, self-help law you champion is: An excellent idea _____ A bad idea _____ Why? (Please elaborate) _____

8. How would you improve the manual? _____

9. My job/profession is: _____

10. I have completed 8-12 _____ 13-16 _____ over 16 _____ years of school.

11. My primary reason for reading this book was: _____

12. I learned about the book through this source or medium: _____

13. The book met my primary need in purchasing the book: Yes _____ No _____

14. It saved me appx. $ _____ using the book to create my Living Trust plan without hiring a lawyer.

15. I bought the book, or read it at this bookstore or library (address in full, please): _____

My Name & Address are: _____

_____ Zip _____ Tel. # _____

Send it to: *Dr. Benji O. Anosike, author* • *c/o Do-It-Yourself Legal Publishers, "Tell It To The Author" Program,* **60 Park Place #1013,** *Newark, NJ 07102*

Index